PUBLISHED BY
Microsoft Press
A Division of Microsoft Corporation
One Microsoft Way
Redmond, Washington 98052-6399

Library of Congress Cataloging-in-Publication Data
Woodcock, JoAnne.
    The ultimate MS-DOS book / authors, JoAnne Woodcock.
        p.   cm.
    Includes index.
    ISBN 1-55615-627-8
    I. MS-DOS (Computer file)   I. Title.
    QA76.76.O63W663   1993
    005.4'469--dc20   93-37566
                                                                  CIP

Printed and bound in the United States of America.

1 2 3 4 5 6 7 8 9   QEQE   9 8 7 6 5 4

Distributed to the book trade in Canada by Macmillan of Canada, a division of Canada
Publishing Corporation.

Distributed to the book trade outside the United States and Canada by
Penguin Books Ltd.

Penguin Books Ltd., Harmondsworth, Middlesex, England
Penguin Books Australia Ltd., Ringwood, Victoria, Australia
Penguin Books N.Z. Ltd., 182-190 Wairau Road, Auckland 10, New Zealand

British Cataloging-in-Publication Data available.

Project Editor: Jack Litewka
Manuscript and Visuals Editor: Eric Stroo
Technical Editor: Jim Fuchs

Contents

CONTENTS

Acknowledgments

Books, at least those at Microsoft Press, are known by nicknames as they travel the road from manuscript to printable pages. This book was known as "hotspud" during the three months in which it took form and grew. The names of the principals are listed at the end of the book, but a simple listing of names and titles is scant acknowledgment for the long days and longer weekends demanded of these people. Here, then, is a more detailed tribute.

In producing this book, thanks go to: Eric Stroo, who not only edited the manuscript but pored over hundreds of photographs to find those you'll see here; Jim Fuchs, who (as always) provided superb support as technical editor; John Sugg, who deftly maneuvered edits, revisions, and rewrites into production-ready form and format; Brett Polonsky, who worked and reworked these pages to make them look better than the text deserves; David Holter, who turned kindergarten sketches and 30-second descriptions into illustrations that do what thousands of words could not; Van Bucher, who turned up hundreds of photographs for us to choose from; Trisha Feuerstein, who kept your needs in mind while combing the book with a professional's eye to produce an index both useful and usable; David Rygmyr, who provided the contacts, tips, and first draft for the "Real Questions, Real Answers" chapter in Section 5; and Jennifer Harris and her colleagues, who quietly did what proofreaders are never praised highly enough for doing well.

This book also benefited greatly from advice and suggestions enthusiastically offered by members of Microsoft's MS-DOS Product Support Services group. In alphabetic order, these contributors included Fletcher Bonds, Greg Brown, Kevin Horst, Randy Ivey, Maher Khabbazeh, Austin Mack, Herschel McPherson, Andrew Mimura, Sam Mitchener, David Parmelee, Dan Penn, Matthew Russell, David Schott, Suzanne Sylliaasen, and Bryan Thompson.

Most of all, however, special thanks go to Peter Lovejoy, who went out of his way to dig up information and provide much of the substance for the "Real Questions, Real Answers" chapter; to Jack Litewka, who served as project editor and, in the process, showed his true colors as day-to-day miracle worker; and to Kate and Mark, who contributed yet another summer to yet another book.

Thanks to them all.

① Places Everyone....

What You See Is What You Get

Start with ABC

ABC. Is that a dumb way to start a book about MS-DOS? Maybe, but think of ABC as standing for A Book [about] Computers, and then think about what those particular letters bring to mind. Exactly. Simple...elementary...nothing to be afraid of. That's the point: The letters, like this book, are meant to help you close your eyes, click your heels three times, and end up not in Kansas, but in a part of the world where computers are as common as fast food (well, almost) and where real people learn quite a bit about using computers while remaining perfectly normal human beings.

Why MS-DOS?

This book is about version 6.2 of MS-DOS, and it's here to help you do two things: use MS-DOS (the easy part) *and* understand it well enough to control your computer (a little more time-consuming, but not much harder). But why MS-DOS? Well...

Some people seem to be born lucky. A computer never causes them to think mutinous thoughts. Never do they have to wonder, "Who's the boss, here, anyway?" Perhaps you aren't one of these. Perhaps you don't always view computers as benign, helpful creatures. In fact, you might sometimes believe your computer has a mind of its own. A mind that sneers at your commands! That coolly and maddeningly responds with some version of "I can't do that" when you know

> **MS-DOS**
> Short for Microsoft Disk Operating System, the set of programs that make your computer "aware" of you, your other programs, and the various gadgets (such as printers) attached to the computer. Without an operating system, a computer is as capable of doing work as a chocolate doughnut.

darn well it can. If you have felt like this, your reaction was probably the same as everyone else's: Snarl.

Because computers are very fast and can beat most humans at chess, people tend to associate computers with intelligence. Wrong. Computers are stupid. They are machines. And like all machines, computers have two ways of operating: fine and make-me-crazy. When the going's good, as it usually is, it's great. But when the going gets rough, you just want to get going...and keep going as far away as possible, hoping that the rough spot will magically disappear in the meantime. It's a very human attitude, but it's not a very realistic one.

This book is about training yourself to control your computer. All you need to understand is that MS-DOS controls the computer, so the surest way to master the machine is to learn how to control MS-DOS. And you don't even have to tango with electronics, programming, and other exotic topics. In fact, the actual knowledge you need is probably much less than you think. Learn to use 10 MS-DOS commands, and you can function perfectly well in almost any situation. Master another 10 commands, and you're approaching power-user status.

Great Expectations

MS-DOS is so very basic to what using a computer is all about that most books on MS-DOS would, at heart, like to be all things to all people. But readers differ, not only in what they know but in what they want to know.

Mostly, this book is for non-experts, but who's to define "expert" in the first place? Instead of running through a list of the types of things you can expect this book to offer, take a short quiz—found in the table at the top of the facing page—to help you decide how useful this book will be for you in particular. Choose the answer that fits you best.

If most or all of your answers were in the middle and righthand columns, you should find this book a good fit. Although you'll find a lot of information here, all of it is geared to help you get started, get confident, and get knowledgeable. You'll also find details and explanations that expand your understanding of computers without taking you into a sea of technicalities.

If most or all of your answers were in the first column, you could probably have written this book, but the coverage of new features in versions 6.0 and 6.2 should still keep your experimenting to a minimum and help you get off to a fast start.

Quiz: Are We Compatible?

Computers:	are fascinating	are OK	are as exciting as a root canal
A port:	is an input/output channel with a name like COM1 or LPT1	is a plug on the back of my computer	is a place where a ship docks
Disks:	are organized into cylinders, tracks, and sectors	are floppy or hard	are round
MS-DOS:	is my operating system, a set of programs that mediate between my hardware and me	is what makes my computer work	is something weird the dealer said I had to have
VGA:	stands for video graphics adapter	is the type of display I have	sounds like a government agency
Memory:	comes in different varieties, including RAM, ROM, and XMS	gets confusing when I see references to different types, such as extended and expanded	is what tells me that 2 + 2 = 4
My keyboard:	contains a microprocessor of its own	is the 101/102 key enhanced version	has lots of keys with funny labels on them
AUTOEXEC:	is a special batch file that MS-DOS runs automatically and that I use to customize startup	is where MS-DOS "remembers" important facts, such as where to find the programs I use	is the head of a car company?

Getting Ready

OK, what, really, do you need in order to put this book and version 6.2 of MS-DOS to work? The list is short, sweet, and simple:

- You need (obviously) version 6 of MS-DOS. The focus of this book is version 6.2, but most of the information will work for you if you have version 6.0. Your version 6 of MS-DOS can have reached you in any number of ways: installed on a new computer, as an upgrade from version 5.0 or earlier, or (if you have version 6.2) as an update disk you either purchased or got from a network, such as CompuServe. However you and MS-DOS joined forces, as long as you have version 6.0 or 6.2, you're in great shape. (By the way, if you have to install version 6.0 or 6.2, don't worry: This book tells you how, in the chapter "First Step: Install MS-DOS," which starts on page 15.)

- You need a computer. You already know that, so look at what kind of computer you need. It has to be what a lot of dealers call "IBM-compatible"— that is to say, it has to be a computer with an Intel-based processor. MS-DOS versions 6.0 and 6.2 run best and most comfortably on IBM-compatibles based on the 80386 and 80486. (Don't worry about SX, DX, and other add-ons to the chip name; the number is the important part.) If your computer is based on the 80286 processor, you can upgrade to version 6.2 of MS-DOS, but you won't be able to take advantage of many memory-conserving features without additional, non-Microsoft software. If your computer is based on the 8088 or 8086 chip, it unfortunately doesn't have the horsepower to work with the newest features of MS-DOS, especially those related to sophisticated memory handling.

WHAT ABOUT FLOPPIES?
Through version 5, it was possible to run MS-DOS from floppy disks, but doing so in the past few years has been as effective as trying to cook a feast in a fireplace. If your computer doesn't have a hard disk, the best advice for you is: Buy one. And while you're at it, ask your dealer to install version 6.2 of MS-DOS on it.

- You need a hard disk. Because versions 6.0 and 6.2 require about 5 MB of storage, your disk should at least be in the 30-MB range, although these days 80 MB and up is considered standard. If your computer is new, your dealer no doubt already installed MS-DOS on the disk. If you're upgrading, the hard disk should already be carrying an older version of MS-DOS—version 2.11 or later. If you're installing the "step-up," specifically from version 6.0 to 6.2, version 6.0 and none other must be currently on the computer.

- You don't need, but can make good use of, a mouse. This is because parts of MS-DOS version 6 are *graphical*—that is, they're based on pictures and lists of commands, all of which are sensitive to mouse actions. If you've never considered a mouse, version 6 is probably not reason enough to get one. If you are suitably equipped, however, you'll find you can mouse around more freely with version 6 than ever before.

That's it. It's not a long list, and there are other items that could be mentioned, such as a printer, a modem, and a CD-ROM drive. But they're not necessary in this context. All you need are a suitable computer, a hard disk, and version 6.0 or 6.2 of MS-DOS. And you, of course. You're critical to the whole thing.

Visual Aids

As you can see from leafing through this book, the pages contain a lot of graphics elements. These elements were put in place to:

- Keep you from falling asleep
- Make the subject as lively as possible
- Help you find things

Of these objectives, it's to be hoped that only the third needs explanation, all of which you can find in the labeled illustration on the facing page.

In a Nutshell

This book has one goal: To put you in charge. With its help, you can learn to control your computer through MS-DOS. Give the book a little of your time and pay some serious (but not brow-furrowing) attention, and both your understanding and your confidence will quickly grow.

Tabs let you turn instantly to the section you need

Tips give you practical advice

Power Play topics take you a little beyond the basics; read them or skip them as you wish

Quick reference cards give you easy-to-find information about MS-DOS commands

"New" icon points out features new to versions 6.0 and 6.2

Troubleshooting topics steer you away from possible hazards or advise you on getting out of a jam

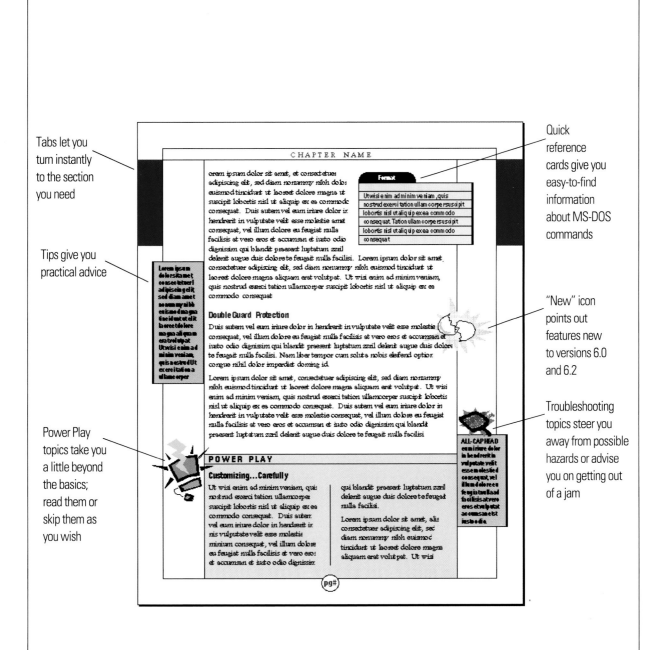

MS-DOS, New and Improved

Cut to the Chase

If you've been using MS-DOS forever, you're eager for someone to cut to the chase and tell you what's new and different about versions 6.0 and 6.2 of MS-DOS. This chapter is where you can separate the songs from the orchestra and figure out which of the new melodies you like best. As you'll see, there's a lot that's new, much of which first showed up in version 6.0. For an alphabetized list of new features, with brief descriptions, read on.

New and Improved Features and What They Do

Choice

Lets you prompt for a choice from inside a batch file. This little command gives you keyboard input—without your having to buy a batch enhancer or write an assembly language program.

For experienced users: See "Choice" in the MS-DOS online Help.

Clean Boot or Interactive Boot

Leaves the driving to you. Press F5 at startup to perform a clean boot (which bypasses CONFIG.SYS and AUTOEXEC.BAT), or press F8 to perform an

CONFIG.SYS
A hardware-related file containing a series of commands that tell MS-DOS how to set up (configure) your computer. MS-DOS looks for this file each time you start or restart your computer. For details on understanding and changing CONFIG.SYS, refer to "Make a File with Edit," in Section 3.

interactive boot (which steps through CONFIG.SYS, prompting for a Yes or No before processing each line). If you like to tinker with your system, remember these keystrokes. Never again will a change to CONFIG.SYS cause your computer to hang—and cause you to wish you'd experimented on a bootable floppy.

If you have version 6.2, the F5 and F8 keys are bolstered by Ctrl+F5 and Ctrl+F8, which perform clean and interactive boots without loading the 30-odd KB of the DoubleSpace disk-compression feature.

See page 299, "Customizing Startup."

Copy, Move, and Xcopy

No longer overwrite (and thus destroy) files on the destination disk that have the same names as files you are copying or moving. All three commands now prompt before overwriting existing files—*if* you use version 6.2.

Defrag

Defragments disk storage, cleaning up all the little storage gaps that appear over time and that can slow disk reads and writes.

See page 199, "Physical Fitness with ScanDisk and Defrag."

Deltree

Lops off an entire directory, including all the files and subdirectories it contains. Deltree frees you from the old chain of commands: change directories, delete all files, change directories again, remove the directory, and (frequently) repeat the process several times. Useful as it is, however, this is not a command for people with hair-trigger reflexes or a tendency to press Enter without thinking. In this case, once gone can mean forever lost.

See page 109, "More About Directories."

DoubleSpace (Dblspace)

Compresses hard and floppy disks, giving you essentially twice as much storage in the same amount of space. If anything, this is *the* hot feature of version 6. If you have version 6.2, also be sure to check out ScanDisk, the new utility that gives extra protection to DoubleSpaced (and other) drives.

See page 271, "Grow Your Disks with DoubleSpace."

Fasthelp

Displays quick information about MS-DOS commands. Fasthelp is the version 6 form of version 5 Help. Fasthelp is for those times when you need "just the facts"—for example, when you can't quite remember how to put a Mode command together. Oh, you can remember? How nice for you....

See page 43, "MS-DOS and What You Do with It."

Help

Displays detailed help on all commands. This form of help is basically the commands section of your old MS-DOS manual, updated for version 6.0 or 6.2, of course, and brought online. Help appears in a full-screen, character-based window (shown here) and responds to either the keyboard or the mouse. Embedded cross-references can take you immediately to related topics, and each command description is accompanied by appropriate notes and examples.

See page 43, "MS-DOS and What You Do with It."

InterInk and Intersvr

Help you transfer files from one computer to another. Interlnk and Intersvr work together, one acting as transmitter and the other as receiver. Using this feature is easy as pie; all you need is a null modem cable.

See page 263, "Transfer Files with Interlnk."

Mem and HIMEM

Display information about memory use. Not new, but definitely improved over the hexadecimal-happy version 5 Mem command, Mem now summarizes nicely, in plain English. And speaking of memory, HIMEM.SYS in version 6.2 now checks for unreliable memory chips that can lead to startup problems, an unstable system, or even loss of data.

See page 171, "More About Memory."

> **AUTOEXEC.BAT**
> A "personal" file of commands that MS-DOS AUTOmatically EXECutes each time you start or restart your computer. AUTOEXEC.BAT establishes a few ground rules: It tells MS-DOS how to behave, essentially customizing certain parts of MS-DOS to suit your preferences. For more on this benevolent BAT, refer to "Customizing Startup," in Section 4.

MemMaker

Optimizes memory use by adjusting the way programs are loaded at startup. MemMaker is for occasional use only, but it takes fine-tuning your system out of the let's-see-whether-CONFIG.SYS-survives category. If you like getting close up and personal with your PC occasionally, you'll enjoy seeing MemMaker tally all the options it's evaluating to find the one that's best for you. Sometimes those alternatives number in the thousands. (But it's fast. Relax and enjoy the show.)

See page 287, "Do It Yourself or Do It with MemMaker."

Microsoft Anti-Virus (MSAV)

Protects your computer from sneak invasion by checking for hundreds of virus programs. Runs under both MS-DOS and Microsoft Windows.

See page 217, "Foil the Bad Guys with Anti-Virus and Vsafe."

Microsoft Backup (MSBackup)

Makes backing up a breeze. Runs in a window and practically runs itself. This version of Backup, unlike any earlier version, both backs up and restores files. It can also remember backup settings and perform selective backups at your command. Works under both MS-DOS and Windows.

See page 233, "Sleep Better at Night with Backup."

Microsoft Diagnostics (MSD)

Checks out your computer and tells you more than you ever wanted to know about its innards, including the processor, disk drives, ports, memory, and attached devices. If a program's installation ever requires you to know about your video adapter, port addresses, or interrupts, this is the place to come. And, of course, if your computer's CMOS battery has ever faded to the point that the machine forgot all about its hard disk, you already know how useful some of this hardware information can be.

MSD is for experienced users. If you call Microsoft Product Support, the specialist you talk to might tell you to start the program.

Move

Moves files from one disk or directory to another. Nothing more need be said to experienced MS-DOS people, except "At last!"

See page 123, "More About Files."

CMOS

Pronounced "sea-moss," this acronym stands for complementary metal-oxide semiconductor (whew). A type of chip that runs very fast but uses little power. In PCs, CMOS chips are typically put to work as special battery-powered memory that's used to hold "unforgettable" information, such as date, time, and the type of hard disk in the computer. CMOS memory chips need a constant, though small, source of power. If the battery fades, a CMOS chip loses the contents of its memory, and you must then replace the battery and help the chip overcome its amnesia by installing a new battery. For help with this, call your dealer.

Numlock

Turns the NumLock key off (or on) at startup. This command goes in CONFIG.SYS, so you have to know how to make changes in your startup files, but it's worth the bother.

See page 299, "Customizing Startup."

Power

Isn't it grand? Actually, this isn't superhero stuff—it's a user-friendly, Earth-friendly command that reduces power consumption when your computer (especially a battery-powered portable) is idle or inactive.

See Power and POWER.EXE in the MS-DOS online Help.

ScanDisk

In version 6.2 only, diagnoses and cures the ailments that disks are heir to. What kind of disks? All kinds: floppy and hard, compressed and uncompressed. The successor to Check Disk, ScanDisk keeps your disks healthy and safe for file storage.

See page 199, "Physical Fitness with ScanDisk and Defrag."

SmartDrive

Not new, but improved over version 5, SmartDrive can load into high memory and now lets you turn read and write caching on and off for specific drives.

See page 151, "More About Hardware."

Startup Menus

Just like Windows...sort of. Several menu options join forces to let you build sets of startup commands that allow you to decide how MS-DOS configures your computer at startup. With a menu, for example, you can concoct one set of commands that connects you to a network, another that gives you lots of extended memory and loads your word processor, and still another that gives you expanded memory and takes you into your spreadsheet program. At startup, all these options will be listed on a menu, from which you pick the one you want. You can also set one menu choice as your default—the startup MS-DOS uses unless you say otherwise. And faithful old MS-DOS even lets you display the menu in color. Eye-popping green on magenta? Sure, if that's your pleasure.

See page 299, "Customizing Startup."

Undelete

Again, not new, but improved, Undelete now offers practically foolproof Sentry protection for deleted files. Runs under both MS-DOS and Windows. The Windows-based version is really nice and can even recover deleted directories and their files—sometimes.

See page 251, "Go Back in Time with Undelete."

Vsafe

Monitors your system for virus activity. Vsafe sits in a small amount of memory and watches for attempts to strike at critical parts of your system. This is a watchdog that can warn you even when Windows is active—a digital Doberman brought to you by MS-DOS.

See page 217, "Foil the Bad Guys with Anti-Virus and Vsafe."

First Step: Install MS-DOS

Who Needs It?

This chapter, that is. Well, you do if MS-DOS version 6.0 or 6.2 is sitting on the desk next to your computer, and you're wondering how to get it from there onto your hard disk. You'll also find this chapter a useful resource if you're thinking of upgrading but aren't sure how much work is involved. (Very little.)

You *don't* need this chapter if you have a new computer and your dealer already installed MS-DOS version 6.2 for you. Nor do you need it if you're so comfortable with computers that you can walk through a typical software installation with your eyes shut.

Change Happens

Anyone who's worked with computers for a while can tell you the one word that describes all computer software (and hardware for that matter): Change. Computer software constantly grows and evolves to match new developments in hardware and, equally important, to provide computer users with new capabilities.

It's axiomatic, then, that change happens. And that's where versions come in. Version numbers tell you how recent a piece of software is. So what about MS-DOS? Well, it's been around since version 1.0, back in 1981. Now it's up to version 6.2. As for what those numbers mean:

- The number to the left of the decimal point signifies a major change in MS-DOS. For example, version 1 became version 2 when MS-DOS gained the ability to recognize and work with hard disks. Maybe that doesn't seem like such a big deal to you, but it was to MS-DOS.

- The number to the right of the decimal point signifies a minor change in MS-DOS—not trivial but not big. For example, version 6.0 became version 6.2

primarily because Microsoft decided to give MS-DOS more ways to protect your data. The change wasn't big enough to warrant a jump from version 6 to version 7, but it was still significant enough to require a shift in the minor version number. (Are you wondering what happened to version 6.1? Don't let it keep you awake nights; Microsoft jumped straight from 6.0 to 6.2. It never released an MS-DOS version 6.1.)

What's Your Version?

Most people know what version of MS-DOS they're using, but if you buy or inherit a computer, there's a chance you might be wondering what you've got. If you want or need to find out what version of MS-DOS you're using, it's really easy: Ask MS-DOS.

1. Turn on your computer.

2. When you see the command prompt, which is probably C:\>, type:

    ```
    C:\>ver
    ```

    and press Enter. MS-DOS will respond with something like the following:

    ```
    MS-DOS Version 6.00
    ```

The command you just used, by the way, is short for *version,* as in "What version are you?" If you're new to MS-DOS, this shorthand form of typing commands might seem a little, well, abrupt. You'll get used to it. MS-DOS is like some people: terse, but willing to go all out for you.

That's enough background information. Time for installation.

Big Step, Little Step

MS-DOS version 6.2 comes in two forms, an *upgrade* and an *update.* For a successful installation, you must be sure you have the version you need:

• The *upgrade* package is a boxed three-disk set that boosts MS-DOS all the way to version 6.2. Prior to upgrading, your computer can be running any

DETOUR
Some original equipment manufacturer's (OEMs) have shipped MS-DOS version 6.0 *without* DoubleSpace, Microsoft Backup, Microsoft Anti-Virus, and Microsoft Undelete. If your version 6.0 does not include these utilities, you *cannot* use the MS-DOS 6.2 Step-Up disk to upgrade to version 6.2. To move up to version 6.2, either purchase the version 6.2 upgrade package or contact your computer manufacturer.

If you have installation disks for MS-DOS version 6.0 rather than 6.2, you have the *upgrade* form of the MS-DOS version that preceded version 6.2. If you need help installing version 6.0, consult your MS-DOS manual and then follow the instructions under the heading "Installing the Version 6.2 Upgrade." Your installation will differ in some respects from the one described there, but not significantly. If you want to go just a little bit further, you can later send for or purchase the MS-DOS 6.2 Step-Up disk, or you can use your modem to download the necessary files from CompuServe or the Microsoft Download Service. At that time, come back and follow the instructions under the heading "Installing the Version 6.2 Update." When you finish, your computer will be running the latest version of MS-DOS available to humankind.

version of MS-DOS from 2.11 through 5.0. The upgrade package retails for about $50, and you should be able to locate it easily at any store that deals in software. If your computer is already running MS-DOS version 6.0, you do *not* need the upgrade package to get to version 6.2; the update is sufficient.

- The *update* is a single disk known as MS-DOS 6.2 Step-Up. This disk takes you from version 6.0 to 6.2 of MS-DOS—no more, no less. This is what you need if your computer is already running version 6.0 and you want to take that extra step to version 6.2. If you don't yet have the update disk yet, you can get it by:
  - Buying it at your local software store
  - Downloading it from either CompuServe or the Microsoft Download Service (more about which is in the tip on this page)

However you get it, bear in mind that you *cannot* use the update disk unless your computer is already running version 6.0 of MS-DOS. Don't think of MS-DOS 6.2 Step-Up as a cheap way to trick MS-DOS into a major upgrade. It won't work.

Although the upgrade and update disks differ in the scope of their jobs, they install in much the same way. There are a few small differences, however, so updating and upgrading are covered separately in the following sections to avoid unintentionally confusing or misleading you. When you finish installing version 6.2, read the advice in the remaining sections of this chapter. Though not as interesting as your horoscope, it's still useful information.

If you have a modem, you can download MS-DOS 6.2 Step-Up from the Microsoft Download Service, a free (except for the phone call) customer support service. Set your modem's communications parameters to 2400 baud, 8 data bits, 1 stop bit, no parity, and then have it dial (206) 936-6735. When your call is answered, register with the service by providing your name, city, and state at the prompts requesting that information. When you're ready, download the version 6.2 update.

The Big "Un"

Whichever type of installation you perform, Setup will ask you to provide an "uninstall" disk. This is a floppy disk to which Setup copies a lot of files that tell it about your current version of MS-DOS. The uninstall disk could be very important, so don't feed Setup some old floppy that's been hanging around gathering dust. You'll need the uninstall disk if, for some reason, you have to undo the 6.2 installation—for example, because your favorite application can't work with version 6.2.

To use the uninstall disk after a successful setup, place the disk in drive A and reboot. Answer Yes when you're asked whether to proceed with the uninstall process. A few seconds later, you'll be done and your world will once again be its old familiar place.

Although it's unlikely to happen, it's also possible that Setup might not complete the installation because of a power outage or an unexpected hardware problem—that sort of thing. If your installation is interrupted, the uninstall disk is, again, your security blanket. Place the uninstall disk in drive A and reboot the computer. When Setup asks whether you want to continue with the installation or recover your old version of MS-DOS, choose whichever is more appropriate. (If you're the kind of person who likes everything just so, you might prefer to choose recover, to get back to home base, and then install version 6.2 again from the beginning.)

Installing the Version 6.2 *Update*

Updating MS-DOS from version 6.0 to 6.2 is not so much an installation procedure as it is a matter of making MS-DOS aware of changes in version 6.2. How you go about teaching MS-DOS about these changes, however, depends on whether you use the version 6.2 Step-Up disk or download the update by way of your modem. If you have the Step-Up disk, skip ahead to the section in this chapter headed "Running the Update Setup." If you get the program files you need for the update from a bulletin board, you go through a few extra steps before swinging into Setup, so continue with the next section.

Downloading the Update

If you download the version 6.0-to-6.2 update, you copy two files named MSDOS62.EXE and README.NOW onto your hard disk. (Copy them into their own directory, as described in the box "Where to Put Them," on the facing page.) MSDOS62.EXE is the working part of your update, a fascinating beast known as a "self-extracting file"—comparable to a science-fiction robot box that turns itself into a spaceship or a house when the owner presses a button. Essentially, what MSDOS62.EXE does is use itself to create the environment that Setup needs to update version 6.0 to 6.2.

Interesting as MSDOS62.EXE is, however, don't forget the file named README.NOW, and don't ignore its plea. README.NOW is a "help" file that tells you about MSDOS62.EXE and the process you go through in updating to version 6.2. README.NOW is stored in plain text—that is, readable characters—so before you start updating, do README.NOW a favor. Turn on your printer and print the file with the following command, substituting for *stepup* the name of the directory to which you downloaded the files:

```
C:\>copy \stepup\readme.now prn
```

Now take a few minutes to read the file. In particular, pay attention to the part that tells you about installing Microsoft Backup, Undelete, and Anti-Virus. As the file says, only the changed parts of these programs are included with the

These instructions were accurate at the time this book went to press. Bulletin-board procedures were, however, still evolving. If you connect to either CompuServe or the Microsoft Download Service and did not find the files described here, check the bulletin board for help or instructions on downloading the version 6.2 Step-Up files you need. If you need more help, contact the bulletin board's system operator or try contacting Microsoft directly.

POWER PLAY

Where to Put Them

As you'll see when you take a look at the file named README.NOW, the recommended home for your update files is a new directory. You can put the files in a home of their own by creating the directory ahead of time. To create the directory, use the Make Directory command:

```
C:\>md stepup
```

In this command, you can substitute your preferred directory name (if you wish) for *stepup*.

If you've already downloaded the files, you can still move them by creating a new directory and then moving the files. For example, if the files are in your \DOS directory, and you create a STEPUP directory, you would move the files with the following command (which wraps to a second line here but won't on your screen):

```
C:\>move c:\dos\msdos62.exe,
c:\dos\readme.now c:\stepup
```

version 6.2 update. That means you can't get updated versions of these programs unless they are already installed on your computer in their version 6.0 incarnations. If you want to run Microsoft Backup, Undelete, or Anti-Virus, follow the instructions itemized in README.NOW.

After you take care of all the preliminaries, you run the version 6.2 update in two stages. The first, which applies only to the downloaded form, is as follows:

1. Change to the directory in which you stored MSDOS62.EXE with the Change Directory command (substituting your directory name if it differs from *stepup*):

   ```
   C:\>cd stepup
   ```

2. Set MSDOS62.EXE running with the command:

   ```
   C:\STEPUP>msdos62
   ```

   When finished, this part of the process will result in two new files named MAKESYS.EXE and SETUP.EXE. Both are necessary, but MAKESYS.EXE comes first.

3. Create the MS-DOS version 6.2 system (core) files that you need with the command:

   ```
   C:\STEPUP>makesys
   ```

4. Now you're ready to run Setup, which you do by typing:

   ```
   C:\STEPUP>setup
   ```

From this point on, everything proceeds as described in the next section, with the text beginning just below the third item in the numbered list. Setup needs practically no description, but if you want a blow-by-blow account, skip down to the paragraph beginning "When Setup begins."

Running the Update Setup

If you're installing version 6.2 from the MS-DOS 6.2 Step-Up disk:

1. Place the disk in a floppy drive; either A or B will do.

2. Make that floppy drive the current drive by typing the letter of the drive, followed by a colon, and then press Enter. If the update disk is in drive A, type:

   ```
   C:\>a:
   ```

   (If the update disk is in drive B, type b:.)

3. Type the command that sets everything in motion:

   ```
   A:\>setup
   ```

When Setup begins, it displays a nice, uncluttered screen headed *Microsoft MS-DOS 6.2 Setup*. The installation begins with a check of your computer and your current version of MS-DOS. (If you installed the version 5 or 6.0 upgrade, this will look really familiar.)

From this point on, about all you have to do is follow the directions on the screen. Basically, you'll be asked to:

BACK AND FORTH

If you use the Step-Up disk to update your version of MS-DOS and find that one or more of your MS-DOS files are corrupted (unusable), you must reinstall version 6.0 and then use the Step-Up disk. For a complete list of steps to follow, refer to "Real Questions, Real Answers," in Section 5.

```
Microsoft MS-DOS 6.2 Setup

        Welcome to Setup.

        The Setup program prepares MS-DOS 6.2 to run on your
        computer.

        • To set up MS-DOS now, press ENTER.

        • To learn more about Setup before continuing, press F1.

        • To quit Setup without installing MS-DOS, press F3.

        Note: If you have not backed up your files recently, you
              might want to do so before installing MS-DOS. To back
              up your files, press F3 to quit Setup now. Then, back
              up your files by using a backup program.

              Before running Setup, you should check the README.TXT
              file for information that pertains to your system
              configuration. For more information, press F1.

ENTER=Continue  F1=Help  F3=Exit  F5=Remove Color
```

1. Provide an uninstall disk (two if you use 360-KB floppies) that fits your drive A. You can't use drive B for this. Don't worry about when to stick the disk in the drive. Setup will prompt you, and it will wait until you press Enter to tell it to go ahead.

2. Verify the manufacturer of your current version of MS-DOS, the name of your MS-DOS directory (MS-DOS path), and the type of display you have. Setup finds this information during its hardware check, so unless you have to change a setting, all you have to do is press Enter.

3. Forge ahead. When installation is complete, remove all floppy disks and reboot the system.

Installing the Version 6.2 *Upgrade*

The version 6.2 upgrade takes longer to perform than the update, but it is remarkably similar; all you really have to do is follow instructions on the screen. About the only real difference between an update from version 6.0 to 6.2 and an upgrade from version 5 or earlier to 6.2 is that you are asked a few more questions at the beginning. All in all, however, you can expect installation to be relatively quick and certainly painless. Before you start the installation, however, you might want to prepare for Setup in two ways:

- Back up your hard disk. This is a peace-of-mind precaution in case something goes wrong (which it most probably won't). If you don't know how to back up, at least find your important files and copy them to floppy disks. (If you need help finding or copying files, refer to the chapter "On to Disks and Files" in the next section of this book.)

- Print the file named README.TXT. This file, which is on Disk 1 of your three-disk upgrade kit, contains a lot of hardware-specific and software-specific information. The first part of this (long) file is about Setup and might contain information related to your computer. To print the file, turn on your computer and your printer, and place Disk 1 of the upgrade kit in your floppy drive. If the disk is in drive A, type the following command:

```
C:\>copy a:readme.txt prn
```

If the disk is in drive B, type:

```
C:\>copy b:readme.txt prn
```

Printing will probably take a while, so just relax. And don't forget to save your printed copy of the file for later reference, too.

Now, for the installation itself. Follow these steps, just as you would for the 6.0-to-6.2 update:

1. Place the disk in a floppy drive; either A or B will do.

2. Make that floppy drive the current drive by typing the letter of the drive, followed by a colon, and then press Enter. For example, if the update disk is in drive A, type:

```
C:\>a:
```

(If the update disk is in drive B, type b:.)

3. Type the command to start Setup:

```
A:\>setup
```

WHAT HAPPENED?

The descriptions of MS-DOS Setup in this chapter apply to the vast majority of MS-DOS upgrades. On some computers, however, Setup will not proceed as described. If Setup stops and tells you to install to floppies, or if it tells you it cannot continue until you take care of some irregularity it found, do what it tells you to do. If you're referred to your MS-DOS manual, check it out. If you're told to read a README file on your MS-DOS disk, print the file as described in this section, and study it carefully. If, after following all instructions, you find yourself more confused than enlightened, call Microsoft Product Support Services and describe your situation to the support engineer who answers your call. The support people are experts—uncommonly nice ones—and will do all they can to help you out.

Once Setup begins, it proceeds as follows:

- The first few screens are the same as those described for the 6.0-to-6.2 update: They give information telling you about Setup and let you know you'll be creating an uninstall disk in your A drive. While you're reading these screens, notice the bottom line, which tells you that you can press F1 for help. When you finish with each screen, press Enter to move on.

- Once the introductions are over, Setup gets down to work and begins asking you to verify your MS-DOS type, your MS-DOS path (directory name), and your display type. As mentioned in the preceding section, Setup finds this

information when it starts up, so all you probably have to do is press Enter to accept the settings shown.

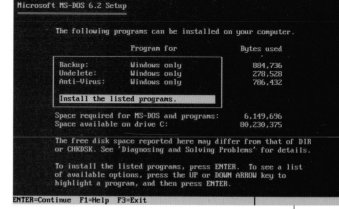

- Next, Setup tells you that it can install Backup, Undelete, and Anti-Virus as MS-DOS programs, Windows programs, or both.

If you don't have Windows, your choice must be *MS-DOS only*. If you have Windows, you can choose *Windows only*, which Setup proposes if it finds Windows on your computer, or you can use the Enter and arrow keys to choose to install one or more of these programs for *Windows and MS-DOS*.

Although installing both Windows and MS-DOS versions takes more room on your hard disk, you might want to choose this option for Undelete. The Windows version is easier to use and can help you recover deleted file categories called directories. On the other hand, the MS-DOS version can recover damaged files that the Windows version cannot. Installing both versions gives you an extra measure of protection you can't get with either version alone.

```
Microsoft MS-DOS 6.2 Setup

     The following programs can be installed on your computer.

                         Program for          Bytes used

       Backup:           Windows and MS-DOS    1,785,856
       Undelete:         Windows and MS-DOS      278,528
       Anti-Virus:       Windows and MS-DOS    1,032,192

       Install the listed programs.

     Space required for MS-DOS and programs:    7,296,576
     Space available on drive C:               80,230,375

     The free disk space reported here may differ from that of DIR
     or CHKDSK. See 'Diagnosing and Solving Problems' for details.

     To install the listed programs, press ENTER.  To see a list
     of available options, press the UP or DOWN ARROW key to
     highlight a program, and then press ENTER.

ENTER=Continue  F1=Help  F3=Exit
```

- If you choose to install the Windows version of Backup, Undelete, Anti-Virus, or any combination of the three, Setup next asks you to verify the name of your Windows directory. This should require nothing more than pressing Enter.

- The preliminaries over, Setup gets down to business with the message:

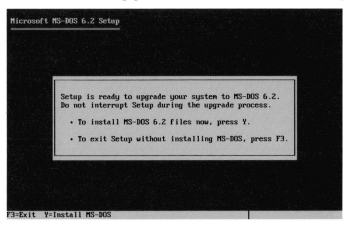

From here on in, the show belongs to Setup. You'll have to insert your uninstall disk when Setup requests it, but otherwise, your job's done. When the process is complete, you'll be told to remove all floppy disks and press Enter. When you do, you see Setup's final message:

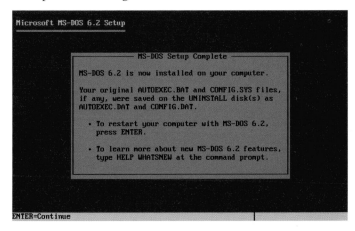

You're done. And don't worry about those references to AUTOEXEC and CONFIG files. You probably won't need them.

About MemMaker and DoubleSpace

During installation, Setup displays different messages telling you about the benefits of using MemMaker to increase available memory and using Double-Space to increase available disk storage. These features are really the "stars" of MS-DOS version 6, and both are highly recommended. If you're uncertain about what they do and how you use them, bear in mind that you *don't* have to run either program right away. MS-DOS versions 6.0 and 6.2 run perfectly well without either, so take your time. If you want to do a little research ahead of time, refer to the chapters "Grow Your Disks with DoubleSpace" and "Do It Yourself or Do It with MemMaker," both in Section 4, for explanations of what these programs do and how you use them.

When Everything's Working Fine...

When Setup installs either an upgrade or the version 6.2 update, it creates a special place for your older version of MS-DOS called the OLD_DOS directory. This directory contains a lot of MS-DOS files and requires several megabytes of disk space, but leave it alone until you've given your new version of MS-DOS a healthy workout. When you're convinced that MS-DOS is working as advertised with your computer, and that your programs have no problems working with MS-DOS, you can get rid of the OLD_DOS directory and regain that storage space with the following command:

```
C:\>deloldos
```

A few seconds later, "ol' dos" will be gone.

② Lights, Camera....

Computers and What They Do

Getting Grounded in Hardware

You couldn't get anyone to believe that pressing the A key on the keyboard causes a little *A* to shoot through the keyboard wire to the computer and from there to the screen, the printer, or the disk drive. But most people, no matter how clever they are at using computers, couldn't give a much better explanation of what happens to that *A* once it's inside the machine. And mostly, not knowing is all right, because a computer is put together in a way that assumes most people are going to "just say no" when it comes to learning about the insides.

Still, knowing a little bit about your computer can give you a practical edge, just as knowing a little bit about your car can. You don't have to know anything about engines or gear ratios to drive to the supermarket, but it's useful to know that when your car coughs to a standstill in the middle of the freeway, a glance

What do you mean, you think you need a graphics accelerator?

at the gas gauge can rule out (or confirm) the source of the problem. So it is with computers. You don't need the type of knowledge that turns you into a fully licensed and pocket-protected computer fix-it person, but knowing a few facts about the equipment gives you an edge in several areas.

First of all, knowing your hardware puts you a little closer to the inside track, where MS-DOS runs. Why? Because MS-DOS works very closely with the hardware. MS-DOS is, in fact, the driving force behind your computer's ability to use the keyboard, monitor, disk drives, and other parts of the machine. Without MS-DOS, your computer knows nothing—nothing about itself, and nothing about you. So knowing something about your computer helps you understand what MS-DOS does for you. And knowing that, you can figure out which version 6 features you need most. In addition, you'll find that understanding both your computer and MS-DOS will help you see new and better ways of using your computer to get a job done.

But the hardware/MS-DOS connection is only part of the story. Knowing about your computer helps you make some very practical decisions:

- Which of the numerous available third-party accessories and add-ons fit your needs? For example, do you need a coprocessor or a graphics accelerator?

- Have you outgrown your old computer? Should you start thinking about moving up to a more powerful machine?

- How well will your computer run that hot new software you've heard about?

This last point is important, because if the fit between your hardware and software isn't good, you won't be happy, and you'll end up blaming everyone from the manufacturer to your mother-in-law. And finally, don't forget that computers are like any other machines: subject to the occasional glitch. When they—and you—hit a bump on the happy road of life, knowing more rather than less often means you can figure out roughly how big a bump you hit.

Who, What, Ware?

In any functioning computer, there are two kinds of "wares" at work: hardware and software. Hardware, of course, is the touchable part. It's what you paid a lot of money for, and it's what you dust and keep clean and feed a diet of floppy disks. Software is what you get when you buy MS-DOS or another program. Software is, in most respects, the opposite of hardware. It's not touchable, or at least not directly. It exists only as coded information on the surface of a disk or, when active, in the computer's memory. And although you can physically handle a memory chip or a disk, you never actually touch a program. Only the computer can use a program directly because only the computer can understand and translate the instructions that make the program go. (Which doesn't make you dumb, by the way; a computer "thinks" in ons and offs, you don't.)

POWER PLAY

Between-ware

Hardware and software are basic, but there's another type of "ware" that's halfway between the two: firmware. Physically, firmware is a read-only memory chip, so it qualifies as hardware. "Mentally," however, firmware is a program, so it also qualifies as software. Unlike typical computer memory chips, read-only memory (ROM) chips don't lose their contents when the power goes off.

They can thus be used to store very basic programs, such as startup instructions, that the computer must be able to find "in the dark"—without having to wait for other parts of the system to "power up" and become available for use.

Oh, there *is* one more type of "ware": liveware. That's you. (Computer humor.)

Hardware

What you think of as a computer is made up of three main—that is to say, indispensable—parts: the keyboard, the monitor, and what's often called the "box." The box, or system unit, functions between the other two parts and is the actual computer. Why do you need these three pieces, even if you have nothing else? To satisfy the three activities that define computing: input (keyboard), processing (computer), and output (monitor). You've heard computers referred to as number crunchers. Well, those numbers are the input, the system unit is the cruncher, and the output is the...um...result of all that crunching.

The system unit is the home of the computer's processor, memory, and disk drives, all of which work together to collect input, process it, and produce output. The keyboard, however, is your primary means of providing input to the computer. It is the principal piece of hardware your computer "watches" to find out what you want to do. Complementing the keyboard is the monitor, your primary means of getting output.

You can, of course, attach all kinds of things to a computer: mice, modems, printers, disk drives (which are essential to you, but not to the computer), joysticks, even microphones and CD players. But no matter how exotic these add-ons—known collectively as *devices*—are, they all provide one form or another of input, output, or both. Both? Sure. A modem can be a source of either input or output, depending on whether it's receiving or sending information. Likewise, a disk drive provides input when you call up a previously saved program or document, but that same drive becomes an output device when you use it for saving a brand-new program or document. Other devices, of course, perform strictly input or output. A mouse, for instance, can't do a thing with output, but it can provide plenty of input when you move the mouse pointer onscreen and click a button. Conversely, you'd grow moldy waiting for a printer to provide input, but that same device is a whiz at making output visible.

Nuts and Bolts

As you've no doubt seen in commercials and glossy advertisements, hardware consists of a lot more than a system unit, a keyboard, and a monitor. Inside each of these pieces, and inside most other computer attachments, is a jungle of circuit boards, metal tracings, and other electronics that make up the truly active portion of the computer.

A circuit board, if you've never seen one up close, looks something like a city as you might see it from a low-flying plane.

Those unexciting black boxes on the board are the chips you've heard so much about, and the "streets" running between them are the pathways along which data and program instructions travel—for example, to and from memory and the processor. Seen from above, chips don't look like much. Seen from the side, they look a little more interesting—like the sort of centipedes that might crawl on a Picasso canvas.

Chips are nondescript but super-essential inhabitants of the motherboard Metropolis.

These chips and boards, along with the associated wires and pins and cables inside the system unit, are what hardware is all about. Now take a closer look at the main pieces. From this point on, by the way, assume that "computer" refers to a computer that runs MS-DOS. Other computers, such as the Apple Macintosh, differ, sometimes dramatically, both inside and out.

The Keyboard

You're pretty familiar with computer keyboards, of course. But remember the old saying that looks can be deceiving? It applies to a computer keyboard really well. While you might consider the keyboard comparable to the keys on an electronic typewriter, it's actually much more. For instance, take a look at the layout and those numerous special keys on the board. Lots of them.

An 83/84-key keyboard. This keyboard, older than the enhanced version (the current standard), is often called an "XT keyboard" after the IBM PC/XT computer with which it was strongly identified.

The QWERTY-style typewriter portion you use most of the time takes up most of the keyboard, but you've also got a series of function keys laid out either across the top (as shown on page 33) or down the left edge of the keyboard (as on the older 83/84-key XT-style keyboard shown above). To the right, on the main portion of an enhanced keyboard, are two groups of cursor-movement keys: a set of six at the top, for moving long distances through a document, and

> **QWERTY**
> The QWERTY keyboard takes its name from the arrangement of the keyboard characters in the top row of letters, starting at the left, next to the Tab key.

POWER PLAY

How Can a Computer (with no eyes) Read the Keyboard?

A keyboard is simple to use, but have you ever wondered how the computer knows which keys you press? The way this works is really interesting, and it explains in part why a new keyboard can be expensive.

When you press a key, any key, the circuitry inside the keyboard (of which there's quite a lot, including a processor that lives to catch your keystrokes) generates a number known as a scan code. For example, the scan code for pressing the right Shift key is 36, and the scan code for pressing the F1 key is 3B. This code not only uniquely identifies the key, it also indicates whether you pressed

or released the key. Each time the keyboard processor detects a scan code, it sends the information off to the computer.

When the scan code arrives in the system, it's taken into custody by a program known as a keyboard handler. This handler converts the code to the character it's supposed to represent and pops the converted character into a portion of memory—sort of a temporary parking lot—known as a buffer. Once parked in the buffer, the character sits patiently until a program, such as MS-DOS, comes along to fetch it and put it to work.

a set of four "arrow" keys below, for moving left or right one character at a time or up or down one line at a time. To the right of these cursor-movement keys is the numeric keypad, which you can toggle between calculator-style numeric entry and cursor movement by pressing the NumLock key.

All right, that's the familiar stuff. Now, what about all the keys with odd names? Take Sys Req, for example. How often do you need that one? Probably never. And then there are the function keys, F1 through either F10 or F12, depending on the keyboard model you use. The function keys are a really special group because they are "programmable"—not necessarily by you, but you've no doubt noticed that application programs use these keys as a means of providing you with fast ways to carry out common tasks. The function of a function key thus varies with the program you are using. A word processor, for instance, might be programmed to recognize the F4 key as a quick way to repeat a command. A spreadsheet, on the other hand, might regard the same key as a cue to recalculate all its formulas.

Keys That Are Special to MS-DOS

If you've used a number of different applications, you know that such programs often rely on special keystrokes (such as Ctrl+Shift+Enter) in addition to the usual cursor-movement keys, function keys, Tab, Caps Lock, and so on. Sometimes, the more exotic keystrokes require a certain amount of finger gymnastics. And mostly, these special keystrokes are so numerous that you wind up remembering only the ones that prove most useful.

MS-DOS doesn't require a great deal of either mental or physical agility where the keyboard is concerned, except for Ctrl+Alt+Del, which restarts the computer and was deliberately chosen for this task because pressing all three keys at once is difficult to do accidentally. But even though you might not have thought that MS-DOS assigns special jobs to certain keys, it does. And knowing those keys and keystrokes can make your work with MS-DOS much easier—especially if you're not always the most accurate typist in the world. The following table lists a set of often-used keys that have special meaning to MS-DOS, along with the jobs these keys do.

MS-DOS, as you probably know, is a collection of many different programs. Some of these, such as Doskey and Edit, respond to keystrokes that MS-DOS proper does not recognize. Many of these keystrokes are covered later in the book, in the chapters dealing with Edit and customizing startup.

Special Keys and Key Combinations

Key	Meaning
1. Esc	The "oops" key. Esc cancels a command, as long as you press it before pressing Enter. When you press Esc, MS-DOS ignores what you've just typed and moves the cursor to a new line so you can try again.
2. F3	Displays the last command you typed. This is especially handy if the command you want to type is almost the same as the last command you used or if you goofed slightly and want to correct your last command.

3. [F6] or [Ctrl] + [Z]

Adds a character, shown onscreen as ^Z, to a file. Useless? Not at all. This ^Z character tells MS-DOS it has reached the end of the file. If, as described in the next chapter, you sometimes create files by typing them directly from the command line, ^Z is the way you tell MS-DOS you're done.

4. [Ctrl] + [Pause/Break]

Cancels a command that MS-DOS is currently carrying out. Remember that Ctrl+Break calls a halt *after* you've pressed the Enter key; Esc calls it quits *before* you press Enter.

5. [Pause]

Stops the screen from scrolling so that you have time to read a long display. If you have a fast computer, however, the screen scrolls so quickly that pressing the Pause key at the right time can make you feel like a contestant on a game show. When you have to stop a long display, think More (the command), rather than Pause. Or, of course, use the /p option of a command like Directory to pause the display.

6. [← Backspace]

Backs up (to the left) one character at a time, wiping out each character it backs over. This is every typist's favorite eraser.

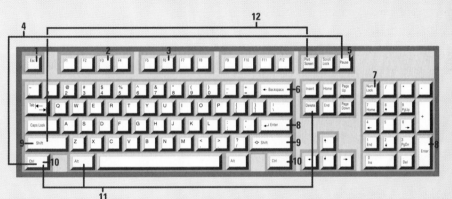

7. [Num Lock]

Doesn't lock anything. This key switches the numeric keypad between numeric entry and cursor movement.

8. [↵ Enter]

The "do it" key. Enter tells MS-DOS to carry out the command you've typed.

9. [⇧ Shift]

As usual, shifts alphabetic keys to uppercase and numeric keys to special characters. MS-DOS usually treats uppercase and lowercase characters as equivalent, but in some commands, such as Find, case can make a difference.

10. [Ctrl]

"Shifts" certain keys to give them a new and special meaning. Ctrl is usually used to send a control command to a program.

11. [Ctrl] + [Alt] + [Delete]

This key combination is accompanied by more cursing than any other because it says, "quit completely and start all over." You seldom need Ctrl+Alt+Del, but it can come in handy when a stubborn program hangs the computer and nothing else will help you get going again. Remember, though, that restarting the computer means losing all data you haven't saved.

12. [⇧ Shift] + [Print Screen]

Sends the contents of the display to your printer. Shift+PrtSc works perfectly with a character-based display (a typical MS-DOS display). If you want to print graphics, or if you have a laser printer, scan the tip to the right about printing screens.

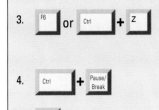

CON

The keyboard makes up half of what MS-DOS refers to as CON, the console. CON, which is not to be confused with the system unit in the middle, contains both an input half—that's the keyboard—and an output half, which is the monitor. Together, the keyboard and the monitor make up the "device" that MS-DOS turns to first when looking for a source of input or a home for output.

About printing those screens. If you use Shift+PrtSc to send screen contents to a laser printer and nothing seems to happen, take the printer offline (press the Online button on the printer to turn it off), and press the Form Feed button. The printer might be waiting for you to tell it when to start printing.

If you have a CGA, an EGA, or a VGA monitor, you can use Shift+PrtSc to copy a graphics screen to the printer. What's a graphics screen? It's the display produced by a program, such as the MS-DOS Shell, that "draws" pictures and characters onscreen rather than using the readable, but rather inelegant, block-type characters you usually see with MS-DOS. To print a graphics screen, first use the Graphics command to prepare MS-DOS for the job. (Type graphics at the MS-DOS prompt.)

The Monitor

A monitor, as you well know, resembles a TV, except that it shows you the work your computer is doing. Even the way it works inside is pretty much the same as a TV: A typical desktop monitor has a coated screen that reacts to the beam from an electron gun, which rapidly sweeps across and down in rows to illuminate small dots (called *pixels,* which is a contraction of *picture elements*). The patterns of dots produce the images you see on the screen. On a monochrome monitor, these pixels are either lit or unlit to form images. On a color monitor, the pixels are laid down in small dots or bands of color—red, green, and blue—and are lit in varying combinations to produce the different shades you see.

Oddly enough, MS-DOS does very little with the monitor, even though *everything* you do with the computer shows up on this device in one way or another. Still, MS-DOS does give you some control over the monitor. You can:

- Change the number of characters per line and lines per screen with the Mode command, as described in "More About Hardware," in Section 3.

- Change the display in the MS-DOS Shell from text (characters) to graphics (pictures). If you have a color monitor, you can also decide what combination of colors you want the Shell to use. For this, all you need are the Display and Colors commands on the Shell's Options menu.

- Adjust color and other aspects of the display when you're using the MS-DOS Editor. For this, see "Make a File with Edit," in Section 3.

POWER PLAY

Giving Yourself More Control

If you're an experienced user of MS-DOS, you probably already know about ANSI.SYS, a program that comes with MS-DOS and that allows you to customize your screen, keyboard, or both. ANSI.SYS is a lot of fun to experiment with, but it's also far beyond the scope of this book—both because it is a long-established feature, by no means new to the version 6.2 upgrade, and because it requires something of a programmer's approach to computers. If you're interested in trying out ANSI.SYS and you upgraded from an earlier version of MS-DOS (from Microsoft), look it up in your old MS-DOS manual.

ANSI.SYS has changed over the years, but not as dramatically as other parts of MS-DOS. What you find in your manual might be enough to get you started. If you can't find information on ANSI.SYS, try some MS-DOS user's magazines or a complete reference to MS-DOS commands or batch files.

Even though MS-DOS doesn't give you much control over the monitor, display-related terms are probably among the most confusing you encounter in dealing with computers. If you want to know a little bit more, read on. If you don't, skip to something that interests you more.

Images and Resolutions

A computer monitor, although it displays an image, doesn't work all on its own. In order to "understand" what it's supposed to display, and in order to create the image properly, the monitor relies either on built-in video circuitry or on a translator known as a display adapter housed on a circuit board inside the system unit. The circuitry or display adapter is what generates the signal that describes the image to be shown. Naturally, this picture-making hardware has to match the capabilities of the monitor.

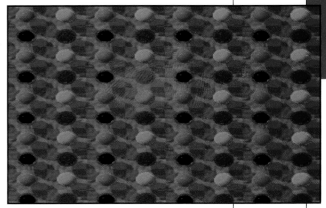

The same image on an SVGA display

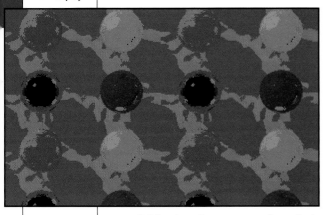

A graphics image on an EGA display

Nowadays, new computers generally come with either VGA or SVGA monitors, both of which can produce up to 256 colors in a range of resolutions. What's resolution? Basically, it's the clarity of the picture, defined in terms of the number of pixels per row and the number of rows per screen that are used to create the image. You can generally assume that the higher the resolution (density of pixels), the clearer the image, but this is not always the case. A typical VGA display uses 640 pixels across by 480 pixels down. SVGA displays are capable of creating images with as many as 1024 pixels across by 768 pixels down, but the characters produced in this mode use the same number of pixels as the lower resolution display and are therefore smaller—too small for easy reading, say some people.

As a computer user, you don't have to know anything more about how display circuitry works. You do, however, have to know that your computer has it, and you should know what kind it is. Understanding video, however, is where people can run into...not trouble, exactly, but an "understanding problem" based on the number of different video configurations, all of which are known by their initials. To wit:

- MDA. Short for Monochrome Display Adapter, this refers to the circuitry used to support the IBM Monochrome Display for the original IBM PC, way back in 1981. The Monochrome Display Adapter, which is not often seen these days, produced very clear characters, but operated only in text mode, meaning that when you typed an *A*, the *A* was created onscreen from a pattern stored in memory. Because the Monochrome Display Adapter relied on such patterns, it could not produce character formats such as italic and script. Also, because these patterns came in one size only, the Monochrome Display Adapter could not change the size or spacing of displayed characters. It showed 80 characters per line and 25 lines per screen, and that was it. This adapter sounds rather old by modern standards, but at the height of its popularity, it was considered state of the art.

- CGA. Short for Color/Graphics Adapter, this was the first entrant in the graphics display department. Like MDA, CGA has been pretty much outdistanced by EGA and, especially, VGA. Still, CGA can display either text or graphics, and can do it in up to 16 colors. MS-DOS still supports CGA, but this type of display adapter is usually seen only on older computers, most of which are not powerful enough to handle recent versions of MS-DOS.

- EGA. Short for Enhanced Graphics Adapter, this refers to an aging (released in early 1984) but still common display adapter that, like CGA, can display either text or graphics. An EGA monitor can display either monochrome or 16 colors. It is noticeably clearer than a CGA screen, but it is not as sharp or as flexible as VGA or SVGA.

- VGA. Short for Video Graphics Array (not adapter), this is really the current standard on new computers. VGA is highly readable and displays either text or graphics. Unlike earlier display circuitry, VGA uses an analog (continuously variable) signal that enables it to produce up to 256 colors. VGA can, however, produce this many colors only at a slightly lower resolution than normal.

- SVGA. Short for Super VGA, SVGA is increasingly common on the latest computers. Like VGA, it uses an analog signal and can therefore generate 256 (or more) colors. As an added attraction, SVGA can produce many color displays at higher resolutions than VGA can.

Local Bus and Video RAM

If you read the Sunday-paper computer ads these days, you often come across references to local bus and video RAM. A local bus can be used with other hardware, such as a disk drive, but most of the time you'll see it, like video RAM, used in connection with computer monitors.

POWER PLAY

Display Details

Video terminology tends to get wrapped up in numbers, many of which apply to more than one kind of video. If you want details, the following table will help you get your pixels straight. These are the common resolutions; there are many more available.

Display Type	Operating Mode	Resolution	Colors
MDA	Text only	80 characters per line, 25 lines per screen	Monochrome
CGA	Text or graphics	40 or 80 characters per line, 25 lines per screen	16
		320 pixels across by 200 pixels down	4
		640 pixels across by 200 pixels down	2
EGA	Text	Same as MDA and CGA	
	Graphics	Same as CGA, plus the following:	
		300 pixels across by 200 pixels down	16
		640 pixels across by 200 pixels down	16
		640 pixels across by 350 pixels down	Monochrome or 16
VGA	Text	Same as MDA, CGA, and EGA	
	Graphics	Same as EGA, plus the following:	
		640 pixels across by 480 pixels down	16
		320 pixels across by 200 pixels down	256
SVGA	Text	Same as MDA, CGA, EGA, and VGA	
	Graphics	Same as VGA, plus the following:	
		640 pixels across by 480 pixels down	256
		1024 pixels across by 768 pixels down	256

First things first. What's a local bus—metropolitan transit vs. Greyhound? Well, in a sense it is. When you use a computer to display lots of colors and graphical images, especially at high resolutions, the machine has to work really hard to draw, refresh, and update the screen—a process that happens many times per second. Normally, the instructions for drawing and redrawing the screen are pumped along with all kinds of other information along the computer's main internal highway, which is called the system bus. Computers that are designed

with local-bus circuitry can effectively bypass the main highway and give video its very own road to travel—one that, like an express lane on the freeway, is designed for high-speed traffic. The result: much faster video, the effects of which you'll hardly notice with MS-DOS and MS-DOS-based applications but which can turbocharge graphics intensive programs, such as Microsoft Windows and programs that make use of art-work, animation, or photographs. (Note that local-bus circuitry must be designed into the computer; it can't be added to an existing computer.)

As for video RAM, that's a special type of memory that lets the processor and the video circuitry gain admission to the video images in memory through separate, but compatible, doorways. What are those images doing in memory to begin with? Well, that's where they sit until it's time for them to go onstage, on the monitor. When you add video RAM to a computer, you provide the machine with high-speed memory specifically set aside for video images. The result: faster displays, which are especially needed by heavily graphic programs. With MS-DOS alone, you're really not going to be handicapped by a machine with little video RAM. But, as with a local bus, you'll gain a lot if you use programs that incorporate a lot of graphics.

The System Unit

Finally, you come to the main part of your computer, that box in the middle. Computer people often use the term *black box* to define a computer or a part of a computer they think of as "that-mysterious-something-that-does-what-I-want-but-in-ways-I-don't-understand"—either because the operation is too technical or because they just don't care. You can go right ahead and think of the system unit as a black box—a machine into which information enters, gets mashed around a bit, and comes out looking the way you want. But if you learn nothing else, at least familiarize yourself with the main pieces of your computer and find out a little about the processor you've got inside the box.

Two Ways to Remember: Disk Drives and Memory

The processor inside the box is what your computer is all about, but the box holds a lot of other pieces too, including two different types of "memory": the disk drives in front and the memory inside.

Maybe you've never thought of disk drives as memory, but that's really what they are. They serve as long-term memory, or storage, for programs and data you want to keep. And the capacity of a disk drive is measured just as memory is—in kilobytes and megabytes and the like. OK, so they're memory of a sort. What else is there to know about them? Well, everyone knows disk drives come in two varieties, floppy and hard. But perhaps you didn't know that floppy and hard disks work in much the same way. The biggest differences between floppy drives and hard disks are that:

- Floppy disks are removable.

- Hard disks actually contain more than one disk and are very finely machined to extremely close tolerances—so close that the disks must be "vacuum-packed" and sealed away from outside contaminants.

POWER PLAY

"Mom, What's a Kilobyte?"

A kilobyte is roughly 1000 bytes. All right, why is it "roughly" 1000 bytes, and what's a byte anyway? Well, the best place to start is at the beginning, with bits. Computers handle all information as electrical signals representing 1s and 0s, the infamous bits that are shorthand for *bi*nary dig*its*. Bits are what computers chew on, but bits by themselves are too small to have any real meaning to people. Why so? Because a two-state signal can basically mean only yes or no, on or off, true or false. To make bits carry meaningful information, they're lumped into groups of eight known as bytes. Each byte is big enough to represent a single character, such as A, B, C or 1, 2, 3 or ! or ; or ". The byte value for an uppercase A, for example, is 10000001.

Even so, bytes are still pretty small doses of data, so larger units come in handy when you begin to talk about thousands or millions or billions of bytes. That's where kilobytes and megabytes and gigabytes come in.

Just as you talk about the number of pages in a book, not the number of characters in it, you talk about how many kilobytes or megabytes or gigabytes of memory or disk storage a computer has. Now here's the kicker. Remember that computers think in ons and offs, 1s and 0s (binary, if you want to be precise). But people think in decimal—powers of 10. To you, then, *kilo*- means 1000, *mega*- means 1,000,000, and *giga*-, if you ever use it, means 1,000,000,000. All nice, round numbers. Because the computer thinks in 2s, however, the familiar *kilo*- means "the power of 2 closest to 1000"; *mega*- means "the power of 2 closest to 1,000,000"; and *giga*- means "the power of 2 closest to 1,000,000,000." To help you keep this straight, here's a quick reference:

bit = 1 or 0

byte = 8 bits

kilobyte = 1024 bytes

megabyte = 1,048,576 bytes

gigabyte = 1,073,741,824 bytes

As for the disk drives themselves, they're amazing in the way they work. Both floppy and hard disk drives contain small read/write heads attached to arms that are very much like the arms on record players. (Does anyone else remember record players?) These heads are attached to a motor that moves them in and out, from the rim of the disk toward the center and back again. At the same time, the disk itself spins rapidly, so that as the heads are moved into position, continuous circular sections of the disk pass beneath them. All this positioning happens very quickly, but that's only part of the story. As the heads are positioned over the spinning disk, they are constantly at work, either transferring a stream of information to the disk surface, or reading a stream of information from it. All this so you don't lose anything when you shut the computer down.

And what about memory? Ah, memory. There's a lot to learn if you want to be an expert with MS-DOS, but if you're satisfied with just getting your computer to work well, all you have to know is this: RAM. That's random access memory, of course, and it's the kind of memory MS-DOS, your programs, and your data all need.

RAM, as you know, is where the computer temporarily stores programs and data as it's working. It is also the kind of memory that goes totally blank when you turn off the computer, so it's what makes you learn, very early on, to save your work before shutting down. Beyond this, if you're going to make good use of version 6 of MS-DOS, you need to know what kinds of RAM are available. (Yes, RAM comes in varieties, just like ice cream, gasoline, and airplane seating.)

RAM comes in three main varieties: conventional, extended, and expanded. Conventional memory is the kind that's included with every computer. For a number of years now, 640 KB of conventional memory has been standard on new machines. Extended memory is RAM that you add to give your computer more than 640 KB. The details get a little tricky, but basically you can think of extended memory as RAM that you pile on top of conventional memory. Expanded memory, which has been declining in popularity, is a special kind of memory that you add to a computer—special in the sense that it's "piped in" to programs that want it and are capable of using it (not all programs can).

Why so many types of RAM? Because both extended and expanded memory are ways of giving an MS-DOS computer more memory to work with. And

KB, MB

Kilobytes (KB) and megabytes (MB) are common units for measuring memory or disk storage. For a full explanation, see "Mom, What's a Kilobyte?" on the preceding page.

why is more memory needed? Because programs, especially current software, love having lots of memory to work in. And why should you bother knowing anything about different types of memory? Because version 6 of MS-DOS can help you free as much memory as possible. It does this by moving both itself and certain types of programs into out-of-the-way places to leave as much memory as possible for your application programs to stretch out in. (For a nice, long look at memory and what MS-DOS can do with it, refer to "More About Memory," which starts on page 171.)

The Processor

Ultimately, all the information that passes through your computer's memory and disk drives has a single destination, the processor. This little chip, only an inch or two on a side, is the brain of your computer, and through it, all kinds of wonders flow in electrical form. The processor is the part of the computer that acts on your data. It does this by following extremely detailed instructions that would drive you crazy. Instructions far more detailed than these:

```
Put hand in pocket

Find key

Hold key with fingers

Remove hand from pocket

Move hand to door

Put key in lock

Turn key
```

You get the idea. Kind of cuts computers down to size, doesn't it? They're fast, and to people who like them, they're great machines, but they need a maddeningly detailed set of directions. Anyway, about those processors.

The processors that power computers that run MS-DOS all come from the same family tree, which is known as the 80x86 (pronounced "eighty-ex-eighty-six") line. Developed by Intel Corporation, these processors (one of which is shown here) have developed over little more than a decade from the ancestral 8088 and its close cousin the 8086 through the currently popular 80486. Along the way, each processor has been made faster and more powerful than its predecessor, but each remains completely capable of running all the same programs as the earlier models. All in all, a look at the family tree yields the following members and the types of systems in which they are found:

Invitation List for Intel Family Reunion	
Processor	Type of System
8088	Older computers, such as the original IBM PC and the IBM PC/XT.
8086	More powerful, but not really high-end machines, such as the IBM PS/2 model 25.
80286	IBM PC/AT-class computers. Typically, these are machines with 1 MB of memory, a 20-MB to 30-MB hard disk, and an EGA display.
80386	Most current systems, including many portables and laptops. A typical desktop system would have 2 MB to 4 MB of memory, a 60-MB to 120-MB hard disk, and a VGA display.
80486	Current high-end systems, including some portables and laptops. A typical desktop system would have 4 MB to 8 MB of memory, a 250-MB hard disk, and a VGA or an SVGA display.
Pentium	Newest and most powerful of the line. The Pentium is just beginning to appear in very high-end computers, such as those needed at the hub of a network that stores files used by many less powerful machines.

Those are the main pieces of your hardware. Now it's time to move on to MS-DOS itself. Along the way, in later chapters, you'll see some of these players again, in bigger roles. For now, though, you should have enough background to set the stage for your work with version 6 of MS-DOS.

Confused by references to DX and SX models of the 80386 and 80486 processors? They're initials used to define the relative capabilities of these chips. SX is used for the "base model" of the 80386 or 80486; DX refers to the more powerful (and expensive) version of each. The SX version of the 80386 chip handles information in smaller chunks and can't use as much memory as its bigger sibling. The SX version of the 80486 chip doesn't perform mathematical calculations as fast as the DX. The DX, by the way, comes in two varieties: the DX and the DX2 (which can work about twice as fast as the DX).

MS-DOS and What You Do with It

Everything You Need to Know

If you've been ambling contentedly through life, using the same (few) MS-DOS commands to do the same (few) things with MS-DOS, here's your chance to find out just how much more you can do with surprisingly little effort or learning. Go beyond Dir. Sweep past Copy. Leave old habits behind, and see how to use

MS-DOS faster, better, and more efficiently. Get through this chapter and the next, and you'll have covered the most important MS-DOS commands—the ones you really ought to know about.

Ready? Take a deep breath, and jump right in. If you're sitting in front of your computer, great. These chapters include a lot of do-it-yourself practices to help you get comfortable with the many ways MS-DOS works and can work for you. Not, of course, that you have to wade through both chapters in one sitting. Each practice brings you back to the same starting point, so you can go through as much or as little as you like at any time.

This chapter and the next are primarily for people who haven't invested a lot of time exploring MS-DOS. But even if you've had a lot of experience with MS-DOS, scan the chapters to see some of what's new in versions 6.0 and 6.2. You'll be introduced to the new clean and interactive boot options, the new Undelete and online Help, and several long-awaited commands, including Move (which finally lets you move files from one disk or directory to another) and Deltree (which neatly snips off a branch of your directory tree).

About MS-DOS

You know that MS-DOS is an operating system. More specifically, it's a *disk* operating system—so called primarily because a lot of the work it does involves disks: preparing them, writing on them, reading from them, and, at a level you cannot see, organizing them to keep your files accurately and neatly stored.

But as important as disks are to MS-DOS, they aren't everything. MS-DOS has a lot of other work to do too. Even though you're

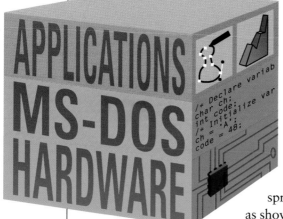

unaware of all its activities, MS-DOS is the one program your computer needs in order to work seamlessly with you and with your other software. MS-DOS controls memory use; MS-DOS controls access to the keyboard and printer. MS-DOS controls most everything. Why is this so? Because an operating system, unlike any other kind of computer program, sits halfway between hardware and the higher-level software, such as word processors and spreadsheets, that put the hardware to work, as shown at left.

People who write books about MS-DOS often try to find some kind of analogy to describe just what position MS-DOS holds in the grand scheme of computing. Frequently, they compare MS-DOS to a traffic cop, a circus ringmaster, or a shop supervisor. But MS-DOS is much more than any of these. It's more like a diplomat or an ambassador who works to bridge the gap between two sometimes very different cultures. In the case of MS-DOS, those two cultures are the intuitive, creative world of humans and the precise, purely logical world of the machine.

That's not an easy job, when you think about it. After all, humans are prone to jump from A to E and assume that everybody knows B, C, and D come between. Computers proceed relentlessly through each step. They cannot function otherwise. But thanks to MS-DOS, you don't have to be anywhere near so single-minded. You don't have to type one machine language instruction after another. You can simply type *dir* and let MS-DOS take over the task of negotiating with the hardware. So, even if you've heard or thought that MS-DOS commands are more lion than lamb, take a longer view. Think of what it would be like if you had to talk to your disk drives directly or squirt out character after character to the printer. Talk about doing things the hard way.

First, You Turn It On

All right, that heading's a joke. This book assumes you've upgraded to version 6.2 (or at least to version 6.0), so it also assumes you know where the on/off switch is on your computer. If you don't, and you've had the machine for a while, you certainly do have an eye for expensive dust collectors....

The news in this section is not how you turn on the computer; it's the different ways version 6 of MS-DOS lets you start the machine—two of which, called a clean boot and an interactive boot, can rescue you in times of trouble. (*Trouble?* Don't panic. It rarely happens, and when it does, it's usually because of something you did. Not entirely consoling, but in most cases, you can do something about the problem. Regardless of the cause, knowing what to do in times of need can be as comforting as knowing there's a spare tire in your trunk.)

Boots and Bootstrapping

You've no doubt heard the expression "boot the computer." Maybe the first time you heard it, you thought someone was telling you to give the computer a swift kick, but you soon realized that "booting" meant starting up. Why do you boot a computer? The term comes from the old saying about pulling yourself up by your bootstraps and refers to the way in which a computer transforms itself from an inert paperweight with the personality of a rock into a humming, interactive appliance.

As it boots, the computer loads a series of programs, each of which gives the machine a little more "awareness." When you turn on the power switch, the computer performs a cold boot: It goes through an extended process that includes a hardware check. When you press Ctrl+Alt+Del to restart the computer, it skips the hardware check. That's a warm boot.

Warm boot or cold, at some point your hard disk light goes on and stays on for several seconds. This happens when you are at the heart of the computer's boot process, the point where MS-DOS itself is moving from disk into memory and taking control of the computer. Important as it is, this takeover occurs quickly, and none of the process is visible to you. You can tell when it's over, however: Strings of messages begin appearing and scrolling rapidly on your screen. These messages, although they might look like gobbledygook to you, are indicators that MS-DOS is active and carrying out the instructions in two very special files you might have heard of, CONFIG.SYS and AUTOEXEC.BAT. These files, which MS-DOS is programmed to look for every time it starts up, contain commands that tell MS-DOS how to customize itself for your particular computer (CONFIG.SYS) and for you personally (AUTOEXEC.BAT).

Finally, after MS-DOS has carried out all its preparations, the screen clears and, unless your computer is set up to start a particular program (such as an application, Microsoft Windows, or the MS-DOS Shell), you see this:

`C:\>_`

MS-DOS is ready to go.

POWER PLAY

Changes in Startup with DoubleSpace and MemMaker

If you ran DoubleSpace after installation in order to gain more storage on your hard disk, part of startup involves making MS-DOS aware of your compressed drive. In a way, running DoubleSpace for the first time is like giving basic MS-DOS a brain boost: The very act of compressing your hard disk causes MS-DOS itself to change, so from then on it will be aware of compressed drives from the minute it starts up. Although all this sounds like too much theory and not enough practice, in fact there's a very real advantage to using DoubleSpace. The fact that this feature is so tightly bound to MS-DOS itself is the reason DoubleSpace is easy to use and requires no work on your part in defining disk volumes or setup files.

In addition to DoubleSpace, your computer's startup might include moving MS-DOS out of conventional memory and into a special part of memory known as the high memory area (HMA). MS-DOS does this to be polite and to leave as much conventional memory as possible open for other programs to use. If you've run MemMaker, you might also be interested to know that your startup probably includes moving some hardware-related software and memory-resident programs into yet another special part of memory called the upper memory area. All this juggling, of course, is for one purpose: To make memory use as efficient as possible on your computer.

Startup in Version 6

When you upgrade to version 6 of MS-DOS, most of the startup process just described remains exactly the same. There are differences, however, some visible and some not, but none of which you really have to understand. What can make a difference are three possible startup options you might want or need to use. One option, which experienced MS-DOS users like a lot, lets you define several alternative startups and choose the one you want from a menu (which you also create). This feature requires a little work on your part, but it's both fun and useful. Here, at the top of the facing page, is what a startup menu looks like:

Menus can be very simple to put together. If you're interested, turn to "Customizing Startup," in Section 4, for a description. A word of advice, however: You should know a little more than how to start the computer before attempting this. If you're still not very surefooted when it comes to tinkering with MS-DOS, work through more of the book before you experiment with alternative startups.

```
MS-DOS 6.2 Startup Menu

   1. Word processor
   2. Spreadsheet
   3. Database

Enter a choice: 1




F5=Bypass startup files F8-Confirm each line of CONFIG.SYS and AUTOEXEC.BAT [N]
```

No Frills: A Clean Boot

Other version 6 startup options—clean and interactive booting—are simple enough that you can try both of them right away. Here's the first:

1. Restart your computer by pressing Ctrl+Alt+Del or by pressing the Reset button (if it has one).

2. When the message *Starting MS-DOS* appears on your monitor, press F5.

You've just performed a clean boot. This told MS-DOS to bypass execution of two files—CONFIG.SYS and AUTOEXEC.BAT—to provide you with a minimal setup: no customizing for a mouse or other devices, no reminders to MS-DOS about where to find your applications, and so on.

Most of the time, you won't need a clean boot, but it can come in handy. If you (or the installation program for a new piece of hardware or software) ever get a little too adventurous and find that MS-DOS won't start properly, you can use a clean boot to bypass CONFIG.SYS and AUTOEXEC.BAT, the two most likely reasons why MS-DOS is misbehaving.

Let Me Decide: An Interactive Boot

Another version 6 startup option is called an interactive boot. If you want to try this option:

1. Reboot the computer with Ctrl+Alt+Del or the Reset button. (Although you normally don't restart the system so frequently, you won't hurt the computer by rebooting twice in a row.)

2. When the message *Starting MS-DOS* appears, press F8.

This time, MS-DOS pauses in the course of its normal startup to display messages, such as the following:

```
DOS=HIGH,UMB [Y,N]?_
```

Don't flinch. MS-DOS reads odd-looking commands like these every time you turn the computer on. Also, don't touch the keyboard until you read a little more.

What's important to you in an interactive boot is that MS-DOS is asking you for advice. Specifically, it's asking whether you want the command carried out. (In this example, MS-DOS wants to know whether it should load itself outside of conventional memory.) The whole point of this startup option is that MS-DOS walks through every line in your CONFIG.SYS file, asking for a Y or an N before it carries out the command. If you type N to say no, MS-DOS skips the command and goes on to the next. CONFIG.SYS, remember, identifies your computer to MS-DOS, so keep this startup option in mind if you (or, once again, a hardware or software installation program) cause MS-DOS to start erratically or not at all.

Oh, right. You're still stuck with that message onscreen. Well, you don't want to monkey around right now, so let MS-DOS carry out each command in your CONFIG.SYS file as it would during a normal startup:

3. Type Y in response to every message MS-DOS displays, whether you understand it or not.

At the end, MS-DOS will ask whether it should process another startup file, AUTOEXEC.BAT. Type Y to say yes, and (if you have version 6.2) type Y in response to all messages from MS-DOS. You'll end up with the fully functional computer you normally get.

MS-DOS Awakes

Now you get to the good part: Telling MS-DOS what to do. This is where you can have some fun and at the same time become much more the doer than the observer. Start right at the beginning, with the very first line of dialog in your ongoing chat with MS-DOS:

```
C:\>_
```

Doesn't look like much, does it? Well, MS-DOS can be pretty terse at times, but that little prompt is still telling you three important facts. It's telling you that:

Both clean and interactive boots are safety measures that enable you to get the computer and MS-DOS going under any circumstances other than broken hardware. Like any emergency measures, know that they're available and hope that you never have to use either. If you do need one or the other, remember that:

• F5 performs a clean boot.

• F8 performs an interactive boot.

For more on this, refer to "Customizing Startup," in Section 4.

- MS-DOS is waiting for a command.
- The current drive is C.
- The current directory is the root directory.

So what? Remember that computers are interactive machines, and they owe that interactivity to MS-DOS. That C:\> command prompt is the operating system's way of saying, "What do you want me to do?" That's a far cry from the room-size computers of old (the 50s and 60s) that sat like idols waiting to be served and tolerated no interruption while they worked. MS-DOS, like all current operating systems, is positively servile by comparison; it lets you be the boss. You can tell it what to do, you can interrupt it with the Esc key, and you can cut it off in the middle of a job with Ctrl+Break. All because of the prompt and what it means: MS-DOS is at your command.

As for telling you the current drive, that's important, too. Your computer undoubtedly has more than one disk drive. Most computers have one or two floppy drives and one hard disk. These drives, as you well know, have names—or at least letters. Your first (probably topmost) floppy drive is A, and your second is B. Your first hard disk is always drive C. Because the command prompt shows you the current drive, it's easy to tell when you have to direct the operating system's attention to a different drive—for example, to the data file you have on the disk in drive B or to the game you're installing from the disk in drive A.

Sending MS-DOS to a Different Drive

You can turn the operating system's attention to a different drive in either of two ways: by changing the current drive or by indicating the drive you want as part of a command you're typing. With either method, you simply type the letter of the drive you want. All you have to remember is to tack a colon (:) on the end.

Changing the Current Drive

When you change the current drive, say from C to A, you start at the command prompt and simply type the letter of the drive you want, followed by a colon. Try it if you want; just be sure to put a formatted disk in drive A so that MS-DOS has something to find (and don't forget to press Enter when you finish typing the command). Your dialog with MS-DOS looks like this:

```
C:\>a:

A:\>_
```

If your computer has a single floppy drive, you normally refer to it as drive A. With certain MS-DOS commands, however, you can use your single floppy drive as both drive A and drive B. For example, when you copy disks with the Diskcopy command, you can use your single floppy drive as both the source (drive A) and the target (drive B). MS-DOS won't get confused, although you might. Commands that refer to your floppy drive as either A or B are noted in the text, when appropriate.

Notice that MS-DOS changes the command prompt to A:\> when it carries out the command. The prompt, remember, shows the current drive, and you've changed the current drive to A. Practice some more by changing back to drive C:

```
A:\>c:
C:\>_
```

Telling MS-DOS Which Drive to Use

As you work, you can tell MS-DOS to leave the current drive as is but to use a different drive when carrying out a command. This is probably familiar territory to you if you've used the Directory, Copy, or Format command. All you do is insert the drive letter (and a colon) in the command to tell MS-DOS which drive you want it to work with. Here are two examples that use one of the first MS-DOS commands everyone learns: Directory. To be sure the examples work as advertised, find a floppy disk you can put in your A drive—a new one will be fine, but one containing lots of files (of any kind) would be better.

First, tell MS-DOS to show you what's on your C drive:

```
C:\>dir
```

Notice that you didn't include a drive letter and colon in your command here. That's because MS-DOS always assumes you mean the current drive, unless you specifically tell it to use a different one. Here, depending on how full your hard disk is, you might see a short list or a very long one that rolls along for screen after screen. How much you see doesn't matter.

Now put the floppy disk in your A drive and use the Directory command again, this time to see what that disk contains. (If the disk is brand-new, be prepared to be underwhelmed.) To add a little variety to the example, you're going to include an option, /p, that tells MS-DOS to pause after each screenful. That way, you'll have time to read the list even if it's long:

```
C:\>dir a: /p
```

> **Remember this: MS-DOS commands that act on files always assume that you mean the current drive, unless you specifically include a different drive letter as part of the command. The distinction can be critical, especially if you're deleting files.**

This time, your command includes a drive letter. You had to put it in because the current drive is C, and you specifically wanted to tell MS-DOS to list the files for another drive, A. If the disk contains a lot of files, notice that /p causes MS-DOS to stop and wait for you to press a key whenever the screen fills up.

Clearing the Screen

By now, your screen is probably a bit of a mess, so it's time to clean up with the Clear Screen command. This has got to be the simplest command in all of MS-DOS. Type:

```
C:\>cls
```

There you have it, a blank slate with the command prompt in the upper left-hand corner. Easy as pie, but better and faster than any eraser. Remember Clear Screen whenever there's too much clutter onscreen.

Clear Screen (Cls)
Clears the screen.
Type:
C:\>cls

About Commands

You control your dog and MS-DOS in the same way: by giving commands. In both cases, you can use slight variations of most commands—for example, either "sit" or "sit now" work with a dog, just as "dir" or "dir a:" work with MS-DOS. As long as the basic command is recognizable, neither the dog nor MS-DOS should have any trouble understanding what you want. The only real difference between computer and canine is this:

- MS-DOS responds instantly to your command, whereas lots of dogs require something along the lines of "Sit. Sit, sit, siiiiiit...oh, come on. Sit!"

Enough of that. Every MS-DOS command has one main part: the command name. You've just seen one of these, Clear Screen, which you type as *cls*. Most commands, however, are more flexible. You can tell them *what* to act on, such as a particular drive or file, and you can control *the way* they behave by including some built-in cues called *switches*. The Directory command provides for both of these, as you can see if you take a look at its basic anatomy, or *syntax*. This diagram shows a simplified form of the Directory command syntax, with labels identifying each of the parts.

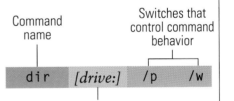

This might look a little forbidding right now, but it's something you'll have to get used to, because this is how MS-DOS commands are always described—not only in this book, but, as you'll see shortly, onscreen when you ask MS-DOS for help. Here's what it all means:

- The command name, *dir* in this case, is shown exactly as you type it. It's always the first part of an MS-DOS command.

- Information that tells the command what to act upon is called a parameter. You provide this information so that you can specify precisely what you want the command to do. Parameters in this book are shown as descriptive words, such as *drive* or *filename*; in syntax lines, they appear in *italics*. When you use such parameters, don't type the description; type an appropriate *drive* letter or *filename* instead. For example, you might type a: or b: to replace the *drive* parameter.

Some commands, such as Format and Copy, require you to include one or more parameters. Other commands, such as Directory, don't require parameters but allow you to include one or more if you want. If a parameter is optional, it's shown in square brackets, like this: [*drive:*].

- Switches, like railroad switches, shunt a command off onto one track or another. A switch is usually a single letter, such as the p and w in the diagram, always preceded by a slash (/).

  Switches are optional. In the Directory command, /p *pauses* after each screenful so that you don't have to have bionic eyeballs to scan the entire list; /w produces a *wide* display that shows the names of files in five columns across the screen. See? The letters aren't arbitrary mind-breakers after all.

- Sometimes, but not frequently, you see switches that use parameters to customize even more. In these cases, a switch looks something like this: /o:[*order*]. When you see such switches in this book, you'll always be told the acceptable values for the switch parameter.

All right, now that you know what a command looks like, you can begin to soar. In fact, if you look back a few pages at the discussion headed "Telling MS-DOS Which Drive to Use," you'll see examples of the Directory command that you can compare with the syntax. The remaining examples in this chapter will stretch your wings a little with some parameters, both optional and required, and some useful switches to remember.

Be sure to use the forward slash (/) for switches, not the backslash (\), which plays its starring role in paths: /p is a switch; \p is a directory named P. Lots more on paths in the next chapter.

Help!

No matter how familiar you are with MS-DOS, there always comes a time when you can't quite remember how a certain command is put together. Or you know you've heard of a command that's exactly right for the job you want to do, but you draw a blank when it comes to the name. Never fear, Help is here. And not just one kind of Help, but two: Fasthelp and Help. Both are help programs that display information about MS-DOS commands and how you use them.

Fast and Lean

Fasthelp, as you can guess, gives you help on the basics of a command. You can ask for Fasthelp for a particular command in either of two ways:

- By typing fasthelp followed by the name of a command for which you want help:

    ```
    C:\>fasthelp cls
    ```

- By typing the name of a command, followed by a slash and a question mark, like so:

    ```
    C:\>dir /?
    ```

If you're interested in speed, you can easily see that the fastest route to Fasthelp is the *command* /? form. To try it for yourself, ask what the Clear Screen command does:

```
C:\>cls /?
```

You see:

```
Clears the screen

CLS
```

The first line tells you what the Clear Screen command does; the second (in capitals) tells you how to type the command.

If you type *fasthelp* without specifying a command, MS-DOS displays a list of the commands supported by Fasthelp.

Almost as Fast, a Lot More Detailed

Fasthelp is great when you already know pretty much what you want and you just want a refresher on how to use or construct a command. Regular Help is a lot more detailed and even includes "pages" of notes and examples. This form of help is basically your MS-DOS manual, computerized, updated, and brought online so MS-DOS can display it.

You ask for Help in either of two ways:

- By typing help to begin with a screenful of command names supported by Help:

    ```
    C:\>help
    ```

- By typing help followed by the name of the command for which you want help:

    ```
    C:\>help dir
    ```

If you have version 6.2, try typing *help whatsnew*. You'll see a nice little summary of all the new features of version 6.2.

Help is far more detailed than Fasthelp. Unlike a lot of MS-DOS, it uses an onscreen "window" and responds to the mouse as well as to the keyboard. The following example gives you a chance to see Help and flip through its pages a little. To get as much information onscreen as possible, use the /h switch, which causes Help to display the maximum number of lines your screen supports:

```
C:\>help /h
```

The resulting screen (the contents screen) lists all the commands in MS-DOS:

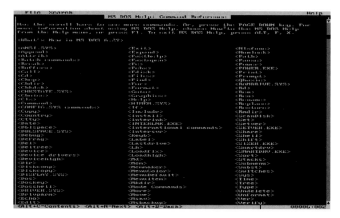

There are a lot, but don't be overwhelmed. Some of these commands (such as Cls) are commonly used; others (such as Break, Fdisk, Nlsfunc, and Switches) are exotic and rarely used. You certainly don't have to know them all, or even a majority of them. All you have to remember is this:

- If you ever need to use a command you don't know, don't sweat it. You can always ask MS-DOS for help.

On the Contents screen, notice that all the command names are enclosed in bright arrowheads, like this: <Cls>. Those arrowheads tell you that you can treat the enclosed topic as a button. It won't exactly hurl you into hyperspace, but it will let you zip directly to information on that topic. To try it:

- If you have a mouse, move the mouse pointer (actually, a square or rectangle) to the entry <Dir>. Press the left mouse button.

- If you don't have a mouse, press the down arrow key until the cursor is in <Dir>. Press Enter.

Bingo. Help on the Directory command. The screen you see here is the Syntax screen—the "page" that describes how you use the Directory command. Notice that the Syntax screen looks a lot like the earlier diagram of the Directory command. The only real difference is that you're seeing the full-blown version of Directory in all its glory. In addition, the syntax you see here encloses both switches and parameters in brackets [ ] and doesn't italicize parameters.

1. To see more, press the PgDn key. Don't worry about understanding all that you see on the screen. Even commands as familiar as Directory often include a lot of extras, but as a rule of thumb, you can assume that the parts you know or find easiest to understand are also the most useful.

2. When you've had enough, press PgUp to return to the beginning of the topic.

Now, see the topics *Notes* and *Examples* enclosed in bright arrowheads at the top of the screen? They're references to additional information about Directory, and they're as easy to turn to as the next page in a book. You can use the arrow keys to move the cursor to the command you want and then press Enter, or you can point and click with the mouse. Or you can take the lazy person's way. Look at the bottom line of the screen. It tells you that Alt+N takes you to the Next (topic). Try it:

1. Hold down the Alt key and press N, or click on the command. The screen instantly changes to show you Notes for the Directory command.

2. Press Alt+N again, and the screen changes to Examples of using Directory. After you've seen all the topics for Directory, pressing Alt+N takes you to the topics for Diskcomp (which is the next command on the Contents screen).

Help also remembers what you've looked at, so if you're researching a particular set of commands, you can also move backward through those you've already consulted. The magic keys for this are Alt+B. And if you want to go right back to the beginning, you can press Alt+C to flip back to the Contents screen.

As a final note, look at the topmost line of the screen. No matter what you're doing in Help, the names of three menus are always displayed here: File and Search on the left, and Help on the right. These are short menus, each of which contains only two commands. Try opening a menu:

• If you have a mouse, point to the menu you want and press the left mouse button.

• If you don't have a mouse, press Alt. This shifts Help's attention to the menus and also causes it to highlight a letter in each menu name. To choose a menu, press the highlighted letter in the name of the menu you want. This is what the menu commands do:

The Exit command on the File menu quits Help. The keystrokes (Alt, F, and X) become automatic after a while.

The Print command on the File menu prints the topic currently displayed. (Check to be sure your printer is turned on before you use this command.)

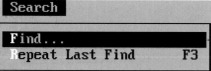

The Find and Repeat Last Find commands on the Search menu let you search Help for each occurrence of a specific word or set of words.

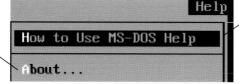

The About command on the Help menu, despite its rather promising name, merely gives you copyright information about Help. You don't need this one.

The How To Use MS-DOS Help command on the Help menu tells you how to use Help itself. You really don't ever have to choose this command, however, because pressing the F1 key does the job for you.

When you choose the Find command from the Search menu, you see this appear:

```
┌──────────────────────── Find ────────────────────────┐
│                                                        │
│  Find What:  [                                      ]  │
│                                                        │
│                                                        │
│     [ ] Match Upper/Lowercase        [ ] Whole Word    │
│                                                        │
│     < OK >          < Cancel >          < Help >       │
└────────────────────────────────────────────────────────┘
```

This is called a dialog box, and it's the way Find asks what you want to find. Type the word or words you seek in the box labeled Find What. As long as the cursor or a dark highlight is in the box, you can just start typing; what you type will replace whatever's in the box.

Next, if you want to search for exact uppercase/lowercase matches, check the box to the left of Match Upper/Lowercase. (With the mouse, just click the box; with the keyboard, tab to the box—repeatedly press the Tab key until the cursor is in the box—and press the Spacebar.) If you want to find whole words only— for example, to start a search for *file* that skips over *filename*—check the box to the left of Whole Word.

To start the search, press Enter or click OK with the mouse. The dialog box disappears, and the help screen reappears with the cursor blinking under the first occurrence of your search text that Find was able to locate. If you want to search some more, choose Repeat Last Find or (much faster) press F3 to search for the next occurrence of the text you specified.

Save Your Fingers with F3

Maybe you're the world's best typist, and you never type something like this:

```
C:\>dit a:
```

when you meant to type this:

```
C:\>dir a:
```

And maybe you never find yourself using the same command over and over, like this:

```
C:\>dir a:
```

Oops, wrong disk, try again:

```
C:\>dir a:
```

Not this one either. Hmm, maybe this one:

```
C:\>dir a:
```

Grrr....

If you're like most people, both of these examples are familiar. If so, you'll appreciate putting one particular function key, F3, to work at the command prompt (as opposed to using it to search in Help). This small, widely unpublicized key tells MS-DOS to display the last command you typed. Try it.

1. Type:

```
C:\>dit
```

2. Press Enter, and MS-DOS complains:

```
Bad command or file name
```

Well, obviously the command isn't bad. It's just wrong; that's all. OK, try again.

3. Press F3 to redisplay the command.

4. Press the Backspace key once.

5. Type r and press Enter.

That's more like it.

Break Time: Fun with Prompts and Hardware

You've seen quite a bit of MS-DOS and its command prompt by now. Have you ever wondered who made the command prompt look like that? MS-DOS did. The command prompt you see is what's called the *default* command prompt, the one that MS-DOS is designed to give you. But if you have a default, can't you also have a nondefault? Absolutely, and with no bother. You can jazz up the command prompt in many ways, like this:

```
Hey, I need input> _
```

this:

```
Today is Sat 12-25-1993_
```

or something more useful, like this:

```
Sat 12-25-1993

Time: 16:30

C:\>_
```

To change the command prompt, you use the Prompt command: Type prompt, followed by whatever you want the command prompt to display. To have MS-DOS display some text, you simply type the text you want. To have MS-DOS display the time, date, or current drive, you use some special abbreviations that tell MS-DOS what you want. These abbreviations are single characters preceded by a dollar sign. For example, the default command prompt, PG, tells MS-DOS to display the drive and path ($P) and a greater-than character ($G). Here is a useful list:

$Q	Displays an equal sign.
$$	Displays a dollar sign.
$D	Displays the date.
$T	Displays the time (on a 24-hour clock, unfortunately, but you can't have everything).
$P	Displays the current drive and path. You'll get to paths in a while; for now, remember that $P is part of the default command prompt—the part that displays *C:*.
$N	Displays the current drive (no path). This might seem more reasonable than $P, but it's actually less useful, as you'll see later.
$G	Displays a greater-than character. This is the rest of the default command prompt, the part that displays *>*.
$H	Backspaces one character. This might seem useless, but normally MS-DOS displays the time in hours, minutes, seconds, and hundredths of seconds. To make the time easier to read, you can use $H to backspace over the parts you don't want to display. You'll see this in a moment.
$_	Moves the next part of your command prompt to a new line.

Now for some fun. If you're sitting at your computer, type the following, pressing the Spacebar where you see *<space>*:

```
C:\>prompt What now, boss?<space>
```

After you press Enter, the command prompt changes to:

```
What now, boss? _
```

Like it? Try this:

```
What now, boss? prompt $d$_The time is: $t$h$h$h$h$h$h$_$p$g
```

Now you've got:

```
Sat 12-25-1993
The time is: 16:39
C:\>_
```

Had enough? Change back to the default command prompt like this:

```
Sat 12-25-1993

The time is: 16:39

C:\>prompt $p$g
```

Prompt

Changes the command prompt. Type:

```
prompt
```

followed by the text you want to display, by an abbreviation consisting of a dollar sign and one of Prompt's special characters, or by a combination of the two. (See the preceding page for a list of commonly used special characters.)

Controlling the Keyboard and the Display

As you know now, MS-DOS works very closely with your computer hardware. It also works very closely with you and gives you a share in its control of the main parts of your computer. Some of this "control" can try your patience, as anyone who's ever used MS-DOS to set up a serial printer can tell you. But that's definitely not true for controlling your keyboard and your display. You can easily work your will on both to make the *personal* in personal computing a little more true for you.

To control either the keyboard or the display, you use a command named Mode. To tell Mode what part of your hardware to work on, you use the name CON, which MS-DOS automatically assigns to both the keyboard and the display. But if you use the same name for both, how does MS-DOS know which one you mean? Remember that the keyboard is input only and the display is output only. Because each has a very definite role to play, MS-DOS can tell from the way you put your Mode command together whether you want to adjust the keyboard or the display. It's simple.

For the keyboard, the Mode command looks like this:

```
mode con rate=x delay=x
```

For the display, the Mode command looks like this:

```
mode con cols=x
```

In each case, all you do is replace *x* with numbers that tell MS-DOS what you want.

Tuning the Keyboard

Keyboard agility varies widely among people, depending on how fast they type and how lightly their fingers dance over the keyboard. Some pound away with the verve of rock musicians; others stroke the keys like a pianist playing Brahms's "Lullaby."

As you type, do you ever wish that a key, such as one of the arrow keys, on your keyboard would move (repeat) a lot faster when held down? Or perhaps you find that keys start repeating too quickly after you press them? With MS-DOS and the Mode command, you can control both the rate at which keys repeat and the amount of time that must pass before the computer realizes you want to repeat the keystroke. The basic Mode command, as you've seen, is:

```
mode con rate=x delay=x
```

So what's *x*? For the rate, which controls how quickly keys repeat, you can use any number from 1 through 32, meaning a repeat rate of about 2 (very slow) through 30 (very fast) characters per second. For the delay, which controls how long you wait for the key to start repeating after you hold it down, you can use 1 for 0.25 second, 2 for 0.50 second, 3 for 0.75 second, or 4 for 1.0 second. To see how this works, try both the slowest and the fastest settings.

To put your keyboard into slow motion, type:

```
C:\>mode con rate=1 delay=4
```

To see the result, press and hold down a letter key, such as R. Slow, steady, and probably irritating. Press Enter to display a new command prompt. (Ignore MS-DOS when it complains *Bad command or file name.* You know that.)

Now shift the keyboard into high gear:

```
C:\>mode con rate=30 delay=1
```

Press and hold the R key again. Now you're cooking. Actually this speed is probably too fast, as you'd see if you tried using an arrow key to move around in a report or some other document. Your cursor would go flying across the screen, and unless you're a typist with a very light touch, you'd probably waste a lot of time overshooting your target and backing up. To reset the keyboard to a more typical setting, press Enter, and type:

```
C:\>mode con rate=20 delay=2
```

POWER PLAY

Reading More, Scrolling Less

Normally, your display shows 25 lines per screen. You can use the Mode command to display either 43 or 50 lines per screen, but you need to do a little preparation first: You have to tell MS-DOS to use a special program called ANSI.SYS to enhance your control. You do this by adding the line:

```
DEVICE=C:\DOS\ANSI.SYS
```

to your CONFIG.SYS file and restarting your computer. The process isn't difficult, but to be sure it works right, you have to know how to edit a file and how to verify that ANSI.SYS is, indeed, in a directory named \DOS on your hard disk.

If you're pretty confident, turn to "Make a File with Edit" (for information about editing files), in Section 3, or "Customizing Startup" (for information about CONFIG.SYS), in Section 4. If you aren't sure about any of this, leave the exploration of ANSI.SYS for later. By the end of the book, you'll know what to do.

Changing the Display

Just as MS-DOS lets you control the rate and delay on the keyboard, it also lets you control the size of the characters on your display. Here you really have only two choices: normal, which is 80 characters per line, or large, which is 40 characters per line. You've seen that the Mode command for controlling the display looks like this:

```
mode con cols=x
```

so change to larger characters:

```
C:\>mode con cols=40
```

and type a Directory command to see what the larger text looks like:

```
C:\>dir
```

Pretty big, isn't it? Well, you know how to reset the display:

```
C:\>mode con cols=80
```

The next chapter takes you into the world of disks and files. The pace picks up a bit, but you're ready. You've seen that MS-DOS is both trainable and controllable. Now you'll see that it's also usable, if not exactly what you'd call pettable.

On to Disks and Files

The Real World

You've covered a fair amount of basic information, all of which you need in order to understand MS-DOS and feel comfortable with it. But now you're ready to move on to control both MS-DOS and the work you create and save on your computer. This chapter shows you around the real world, where you're going to spend most of your quality time with MS-DOS, now and in the future.

Most of the examples in this chapter build on one another to show you how the different aspects of your work with MS-DOS are related. The examples are not complex, and none takes more than a few minutes to try, but because example C assumes you've completed examples A and B, you don't have as much freedom to skip around as you did (or could have done) in the preceding chapter.

If you've been trying examples on your own computer but don't have lots of time or patience, don't worry. No one figures you're going to want to chain yourself to the machine until you reach page 91. To help you plan your time with MS-DOS, the chapter is studded with breakpoints, all of them clearly indicated. You can pause for coffee, quit, or go on vacation at any of these points, and whenever you choose to return, you can pick up exactly where you left off.

That said, it's on to disks.

Disks

In a way, disks are a kind of computer "memory." What? Sure. They're *permanent* memory. Unlike RAM, which goes blank as soon as you turn off the computer, disks hold information for as long as you want—or at least until you boil them, scrape your windshield with them, or use them in a Science Fair project on magnetism. Disks are where you save anything and everything you don't want your computer to "forget"—from MS-DOS itself right on through application programs and letters to Aunt Maude. If you didn't have disks, you would have to educate your computer from the ground up every time you started it.

Although hard disks and floppy disks differ mainly in the amount of information they can hold, their care and feeding is somewhat different. Floppy disks are far more portable than hard disks, but because they can be taken out of the drive and carried around, they are also hostage to your own good intentions. This is especially true of 5.25-inch disks because they really are floppy compared to the smaller, stiffer, 3.5-inch variety.

POWER PLAY

Disk Capacity

A hard disk is a hard disk is a hard disk. About all you have to know about it is how big it is. And actually, you don't even have to know that; MS-DOS can tell you with the Check Disk command. Floppy disks, however, are a slightly different matter because they come in two sizes and five varieties, distinguished by their carrying capacity:

- 5.25-inch floppies capable of holding 360 KB of information. These are usually called double-sided, double-density, or DD.

- 5.25-inch floppies capable of holding 1.2 MB. These are often called double-sided, high-density, or HD. If your dealer said your computer has a "high-capacity" 5.25-inch drive, these are the disks you use.

- 3.5-inch floppies capable of holding 720 KB. These are the 3.5-inch version of double-density disks. Despite their name, 3.5-inch disks are pretty unfloppy floppies.

- 3.5-inch floppies capable of holding 1.44 MB. These are the 3.5-inch version of high-density disks.

- 3.5-inch floppies capable of holding 2.88 MB. These are not widely used. If they had a common name, it would probably be something like super-high-density.

You can use a low-capacity floppy disk in a high-capacity drive, but you cannot reverse the situation and read a high-capacity disk in a low-capacity drive. Doing so won't break your computer, but the drive will not be able to use the disk properly. At best, the disk will have a lot of bad (unreadable) spots on it. At worst, and most commonly, the disk will be completely unreadable. To avoid causing yourself headaches, you should generally match disks to the maximum drive capacity. That is, use 1.2-MB disks in a 1.2-MB drive and 1.44-MB disks in a 1.44-MB drive.

With either type of floppy disk, careful handling means:

- Keeping them away from magnets, which can thoroughly scramble their data.

- Protecting them from being stabbed by sharp objects. This warning includes ballpoint pens, if you use them to write labels for 5.25-inch floppies. Always try to fill out the label before sticking it on the disk. If you have to add to a disk label, use a felt-tip pen.

- Not letting your disks get dusty or dirty. Cleanliness here doesn't mean antiseptic. Dust-free and off the floor will do fine. Storing your 5.25-inch floppies in their sleeves is a worthwhile precaution.

- Storing your disks in disk boxes or other containers. Do this not only to keep the disks clean, but to keep them organized. This is the voice of harsh experience speaking.

And what about hard disks? How do you care for them, or do you even have to? Well, all hard disks are sealed in airtight cases to keep dust and contaminants away from the insides, especially the disk surfaces and the read/write heads. This protection is important, because during operation those heads literally float on air, a tiny fraction of a hair's breadth above the disk surface.

To a hard disk, a dust particle or similar-size obstacle is like a boulder. And the read/write heads are no happier about crashing into such objects than you would be about slamming into a boulder while running or driving at top speed. Ouch! to say the least. You're probably looking at a damaged disk and lost data in such circumstances.

Although its airtight case protects the hard disk from dirt, *you* must keep the disk's close tolerances in mind, too. Normally, hard disks don't mind being moved (carefully) when you move your system, but on a day-to-day basis, keep several points in mind:

- Keep your computer area relatively clean and dust-free. If you can, take smoke breaks away from the machine. (Doing so helps keep the screen clean, too.)

- Don't jostle the system while the hard disk is working. The disk is spinning at about 3600 RPM, and the heads are truly flying, so be as careful about bumps as you would be with a record turntable or a cake in the oven.

- Don't turn off the computer until the hard disk settles down. Waiting until the drive light goes off guarantees that the heads are safely in their own parking zones.

REVIVING YOUR SYSTEM

If a problem, such as a program "bug," causes a drive light to go on and stay on, you can't very well sit for eternity waiting for the drive to settle down. If such a thing happens and you're pretty sure you've encountered a problem, wait a good long time—a minute or two—to see whether the system quiets down on its own. If it doesn't, try Esc and then Ctrl+Break to see whether either can call a halt. If they can't, Ctrl+Alt+Del might do the job. If even that doesn't work, your final recourse is to switch off the power and reboot.

When you're labeling 3.5-inch floppy disks, your instinct might be to stick the labels on "right side up" so that the lettering on the disk and the lettering on the label face the same direction. Instead, stick each label on "upside down," as shown in the illustration on the facing page. The reason: When you store those disks in a box, you'll want to be able to read the labels easily as you flip through the disks. So the "upside-down" labels will magically turn right side up.

Preparing Disks with Format

You might have little or no occasion to format new floppies; these days many come preformatted and ready to go. And chances are you'll never have to format a new hard disk because they're almost always formatted by the manufacturer or dealer that installs them. Still, formatting is a necessary first step to making a disk usable, for two reasons:

- So that MS-DOS can store and retrieve information with pinpoint accuracy. (No minor task when you consider how large a hard disk can be and how very small a single byte is.)

- So that MS-DOS can always tell exactly how much storage remains available on that disk.

Important as it is, formatting is a process that MS-DOS handles pretty much on its own. Your main contribution is supplying the disk, closing the drive latch (if necessary), and pressing a few keys when MS-DOS asks you to. During formatting, your drive light goes on and remains on, as MS-DOS checks the disk and then proceeds to turn it into the electronic equivalent of a neatly ruled sheet of paper, ready for whatever you want to "write" on it.

When formatting disks, your only real decision comes in figuring out what type of format you want. Uh-oh, you just *knew* this was going to get complicated, right? Nope, it's simple. MS-DOS supports three basic types of formatting:

- Standard. This is the easiest, a real no-brainer you can turn to anytime, with any disk, but it's typically what you would choose with a never-before-formatted disk. You can reverse a standard format with the Unformat command.

- Quick. This is really easy, too. Much faster than a standard format, a quick format is *the* choice when you want to recycle a used disk. A quick format, too, can be reversed with Unformat.

- Unconditional. This is very thorough, relatively lengthy, and—remember this—irreversible: You can't undo the process as you can with either standard or quick formats. Choose an unconditional format when you want to make the contents of a used disk unrecoverable. Otherwise, forget this option.

Now to get to work. You'll need a floppy disk, of course. Find one that fits your A drive, and check to be sure it is the type your drive was designed to use—if you have a 1.2-MB drive, use a 1.2-MB floppy; you get the idea. Although you can format a high-capacity disk for a lower capacity, make life simple right now by matching the disk to the drive.

Start with a standard format, which is very likely what you've been using all along in your work with MS-DOS:

Although MS-DOS requires you to confirm your intention before it will format a hard disk, think carefully before you take the plunge, and think especially deep thoughts if the hard disk is your C drive. "Do I really want to do this to the disk that boots my system?" With version 6 of MS-DOS, it *is* possible to reverse a format, but even experienced MS-DOS users hesitate before formatting a hard disk.

1. If you're using a new disk (which will do just fine), put it in drive A. If you're formatting a used disk, put it in drive A and check it with the Directory command to be sure it doesn't contain any files you want to keep:

   ```
   C:\>dir a: /p
   ```

2. Now, type the plain-vanilla Format command:

   ```
   C:\>format a:
   ```

Unlike most MS-DOS commands, Format carries on a dialog of sorts with you. First, in response to your command, it asks you to be sure there's a disk in drive A:

```
Insert new diskette for drive A:
and press ENTER when ready...
```

Press Enter, and Format begins with a message telling you what it's doing:

```
Checking existing disk format.
Saving UNFORMAT information.
```

The first line means that Format is finding out whether the disk has been formatted previously and, if so, to what capacity. The second line tells you it's saving a record of what, if anything, is on the disk so that you can later undo the format if necessary—for example, if you got distracted and accidentally formatted the disk containing the only record of reconstructed dinosaur DNA in existence. (Yeah, sure.)

When the initial check is over, Format goes on to the main part of its job and tells you it's doing so like this:

```
Verifying 720K
```

As it works, it gives you an ever-changing status report such as this:

```
22 percent completed.
```

Disk capacity, of course, depends on the size of the disk you're formatting. When all is done, Format informs you:

```
Format complete.

Volume label (11 characters, ENTER for none)?
```

This last line looks pretty meaningless if you don't know what a volume label is. Fortunately, you're about to find out: A volume label is a name you assign to a disk so that you can identify it later on. As the message states, you can assign a name of up to 11 characters, or you can press Enter to skip the name. If you give the disk a volume label (recommended so you can use the name as a guide to the disk's contents), you can include spaces but none of the following characters:

```
" * + , . / : ; < = > ? [ \ ] |
```

When this message appears on your screen, assign a volume label like this:

```
Volume label (11 characters, ENTER for none)? my disk
```

To finish up, Format then reports on the disk:

```
        730112 bytes total disk space
        730112 bytes available on disk

          1024 bytes in each allocation unit.
           713 allocation units available on disk.

Volume Serial Number is 3722-0FC9

Format another (Y/N)?
```

Type **N** in response to the (ultimate) question, and then take a look at those other messages.

Compared to much of MS-DOS, Format is downright chatty when its work is done, what with all those comments about bytes available and allocation units. Here's what it all means:

- Total disk space tells you how much the disk can hold.

- Bytes available on disk tells you how much free storage space remains. In this case, because the disk is newly formatted, total and available space are the same.

- The size and number of allocation units give you a glimpse at how MS-DOS actually stores files. Because transferring information to and from disk one byte at a time would be both inefficient and time-consuming, MS-DOS stores information in chunks, each of which occupies one allocation unit (which, in this example, is 1024-byte size).

- The volume serial number is a unique number (based on the date and time) that MS-DOS assigns to every formatted disk. Even though volume serial numbers, such as 3722-0FC9, don't look much like numbers, they are. For its own work, MS-DOS uses special arithmetic known as hexadecimal, or base-16, numbering.

Need a rest? You can stop here, if you want. Keep the disk you just formatted, though. You'll use it again.

As described in the next chapter, you can use Format's /v switch to assign a volume label at the time you type the Format command. Here's a tip, though: When you type the label as part of the command, you cannot use spaces; when you type the label in response to Format's prompt, as shown here, spaces are perfectly legal. Thus, you could assign the label MY-DISK or MY_DISK with the /v switch, but you could use MY DISK if you let Format prompt for a volume label.

If Format reports bad sectors on a floppy disk, be suspicious. Either avoid using the disk or use it for your least sensitive data files.

Reformatting Disks

Reduce, reuse, recycle. That advice applies to floppy disks as well as soda cans and milk jugs. Format is not only good for preparing disks for the first time, it's also a way to use MS-DOS to clean up your environment and save you money. As you work, it's really easy to grab for a new disk whenever you want to store or transport work on a floppy. But eventually, you end up with piles of disks—some useful, others not, possibly most of them unlabeled, and most likely none full. What to do with them? The obvious first answer is to organize them and store more than a few files on each one. The next solution is to recycle old disks by reformatting them. This is easy, because you can do a quick format.

Before you try a quick format, do a little preparation for the unformatting that you'll be doing immediately after:

1. Leave the disk you just formatted in drive A, and type:

   ```
   C:\>copy c:\autoexec.bat a:
   ```

   That puts a file on the disk. You'll use it to check up on MS-DOS in a minute or two.

2. Now, to establish good habits, check the disk:

   ```
   C:\>dir a: /p
   ```

   MS-DOS responds by showing one file, AUTOEXEC.BAT. Before you go on, also note the first two lines of output from the Directory command; they give the disk's volume label and volume serial number. Reformatting will cause both of these to change.

3. All right, now reformat the disk:

   ```
   C:\>format a: /q
   ```

   Quick is right. After the initial messages appear, formatting is over practically before it begins. In preparation for the next demonstration (unformatting), change the volume label:

   ```
   Volume label (11 characters, ENTER for none)? new disk
   ```

   Respond N when Format asks whether you want to QuickFormat another disk.

4. To check the result, use the Directory command to check the disk:

   ```
   C:\>dir a:

   Volume in drive A is NEW DISK
   Volume Serial Number is 2D38-10D5
   Directory of A:\

   File not found
   ```

When you reformat a disk, always review its contents with the Directory command to be sure you're not about to wipe out valuable information. For example, check the disk in drive A with `dir a: /p`.

Although it sounds contradictory, you can, in fact, do a super-fast format on a recycled disk. The trick is to perform both a quick and an unconditional (quickly unconditional? unconditionally quick?) format on it. Use the command `format [drive:] /q /u`. The quick part tells Format to do nothing more than wipe out the disk's "index" to stored files; the unconditional part does the rest of what needs to be done.

Not only have the volume label and serial number changed, the copy of AUTOEXEC.BAT on the disk is now gone.

Oh, No. I Didn't Mean to Do That.

Before you leave the subject of formatting, consider the following (not entirely impossible) situation: You grab a disk and format it, only to find out after the fact that you (a) forgot to check what was on it or (b) overlooked that one file, hidden among the others, that you really, really needed. The solution: Unformat, a command that needs no further introduction. Here's how you use it:

1. Place (or leave) the floppy disk you just formatted in drive A. Remember that AUTOEXEC.BAT has disappeared and that you changed the volume label to NEW DISK when you reformatted the disk.

2. Type the Unformat command:

   ```
   C:\>unformat a:
   ```

   First you see the message:

   ```
   Insert disk to rebuild in drive A:
   and press ENTER when ready.
   ```

3. You're ready, so press Enter. Now you see a screenful of words, dominated by *WARNING!! WARNING!!*

   Even though Unformat is asking a question (at the bottom), take the time to read the screen. Some of it might not make sense to you, but the important paragraph starts out *This command should be used only to recover from the inadvertent use of the FORMAT command....* Remember this warning. It's telling you that Unformat, valuable as it can be in recovering files you

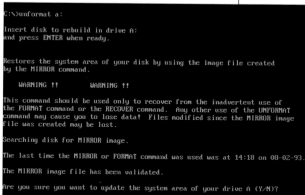

lost with a careless Format command, is not infallible. Unformatting a disk can lead to data loss. Do not assume that Unformat is a replacement for using your gray matter.

4. In this case, however, you really do want to unformat the disk in drive A, so type Y in response to the question *Are you sure you want to update the system area of your drive A (Y/N)?*

Your disk drive goes into action for several seconds, and at the end, you see messages telling you that:

```
The system area of drive A has been rebuilt.

You may need to restart the system.
```

When you unformat a floppy disk, you don't have to restart anything. You're done. If you use the dir a: command, you'll see that the volume label is now MY DISK, the label you assigned before you formatted the disk. In addition, your copy of AUTOEXEC.BAT is back. If you needed proof that Unformat works, there it is.

Take a break if you want, but keep the disk you just used. See you later.

And Disks Are for Files

The whole reason for having disks is to save files on them. You hear a lot about files when you use a computer, so start at ground level here with the definition of a file, according to MS-DOS:

A file is any collection of information, small or large, that you want MS-DOS to handle as a single unit.

This definition holds true for any information you store on a disk, no matter whether it represents a program, a letter, a spreadsheet, a game, a picture, or anything else. But how does MS-DOS, eyeless and brainless, tell one file from another? By its name. Every file you store must have a name. Because of the way MS-DOS is built, this name can be made up of two parts, called the filename and the extension, as shown in this illustration:

When you name files, you have to follow certain rules, to wit:

Filename

Extension

MYDATA.DOC

- The filename can contain up to 8 characters but cannot include spaces. In addition, because MS-DOS has special uses for them, the filename cannot include the following characters:

    " * + , . / : ; < = > ? [\ ] ¦

- The extension, which is separated from the filename by a period, can be up to 3 characters long. No spaces allowed, of course, and don't try to slip in one of the "illegal" characters shown for filenames.

The following table shows some legal and illegal filenames and extensions:

File Naming		
OK	**Not OK**	**Why**
RIGHT-ON.DOC or RIGHT_ON.DOC	RIGHT ON.DOC	Hyphens and underscores are acceptable, spaces are not.
TAXES.93, 93TAXES.XLS, or 1993.TAX	TAXES.1993	Extension can't be more than 3 characters.
WHY.NOT	????.NOT	Question marks are not allowed.
A-PLUS.RPT	A+.RPT	Although MS-DOS doesn't exactly choke on plus signs, avoid them. They cause errors and unexpected results when used to specify a file in an MS-DOS command.

When it comes down to naming files, there are only three more things you really need to know:

- MS-DOS will not allow two files on the same disk to have the same filename and extension. (If you already understand directories, you know this is not strictly true, but accept it for the present.)

- If an application program suggests a particular extension, accept it. Your word processor, for instance, might automatically assign the extension DOC to all the files it saves for you. Let it. The program is designed to search for that extension, so accepting the default makes finding files with the program a lot easier.

- If you make up your own extensions, avoid using those your programs recognize as defaults. In particular, avoid COM, EXE, SYS, and BAT, which MS-DOS assumes refer to executable (program) instructions rather than data.

Copying to Create a File

All right, time to get to work. How? You're going to use MS-DOS to create a sample file you can use in later examples. Actually, you'll use the Copy command—probably an old friend—to "copy" your typing from the keyboard into a file. When you use Copy in this way, you can backspace to correct errors, but you can't return to a line after you press the Enter key. Don't worry if you miss a typo, though; this is just a practice file.

Some people feel that the 8-character and 3-character limits on filenames and extensions cramp their style a bit, and in some respects, they do. But don't let it get you down. Look at the bright side: Short names are easy to remember and easy to type. Which would you prefer: THIS-IS-THE-LETTER-I-SENT-TO-THE-PRESIDENT or PREZ.LTR? Besides, you can't do anything to change the situation....

Here's what you do:

1. Place the floppy disk you've been experimenting with in drive A.

2. Type the following lines, pressing Enter where you see <Enter> and pressing the F6 key where you see ^Z (which is what will show up on your screen):

```
C:\>copy con a:testfile.txt<Enter>
Jack be nimble, Jill be quick,<Enter>
Make DOS jump over the candlestick.<Enter>
^Z<Enter>
```

MS-DOS responds *1 file(s) copied*.

That's it. Simple, right? You can use this rather odd feature of the Copy command whenever you want to create a short file without bothering to start an application program. Remember your limited editing capabilities, though.

Viewing a File with Type

The file you just created is stored on disk as a text file. Wait, don't think to yourself "Of course it's a text file, dummy." There's more to this than meets the eye. Text in this case does not mean the opposite of numbers or pictures. It means that the file consists of ASCII characters, which constitute what might be called the common alphabet of computers. What's important about ASCII is that it enables a computer to save text in a universally accessible form, as opposed to documents saved by word processors and other applications, which tend to produce files that only they or other programs specifically designed to do so can use.

Now that you've been introduced to ASCII, meet Type, a command that can save lots of time when you're sifting through files looking for that elusive passage tucked away in that file with the oh-so-self-descriptive (completely opaque) name.

Despite its name, Type doesn't type anything. It *displays* files for you. Is this weird computer talk again? Well, yes. Just think of it as MS-DOS "typing" characters on the screen. Type is a simple command that takes only one parameter: the name of the file you want to see. Try it with your practice file:

```
C:\>type a:testfile.txt
```

and you see:

```
Jack be nimble, Jill be quick,
Make DOS jump over the candlestick.
```

ASCII

Pronounced "askee." Short for American Standard Code for Information Interchange, ASCII is a code that assigns numbers to letters, numerals, punctuation marks, and certain special characters (such as a carriage return).

POWER PLAY

What, Exactly, Is ASCII?

In many ways, ASCII is much like Morse code in the sense that it describes how A, B, C and 1, 2, 3 are to be represented (in a binary system). More specifically, however, ASCII is a code that assigns numbers to characters, thereby defining a standard means of representing text stored on or transmitted by computers (which, remember, crunch numbers, not letters). In other words, ASCII decrees that the numeric code 65 shall always and forever stand for the capital letter *A*, 66 shall stand for the capital letter *B*, and so on. Because ASCII lays down the rules, any computer that can understand ASCII, and that's virtually every one in existence, can therefore use any file saved as ASCII characters.

ASCII files are often called plain-text files because they don't contain the coded, unreadable instructions that application programs normally use to store *formatting*, a term that covers everything from character attributes, such as italics and boldfacing, to complex page layouts. ASCII files can contain some basic formatting, such as page breaks and tabs, but overall they are definitely in the plain-text category. This lack of sophisticated formatting, however, means that ASCII files, though not as pretty as other documents when printed, are totally readable because they contain only the essential characters needed to create a document. ASCII files are to formatted documents what fish bait is to caviar—essential, but...

Easy, right? And Type even works with very long files, if you add the MS-DOS More command. You can try this too by displaying the README.TXT file, which is shipped with MS-DOS and should be on your hard disk. The following command assumes you installed MS-DOS in a \DOS directory, as Setup suggests. If you chose to install MS-DOS in a different directory, substitute your directory name for **dos** in this command:

```
C:\>type c:\dos\readme.txt | more
```

Press any key when you see the —*More*— prompt to see the next screenful of information.

When you've seen enough, press Ctrl+Break to end the command.

Now, if Type is so easy to use, why was the beginning of this section complicated with all that stuff about ASCII? Because Type works best with ASCII files. You *can* use Type with other kinds of files, including those you create with your application programs, but in some cases, you'll be in for a (non-electrical) shock and not a few beeps from your computer. For instance, program files contain little or nothing readable (unless you happen to be a computer).

If you use Type with a program file, such as FORMAT.COM, this is what you see:

Yuk. And even a document file created by an application program can be bizarre when displayed by Type. That's because such document files generally contain a combination of ASCII characters and special embedded codes that ASCII can't even "pronounce." They help the program change type styles, adjust line spacing, and so on to give you an attractive printed document. Those embedded codes show up onscreen when you use Type, and the result can look something like this:

Recognizable. Sort of.

Printing a File

Most of the time, you'll use your applications to print files, but you can use MS-DOS and its Print command for plain ASCII files. A longtime resident of the MS-DOS command corral, Print is different from most of its stablemates in being what's called a memory-resident program. That is, when you use Print, MS-DOS loads it from disk into memory, where it stays, ready to do your bidding, until you shut down or restart the computer. Also unlike most MS-DOS commands, Print starts up by asking you a question, as you'll see. To try Print, turn on your printer and place the floppy disk containing TESTFILE.TXT in your A drive. Now:

1. Type the Print command:

   ```
   C:\>print
   ```

   Print responds with:

   ```
   Name of list device [PRN]:
   ```

   It's asking for the name of your printer (list device). By this, Print is not asking whether you have a LaserJet or an Epson printer. Nor does it want to know whether you privately call your printer SlowPig or Speedy. What Print is prompting for is the name of the port—the plug on the back of the computer—

that the printer is connected to. Print needs this information so that it can send your file through the correct outlet, to the correct device. By default, Print assumes you have a printer connected to the main parallel printer port, LPT1 (also known, as you can see, by the nickname PRN). LPT1, or PRN, is the correct printer port on almost all systems.

2. If you know your printer is connected to LPT1 (or if you don't know, but you have a pretty standard computer setup without a lot of added hardware), press Enter.

If you know your printer is connected to a different port, type the port name and number at the prompt, like this:

```
Name of list device [PRN]: lpt2
```

Print responds:

```
Resident part of PRINT installed
PRINT queue is empty
```

3. To actually print a document, you use the Print command again, this time including the name of the file to print. Verify that your printer is turned on and online, and then type:

```
C:\>print a:testfile.txt
```

Print responds:

```
A:\TESTFILE.TXT is currently being printed
```

and a few seconds later, a copy of the file pops out of the printer.

Just Don't Need You Anymore

Some of the files you create you want or need to keep forever. Others, like that mash note to your old flame, become, well, expendable after a while. Beyond such emotional highs (or lows), of course, you also have to face the more mundane tasks of life, like housekeeping. Yes, even computer disks need cleaning up now and then. Your tools: the Delete command, to sweep out what you don't want, and the Undelete command, to guard against losing any valuables you overlook because they're tangled up with the trash.

When you use Delete and Undelete, you always start the "un" before the "do," like so:

1. Place your sample floppy disk in drive A.

Even if you've never tried Undelete before, it's possible you'll see the following message when you try the Undelete example here:

```
Cannot load with
UNDELETE
already resident.
```

That means someone set up your computer to give you Undelete protection automatically, at least for drive C. If you want to try the example, you can. Just prepare for it with this command:

```
C:\>undelete /unload
```

to tell MS-DOS you want to start over. And don't worry about destroying whatever protection you had going. The next time you start your computer, everything will be back the way it was.

POWER PLAY

Which One's the Printer Port?

If you have a printer, you should already know which port it is connected to. If you don't know, there are a few ways to find out. The first, and easiest, is to take a look at the back of your computer. If the sockets on the back are labeled, find the cable that connects the computer to the printer, follow the cable to the computer, and check the name of the socket. Be sure to remember not only the name (LPT or COM), but also the number (such as LPT1, LPT2, COM1, or COM2). That's your printer port.

If the sockets on your computer are not labeled, start the Microsoft Diagnostics utility by typing msd. When the list of options appears, type L to see a list of your LPT ports. If you have a parallel printer, you'll see a line such as this telling you about your printer and the port to which it's connected:

Port	Port Address	On Line	Paper Out	I/O Error	Time Out	Busy
LPT1:	03BCH	Yes	No	No	No	No

If you have a serial printer, do one of the following:

- Display your AUTOEXEC.BAT file with the following command:

```
type c:\autoexec.bat | more
```

Scan the commands in the file for one that looks like this:

```
mode lpt1=com1
```

The COM port in the command (COM1, COM2, COM3, or COM4) is your printer port.

- Check your printer manual for instructions that tell you what baud, parity, data bits, and stop bits you set with an MS-DOS Mode command. Then start MSD and choose COM Ports from the list of options. Check the list that appears for the settings that match those for your printer. That's your printer port.

Now, tell MS-DOS you want its highest level of delete protection. This is called Delete Sentry, and it's started with the Undelete command, an adaptable animal that both provides protection and, if you need it later, rescues protected files from oblivion. To start Sentry protection, type:

```
C:\>undelete /sa
```

MS-DOS responds with copyright and other information, followed by:

```
UNDELETE loaded.

Delete Protection Method is Delete Sentry.
Enabled for drives : A C
Initializing SENTRY control file on drive C.
```

What all this means is that Undelete has moved into memory (*UNDELETE loaded*) and has established Sentry protection for drive A and (by default) drive C.

2. Now that you've got Undelete guarding your flank, you can try the Delete command, which is a simple command name (Del) followed by the name of a file you want to delete—in this case, your sample file:

```
C:\>del a:testfile.txt
```

Your drive light winks on, and a second or two later, the command prompt returns. The file's gone.

3. To verify the deletion, use the Directory command on drive A:

```
C:\>dir a:
```

MS-DOS replies:

```
Volume in drive A is MY DISK
Volume Serial Number is 3722-0FC9
Directory of A:\

AUTOEXEC BAT        171   07-25-93      11:10a
        1 file(s)       171 bytes
                     729088 bytes
```

Come Back Little File

Did you notice how quickly your sample file disappeared? One simple command, and bam! No messages from MS-DOS like "Gee, boss, are you sure about this?" or "I'm going to do it, I'm really going to do it, right now." Now you can see the value of delete protection, and now that you've deleted a file, you can see how Undelete can help you recover it:

1. Type:

```
C:\>undelete a:testfile.txt
```

Here's the screen you see:

> When you delete files, MS-DOS gives you a chance to reconsider, but only in one situation: When you tell it to wipe out every file in the current directory with the shorthand command del *.*, which is covered in a later chapter, "More About Files." For now, remember this: When you delete anything less than every file in a directory, MS-DOS goes ahead and does the deed as soon as you press Enter.

```
C:\>undelete a:testfile.txt

UNDELETE - A delete protection facility
Copyright (C) 1987-1993 Central Point Software, Inc.
All rights reserved.

Directory: A:\
File Specifications: TESTFILE.TXT

    Delete Sentry control file contains     1 deleted files.

    Deletion-tracking file not found.

    MS-DOS directory contains   1 deleted files.
    Of those,    0 files may be recovered.

Using the Delete Sentry method.

      TESTFILE TXT       7 8-02-93  2:51p  ...A  Deleted: 8-02-93  3:00p
This file can be 100% undeleted. Undelete (Y/N)?
```

Those lines about a deletion-tracking file and the MS-DOS directory are reports on two less secure methods of undeleting files. They're covered in an upcoming chapter, "More About Files." For now, note the bottom of the screen, where you see:

```
Using the Delete Sentry method.

TESTFILE TXT      7  8-02-93  2:51p  ...A  Deleted:  8-02-93  3:00p
This file can be 100% undeleted. Undelete (Y/N)?
```

When you use Undelete to recover files, it lists the name of every deleted file it finds and prompts you for a Y or an N before undeleting each one. Here, you see the name of the one file you've deleted. You want to get it back, so...

2. Type **Y**, and a few seconds later, Undelete responds:

```
File successfully undeleted.
```

3. To verify, use the Directory command again:

```
C:\>dir a:
```

There it is, safe and sound.

Simple, wasn't it? But now it's time for a little advice before you go getting all cocky and thinking that Undelete will unfailingly gallop to your rescue like the Lone Ranger. Sentry protection is as good as you can get, but it is *not* 100 percent safe. When you start Sentry protection, Undelete works behind the scenes to move all the files you delete into a hidden area on the disk they occupied. Because these files have been moved rather than wiped out, they are recoverable. But be warned: That hidden area is not endless, and as you delete more and more files, it fills up. When the hidden area becomes too full, Undelete purges it, deleting (for good) the oldest files there. Because Undelete works this way, bear two things in mind:

- When you must undelete a file, do it promptly (as soon after the deletion as possible).

- If you're deleting a lot of files at one time, *pay attention!* Look before you leap, and all that.

Break time, if you want. If you shut down your computer, be sure to start Undelete again when you come back. You'll need it later.

> If you're the forgetful type, you can ensure that delete protection is enabled whenever you start your computer. To do this, you add an Undelete command to your AUTOEXEC.BAT file, naming every drive you want to protect (including drive C if you don't trust MS-DOS to remember). If you don't know how to change your AUTOEXEC.BAT file, refer to the chapters "Make a File with Edit" (in Section 3) and "Customizing Startup" (in Section 4).

Handling Groups of Files

Earlier in this chapter, you used the Copy command to create your sample file. If you've been using MS-DOS for a while, you know that Copy is really a work-horse command and that its main job is to duplicate files on other disks, as you did when you copied your AUTOEXEC.BAT file to your test floppy. You use Copy anytime you want to leave a file in its current location but you also want an identical version somewhere else—for example, on a floppy disk you plan to give to a friend or take home. (Using Copy to duplicate *programs* to give away, however, is not kosher; selling their work is how programmers make a living.)

What you've not yet seen are ways to make your work easier and faster by using Copy (and Delete, and Undelete, and all kinds of other commands) on more than one file at a time. You can, and it's simple, thanks to two special MS-DOS characters known as wildcards. If you haven't met them before, these characters are the asterisk (*) and the question mark (?):

- Whenever you include an asterisk in a filename or as an extension, MS-DOS interprets it as meaning "let this asterisk stand for *any acceptable number* of characters, of any kind whatsoever."

- Whenever you include a question mark in a filename or an extension, MS-DOS interprets it as meaning "let this question mark stand for *one* character, of any kind whatsoever."

The following table shows you some ways to use both characters:

Wildcard Decoding		
File Specification	**Meaning**	**Examples**
?OA?.DOC	Any four-character filename with OA as the middle two characters and the extension DOC	LOAF.DOC, MOAT.DOC, SOAP.DOC (but not OAF.DOC or BOA.DOC, which are one character too short)
LETTER.??T	Any file named LETTER with a 3-character extension ending in *T*	LETTER.TXT, LETTER.LST, LETTER.BAT
DO*	To the Directory command only: any filename starting with DO, regardless of length or extension	DO.DOC, DONT, DOUBLE.DIP, DOOBY.DOO
DO*	To commands other than Directory (such as Copy and Delete): any filename of any length starting with DO, but having no extension	DO-IT, DONUTS, DORMOUSE, but not DOOR.BIG or DO-SI.DO
*.DOC	Any filename of any length with the extension DOC	ME.DOC, YOU.DOC, THEM.DOC, BONES.DOC
.	Any file of any length with any extension	All files on the current disk or (as you'll soon see) in the current directory

Here are some examples that let you try out some wildcard file specifications:

1. First, try copying more than one file from your hard disk to your test floppy. To include several files in the same command, you'll specify some text files in your \DOS directory. If you installed MS-DOS to a place with a path other than \DOS, use the name you assigned instead of **dos** in the following command:

   ```
   C:\>copy c:\dos\*.txt a:
   ```

2. Now list the files you just copied:

   ```
   C:\>dir a:*.txt
   ```

3. Next ask to see the names of all TXT files that have *E* as the second letter of the filename:

   ```
   C:\>dir a:?e*.txt
   ```

   Here you should see the names TESTFILE.TXT, NETWORKS.TXT, and README.TXT. (People hardly ever use such contrived file specifications as ?e*.txt, but at least you know you can if you want.)

4. Now put some of your hard-won knowledge to work. To be sure this turns out right, check that Undelete is offering Sentry protection with the command:

   ```
   C:\>undelete /status
   ```

   If Undelete isn't running, start it up. You remember how.

5. OK. First, delete all TXT files on the disk in drive A:

   ```
   C:\>del a:*.txt
   ```

6. Whoops! You just deleted your TESTFILE.TXT along with the MS-DOS files you copied. See how easy it is to overlook one file among many? Luckily, you've got Undelete running, so you can get that file back:

   ```
   C:\>undelete a:
   ```

   Answer **Y** when Undelete asks whether you want to recover TESTFILE.TXT. Answer **N** to all the other questions.

7. Verify that your sample file is back:

   ```
   C:\>dir a:*.txt
   ```

   All's right with the world once more.

Had enough for a while? Break time.

Help! I Know My File's Here Someplace

So far, you've been working with a few files and a floppy disk. That's not how you work in real life, though. As you commit more and more files to MS-DOS and your computer, those files fill your disks, especially your hard disk, at an astounding rate. After all, programs put program files—often lots of program files—on your hard disk. And when you use those programs, they make more files, all the data files you create and save.

To help you keep all your program files and data files straight, MS-DOS allows you to organize storage on your disks by sorting files into categories called directories. You've seen one such directory—the one called \DOS, which MS-DOS creates for itself on your hard disk. If you've installed applications, games, and other programs, you've no doubt seen other directories, because programs these days generally do what MS-DOS does and install themselves in their own directories. Perhaps you weren't aware, however, that you can create, move around in, and even reorganize your own data directories at will.

First, what exactly is a directory? It's a compartment that you create and name—a kind of electronic folder into which you can put other files and directories. You can create a directory on any disk, floppy or hard. Of course, hard disks are so very large and can contain so many files that directories seem unavoidable. Without them, you'd be hard pressed to keep a hard disk full of files organized to view and find the files easily. You might picture directories as bins or boxes into which you sort related files. That picture, although helpful, is not the most accurate. It's back-to-nature time.

For Every Disk, a Tree

Organization...compartmentalization...neatness. They're the keys to understanding directories. But the question is, how does MS-DOS envision these things? Not as boxes or file folders, but as the branching roots of a tree.

Every disk you format, every disk that MS-DOS uses, starts life with a single, very important directory known as the root. When you (or your programs) start creating directories on that disk, MS-DOS sets them up so that they branch off from the root. Furthermore, just as the roots of a tree can branch and branch again, so can directories. To picture this, think of tree roots from a worm's eye view. No matter how much the roots divide and subdivide, you can always trace them back to the main root. It's the same with your directories and the directories (sometimes called subdirectories) within them. Everything goes back to the root directory, as you can see in the illustration on the facing page.

When you create directories, you can put files in any one you want. Suppose, for example, you're the famous author of many horror novels. Imagine having to track down all the chapters of, say, *Werewolf Come Home,* on a large hard disk without any directories. No thanks. Wouldn't it be better by far to have a directory named WEREWOLF that contained all the chapters for that book? And wouldn't it be even better to have two directories within it? One named DRAFTS and the other named FINAL? No problem then if your publisher called out of the blue and asked for the original draft of chapter 22.

Although the diagram doesn't show it, a directory is not limited to holding a certain number of files. As you create more and more files, your directories expand to hold them all. The only time this isn't quite true is when you're saving files in the root directory, which is usually limited to 512 files. But then, once you begin creating directories, you should use the root mainly as a starting point for reaching the directories where you do keep your programs and data files.

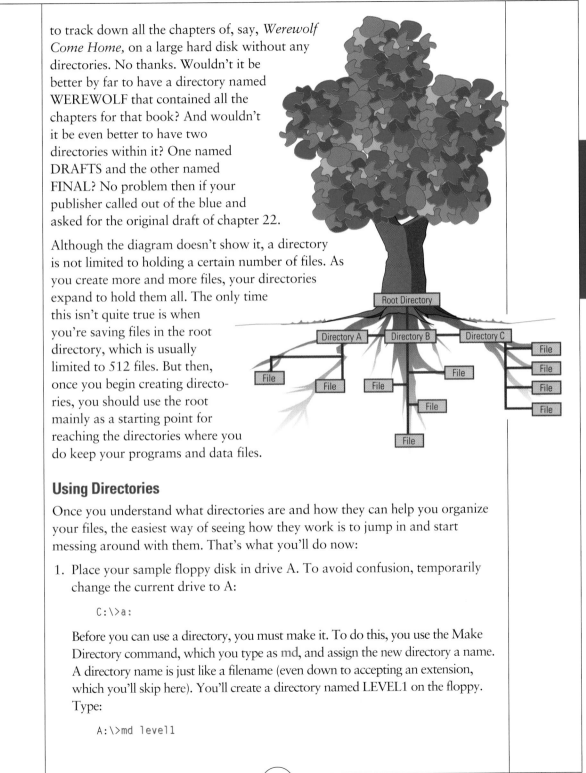

Using Directories

Once you understand what directories are and how they can help you organize your files, the easiest way of seeing how they work is to jump in and start messing around with them. That's what you'll do now:

1. Place your sample floppy disk in drive A. To avoid confusion, temporarily change the current drive to A:

   ```
   C:\>a:
   ```

   Before you can use a directory, you must make it. To do this, you use the Make Directory command, which you type as **md**, and assign the new directory a name. A directory name is just like a filename (even down to accepting an extension, which you'll skip here). You'll create a directory named LEVEL1 on the floppy. Type:

   ```
   A:\>md level1
   ```

2. Use the Directory command to see your new directory:

    ```
    A:\>dir
    ```

    There it is. As you can see, MS-DOS uses *<DIR>* to tell you which entries in a directory listing are themselves directories.

3. Now that you've got a directory, how do you use it? The easiest and most foolproof way is to change to the directory you want with the Change Directory command, which is typed cd. Change to the new directory:

    ```
    A:\>cd level1
    ```

    If you're using the default MS-DOS prompt, notice that your command prompt changed from *A:\>* to *A:\LEVEL1>*. To help you get and keep your bearings, the default prompt always shows you the name of the current directory.

4. Next, to give yourself something to look at, copy TESTFILE.TXT from what you now know is the root directory of the disk in drive A. Remember that MS-DOS is now focusing its attention on your LEVEL1 directory, so you have to tell MS-DOS where to find the file to copy. Do this:

    ```
    A:\LEVEL1>copy \testfile.txt
    ```

    The backslash (\) is a shorthand "name" that MS-DOS uses for the root directory of any disk. By typing a backslash in front of testfile.txt, you told MS-DOS to go look for the file in the root directory.

5. Now, create another directory, this time within the new LEVEL1 directory:

    ```
    A:\LEVEL1>md sub1
    ```

6. Use the Directory command again to see the new directory and to verify that the file, TESTFILE.TXT, has been duplicated in LEVEL1:

    ```
    A:\LEVEL1>dir
    ```

    Notice that MS-DOS is now allowing two identically named files to exist on your disk: TESTFILE.TXT in the root directory and TESTFILE.TXT in your LEVEL1 directory. That happens because MS-DOS has no trouble whatsoever dealing with identical filenames, *as long as* they are in different directories.

7. Even though two identically named files will cause MS-DOS no problems, you might start feeling like you're stuck in a hall of mirrors, so use yet another handy MS-DOS command called Rename to change the name of TESTFILE.TXT in your LEVEL1 directory:

    ```
    A:\LEVEL1>ren testfile.txt newfile.txt
    ```

    As you can see, the Rename command is really simple: After the command name, just type a space, the current name of the file, another space, and the new name you want to assign. Easy as pie.

8. Getting the hang of it? Good. Before you try the next step, return to the root directory:

```
A:\LEVEL1>cd \
```

9. Make your tree a little bushier. Create another directory to match LEVEL1, and then create a subdirectory of the new directory to match SUB1. The first command is:

```
A:\>md level2
```

The second is:

```
A:\>md level2\sub2
```

This is what your directory tree looks like now:

Break time. You've covered a lot here, so you might be feeling like you need one.

When you use directories, no matter how organized you are, it isn't hard to lose track of a file. Whenever you feel like banging your head on the keyboard because you can't find a file you know you saved somewhere, call on the Directory command. As described in a later chapter, "More About Files" (in Section 3), Directory includes a /s switch that searches the current directory and all subdirectories for a file you specify. This is the magnet you use to pull a lost needle out of the haystack. Here's the command form:

```
dir file-specification /s
```

file-specification here includes whatever combination of drive, path, and filename you need in order to tell MS-DOS where to look. If you're looking for URGENT.DOC and you haven't got a clue, type the command as:

```
C:\>dir \urgent.doc /s
```

That tells MS-DOS to search every directory on the current disk, from the root on down, for the file specification you include.

Finding Your Way Around

The tiresome thing about working with directories is that you always have to tell MS-DOS which directory you want. Especially if you created directories within directories within directories. Fortunately, MS-DOS provides two different ways for you to go swinging through a directory tree:

- You can quickly move up and down from one level to another with the help of two special symbols. The first, a pair of dots (..),

moves you up one level in the tree, and the second, a backslash (\), always takes you directly to the root.

- You can tell MS-DOS the *path* to the directory you want. This involves some typing because, essentially, you tell MS-DOS how to find its way through the chain of directories from your present location (the current directory) to the directory you want. This is what the path to your SUB1 directory looks like:

```
\LEVEL1\SUB1
```

And this is the path to SUB2:

```
\LEVEL2\SUB2
```

Notice that a \ (backslash) character starts each pathname. That character indicates that the pathname begins with the root directory. Ah, but a \ character also separates LEVEL1 from SUB1 and LEVEL2 from SUB2. These backslashes, somewhat confusingly, do not represent the root. When a \ appears *within* a path, interpret it as a separator between two directory names.

Once again, a short practice session will teach you more than a flood of words, so try it for yourself. You'll use your sample disk again.

1. First, change the current drive to A: if necessary.

2. Now, change to the SUB1 directory:

   ```
   A:\>cd level1\sub1
   ```

3. Next, use the double dots to move up the branch one level:

   ```
   A:\LEVEL1\SUB1>cd ..
   ```

   The command prompt changes to *A:\LEVEL1>*. Fast, eh?

4. Change back to the SUB1 directory. MS-DOS doesn't include a "down" button, so you'll have to do it the hard way:

   ```
   A:\LEVEL1>cd sub1
   ```

5. Now, go all the way back to the root with a single command:

   ```
   A:\LEVEL1\SUB1>cd \
   ```

   Neat, quick, and painless. Remember this command. You can use it to go straight to the root no matter how far down a complex directory tree you happen to be.

6. Go down again, back to SUB1:

   ```
   A:\LEVEL1\SUB1>cd level1\sub1
   ```

7. Finally, take another look at how you type a path with the Change Directory command. This time, you're going across to LEVEL2\SUB2:

   ```
   A:\LEVEL1\SUB1>cd \level2\sub2
   ```

The reason for this last command was to show you one little subtlety you might otherwise overlook. Notice that earlier you specified the path to SUB1 as level1\sub1. You didn't start the path with a backslash. Why? Because the directory you wanted was farther down the branch you were in. In the last example, however, you started the path with a backslash. Why again? Because you weren't moving *within* the current branch in the last example—you were

Change Directory (Cd)

Changes from the current directory to a different directory. When typed without any parameters (plain **cd**), the command displays the name of the current directory. The command form is simple:

```
cd [drive:][path]
```

drive is the drive on which you want to change directories.

path is the pathname of the directory to which you want to change. Remember that you can use the .. symbol to move up one directory level and the \ symbol to move directly to the root.

moving across to a different branch. Confused? Here, take a pictorial look at what you did. Here's your directory tree:

From the root directory, you can get to the SUB1 subdirectory by specifying the path as:

```
A:\>cd level1\sub1
```

To change the directories from SUB1 to SUB2, specify the complete path to SUB2 from the root: cd \level2\sub2.

MS-DOS can then follow the path from the root through LEVEL1 and on down to SUB1. When the current directory was SUB1, however, the only way you could get to SUB2 was by telling MS-DOS to start at the root and then go down through LEVEL2. To do this, you told MS-DOS to back up all the way to the root and then start following a different branch of the tree. See the difference? The explanation might sound complicated, but the moral of the story is really very simple and practical:

- If MS-DOS ever announces *Invalid directory* in response to a Change Directory command and you know that the directory exists, repeat your Change Directory command, but this time, begin it with a backslash. The pathname is almost sure to be the problem.

Break time again.

Listing Files

Directory tells what's on a disk—by name, by size, even by date and time. Specifically, as the name suggests, Directory tells you what's in the current directory or in the directory you specify. You've probably used Directory a zillion times or more, but perhaps you weren't aware of two really useful little switches:

```
dir [drive:] /p /w
```

So that you can see how these switches work, the following examples use your MS-DOS files, even though shorter listings would be preferable. The reason for using MS-DOS in the examples is, of course, that everyone using this book has got to have MS-DOS files.

Your MS-DOS files are in a special place on your hard disk, grouped in a directory of their own. If you accepted MS-DOS Setup's recommendation, this directory is named \DOS. If

Directory (Dir)

Lists the files on a disk or in a directory. The Directory command can be customized in many ways, as described in the upcoming chapter, "More About Files." The basic command form, however, is:

```
dir [drive:][filename] /w /p
```

drive is the name of the drive containing the disk for which you want a listing. You can omit this to see a list for the current drive or directory. For example:

```
C:\DOS>dir
```

lists the files in the \DOS directory.

filename is the name of a particular file or group of files you want to check on. You can use wildcards for this. For example:

```
C:\>dir *.doc
```

shows the names, sizes, and other information about all files on the current disk or in the current directory that have the extension DOC.

/w produces a wide listing five columns across.

/p pauses the display after each screenful so you can read a long listing.

you decided to install MS-DOS in a different directory, you should know what directory you chose. Either way, to make your commands easy to type, begin by changing to your \DOS directory as follows (substitute your directory name for **dos** in this Change Directory command if you installed in a different directory):

```
C:\>cd \dos
```

All right, now you're ready to go. First, for the sake of comparison, take a look at a normal directory listing:

```
C:\DOS>dir /p
```

The listing could go on for screen after screen, but all you need is a reasonably good look at part of the list, so when the /p switch causes MS-DOS to pause at the end of the first screenful, notice merely that there doesn't seem to be any order to the way the files are listed. Actually, they're shown in the order in which they appear on the disk, but never mind; the important thing is that the order isn't readily apparent.

You don't have to see any more, so press Ctrl+Break to cancel the command. Remember to use this key combination whenever you want to avoid having to page through screenful after screenful.

```
Volume in drive C is MS-DOS 6
Volume Serial Number is 1DE8-0D1E
Directory of C:\DOS                 o

.               <DIR>     12-07-92    9:08a
..              <DIR>     12-07-92    9:08a
EXTRA           <DIR>     12-07-92    7:34p
MOUSE    CHD     48685    10-05-92    6:20a
DBLSPACE BIN     51214    03-10-93    6:00a
README           3002     09-30-92    7:25a
FORMAT   COM     22717    03-10-93    6:00a
GORILLA  BAS     29434    07-17-92    5:00a
INTEREST BAS       379    07-17-92    5:00a
MONEY    BAS     46225    07-17-92    5:00a
NIBBLES  BAS     22579    07-17-92    5:00a
REMLINE  BAS     12314    07-17-92    5:00a
REVERSI  BAS     17492    07-17-92    5:00a
SORTDEMO BAS     23753    07-17-92    5:00a
NLSFUNC  EXE      7036    03-10-93    6:00a
DOSSHELP CHD     49338    07-17-92    5:00a
UPDHELP  CHD    131935    09-30-92    7:25a
ADAPT    COM     39977    09-30-92    7:25a
ASSIGN   COM      6399    07-17-92    5:00a
Press any key to continue . . .
```

Now, take a look at what the /w switch can do. You'll be using /p again, and you already know what it does, so here's /w, which produces a wide listing:

```
C:\DOS>dir /w /p
```

The first screenful looks like this:

As you can see, the /w switch packs a lot more onto the screen, but you do lose the size, date, and time information displayed in a normal listing.

```
Volume in drive C is MS-DOS 6
Volume Serial Number is 1DE8-0D1E
Directory of C:\DOS

[.]           [..]          [EXTRA]       MOUSE.CHD     DBLSPACE.BIN
README        FORMAT.COM    GORILLA.BAS   INTEREST.BAS  MONEY.BAS
NIBBLES.BAS   REMLINE.BAS   REVERSI.BAS   SORTDEMO.BAS  NLSFUNC.EXE
DOSSHELP.CHD  UPDHELP.CHD   ADAPT.COM     ASSIGN.COM    COUNTRY.SYS
CV.COM        KEYB.COM      KEYBOARD.SYS  ANSI.SYS      ATTRIB.EXE
CHKDSK.EXE    EDIT.COM      GRAFTABL.COM  EXPAND.EXE    CHKLIST.MS
MORE.COM      MSD.EXE       KP.COM        QBASIC.EXE    MIRROR.COM
RESTORE.EXE   SYS.COM       MSHERC.COM    PWRCON.COM    README.COM
UNFORMAT.COM  NETWORKS.TXT  README.TXT    4201.CPI      4208.CPI
5202.CPI      OS2.TXT       EGAGR.CPI     EGA_THIN.CPI  LCD.CPI
LCD_THIN.CPI  README.CPQ    README.EGA    DEBUG.EXE     FDISK.EXE
DOSSHELL.VID  CACHE.EXE     CEMM.EXE      CEMMP.EXE     DELOLDOS.EX_
COMP.EXE      CPQXPAND.EXE  DOSSHELL.INI  DOSSHELL.GRB  CHOICE.COM
EDLIN.EXE     EXE2BIN.EXE   EXMEM.EXE     FASTART.EXE   MODE.COM
DEFRAG.EXE    DEFRAG.HLP    DOSSWAP.EXE   EGA.CPI       EGA.SYS
JOIN.EXE      HIMEM.SYS     MEM.EXE       XCOPY.EXE     DELTREE.EXE
MOVE.EXE      RECOVER.EXE   RAMDRIVE.SYS  SMARTDRV.EXE  RUMHI.EXE
DOSSHELL.BAK  DOSSHELL.EXE  HELP.COM      APPNOTES.TXT  TU.EXE
UILIB.EXE     DISPLAY.SYS   UPCU.EXE      DOSHELP.EXE   CGA.GRB
Press any key to continue . . .
```

Begone

Once you start working with directories, you'll probably never go back to stuffing files on a disk any which way. You'll be able to keep your important documents separate from those belonging to everybody else: the kids, your roommate, your spouse, your parents, your in-laws.

But times change, and so do people, and a directory tree should never become petrified. Thanks to two simple commands—Remove Directory and Deltree—you can lop off branches of the tree whenever you want. Of the two, you should use Remove Directory most often. The reason: Remove Directory will not allow you to get rid of a directory until you've deleted all the files in it; Deltree (which is new with version 6) takes a chainsaw to the branch and cuts it off, whether the directory contains files or not. For this reason, Remove Directory is safer. Even though you might mistakenly delete a file you need, at least Remove Directory makes you think about the matter. Deltree assumes you know what you're doing. (Big mistake sometimes, no matter how experienced you are.)

To see how these commands work, use your test floppy again. Change the current drive to A and change the current directory to the root if necessary.

1. Start by putting a file in your LEVEL2\SUB2 subdirectory. To make this quick, you'll use a new version 6 command called Move, which literally moves a file from one disk or directory to another. Here's the command:

   ```
   A:\>move testfile.txt level2\sub2
   ```

   MS-DOS displays:

   ```
   a:\testfile.txt => a:\level2\sub2\testfile.txt [ok]
   ```

   Like it? This is a command you should check into a little more. To see all that Move can do, you should read up on it in "More About Files." It's a great bonus in version 6. End of commercial.

2. If you're a show-me type and want to be sure the file was actually moved, use the /s switch of the Directory command described in an earlier tip. Search all subdirectories on the disk for TESTFILE.TXT by typing:

   ```
   A:\>dir testfile.txt /s
   ```

3. All right, now get down to business. First of all, it's important to remember that neither Remove Directory nor Deltree will remove the current directory, and neither can ever remove the root directory of a disk. Need proof? Use the Remove Directory command (which you type as rd) to get rid of the current directory—which also just happens to be the root directory. Type:

   ```
   A:\>rd \
   ```

Be very careful when you delete directories and the files they contain. Even though MS-DOS includes an Undelete command, you cannot necessarily recover a deleted directory or the files in it. In fact, the only time you can recover a deleted directory and its files relatively easily is when you use the Windows version of Undelete immediately after deleting the files and directory. Trying to recover files in a deleted directory is much trickier at the command prompt and can be done only if you've enabled Sentry protection for the disk. Be warned. For more on this, refer to "Go Back in Time with Undelete," in Section 4.

No way, says MS-DOS:

```
Attempt to remove current directory - \
```

4. Now see what happens when you try to get rid of a directory that contains another directory. That's a no-no too. As you know, LEVEL1 contains a subdirectory, SUB1. Try to remove LEVEL1:

```
A:\>rd level1
```

MS-DOS responds with a different complaint:

```
Invalid path, not directory,
or directory not empty
```

Enlightening, isn't it? Well, MS-DOS isn't being surly. It's telling you there are three possible reasons why it wouldn't carry out your command. Your mission is to spot the right one. Here, of course, you know that the problem is "directory not empty." In real life, the easiest way to figure out what's what is first to check your typing, then to check for the directory with a Change Directory command, and then to check the contents of the directory to see whether it's empty.

5. Assuming you typed the last Remove Directory command correctly, change to LEVEL1 so you can verify that it is a directory and then see what's in it:

```
A:\>cd level1
```

It's a directory, all right. Is there anything in it?

```
A:\LEVEL1>dir
```

Oh, yeah. There's SUB1, big as life.

6. Well, now you know what to do:

```
A:\LEVEL1>rd sub1
```

List the contents of the directory again, and you can see that SUB1 is gone.

7. As a final exercise with Remove Directory, try it with a directory that contains a file. Way back when, you copied a file to LEVEL1 and named it NEWFILE.TXT. Change to the root directory, and try to remove LEVEL1:

```
A:\LEVEL1>cd ..
A:\>rd level1
```

There's that message again. This time, the *directory not empty* part means you have to do something about that file.

8. Delete the file and try again:

```
A:\>del level1\newfile.txt
A:\>rd level1
```

Success.

And now, what about Deltree? As already mentioned, Deltree can be a dangerous command because it cares not a whit about whether a directory contains
files. You can see the difference between Remove Directory and Deltree very
easily. Remember that you moved TESTFILE.TXT to LEVEL2\SUB2? All right,
try to remove LEVEL2, its subdirectory, and TESTFILE.TXT:

1. Type the Deltree command:

```
A:\>deltree level2
```

MS-DOS responds with a question:

```
Delete directory "level2" and all its subdirectories? [yn]
```

Here, you know that's exactly what you want to do, but in real life, *think about it.*
If you're at all uncertain, cancel the command by typing N. It's your last chance.

2. This time, you're safe, so go ahead and type Y.

```
Delete directory "level2" and all its subdirectories? [yn] y
```

Press Enter, and a simple acknowledgment appears:

```
Deleting level2...
```

When the command prompt returns, LEVEL2 is gone, LEVEL2\SUB2 is gone,
and TESTFILE.TXT is gone.

That winds up the practice sessions for this book. Your certificate will come by
mail within the week. You've had a good look at different ways to use MS-DOS
and, more important, you've been through the basics of the most important job
you'll ever give to MS-DOS: management of the files and disks to which you
entrust all your programs and data. The remaining chapters cover the multitude
of ways that MS-DOS can help you get things done. You don't have to tackle
them all in order, in one sitting or even in one month or year. Like MS-DOS
itself, those chapters will be ready when you are.

③ Action!

More About Disks

Tracks Aren't Just for Trains

Whenever MS-DOS saves a file for you, whether you created that file with MS-DOS or, as is much more likely, with an application program, it lays your data down in tracks on the disk. Tracks. That's how MS-DOS organizes storage so it can find and retrieve the file you want the next time you call for it.

To picture how this all works—roughly speaking, at least—imagine a large, flat circular plane divided into rings. This is your disk, and each of those rings is a track. On each track are tens of thousands of small, slender magnets, one right next to the other. Some magnets are lying with their "heads" facing north; others are lying with their heads facing south; still others are lying randomly, waiting to be told which way to turn. This is basically what the surface of a formatted computer disk is like. The magnets lying in ordered, north/south patterns represent bits. And together, those bits represent bytes and kilobytes of stored information. As for the magnets that haven't been told what to do yet, they represent areas of available storage on the disk.

As organized as this all sounds, something's missing. Have you figured it out? Think about those tracks full of bits from your operating system's point of view. If each track can hold thousands and thousands of bits, a single track represents a lot of information. For MS-DOS to have to transfer files to and from your computer's memory in track-size units would be as efficient as you hauling the rails for your model train in one fully assembled piece from the basement to the attic. There must be a better way, right? "Divide the track into smaller, more manageable pieces," you say. That's exactly what MS-DOS does, and it calls those pieces *sectors*. This is what you end up with, as shown here:

Sectors

Tracks

2 Sides

Tracks and sectors—those are the basic units of disk storage under MS-DOS. The only other terms you need to know are *side* (two per disk, obviously), *cylinder*, and *platter*. Cylinder applies only to hard disks and only because such disks consist of two to eight (or more) shiny disks called platters. Because a hard disk contains more than just a single two-sided platter, it gains a dimension of depth that doesn't apply to floppies.

As you can see from this diagram, a hard disk is basically a stack of platters, each divided into tracks and (although you don't see them here) sectors. Because the tracks on each platter align neatly, one above the other,

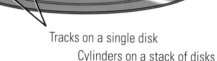

the term cylinder is used

Tracks on a single disk

Cylinders on a stack of disks

to describe what is basically a stack of tracks. That is, if you could look down on a cylinder from above, you would see something closely resembling a Slinky toy. Each "ring" of the toy would correspond to one track, and all the tracks combined would represent one cylinder. The only difference between the toy and the cylinder is that the rings of the toy actually form a spiral, whereas each track in a cylinder is separate from all the others.

Because disks differ in size and capacity, the number of tracks and sectors on those disks differs too. You don't have to care about how many tracks and sectors there are on a hard disk because the number of megabytes it can hold is the most important piece of information you need about it. Floppy disks are a somewhat different matter, however, because the number of tracks and sectors they contain is directly related to the amount of information they can hold. For a detailed rundown, see "Slicing and Dicing Floppy Disks," below.

POWER PLAY

Slicing and Dicing Floppy Disks

In your everyday work with MS-DOS, you don't have any burning need to remember how many tracks and sectors a disk has. The Format command allows you to use these numbers if you want, but otherwise, you can just take satisfaction in knowing that you know.

The following table lists the various floppy disk capacities, along with the number of tracks and sectors on each. If you study the table, you can see that a 720-KB disk contains twice as many tracks as a 360-KB disk and, not surprisingly, holds twice as much information. Similarly, a 2.88-MB disk has twice as many sectors as a 1.44-MB disk and, again predictably, has twice the capacity. Notice that the physical size, in inches, of the disk is not a critical factor.

Disk Size (inches)	Capacity	Tracks per Side	Sectors per Track
5.25	360 KB	40	9
5.25	1.2 MB	80	15
3.5	720 KB	80	9
3.5	1.44 MB	80	18
3.5	2.88 MB	80	36

The rest of this chapter describes the workhorse MS-DOS commands most often used with hard and floppy disks. The names of the commands and what they do are as follows:

Disk Management Commands (in this chapter)

Command	Description
Check Disk	Checks file storage on a disk
Diskcopy	Duplicates a disk
Format	Prepares a new disk or recycles a used disk
Label	Displays and changes a disk volume label
System	Copies the MS-DOS startup files to a disk
Unformat	Reverses an accidental disk format
Volume	Displays a disk's volume label

Disk compression and virus protection are handled by their own applicationlike programs (unlike typical commands typed at the command prompt). For more information, refer to the chapters listed in the following table:

More Disk Management Commands (in Section 4)

Command	Description	Covered in the Chapter...
Defrag	Neatens storage on a disk	"Physical Fitness with ScanDisk and Defrag"
DoubleSpace	Compresses a disk so it can hold far more information	"Grow Your Disks with DoubleSpace"
Microsoft Anti-Virus	Checks for and destroys computer viruses	"Foil the Bad Guys with Anti-Virus and Vsafe"
ScanDisk	Checks and corrects file storage on a disk	"Physical Fitness with ScanDisk and Defrag"
Vsafe	Monitors a computer for signs of virus activity	"Foil the Bad Guys with Anti-Virus and Vsafe"

Check Disk

If you have version 6.2, your disk checker of choice should be ScanDisk—at least where concerns about accurate file storage and general disk health are at issue. If you don't have version 6.2, however, the long-time MS-DOS workhorse named Check Disk is what you use. The Check Disk command, which you type as chkdsk, produces a report like this:

```
C:\>chkdsk

Volume MS-DOS 6      created 07-21-1993 3:00p
Volume Serial Number is 1DE8-0D1E

172769280 bytes total disk space
    90112 bytes in 3 hidden files
   581632 bytes in 69 directories
142376960 bytes in 1715 user files
 29720576 bytes available on disk

     8192 bytes in each allocation unit
    21090 total allocation units on disk
     3628 available allocation units on disk

   655360 total bytes memory
   515040 bytes free
DoubleSpace is checking drive C.

DoubleSpace found no errors on drive C.

C:\>
```

Check Disk (Chkdsk)

Checks and reports on disk storage, including fragmentation and lost clusters. The command form is:

    chkdsk [drive:][file-specification] /f /v

drive is the drive you want to check. If you omit this, Check Disk checks the current drive.

file-specification specifies one or more files you want to check for fragmentation. You can include a path and wildcards here. For example:

    C:\>chkdsk c:\mystuff*.doc

/f collects lost clusters into files with names such as FILE0000.CHK, FILE0001.CHK, and so on. You can use the MS-DOS Editor to check the contents of these files to see whether the lost clusters represent any information you want to keep.

/v causes Check Disk to display the path and filename of every file on the disk (volume). You see them all, even if you specify a particular path or set of files, although in this case, Check Disk also reports on whether the specified files are contiguous.

(What you see here is the version 6.0 Check Disk report. If you have version 6.2, your report looks a little different—and a lot more readable because the numbers contain commas.)

Until the Mem (Memory Display) command came along in version 5 of MS-DOS, Check Disk provided a quick and easy way to check not only disk capacity and available storage but also available memory. Check Disk's main job, however, is to report on disks. In addition to the disk stats it normally provides—size, number of directories and files, and available room—Check Disk can also tell you about two less visible aspects of disk storage: file fragmentation and some pitiful little waifs known as lost (or orphaned) clusters.

File fragmentation, dire as it sounds, actually happens naturally as you save and delete files. When you delete a file, a "hole" opens where the file used to be stored. To avoid leaving holes all over, MS-DOS breaks files into consistent-size pieces and store these pieces in whatever holes open up on the disk. Neat solution, especially because MS-DOS does all the tracking of all the pieces of every one of your files, to guarantee that it can find and reunite the file on demand.

Never, never run Check Disk from Windows. The consequences are severe—as in, "Do you really want to reformat your hard disk?"

File fragmentation, then, occurs on an active disk as MS-DOS ends up breaking more and more files and stores their various parts in different, and sometimes widely separated, areas. None of this is a concern, but when too many files are fragmented, your disk processes become slower for the simple reason that MS-DOS must take more time to locate and reconnect the pieces. Although Check Disk (like its colorful offspring, ScanDisk) can't cure fragmentation—Defrag does that—it can tell you whether a particular file or set of files is fragmented. To find out about fragmentation, all you do is include the name of a file or files to check as part of your Check Disk command, like this:

```
C:\EGGS>chkdsk humpty.doc
```

If the file is fragmented, MS-DOS reports:

```
C:\EGGS\HUMPTY.DOC Contains 2 non-contiguous blocks.
```

And what of lost clusters? These little guys are pieces of information that become disconnected from their files. Lost clusters generally happen only when something goes wrong: for example, the power goes out suddenly or a program misbehaves so badly that you must shut down and reboot your computer. At such times, open files are not properly put away, and bits and pieces can get lost, or orphaned. Check Disk—again, like ScanDisk—automatically checks for lost clusters and, if it finds them, shows you a message like this:

```
Errors found, F parameter not specified
Corrections will not be written to disk
4 lost allocation units found in 1 chains.
8192 bytes disk space would be freed.
```

Sounds like you're being told off, doesn't it? Well, oddly enough, MS-DOS does nothing about lost clusters unless you include a special switch, /f, in the command that starts the check in the first place. So all this message really means is that you didn't include the switch, but if you had, 4 orphans (never mind the chains) would be recovered and you would gain 8192 bytes of storage. Although the message doesn't tell you so, those orphans would be given a home in the root directory, in a file named FILE0000.CHK. (If CHK files already exist, MS-DOS creates a new file named FILE0001.CHK, FILE0002.CHK, FILE0003.CHK, and so on.) And once the file is saved on disk, you can take a look at its contents with a command like this:

```
C:\>edit file0000.chk
```

If you don't see anything you need, as is probable, you can use the Delete command to delete the file.

The following table shows some common ways to use Check Disk:

Although DoubleSpace adds its own report to the one Check Disk produces, if you don't have version 6.2, you can (and should) use the Dblspace /chkdsk command, which has its own /f switch, to check a compressed drive and fix any storage errors on it.

Check Disk

Type:	To:
C:\>chkdsk	Check the current drive (C)
C:\>chkdsk /f	Check drive C and fix storage errors
C:\>chkdsk a:*.doc	Check all DOC files on the disk in drive A for fragmentation
C:\CASTLE>chkdsk *.*	Check all files in the CASTLE directory for fragmentation
C:\>chkdsk /v	Check drive C, displaying the names of all files in all directories on the disk (volume)

Diskcopy

Diskcopy clones a floppy disk, making an exact copy of the original—right down to giving the duplicate the same unused sectors and, if they exist, the same fragmented files. So what, you might think, is the point of using Diskcopy? Well, if the original is in good shape, as all but the most-used floppies are, Diskcopy is an easy way to create a spare to take along on a trip, hand over to someone who needs it, or—and this is important— guarantee that some valuable information isn't lost if the original disk is damaged by fire, flood, or a drooling two-year-old (of either the two-legged or four-legged kind). Furthermore, because Diskcopy duplicates everything on a disk, including files used by MS-DOS at boot time, you can use Diskcopy to duplicate a program's startup disk. (This, of course, is for purposes of making a spare or a backup; duplicating programs—other than those in the public domain—so that you can give them away is called piracy.)

When you use Diskcopy, it prompts you through the entire process. In fact, if your target disk isn't yet formatted, Diskcopy will even do that for you. So all you really have to remember is to copy from and to floppy disks of the same size and capacity. You cannot, for example, use Diskcopy to copy from a 3.5-inch 1.44-MB drive to a 5.25-inch 1.2-MB drive. And herein lies what is probably Diskcopy's main drawback in all but version 6.2 of MS-DOS.

Diskcopy

Makes an identical copy of a floppy disk, duplicating not only the files on it but also the on-disk locations of those files. You cannot use Diskcopy on a hard disk, nor can you use it to copy one floppy to another that's a different size or capacity. The command form is:

```
diskcopy [source-drive:]
    [target-drive:] /v
```

source-drive is the drive containing the disk to be copied.

target-drive is the drive containing the disk to copy to.

/v verifies that the copy is accurate. Using this switch makes the copy process longer, but it can be useful if you absolutely have to know that the duplicate is identical to the original. (If you want, you can skip /v and use the Disk Compare command instead.)

If you have a single floppy drive or two floppy drives of different capacities, you must use the same drive for both *source-drive* and *target-drive*.

Version 6.2 uses your hard disk as a temporary home for disk contents being copied, so as you'll see on the next page, a single Diskcopy command and a small amount of floppy swapping can easily produce not only twins, but triplets...quadruplets...however many identical copies you want. In contrast, Diskcopy in versions of MS-DOS through 6.0 uses your computer's RAM to hold disk contents during a copy. As a result, if you have a single floppy drive or two floppy drives of different sizes, you will have to flip floppies in and out of one drive until Diskcopy is done. It will tell you when it needs the original and when it needs the disk it's copying to, but with high-capacity floppies, you can be in for a lot of swapping.

In version 6.2, Diskcopy's prompt for the original (source) and destination (target) disk looks like the following—where the specifics, of course, depend on the disk size and drive you're using:

```
Copying 80 tracks, 18 sectors per track, 2 side(s)
Insert SOURCE diskette in drive A:
Press any key to continue . . .
Reading from source diskette . . .
```

When Diskcopy (in version 6.2, remember) has taken all the information it needs from the source disk, it then prompts for copies to the target disk:

```
Insert TARGET diskette in drive A:
Press any key to continue . . .
Writing to target diskette . . .
```

If you're a longtime user of MS-DOS, here's the good part:

```
Do you wish to write another duplicate of this disk (Y/N)?
```

Type Y, and this time there's no prompting for the source. Diskcopy now simply tells you to:

```
Insert TARGET diskette in drive A:
```

and forge ahead.

Remember: Diskcopy works only on floppy disks and requires you to tell it which is the source disk and which is the target, so the way you type the command depends a lot on your current drive. Pay attention here, if only to avoid this message:

```
Invalid drive specification
Specified drive does not exist, is non-removable,
or is compressed. (To duplicate a compressed drive
specify the host drive letter as the source.)
```

In MS-DOS versions 6.0 and earlier, Diskcopy's prompts appear in a different order and might be repeated many times. The basics are similar enough to what you see here, however, that you shouldn't have any trouble figuring out what to do. Diskcopy has never been either devious or subtle.

MS-DOS also includes a Disk Compare command, typed diskcomp, which can verify that disks copied with Diskcopy are identical.

Disk Compare is almost the same as Diskcopy, so it's not described in detail here. Specify *source-drive* and *target-drive* after the command name, just as you do with Diskcopy. Disk Compare will prompt you the rest of the way.

Kind of ugly-sounding, but it usually amounts to this: The hard disk is your current drive, and you didn't type your Diskcopy command quite right. Depending on how many floppy drives you have and their size and capacity, your Diskcopy command can take any of several forms. The easiest and surest ways to proceed, however, are as follows:

- If you have two floppy drives of the same size and capacity, keep your hard disk as the current drive, put the source disk in drive A, the target disk in drive B, and type the command as:

```
C:\>diskcopy a: b:
```

- If you have one floppy drive or your floppy drives are different capacities, leave the hard disk as the current drive, place the source disk in the floppy drive (assume drive A in this example), and type the command as:

```
C:\>diskcopy a: a:
```

(Of course, if you're copying a compressed floppy, read the message and do as it says.)

Format

One of the oldest commands in MS-DOS, Format is used to prepare new disks for use or to erase and recycle used disks. Format is less often needed these days than in earlier times because both hard and floppy disks often come preformatted and ready to go. It is, however, not only valuable but essential with blank, new, unformatted disks.

When you format a disk, you can choose to perform one of three kinds of format:

- Standard. This type of format is thorough, but it's a safe choice because MS-DOS preserves a record of what—if anything—exists on the disk. This record can then be used by Unformat if it becomes necessary to reverse the format. A standard format is typically what you get with a plain Format command, such as format a:.

Format

Prepares a new disk for use or wipes out the contents of a used disk so it can be reused. The command includes a number of parameters and switches, among them:

```
format drive: /v:[label] /q /u /f:size /s
```

drive is the drive to format. You must include this.
/v:[label] assigns the newly formatted disk the volume label you specify as *label*. For example:

```
C:\>format a: /v:songs
```

/q performs a quick format. You can't change the capacity of a disk (for example, format a high-density floppy to double-density) during a quick format.
/u performs an unconditional (nonreversible) format. For a new disk, using the /u switch with the /q switch can speed up formatting.
/f:size formats the disk to the capacity you specify as *size*. You can specify 360, 720, 1.2, 1.44, or 2.88. (There are various other ways to specify *size*—for example, 1200 and 1.2mb—but those shown here are the simplest and fastest to type.) For example:

```
C:\>format a: /f:720
```

/s formats the disk as a system disk, meaning that at the end of formatting, MS-DOS copies some hidden system files to it so the disk can be used for startup. Switches can, of course, be combined. For example:

```
C:\>format a: /q /s /v:startup
```

quick-formats the disk in drive A, transfers the system files to it, and labels the disk STARTUP. Format can be reversed with the Unformat command, but data might be lost if files are deleted or saved between the times of doing and undoing, so check used disks thoughtfully with the Directory command before reformatting them.

- Quick. This wipes out the disk's existing record of its contents (called the file allocation table, or FAT) but saves this information so that Unformat can reverse the process. A quick format is quick because it does the minimum necessary to prepare the disk for use (no checking for bad spots and things like that).

- Unconditional. This is the most thorough type of format, but—importantly—it cannot be reversed. Use an unconditional format if you have trouble formatting a disk for the first time, if you want to make the previous contents unrecoverable, or if MS-DOS has difficulty using the disk. Otherwise, rely on standard and quick formats.

Regardless of the type of format you choose, remember this advice, which cannot be repeated often enough: Think before you format a hard disk. Think once, think twice. Get up and take a break. Even though you can reverse a format, you can also end up losing data by the time you realize there's a problem. Be very sure you want to format your hard disk—especially drive C—before you press Enter to tell MS-DOS that you do, indeed, know what you're doing.

One final note about Format: Remember that it allows you to assign a volume label to the formatted disk. Volume labels can be really useful in helping you keep track of what's on your disks, especially your floppies. Whenever you use the Directory command, for example, the volume label is shown at the beginning of the display. If your filenames tend to monotony (for example, REPORT1.DOC, REPORT2.DOC, REPORT3.DOC), descriptive volume labels can help you easily tell that all the REPORT files on one floppy relate to ACME CO, while those similarly named reports on another disk all concern BANANAS INC. A volume label can contain up to 11 characters but can't include any of the following:

```
" * + , . / : ; < = > ? [ \ ] ¦
```

Remember too that if you assign a volume label with the /v switch, you can't include spaces in the label. If you let Format prompt for a label at the end of formatting, spaces are perfectly acceptable. You decide.

The following table shows some common uses of the Format command:

Format

Type:	To:
C:\>format a: /q	Quick-format the disk in drive A
C:\>format a: /v:mydisk	Format the disk in drive A and assign it the volume label MYDISK
C:\>format a: /f:720	Format the disk in drive A to hold 720 KB
C:\>format a: /u	Unconditionally format the disk in drive A

DOUBLE TROUBLE
If you try to format a disk, floppy or hard, that has been compressed by DoubleSpace, you can't use the normal Format command. MS-DOS will tell you to use the Dblspace /format command instead, displaying a message like this: *You must use "DBLSPACE /FORMAT C:" to format that drive.*

You can format a high-capacity floppy disk to a lower capacity—that is, you can format a 1.44-MB floppy to hold 720 KB instead, or format a 1.2-MB floppy to hold 360 KB. Do not, however, attempt the reverse, such as formatting a 720-KB disk to hold 1.44 MB. Your disk drive will grind on and on, make awful noises, and end up giving you an unusable disk. You wouldn't try to stuff a tree into an acorn, would you? Well, don't try this either.

Label and Volume

The closely related Label and Volume commands let you mess around with disk volume labels. The Label command allows you to display the label, change it, or delete it. The Volume command merely tells you what the label is. To keep these commands straight, think "Volume is for information, Label for manipulation."

To see these commands in action, start (in nonalphabetic order) with Volume because it's so simple. When you use the command, MS-DOS responds with something like this for the drive you specify:

Label
Displays or changes the volume label of a disk. The command form is:
label [*drive*:][*label*]
drive is the drive for which you want to check or change the label. If you omit *drive*, Label assumes the current drive.
label is a volume label you want to assign to the disk you specified. If you omit *label*, the command prompts for one. For example:
C:\>label c: dos upgrade

```
C:\>vol
Volume in drive C is MS-DOS 6
Volume Serial Number is 1DE8-0D1E
```

Volume
Displays the volume label and volume serial number of a disk. The command form is:
vol [*drive*:]
drive is the letter of the drive for which you want to check the label.

That's it. Now take a look at what happens with Label.

First, if you include a new volume label in the command, you get: Nothing. That's right. The drive light goes on for a short while, and then the command prompt reappears. However, the volume label on the disk you specified did, indeed, get changed. So, for example, if the label of the disk in drive A is PEACHES and you type:

```
C:\>label a:kumquats
```

A quick Volume command will get you:

```
C:\>vol a:
 Volume in drive A is KUMQUATS
 Volume Serial Number is 1268-12D3
```

And what if you type the Label command all by itself? This happens:

```
C:\>label
Volume in drive C is MS-DOS 6
Volume Serial Number is 1DE8-0D1E
Volume label (11 characters, ENTER for none)?
```

Label stops in midstride and asks you to either type a new volume label or press Enter to delete the existing label. If you type a new volume label, the command finishes and Label renames the disk. If you press Enter, however, Label displays yet another message:

```
Delete current volume label (Y/N)?
```

Cautious, isn't it? Press Y or N as necessary to tell it what you want.

System

The System command has one goal in life: to copy to a disk the files MS-DOS needs at startup so that you can later use that disk to boot your computer. As you no doubt already know, you can transfer the system files when you format a disk by including Format's /s switch in your command. System gives you another way to skin the same cat, but with a slight difference: System doesn't format the disk as Format does.

> **System (Sys)**
>
> Transfers the MS-DOS system files to a disk that can then be used for starting the computer. The form of the command is simple:
>
> sys [*source-drive*:] *target-drive*:
>
> ***source-drive*** is the drive and path of the system files. For normal use (copying system files to a floppy disk), this is your startup hard disk. If your startup hard disk is the current drive, you can omit this parameter.
>
> ***target-drive*** is the drive containing the disk that is to receive the system files. You must include this.

When you work with MS-DOS a lot, you hear about system files all the time. What, exactly, are these things? Well, they are a group of program files that absolutely must be on any disk you use for startup. What do they do? It's more a matter of what they are. They are the heart of MS-DOS. Three of these files are on every startup disk: IO.SYS, MSDOS.SYS, and COMMAND.COM. If you've DoubleSpaced your hard disk, another file named DBLSPACE.BIN joins the crowd. Here's roughly what these files do:

- IO.SYS provides MS-DOS with a basic set of input/output devices at startup. This is what enables MS-DOS to find and recognize your keyboard, hard disk, and monitor.

- MSDOS.SYS provides MS-DOS with the ability to run your hardware—control memory, read from and write to disks, and so on. This file is often called the MS-DOS *kernel,* the real core of the operating system.

- COMMAND.COM provides MS-DOS with the ability to interact with you. Known as the command interpreter, COMMAND.COM is the part of MS-DOS that looks for, and carries out, your commands.

- DBLSPACE.BIN provides MS-DOS with the ability to use DoubleSpaced drives. Files on DoubleSpaced drives are compressed to make the smallest possible bundles of bytes for storage. To be used, however, they must be fattened up again. That's what DBLSPACE.BIN does: Unnoticed by you, it works away in the background, compressing and uncompressing files for you and your programs to use.

Because these files are so important and should never be deleted, the system files, except for COMMAND.COM, are assigned certain attributes that keep them tucked out of sight and protected from normal efforts to change or delete them. These attributes are as follows: hidden, which keeps files out of typical directory listings; read-only, which protects files from change; and system, which applies mostly to programs and, like the hidden attribute, keeps files out of sight. If you want, you can see these files on a disk:

Put a formatted floppy disk in drive A, and copy the system files to it with the command:

```
C:\>sys a:
```

When MS-DOS reports *System transferred,* type a Directory command (which is covered in "More About Files") that tells MS-DOS to display the names of all hidden files on the disk:

```
C:\>dir a: /ah
```

There they are, with the exception of COMMAND.COM, which you can see with a plain Directory command.

> The System command is pronounced "sis" and is usually used (be still, guardians of grammar) as a verb, as in "Go ahead and sys the disk."

Unformat

Unformat, the last command covered in this chapter, is your friend in time of need. All you need to know about it is that Unformat can reverse an ill-considered format...maybe. As mentioned in the previous chapter, which introduced many of the essential MS-DOS commands, Unformat works well but cannot guarantee recovery of all your data. There are three complicating factors you should keep in mind:

- First, if you used the /u switch of the Format command, the format can't be undone no matter how sincerely you wish it could.

Unformat

Reverses a format to allow you to regain access to information lost when the disk was formatted. The Unformat command lets you either do the job or take a test run to see what will happen. If you're unformatting your hard disk(!), you can try a test run to see how successful you'll be. The alternative to turning Unformat loose, however, is the loss of all information on the disk, so the choice is not a particularly pleasant one. The form of this command is:

```
unformat drive: /l /test /p
```

drive is the drive containing the disk to unformat. You must provide this information.

/l (lowercase L, not the numeral 1) lists every file in every directory Unformat finds. For example:

```
C:\>unformat a: /l
```

/test tells Unformat to show what will happen if you unformat the disk, but does not actually do the unformatting. This is the switch you use for a test run.

/p sends the output of the command to the printer. For example:

```
C:\>unformat a: /test /p
```

- Second, when you perform a standard or a quick format on a disk, MS-DOS "pretends" that the disk is now blank but does not actually erase anything on the disk. Files remain there, and remain recoverable, but only until they are replaced by new data. Thus, if you save even a small file after formatting, that file might well replace—and make unrecoverable—all or part of one or more of the files that used to be on the disk. If you have to unformat, do it without delay.

- Third, Unformat can't recover all parts of a fragmented file. It will find and recover all of the file up to the first fragmented section, but at that point, Unformat will tell you it can't go any further and will ask whether you want to get back the part of the file it has found, incomplete though it is. (Another endorsement for using Defrag routinely.)

See? If it works, Unformat can come to your rescue better than (or at least as well as) any knight who ever helped any distressed damsel. At such times, Unformat can be everything you ever wanted in an MS-DOS command. If it can't complete the job, though, nothing else can. In those cases, you end up wishing there were such a thing as time travel so that you could go back to the second before you pressed the Enter key after typing that Format command. Even  though Unformat gives you insurance, and plenty of it, the best policy when formatting disks is still the one that's been in effect since MS-DOS began: Think first, format second.

Unformat can reverse an ill-considered format.

If you do need Unformat, bear the following in mind when deciding whether to use any of the switches it supports:

- Use the /l switch to list all files and directories. If you omit this switch, Unformat lists only directories and fragmented files (which you can't recover, remember). If the list is long, you can control scrolling by pressing Ctrl+S to stop the display and pressing any key to continue.

- If you use the /test switch, be prepared for a long wait, especially if you are checking your hard disk. Unformat doesn't rely on any saved records of prior disk contents, but instead reads the disk directly. The process can take five nerve-wracking minutes or more, even on a floppy disk.

- Unformat assumes the printer is connected to LPT1, so verify that this is so before using the /p switch. If you're using the /l or /test switch, you can use /p to print a copy of the results.

POWER PLAY

The Version 5 Mirror Command

If you upgraded to version 6 of MS-DOS from version 5 and you're a pretty advanced user, you might be wondering about all those Unformat switches in version 5 that no longer appear in version 6—switches like /partn, for example, that can restore a damaged disk partition table. Well, don't worry. Those switches are still supported by version 6, even though they're not officially part of the command anymore. As to why they're not part of the command, the reason is that Mirror went from being a separate program to being part of Undelete.

More About Directories

To Think That I Might Someday See a Disk That Doesn't Have a Tree

Directories first appeared in version 2 of MS-DOS to support the vast storage capacity of the 5-MB to 10-MB hard disk in the IBM PC/XT. Are you laughing? Well, before the XT showed up, you have to remember that *disk* to a personal computer owner meant *floppy disk,* and *floppy disk* in those days meant at most 360 KB of storage. That puts the XT's "large" hard disk in perspective, at least for its time.

Nowadays, of course, hard disks hold much more than a stack of XTs could hold. In fact, modern hard disks easily store more than the XT and version 2 could even have handled. They have grown in storage capacity by orders of magnitude. New computers commonly have hard disks that hold 80 to 100 MB. Higher-end machines often have hard disks that hold 150 to 300 MB. And powerhouse computers can be equipped with mammoth hard disks that hold 1 GB (gigabyte) or more.

But the subject here is directories, not hard disks. And the point of all this is that if directories were considered necessary for the hard disk of an XT, imagine how much more important they are to the hard disks in the XT's descendants. Even if the root directory of a hard disk could hold an unlimited number of files (which it can't—512 remains the limit), just imagine having to sort through a single directory listing that contains all the files on a full 150-MB hard disk. Talk about Excedrin headaches.

Who Needs Directories? You Do

Back in the golden days when computers in the 80286 class abounded, directories could be—and usually were—matters best left in the hands of the knowledgeable and often nerdy. These days, especially because floppy disks as well as hard disks hold so much information, directories are for everyone—so much so that MS-DOS commands automatically assume that, likely as not, you'll precede a filename with the path to the directory in which the file is stored. Luckily, directories are easy to manage and easy to use. Use directories freely, and you'll find that they make the difference between a well-organized disk and a disk like that embarrassing drawer—you know, the one in your kitchen or garage that ends up full of stuff like screws, washers, scissors, dried-up bottles of glue, balls of string, old keys....

Trees Revisited

An earlier chapter, "On to Disks and Files," introduced the concept of directory trees. The term *tree* is often used in computing to help give you a mental picture of a structure that starts at one level and branches out from there. You can visualize the tree structure moving downward into the root system.

Basically, a directory tree is just like your family tree or your company's organization chart: It starts at a "top" level, the root, which is comparable to the ancestral parent or the top boss, and it branches out through succeeding levels (family generations or company executives). What's important to note about these levels is that each one below the top is subordinate to, but related to, the one above it. (A directory inside another directory is often called a *subdirectory*.) And it's this *hierarchical* structure that allows you to organize your own directory tree into levels and sublevels that sort files successively into more and more closely related groups, like this:

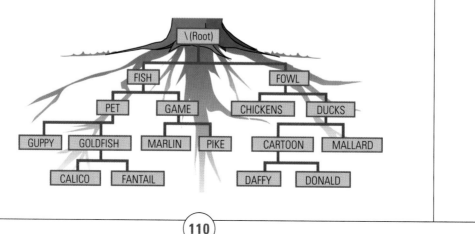

Show Me the Way…

Because a directory tree can contain many branches arranged on many different levels, you need to have a way to tell MS-DOS exactly where a particular file is stored. That way is called a path, or pathname. A path, as described earlier in this book, lists the string of directories leading to a particular file. Remember grammar-school English, when you had to diagram sentences? Pathnames are similar sorts of diagrams but much simpler because you don't have to figure out subjects, verbs, and objects. Pathnames diagram a branch of the directory tree by showing you how one level leads to the next, and the next, until you reach a particular file. For example, suppose the branch of your directory tree leading to the file EARTH.DOC looks like this. (Imagine yourself walking up or down stairsteps representing the various levels.)

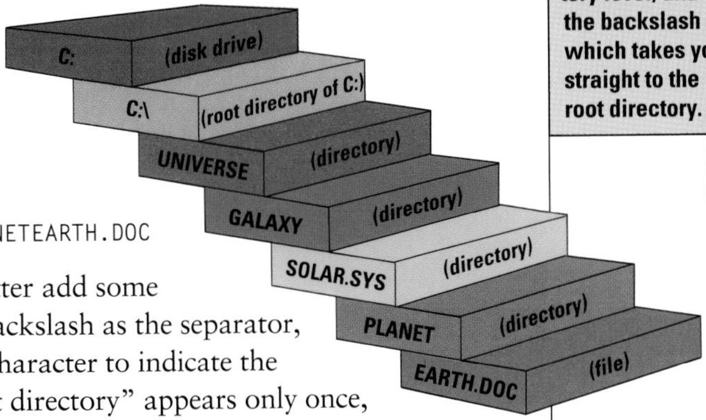

If you flatten the stairs and pull the directory names together on a single line, you get something like this:

```
C:\UNIVERSEGALAXYSOLAR.SYSPLANETEARTH.DOC
```

Hmmm. Not very readable, is it? Better add some separators. In MS-DOS, you use a backslash as the separator, even though you normally use that character to indicate the root. (Because the \ that means "root directory" appears only once, as the very first character in a pathname, MS-DOS doesn't get confused.) Now your pathname looks like this:

```
C:\UNIVERSE\GALAXY\SOLAR.SYS\PLANET\EARTH.DOC
```

Much better.

As you can see, a complete pathname begins with the drive on which the file is found, and then describes the successive directory levels MS-DOS must follow to find the file (EARTH.DOC) at the end of the path. Each of the directories in these pathnames can, of course, contain files of their own, but that's irrelevant here. If you were listing the path to one of those files, it would simply end at whatever directory the other file was in. The point to remember is that when you store files in directories, each file has a unique pathname, which consists of the string of directories leading to its particular storage location.

The sample pathname shown above is pretty long—counting the root, you go down through five directory levels before you reach EARTH.DOC. Not to worry. MS-DOS can handle directory trees that make a brier patch look tame. Altogether, a single pathname, including the filename and extension at the end,

> When you want to play Tarzan and go swinging through your directory tree, don't forget a few special characters. Used with Change Directory and other commands, they can save a lot of typing: two dots (..), which take you up one directory level, and the backslash (\), which takes you straight to the root directory.

The stairstep diagram labels:
C: (disk drive)
C:\ (root directory of C:)
UNIVERSE (directory)
GALAXY (directory)
SOLAR.SYS (directory)
PLANET (directory)
EARTH.DOC (file)

can go as long as 63 characters. So this pathname, for instance, is perfectly valid to MS-DOS:

```
\A\B\C\D\E\F\G\H\I\J\K\L\M\N\O\P\Q\R\S\T\U\V\W\X\Y\Z\ALPHA.DOC
```

You probably don't want anything quite so elaborate. If you created such a bizarre mess, this is what Change Directory and Directory commands would look like:

Yeah, sure.

Although MS-DOS can wind its way down and down through many directory levels, you not only don't have to create such mazes, you really shouldn't. Long pathnames are a nuisance to type, and files can be just as hard to find on an overorganized disk as they are on an underorganized one. Once you decide you want to use directories to organize your files, think about how you work and how you want your programs and files organized before you run off like Johnny Appleseed sowing tree seeds everywhere. Here are two basic rules that can help you out:

- If a program suggests installing itself in its own directory, accept graciously. You're free to organize programs any way you want, but generally if you keep programs separate, you'll find that reinstalling and upgrading are simple. If you have a lot of programs, you might want to consider grouping their directories in a directory named PROGRAMS (or something similar), but in general, try to keep your programs separate from one another. You'll be able to tell at a glance what files the program considers its own, and if you ever have to delete the program, you can do so easily.

- As you organize your data files, try to keep the master plan of your directory tree fairly simple and flexible. Most people can do wonders with about three or four directory levels. If you find yourself going much further down, think about whether you might be overdoing it. For instance, all of this book, comprising dozens of files, was stored in one book directory with two subdirectories, like this:

Remember, you use directories to make your work simpler. If you end up spending half your time typing pathnames and the other half searching one level after another for a file you know is stowed away somewhere in there, you're not being very effective.

POWER PLAY

The Low-Key Approach to Typing Commands

In addition to the .. and \ characters described in the margin on page 111, MS-DOS recognizes a third "shortcut" character, a single dot (.), which you can use to refer to the current directory. Most of the time, you don't have to tell MS-DOS anything about the current directory because that's where its attention is focused. But the single dot, like the .. and \, can be used in all kinds of creative ways, with various MS-DOS commands, to get work done quickly, without the hassle of typing long pathnames. Here are some examples to show you how it's done:

```
C:\DOWN1\DOWN2\DOWN3>dir \
```

lists the files in the root directory without your having to leave the current directory.

```
C:\DOWN1\DOWN2\DOWN3>dir ..
```

lists the files in the directory (DOWN1\DOWN2) immediately above the current directory.

```
C:\DOWN1\DOWN2\DOWN3>copy . a:
```

copies all the files in the current directory (.) to the disk in drive A.

```
C:\DOWN1\DOWN2\DOWN3>copy . ..
```

copies all the files in the current directory to the directory one level up.

```
C:\DOWN1\DOWN2\DOWN3>cd
..\across1
```

changes the current directory from DOWN1\DOWN2\DOWN3 to the ACROSS1 directory in DOWN1\DOWN2. (The .. tells MS-DOS you want it to look one level up, at the DOWN2 directory, and the \across1 tells MS-DOS to find the ACROSS1 directory in DOWN2.)

Had enough? All right, it's on to the MS-DOS commands you need for dealing with directories. There aren't many.

Change Directory

One of the simplest yet most useful of MS-DOS commands, Change Directory turns the operating system's attention to the drive and directory you want to work with. Most people type the command as cd, but you can also use chdir if you like typing.

Although Change Directory is easy to use, it does have a couple of subtle characteristics that are good to know about:

- When you change directories on a drive, the new directory remains the active directory for that drive, even after you change to a different drive. This can cause a little confusion if MS-DOS responds *File not found* about a floppy because you assumed one directory to be its active directory, but MS-DOS was looking at another.

- You can change the active directory on a drive other than the current drive. Just precede the path with a drive letter.

- You can use the . and .. and \ characters to cut down on typing.

Here are some examples of ways to use Change Directory:

Change Directory	
Type:	**To:**
C:\>cd	See the current directory. (Not a big deal because it's shown by the prompt anyway.)
C:\>cd b:	See the current directory of the disk in drive B. Note the difference (the backslash) between this and the next example.
C:\>cd b:\	Change to the root directory of the disk in drive B without changing the current drive or directory (C:\).
C:\CATS>cd lions\zoo	Change to the CATS\LIONS\ZOO directory. Notice that the path does not start with a backslash. That's because LIONS is a subdirectory of CATS. You need the backslash only when the path must start at the root.
C:\CATS\LIONS\ZOO>cd ..	Change to the LIONS directory (one level up from the current directory, ZOO).
C:\CATS\LIONS\ZOO>cd ..\pumas	Change to the CATS\LIONS\PUMAS directory from the CATS\LIONS\ZOO directory. Notice that you're going to a different "branch" of the directory one level up.
C:\CATS\LIONS\PUMAS>cd \	Change to the root directory of drive C.

Deltree

The Deltree command is your version of a pair of pruning shears: You use it to turn a shaggy directory tree into a bonsai work of art. With Deltree, you can clip here and there to shape your directories with little time and effort. BUT:

• You must do so *carefully*.

Take this warning seriously. Deltree, unlike the Remove Directory command, is perfectly willing to lop off not only a directory, but all the files it contains. And normally, you cannot get those files back. There are ways, as you can see from the accompanying item headed, "Undo Deltree? Maybe." But don't count on them. Deltree assumes you're smarter than it is. Be sure you are.

Deltree

Removes a branch of your directory tree, *including* all files and subdirectories contained in the directory. Be sure a valuable file isn't hiding in a pile of unwanted ones before you use Deltree. Form this good habit: Always precede Deltree by two Directory commands, **dir /p** and **dir /ahsr /p**. These two commands, taken together, display every file in the directory, even hidden and system files (which Deltree deletes right along with everything else).

The command form is simple:

    deltree /y [drive:]path

/y turns off Deltree's normal prompt for confirmation before it deletes a directory or file. To enjoy a long, serene life, don't use this switch.

drive is the drive containing the directory to delete. Omit this if the directory is on the current drive.

path is the path to the directory. You must include this. If you're the adventurous type, you can use wildcards, but you'd better know exactly what you're doing.

POWER PLAY

Undo Deltree? Maybe

If you use Deltree and realize that you made a mistake, it's possible to recover your deleted directories and files, but only under certain circumstances, and only if you act quickly.

• If you use Microsoft Windows and you chose to install the Windows version of Undelete, you might be able to get your directories and files back by first undeleting each directory you want to recover and then undeleting the files in each of the directories.

• If you didn't install the Windows version of Undelete but you started

the MS-DOS version of Undelete *with the Delete Sentry option,* try using the Make Directory command to reconstruct the deleted branch of the tree. Use the exact same directory names. After you re-create the directories, recover the files in them, directory by directory, with the Undelete command: Use Change Directory to make one reconstructed directory the current directory, undelete the files in it, change to the next reconstructed directory, undelete the files in it, and so on. Remember, this works only if you started Delete Sentry.

If you've used MS-DOS in the past to reorganize your directory tree, the easiest way to understand and appreciate Deltree is to think that this single command:

```
deltree [unwanted directory]
```

replaces these commands (or perhaps a series of these commands):

```
cd [unwanted directory]
del *.*
cd ..
rd [unwanted directory]
```

When you use Deltree, it normally prompts for confirmation before deleting a directory and the files in it:

```
Delete directory "adios" and all its subdirectories? [yn]
```

If you type Y, Deltree will display:

```
Deleting adios...
```

When the command prompt reappears, ADIOS will be gone, amigos.

Here are some examples of ways to use Deltree:

Deltree	
Type:	**To:**
C:\>deltree oldstuff	Delete the OLDSTUFF directory, including all subdirectories and files in it.
C:\>deltree ???stuff	Delete every directory whose name begins with three characters and ends with *STUFF*—for example, OLDSTUFF, NEWSTUFF, and BIGSTUFF. All subdirectories and files in all matching directories will also be deleted. Deltree will prompt before deleting each matching directory, but that's all the warning you'll get. Pay attention.
C:\>deltree /y a:bigtree	Delete the BIGTREE directory on the disk in drive A, including all subdirectories and files, but without prompting for confirmation. This command's /y switch is for the supremely confident or the habitually reckless.

Make Directory

The Make Directory command, typed as either md or mkdir, creates a directory. Make Directory is easy to use and, because it creates directories as opposed to changing or deleting them, it is an extremely safe command to experiment with. All you really need to understand about Make Directory is this: If you don't specify a drive, a path, or both, Make Directory creates the new directory within the current directory. To create a directory on a different drive or on a different

When you use Deltree, bear this in mind: Deltree will not remove the current directory. It will, however, delete all subdirectories and files in the current directory. To avoid unexpected results, never use Deltree on the current directory.

branch of your directory tree, include the drive and path in
the command, as shown in the following examples:

Make Directory

Type:	To:
C:\>md new	Create a directory named NEW in the current (root) directory of drive C.
C:\>md new\newer	Create a directory named NEWER in the NEW directory of drive C.
C:\OLD>md \new\newer\newest	Create a directory named NEWEST in the NEW\NEWER directory on drive C. Notice that the path begins with the root directory because the new directory is being created in a different branch of the directory tree than the current directory (OLD).

Path

The Path command is unlike the other commands described in this chapter in that it is typically used only in
your AUTOEXEC.BAT file and is ready and willing to be
ignored until you need to modify it. And in real life, you seldom need to do that.
Why? Because normally, the only time you need to change your Path command
is when you install a new program, and most programs come with installation
software that modifies the Path com-
mand in AUTOEXEC.BAT for you.

If Path is so unassuming, you're
probably wondering why you need
to know about it at all. Well, for the
simple reason that Path is the command
that tells MS-DOS which directories to
search for your program files. Remember that most programs these days
install themselves in their own directories. Remember too that MS-DOS
searches the current directory only,
unless told otherwise. Combine these
two facts of life, and you come up with
a great reason for using Path: With it,
you don't have to type a pathname
each time you start a different program.
Furthermore, because Path sits in your
AUTOEXEC.BAT file (which MS-DOS

Make Directory (Md or Mkdir)

Creates a new directory. If you don't specify a drive or path, the directory is created in the current directory. The command form is:

    md [drive:]path

drive is the drive on which to create the directory. Omit this if you're creating a directory on the current drive.
path is the path to the new directory. To create a directory in the current directory, include only the name of the new directory. To create a directory elsewhere in the directory tree, precede the name of the new directory with the appropriate path. Don't forget to start the path with a backslash if MS-DOS must start at the root directory.

Path

Displays, deletes, or sets the search path MS-DOS uses to find executable program files. This command is normally placed in AUTOEXEC.BAT, but you can use it from the command prompt to display, delete, or set the search path.
To display or delete the search path, the command form is:

    path [;]

path, typed all by itself, displays the search path.
path followed by a semicolon deletes the search path. You shouldn't use this command! It causes MS-DOS to search only the current directory for program files, and chances are that many, if not most, of your programs are in their own directories.
To set a search path, the command form is:

    path [drive1:][path1];[drive2:][path2];
        ...[driveN:][pathN]

drive1 and **path1** are the drive and path leading to the first directory you want MS-DOS to search; **drive2** and **path2** are the drive and path leading to the second directory; **driveN** and **pathN** are the drive and path leading to the Nth directory. Separate each drive/path pair from the next with a semicolon. Don't forget this.

processes every time you start or restart the computer), you don't have to bother typing in the paths to all your programs at every startup. Nice.

Even though you don't have to tinker much with Path, you should know a few things about it. For instance:

- The MS-DOS version 6 Setup program searches AUTOEXEC.BAT for a Path command and either creates or modifies it to point to your \DOS directory. All other pathnames remain untouched, so you don't have to worry about your new version of MS-DOS being unable to find applications that were on the hard disk before you upgraded the operating system.

- You can include as many pathnames in the search path as you want, up to a maximum of 127 characters, including the semicolons that separate the pathnames.

- Each pathname you specify must be complete—that is, it must start with the root directory.

- If a program installs itself in a directory with multiple subdirectories, you generally need to specify only the main program directory. As long as MS-DOS can find the file it needs to start the program, you can usually let the program figure out the rest on its own.

You can see what your search path looks like by typing path at the MS-DOS prompt. A typical path looks something like this:

```
PATH=C:\DOS;C:\WINDOWS;C:\WORD
```

Your search path, of course, might be much longer and, except for C:\DOS, will probably list different pathnames. Oh, and don't worry about the equal sign; that's optional. The all-uppercase look is produced by MS-DOS, so your search path is always displayed in uppercase, even if you type it entirely in lowercase.

If you have to change your search path in AUTOEXEC.BAT, you have to be able to use a text-file editor, such as the MS-DOS Editor. It's easy, but it's grist for another chapter. For details, refer to "Make a File with Edit," in Section 3.

Remove Directory

Remove Directory is a safer, if more time-consuming, way to remove directories than Deltree. Remove Directory works only if the directory to be removed contains no files or subdirectories and is not the current directory. If you don't feel particularly confident with computers or MS-DOS, opt for Remove Directory over Deltree until you feel you've earned your wings.

ENVIRONMENT
Your search path is one piece of information that MS-DOS "keeps in mind" as it works. It also keeps a number of other facts in memory, including what the command prompt is supposed to look like. This collection of information is what's called the *environment*. You can see your current environment settings very easily by typing set at the command prompt.

When you use Remove Directory and all goes well, MS-DOS responds by merely redisplaying the command prompt. If you use Remove Directory and all does not go well, you see:

```
Invalid path, not directory,
or directory not empty
```

MS-DOS is asking you to recheck your command because:

- The path does not exist, at least not as you typed it.

- You didn't type the name of a recognizable directory.

- You typed the pathname and directory correctly, but the directory still contains subdirectories or files that you must remove.

Assuming the problem was not a typing error, use the Directory command to see what's in the directory. If you see files there, delete them (if they're expendable), and try the Remove Directory command again. Remember, however, that Remove Directory will not delete the current directory, so if you changed to the directory you want to remove, be sure to issue the command from a different directory.

Remove Directory (Rd or Rmdir)
Deletes a directory as long as it contains no files or subdirectories and is not the current directory. The command form is simple:
rd [*drive:*]*path*
drive is the drive containing the directory to be removed. Omit this if the directory is on the current drive.
path is the path to the directory to be removed. If you type only a directory name, MS-DOS assumes the directory is a subdirectory of the current directory. To remove a directory elsewhere in the directory tree, type a pathname. Be sure to start the pathname with a backslash if it begins at the root.

POWER PLAY

It Looks Empty, But...

At times, Remove Directory can become exasperating because it keeps displaying its error message, even though repeated Directory commands show a seemingly empty directory. The solution: Check for hidden or system files. Neither of these types is listed by a normal Directory command, but files of both types are just as real as any other files. Change to the directory and type attrib, which displays the at- tributes of all files in the directory:

```
C:\>JUSTME>attrib
     SHR      C:\JUSTME\HIDEME.SYS
      H       C:\JUSTME\PERSONAL.DOC
```

If the listing shows hidden files, do think twice about deleting them, especially if their extensions are COM, EXE, SYS, or BIN. Pro- gram files have these extensions, and deleting program files can be nasty.

And unless you're an expert, never delete the following: COMMAND.COM, IO.SYS, MSDOS.SYS, or any files named DBLSPACE.

Tree

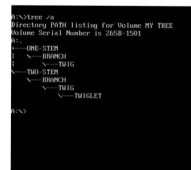

Tree

Displays the directory tree of the drive specified, including filenames if requested. The command form is:

> tree [*drive:*][*path*] /f /a

drive is the drive for which you want to see the directory tree.

path is the path to the directory for which you want to see a tree. If the current directory is not the root and you want to see the structure of the entire disk, specify *path* as the root directory (\).

/f displays the names of the files in each directory.

/a uses ASCII characters to create lines diagramming the tree. Use this switch if you have trouble displaying or printing a tree.

Tree, which is both descriptively named and a lot friendlier sounding than many MS-DOS commands, draws a diagram of a directory tree on the screen so that you can see the parts in relation to the whole. Better yet, Tree can also work with a special character (>) known as a redirection operator to send a picture of the directory tree to your printer.

When you use the Tree command, you can choose to display directory names only or both directory names and filenames. You can display all of the tree or just part of it. And you can display the result with graphics characters that produce neat, solid lines like the ones shown in the lower left screen.

As an alternative, you can specify ASCII characters that produce universally displayable and printable lines and "corners" like the ones shown in the lower right screen.

Oh, yes. To print a copy of your tree, type the command and follow it with the redirection operator and the name MS-DOS recognizes for the printer, like this:

> C:\>tree > prn

You can also save a copy of the directory tree in a file in much the same way, with a command like this:

```
C:\>tree > mytree.txt
```

where MYTREE.TXT is the name of the file in which to save the tree diagram.

Here are some examples of ways to use the Tree command:

Tree

Type:	To:
C:\>tree	Display the directory tree of the current drive, using graphics characters.
C:\>tree /a	Do the same as above, but use ASCII characters.
C:\PINE\CONE\NEEDLE>tree \pine	Display a tree of the PINE directory, including CONE, NEEDLE, and any other subdirectories in PINE. Notice that this command is being issued when the current directory is a few levels down in the directory tree being displayed.
C:\PINE>tree /f	Display a tree of the PINE directory and all its subdirectories, listing the files in each directory.
C:\>tree a: > prn	Print the directory tree of the disk in drive A. (This assumes you have a printer that can handle graphics characters.)
C:\>tree a: /a > prn	Print the directory tree of the disk in drive A, using ASCII characters. (This is what you do if your printer cannot handle graphics characters.)

More About Files

And It All Boils Down to These

No matter what kind of hardware you have, you can't get it to do anything without files. Files are what all computing is about. Without files, your computer's processor has nothing to think about—and, in truth, nothing even to think with. The processor might have the calculating potential of an Einstein, but without files, it has the brainpower of a sponge.

So what is it about files that makes a computer compute? Well, you know that all computer information is stored in files. MS-DOS is stored in files. Application programs are stored in files. Your documents, pictures, and games-in-progress are stored in files. What makes your computer unique is the way it combines two different types of files to make things happen. In a way, your computer is the catalyst that brings two elements together to create something new (with your help, of course). Those two elements are programs and data. Although both are stored in files, they're vastly different:

- Program files contain instructions that tell the computer what to do.

- Data files contain information that gives the program files something to do unto.

Come Up and See My Files Sometime

People use the word *cryptic* to describe things that are mysterious. Program files are the ultimate in cryptic. To prove it to yourself, take another look at a familiar program—Format—as MS-DOS shows it to you. If you're at your computer, type the following command, substituting the name of your MS-DOS directory if it's not called dos. Oh, and don't jump when the computer beeps; you're not breaking anything:

```
C:\>type c:\dos\format.com
```

```
C:\>type c:\dos\format.com
⌐@Ü‖"Ü:-sⁱⁱ—D♦É:≡ ⁱ"‖6 Éⁿ▀©M<Ñⁱ╫╞▄ⁿ⌐ô᷃J♪J³╗Ṣ╗J⮹PKLITE Copr. 1992 PKWARE Inc. Al
l Rights ReservedNot enough memory⌐₁      ‖a⌐─!≈ Éⁿⁱ"00ᴶↀ@♥₂ⁱ╨⌐◊Ñⁿç≈FF⌐ ⌐iⓄ‖▶ ô2
ÉⁱⓄ‖▶ ô:ⁱⓄ‖▶ ô<ⁱⓄ‖▶ ôÑⁱⓄ‖▶ ôcⁱⓄ‖▶ ôdⁱⓄ‖▶ ôeⁱⓄ‖▶ ôfⁱⓄ‖▶ ╥╥⌐Jⁱ╥⌐s"3⌐╥⌐Jⁱ╥⌐t⌐J⌐╥₁⌐t♯⌐J
╫┌⌐çJ♦rô⌐╥Ju♦ⁱⓄ‖ ⌐╥╨.cₐ─⌐Ç.
                            t:3ℸâ·Ⓞt♌╥─♪Jtür▼╥♪Jtü⌐╥♪Jtôⱦ⌐╥♪Jtoⱦ⌐╥CJⓄsⅰ.c₁,Ⓞ¼╨ⁱÜⁱ⌐
♦<<ñ^ôⱦ¼Ø╫Ç⌐ < u⌐ô3⌐♪Ju♦ⁱⓄ‖ ⌐╥╥Çrⱦ╥♪Ju♦ⁱⓄ‖ ⌐╥╥çⱦⱦ⌐╥♪Ju♦ⁱⓄ‖ ⌐╥╥ⁿu╥ⱱ ã╨ô¦3ⱦⱦ¼ ⌐Sⁱⱦⁱⁿⱦ
╨ⁱôⁱ≈ⁱⱦ╥▼ Ⓞ
      ♦ⱷ  ♦♦⬨♦
ⱷYDⁿ ôp♦ⱷ ⌐Converted AⒷⱸM2ⱦ  ⒷⒷ HÉ ⌐    ç♀▸ ▲‖ᴬ "ⒶⒷç ᶜ¶ô ⌐ θⁱⱷⱷ ôⁿ↓LJK
        ⌐‖ⱦⱷt ôⁱ ôÇ‖l ⱷⒷBá—ôⁿⁱ▶ⒷⒶⱷèⱦⁱôâ¦a ,ᴶôⱼüt◆◆ôᴹↄ¼Ⓞↄ Vaↄ♀Ⓞↄ ▶¶ⱦₛ̣БH,◊◊óLⱼ1◊ÑÑóᴵ
J, ô 7PJ1BⁱⁿⒶᵔ "E⌐ⓜⒶ‖çⱦ‖ⓄVB.1£♀◆"╥─9♀9♀1♦‖ ↓ó─ⱷ¶─,‖◆♀    Ⓑ↑
⌐ⓥJↄ◊ↄⱷ◊♀◆ⱱ◐‖◀♥◁♥◆♥ⁱↄ‖◐♀Vⱷ♀VⱷⒷ◐ⱼ◀◐ⱷↄ◊♀◐‖◀◆♀◐♀
C:\>
```

As the illustration shows, a program file can contain readable words (like the copyright information at the beginning), but most of the file is "displayed" as a jumble of strange-looking symbols and, as you heard, long or short beeps. Weird, isn't it? But that's a working—rather, a workable—program. Those odd characters you see and hear are the instructions that actually make up the program. The reason you can't read any of it is that the program is stored on disk as an executable (runnable) file, rather than as a set of people-readable instructions. While it was being created, the program was readable—at least by its programmers—but in the process of being converted to a working part of MS-DOS, FORMAT.COM lost its human connection in order to take on a form that the computer could easily use.

Now, for comparison, take a look at a data file—that is, a file other than one that contains instructions telling the computer how to do work. Your \DOS directory includes a data file as well, so use the Type command again, this time to display the file named README.TXT. The file is quite long, so tack a More command on the end to pause scrolling after each screenful:

```
README.TXT

NOTES ON MS-DOS 6.2
===================

This file provides important information not included in the
MICROSOFT MS-DOS 6 USER'S GUIDE or in MS-DOS Help.

This file is divided into the following major sections:

1. Setup
2. MemMaker, EMM386, and Memory Management
3. Windows
4. Hardware Compatibility with MS-DOS 6.2
5. Microsoft Programs
6. Third-Party Programs
7. DoubleSpace

If the subject you need information about doesn't appear in
this file, you might find it in one of the following text
files included with MS-DOS:

* OS2.TXT, which describes how to remove and save data on your
  computer when you upgrade from OS/2 to MS-DOS 6.2.
-- More --
```

```
C:\>type c:\dos\readme.txt | more
```

Aaah. That's more like it. Real words.

PRINTING README.TXT

If you haven't read all of README.TXT, you should do so. The file contains information about version 6.2 that you won't find in your MS-DOS documentation (although you will find it in the online Help and in this book). To make life easy, print a copy of README.TXT with the command:

```
C:\>copy c:\dos\readme.txt prn
```

Right, the Copy command can do a lot more than copy files from disk to disk. More about this later.

POWER PLAY

More about ASCII

Earlier in this book, ASCII was described as a coding scheme in which characters are assigned numeric values. This works pretty much the same way as you being assigned a number, say 151, in the next marathon you run. For the time you're in the race (during processing as it were), you'd be 151 rather than Len or Lekeshia. When the race ends and you're "output," you'd once again revert to your real name. That's what happens to ASCII characters.

Now, what wasn't explained earlier is that ASCII provides for a possible 256 characters, but that standard ASCII of the sort used in putting plain-text files together accounts for only 128 of those characters. These standard ASCII characters are rigidly defined and never vary. That's why they're so useful as a "universal" computer alphabet. The remaining 128, known as extended ASCII, are a little more flexible. They can be assigned to characters that are somewhat out of the mainstream (at least the English-language mainstream). Extended ASCII characters include accented letters, Greek letters, currency symbols, mathematical symbols, and so on. Where MS-DOS is concerned, extended ASCII is generally assigned to what is called the IBM extended character set.

To type standard ASCII characters,

all you do is use the main part of your keyboard: the letter keys, number keys, and special keys such as Shift, Tab, and the Spacebar. You can also, if you want, "type" ASCII characters by holding down Alt and using the numeric keypad—not the number keys at the top of the keyboard— to "key in" the ASCII code of the character you want. This Alt+numeric keypad approach is, in fact, the way to create extended ASCII characters with MS-DOS. If you've never tried this, you might find it fun to play with, either at the MS-DOS command line or, if an application program allows, as a means of inserting special characters in a letter or other document. To figure out which numbers refer to which characters, see the table in this book's last chapter.

To experiment with extended ASCII characters, create a small test file— call it TESTFILE.XXX. Rename TESTFILE.XXX as ¥4.DOS with the following command. To produce the yen character (¥), hold down Alt and type 157 on the numeric keypad (the characters shown in [ ] brackets):

```
C:\>ren testfile.xxx
   [Alt+157]4.dos
```

To delete the file, use the same characters:

```
C:\>del [Alt+157]4.dos
```

Even though readability is a basic difference between program files and data files, don't go getting the idea that all program files are gobbledygook and all data files are as clear as mountain water. That's just not so. Program files *are* unintelligible onscreen, but so are some of the data files. What you see in README.TXT is a file stored in plain-text, or ASCII, format. ASCII files are sort of the computer equivalent of Dick and Jane readers: simple and limited to very basic characters and formatting (such as tabs and carriage returns), all of which any computer can easily display. Other data files, even such everyday files as your word-processed documents, contain special codes embedded by the word processing program. These codes tell the program how to display, print, and otherwise manage the file to produce exactly the output you want.

A word-processed document, for instance, contains codes that describe the way your finished document is to look: the typeface (font) used for printing, the size of the margins, the words you want italicized, the way you've set up column layouts, and so on. More exotic data files, such as graphics images, are coded and stored in a way that makes them completely unrecognizable when you use the Type command, but also in a way that makes those files completely visible when you use a program designed to interpret them.

The Eight-Dot-Three Rule

Eight-dot-three. That's the rule for filenames and extensions under MS-DOS: up to eight characters for the filename, followed by a dot (optional) and an extension (also optional) of up to three characters. As explained earlier in this book, filenames and extensions can contain any printable characters you want, except spaces (yes, they're considered printable) and the following, all of which MS-DOS reserves for its own use:

```
" * + , . / : ; < = > ? [ \ ] |
```

These same rules, by the way, also apply to directories, which MS-DOS really considers special-purpose files: files that contain lists of other files. So, for example, you could use any of the names in the left column below as either a filename or a directory name, but those in the middle column would all be considered illegal by MS-DOS:

File Naming Dos and Don'ts		
Good	**Bad**	**Reason for Ugly**
COGITO	I THINK	No spaces, remember?
ERGO.SUM	THEREFORE.IAM	Filename too long.
EUREKA.AHA	FIGURED.ITOUT	Extension too long here.
RIGHT-ON.!!!	"WAY-TO.GO"	No quotation marks allowed.

You can have some fun playing with filenames by using extended ASCII characters. If you do this, however, either memorize the ASCII values for the characters you use (boring) or have an extended ASCII table handy to help you "decode" the filename the next time you want to use the file. Caution: Playing around like this is a pretty trivial use of your time, but if you do try such tricks, avoid assigning oddball names to files you want to use with your programs. In particular, don't mess around with files you'll try to use with Microsoft Windows. Windows recognizes a different extended character set (the ANSI set) and won't be able to find your file until you return to MS-DOS and rename the thing.

Other than remembering eight-dot-three and a few off-limits characters, you need remember only one practical fact about filenames: MS-DOS does not allow two files with the same name and extension to exist on the same disk in the same directory. This is not, however, the same as saying you always need to come up with unique filenames. You don't. Remember that to MS-DOS, a filename (and extension) are part of a file specification. The entire thing also includes the path to the file. Thus, it has no problem working with two identically named files as long as they are on different disks or in different directories. You can see this easily in the following two examples, both of which include a file named REPORT.DOC:

```
C:\BILL\PLAYS\HAMLET\REPORT.DOC
C:\SEUSS\BOOKS\CAT-HAT\REPORT.DOC
```

The paths are entirely different, though both lead to files named REPORT.DOC, so MS-DOS would have no trouble finding one or the other file.

Extensions Are More than Just Extenders

When you first start using MS-DOS, it's easy to ignore extensions and just assign filenames to your files. This is one case in which the beginner does through inexperience what the "pro" sometimes lives to regret. Even though an eight-character limit on filenames is sometimes irritating, it's generally best not to assign extensions unless you really need them. There are two reasons for this: First, application programs have their own expectations regarding extensions; second, so does MS-DOS.

Application programs—word processors, spreadsheets, games, and most everything else—are built to expect their data files to have a particular extension. The extension differs from one program to the next, but each program does assign a particular extension by default. This extension is also the one the program searches for by default. Your word processor, for example, probably assigns the DOC extension (for *document*) to its files. So when you tell it to save a file, it expects to tack DOC onto the end of the filename. Furthermore, and this is the important part, the program will also automatically search for DOC files when you tell it to find a file. The program will, no doubt, gracefully accept SHOTS.VET instead of SHOTS.DOC, but when it's time for a booster and you tell the program to find the file again, you'll have to make a point of including the VET extension. SHOTS alone will not be enough to help the program find the file. That, of course, means extra typing—either because you have to type both the filename and the extension or because you have to tell the program to list all files (*.*) or all files with the VET extension (*.VET). Why bother?

About the only time you might want to assign an extension is when you're creating a plain-text file. By convention, these files are given the extension TXT, and you might very well want to march to the beat of everyone else's drum by following the same practice. That way, your ASCII files will be immediately recognizable to anyone who knows what a TXT file normally contains.

POWER PLAY

Already Taken; Some Extensions to Avoid Using

Given the multitudes of MS-DOS programs in the world, it's impossible to give you a list of all extensions recognized by all programs. Some, however, are pretty standard in the MS-DOS environment. The following list briefly describes those you're most likely to encounter (and wise to avoid in your own filenames):

COM: One of the basic types of executable files MS-DOS searches for in trying to run a program.

EXE: The second type of executable program file MS-DOS searches for. The differences between COM and EXE files have to do with the way they're loaded into memory at startup.

BAT: The third type of program file MS-DOS searches for. BAT is short for "batch" and refers to the special nature of files of this type: They are, essentially, collections of MS-DOS commands that you can save and run as a group instead of typing the same sequence repeatedly. Batch files are for intermediate to advanced users. You'll see a little bit about them in "Make a File with Edit," in Section 3, but most of this subject is beyond the scope of such a short book as this.

BAS: A Basic program. This is what you create when you program in the Basic language.

BIN: A binary file. Strictly for programs to use, and definitely not to be messed with. DBLSPACE.BIN, for example, is the file that tells MS-DOS how to use compressed drives. Without it, you're sunk.

DAT: A data file, but one probably created by a program, not by you. Leave DAT files alone.

DLL: A "library" file needed by Windows-based programs, such as the Windows versions of Backup, Undelete, and Anti-Virus. Don't touch these, and don't move them.

HLP: A help file. This is the type of file in which the online MS-DOS Help is stored.

INI: A startup (initialization) file. Like BAT files, INI files are readable and editable. Do not change one, however, unless you know exactly what you're doing. You could make it difficult or impossible for the program that needs that INI file to start up, or at least to start up properly.

SYS: A hardware-related program file. Consider a SYS file off-limits.

And then, of course, there's the whole program-file department. MS-DOS itself expects a standard executable file to have one of three extensions. When you tell it to run a program, it searches for a file with the name you type and the extension COM, EXE, or BAT. This is why the Format command, which is a program stored on disk, is named FORMAT.COM. For the same reason, other

MS-DOS program files have names that end in EXE. And, of course, your AUTOEXEC file (which is a special case) has the extension BAT.

COM, EXE, and BAT. That, in a nutshell, is how MS-DOS tells an executable file from a document file. If you dig into it a little further, you find that MS-DOS recognizes other extensions too: SYS, INI, BAS, HLP, and so on. All of these, however, end up as variations on the COM-EXE-BAT foundation that forms the executable world of MS-DOS. Very few things in life are as clear-cut as they ought to be, and here you see one of them. But the point is really not how many extensions MS-DOS can recognize. The point is that some extensions have special meanings to MS-DOS and to application programs, and where those are concerned, you're advised to follow two rules:

- For data files, let your applications assign extensions.

- For any files, avoid extensions that MS-DOS expects to find attached to program-related files.

Wildcards

When you work with files, don't forget about the MS-DOS wildcard characters, * and ?. If you skipped over the earlier chapter "On to Disks and Files," here's a quick refresher.

The asterisk (*) can be used to represent any number of characters in a filename or an extension. Do not, however, use it as the first character in a filename; if you do, MS-DOS won't read any further than the asterisk and will interpret the file specification as simply "all filenames." For example:

- SEPT* refers to all filenames beginning with SEPT and ending with any number of characters up to the limit of eight. This, then, would match SEPT, SEPTACCT, SEPTRPT, SEPT93, SEPTNEWS, and SEPTIC.

- *SEPT refers to all filenames, period. Not only ACCTSEPT, QUIZSEPT, and CONSEPT, but APPLE, ORANGE, BUTTER, and JAM.

- *.* refers to all files, regardless of filename or extension. This common and useful way to employ asterisks is widely called "star-dot-star."

- *. refers to all files that don't have an extension (notice the dot). This would match NIGHT, DAY, ALPHA, and BETA but would not match NIGHT.DOC, DAY.TXT, ALPHA.NUM, or BETA.WRI.

The question mark takes the place of any single character in a given position within a filename or an extension. For example:

- BIG???? would match any filename starting with BIG and ending with up to four additional characters. Possible matches would include BIGFOOT and BIGWIG, but not BIGMOUTH (more than four additional characters).

- REPORT?.DOC would match any filename starting with REPORT and ending with zero or one additional character and the extension DOC. Among these: REPORT1.DOC, REPORT2.DOC, REPORT.DOC, REPORTX.DOC, and so on.

- *.?U? would match any filename with any extension in which the second of three characters is U. According to these rules, any of the following would qualify: ATTILA.HUN, KING.TUT, DOS.FUN, SECRET.MUM, and TAXES.JUL.

The rest of this chapter covers some basic file-related MS-DOS commands. Although you might expect to find MSBackup and Undelete here with the rest, they're more involved than most commands and, because they both have big jobs to do, they have their own chapters in Section 4: "Sleep Better at Night with Backup" and "Go Back in Time with Undelete."

No See, No Touch: Attribute

Attribute (Attrib)

Displays or changes the attributes of one or more files. You can use the Attribute command on directories as well. The basic command form is:

```
attrib [+attribute][-attribute]
     [drive:][file-specification] /s
```

attribute is the letter standing for the attribute to assign or remove. Precede the attribute with a + to apply it, a – to remove it. The attributes are: R for read-only, H for hidden, S for system, and A for archive. (See the text for details.)

drive is the letter of the drive containing the files, and *file-specification* is the path, filename, and (if applicable) the extension of the files to view or change. You can use wildcards to list or change the attributes of a number of files at once.

/s applies an Attribute command to all matching files in all subdirectories of the directory you specify.

When you save a file, that file goes on disk for all the world to see (with Directory) and, if anyone wants, to copy or change or delete. Sometimes, you'll want to make files a little harder to get at. You might, for instance, want to be sure your 12-year-old future rocket scientist doesn't remove your tax records to make room for a new game. Or you might want to make specific files invisible to casual onlookers. In such cases, you can apply the Attribute command. It's not foolproof, and anyone who knows MS-DOS well can get around your precautions, but it's still a simple and useful means of giving files some extra security. (If you do have a rocket scientist in the house, he or she probably knows all this already, so you might as well know it too.)

The Attribute command applies and removes any of four attributes—essentially, descriptions—that determine how MS-DOS (and your applications) treat a file. These attributes, by the way, can be applied to directories too, although the only one you're likely to use is the hidden attribute, to prevent the directory from being listed by casual users. The attributes are:

- Read-only (R). This means the file can be shown in a directory listing and opened and used by a program, but it cannot be deleted, nor can it be changed and then resaved with the same name. (If you change a read-only file, you must save the changed version under a different name.)

You can apply the read-only attribute to a directory, but there's not a lot of point to it. Read-only does not protect the directory from deletion.

- Hidden (H). This means the file is not shown in an ordinary directory listing. The file might also be invisible to your application programs, so keep this in mind if you decide to apply the hidden attribute. If you apply the hidden attribute to a directory, the attribute applies only to the directory. It is not automatically extended to the files in the directory. The Directory command includes a switch that lists hidden files and directories, so bear in mind that the hidden attribute really doesn't provide top security.

- System (S). This means the file is "tagged" as a system file. Such files are not shown in normal directory listings. This attribute is normally given to program files but can be applied to data files too. Because the hidden attribute is more commonly used to hide a file, using the system attribute can make the file slightly harder to find.

- Archive (A). When turned on, this attribute tells programs that look for it (such as MSBackup and Xcopy) that the file has been created or changed since your last backup. Because this attribute has special meaning to programs, leave it alone.

When you use the Attribute command, it lists the attributes for the files (or directory) you specify. For example, if you were to use Attribute to check the files on the disk in drive B, you might see something like this:

```
A              B:\OUTLINE1.DOC
A              B:\CH1.DOC
A    H         B:\CONTRACT.DOC
A  S R         B:\PROGRAM.SYS
A    R         B:\FINAL1.DOC
A              B:\NOTES.DOC
```

Here you can see that neither the hidden nor the system attribute provides absolute protection, because files with both attributes are listed.

The same command, of course, not only lists attributes, it also applies and removes them. To apply an attribute, you use a plus sign (+) followed immediately by the letter of the attribute. To remove an attribute, you use a minus sign (–) instead. For example, if you wanted to apply the hidden attribute to NOTES.DOC, the command would be:

```
C:\>attrib +h b:\notes.doc
```

From that point on, NOTES.DOC would disappear from normal directory listings.

To remove the hidden attribute from NOTES.DOC, the command would be:

```
C:\>attrib -h b:\notes.doc
```

Here are some more examples of ways to use Attribute:

NO SEE, NO CHANGE

If you've set the hidden or system attribute for a file and then try to set another attribute, such as read-only, MS-DOS refuses with a message like this:

```
Not resetting hidden file B:\HIDDEN.DOC
Not resetting system file B:\SYSTEM.SYS
```

To change the attributes of such files, you must first remove the hidden or system attribute and then apply the new attribute.

If you use Attribute with directories, you must specify each directory separately by including its particular drive and path. Omit the file specification, however, so that Attribute does not apply the command to the files in the directory. Because you must specify the directory you want, Attribute affects directories one at a time. A single Attribute command does not affect more than one directory, even if you include the /s switch.

Attribute

Type:	To:
C:\SEEME>attrib	Display the attributes of all files in the SEEME directory.
C:\SEEME>attrib c:\seeme	Display the attributes of the SEEME directory. Notice that you must type the complete path, even though SEEME is the current directory.
C:\README>attrib +r *.doc	Apply the read-only attribute to all DOC files in the current directory, README.
C:\NOT-HERE>attrib +h \here*.* /s	Apply the hidden attribute to all files in the HERE directory and all its subdirectories. Notice that the target directory in the example is not the current directory.

The All-Purpose Duplicator: Copy

Copy is one of the most commonly used commands in all of MS-DOS. Dating back to the first version of MS-DOS, Copy has always existed as your MS-DOS equivalent of a photocopy machine. Copy is easy to learn, easy to use, relatively quick, and effective in duplicating files. What many people don't know, though, is that Copy is both more and less than they think it is:

- It is more than just a means of duplicating files. You can also use Copy to create a file, pretend your computer is a typewriter, print a file, and even combine several files into one.

- It is less than the Xcopy command, which can duplicate an entire branch of your directory tree at one go. (Copy can't see beyond the current directory or the path you describe when you give the command.)

A complete description of Copy in all its guises could go on for pages, but all that detail isn't really necessary. The descriptions here will cover its main uses and give you more than enough to use Copy confidently. If you want to explore its nature further, fire up the online MS-DOS Help. You'll get a blow-by-blow account there.

Make a Copy, Copy

Duplicating files is Copy's most-used talent, so it's the obvious place to start. When you duplicate files, you specify two simple things: the files to copy and the place to copy them to. That's it.

Here's what you have to know about using the Copy command:

- To copy to the current drive and directory, all you need to specify are the files to copy. For example:

        C:\COPIES>copy b:*.*

    copies all files from the current directory of the disk in drive B to the current directory, COPIES.

- To copy files from the current drive and directory to another location, specify both the files to copy and the disk or directory to copy to. For example:

        C:\ORIG>copy *.* b:

    copies all files in the ORIG directory to the current directory of the disk in drive B.

- To change the name of the copied file, include the new filename with the destination. To change part of the names of a group of copied files, use wildcards. For example:

        C:\COPIES>copy b:*.new *.old

    copies all files with the extension NEW from the current directory of the disk in drive B to the current directory and at the same time changes their extensions to OLD. (Don't try to specify the files to copy as *.* because that file specification could include two or more files with the same names but different extensions, and only the first copied file could have its extension changed to OLD.)

If you're an experienced user of MS-DOS, you know that through version 6.0, Copy could be dangerous when used to duplicate files. It never told you whether a file you were copying had exactly the same name and extension as a file already on the disk or in the target directory, and so your Copy command could end up replacing an identically named but possibly much different file. With version 6.2, however, you no longer have to care about all this, because the new, improved Copy now refuses to overwrite blindly (and thus destroy) one file just because you inadvertently copied another with the same name. Good—and welcome—news. Now, here are some examples (in the table on the next page) that use Copy to duplicate files:

Copy (to duplicate files)

Copies one or more files from one disk or directory to another. The basic command form is:

    copy *files* [*destination*] /v

files are the files to copy. You can include a drive and path, and you can use wildcards to copy a group of files.

destination is the disk or directory to copy to. Defaults to current drive and directory.

/v verifies the copy. Copy is very reliable, so you don't need this unless you're really nervous about the result. Using /v will slow you down.

Copy	
Type:	**To:**
C:\DOS>copy readme.txt a:	Copy the MS-DOS README.TXT file to the current directory of the disk in drive A.
C:\>HERE>copy a:\movem*.*	Copy all files in the MOVEM directory on the disk in drive A to the current directory, HERE.
C:\>copy a:qtr?.doc \realstuf	Copy all DOC files in the current directory of the disk in drive A that have four-character filenames beginning with QTR to the REALSTUF directory on drive C.

Copy (to print files or your typing)

This use of Copy sends the contents of a file or your typing to the printer. If you copy a file to the printer, be sure the file is saved as text-only (ASCII). Sending a formatted document, such as a word-processed letter, to the printer with Copy results in botched output because Copy can't interpret the word processor's internal formatting codes correctly. This form of the command is as follows:

    copy source target

source is the source of the characters to copy. To copy from the keyboard, specify source as con. To copy from a file, specify source as the drive, path, filename, and extension of the file to copy.
target is the device to copy to. This is almost always the printer, which you specify as prn.

Take a Letter, Copy

You say you're not likely to need to use Copy to turn your printer into a glorified typewriter? Admittedly, this use of Copy is something you'd do primarily for the fun of it, but fun is a legitimate activity, too. Even so, what this section actually shows is a way of using Copy to copy characters to a device. That makes it sound serious enough. And because the target device is almost always the printer, you might think of this variation as "copy-to-printer."

Using Copy to print a file is quick and easy. You don't even have to know what port your printer is connected to.

To "copy" a file to the printer, use a command like the following:

    C:\>copy c:\dos\readme.txt prn

To copy directly from the keyboard to the printer, use the command:

    C:\>copy con prn

and then start typing. When you want to quit, press F6 or Ctrl+Z to tell MS-DOS you're done. (If you have a laser printer that doesn't automatically eject the page when you print from MS-DOS, press Ctrl+L before you press F6 or Ctrl+Z. The Ctrl+L, displayed as ^L, sends a control character that tells the printer to eject the page.)

Make a File, Copy

Using Copy to create a file is basically the opposite of using Copy to print to the printer. What you do here is tell MS-DOS to copy *from* a device to a filename. The device, in this case, is the keyboard, CON.

There's really nothing to using Copy in this way, but you should remember your very limited editing capabilities. Some people use Copy to bang out quick batch

If you're concerned about conserving memory, Copy gives you a slight edge. The Print command requires a small amount (about 6 KB) of memory to live in, and once you use it, Print stays in memory until you turn off or restart your computer. With Copy, you save that memory for other uses.

files (collections of MS-DOS commands), but even they often find that the results eventually need to be pulled into a text editor, such as the MS-DOS Editor, for polishing. Also, remember to end the file by pressing F6 or Ctrl+Z. Or, if you plan to print the file on a laser printer, end it with Ctrl+L (displayed as ^L) followed by F6 or Ctrl+Z.

Here's an example:

```
C:\>copy con c:\samples\sample.txt
A B C D
As you write
Remember each
Becomes a byte.
^L^Z[Enter]
```

Merge Them for Me, Copy

And here you have the last and least simple application of the Copy command: using it to combine files. When you use Copy this way, what you're doing is called *concatenating* the files (a word you can pull out to impress your friends and neighbors). Concatenating is basically just a fancy way of saying "tacking one thing onto another." Lots of concatenating goes on in computing, but this is the only use of it you'll see here.

What Copy does when you combine files is merge them by adding each one to the end of a given file. There are two ways to tell Copy to combine files. First, you can tell Copy to take a group of files you specify with wildcards and combine them into a single target file, like this:

```
C:\>copy a:*.doc combo.doc
```

Copy (to create a file)

This use of Copy copies characters from the keyboard to a file on disk. It's a quick and easy way to produce a short, completely unformatted file, but do remember that correcting typos is limited to backspacing and retyping, and you can't go back to correct a line after pressing Enter. To end the file, press F6 or Ctrl+Z. The command form is:

    copy con *filename*

con, of course, is the name MS-DOS uses for the keyboard.

filename is the drive, path, filename, and extension that you want to assign to the new file.

Copy (to combine files)

Combines several files into one by appending them to a target file. The command takes one of three forms:

    copy *source-files target*

In this form of the command, you use wildcards to specify a group of files. *source-files* are the files you want to combine, and *target* is the file in which they are to be combined. If the target filename does not exist, MS-DOS creates it. If the target does exist, version 6.2 (and only 6.2) asks if you want to overwrite it. Example: copy *.doc all.doc.

    copy *source1+source2+...sourceN target*

***source1**, source2,...sourceN* are the files to be combined. Each can include a different drive and path, as well as filename and extension.
target is the file in which the source files are to be combined. Here, too, if the target doesn't exist, MS-DOS creates it. If the target does exist, version 6.2 asks whether you want to overwrite it.

    copy *source1+source2+...sourceN*

***source1**, source2,...sourceN* are, again, the files to be combined. This form of the command does not include a target filename, however. Here all files are combined, in the order in which they appear, into the first source file, *source1* (which must exist).

This command takes all the DOC files from the current directory of the disk in drive A, appends them (one after the other), and writes them to the file named COMBO.DOC on drive C. If the target file you specify doesn't exist, MS-DOS happily creates it for you. If the file does exist, previous versions of MS-DOS would simply overwrite the existing file. Version 6.2, however, tells you the file exists and then asks whether you want to overwrite it:

If you don't have version 6.2, safe-guard existing files by checking for matching filenames with the Directory command.

```
Overwrite COMBO.DOC  (Yes/No/All)?
```

Choose Yes to overwrite (and thus destroy) the existing file, or choose No to avoid copying the file. Choose All to tell Copy to overwrite all matching files on the destination disk directory. This option is really only for use when you copy multiple files and you really, truly, don't care if files with identical names are destroyed at the destination.

The second way to tell Copy to combine files is to separate the filenames with plus signs. This method is what you use when you need to control file order or when you can't use wildcards to specify a group of files. When you use Copy this way, you have two (more) alternatives. If you specify a target file, such as FOUR in this example:

```
C:\>copy one+two+three four
```

MS-DOS copies files ONE, TWO, and THREE, in that order, into a file named FOUR. Here, too, Copy in version 6.2 prompts before overwriting if the target file exists. If you don't have version 6.2, use the Directory command, as noted in the tip in the margin, to find out if the target file exists.

If you do not specify a target filename when you use plus signs, Copy appends each file to the *first* file you specify. So, for example:

```
C:\>copy A+B+C+D
```

appends files B, C, and D to file A, as shown in the illustration. Notice the order, and notice that you do not include a target filename. As usual, version 6.2 prompts if the file exists.

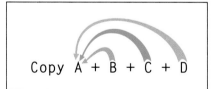

Get Lost: Delete

The Delete command, which can be typed either del or erase, is an old-timer, present in MS-DOS since version 1. Delete has only one job to do: delete files on both normal and DoubleSpaced drives. Delete does not affect directories (for that, you use Remove Directory or Deltree), nor does it remove DoubleSpaced drives. (For that, you need Dblspace /delete.)

Delete has plodded contentedly through the years with only one significant change: the addition of a /p switch in version 4 that prompts for confirmation before deleting each file you specify. If you've got a disk full of files or—especially—if you use wildcards to specify the files to delete, remember /p. It takes a little longer but guarantees that Delete removes only the files you know you want to get rid of.

If you don't use /p, Delete prompts for confirmation in only one instance: when you specify the files to delete as *.* (or just .), meaning every file on the disk or in the directory you specify. Because this is such a sweeping act, Delete displays the message:

```
All files in directory will be deleted!
Are you sure (Y/N)?
```

If you already know that you want to delete all the files—for instance, when you're wiping out a directory and plan to use Remove Directory instead of Deltree—answer in the affirmative. If you're not sure, however, reply N, and MS-DOS will end the command and return you to the command prompt. (If something held you back from typing Y, you can quickly check the file specification with the Directory command; if you see no surprises, go ahead and use Delete again.)

Here are some examples of common ways to use Delete:

Many applications create backups automatically, usually assigning them the extension BAK. Check your own document directories for such files; they can end up occupying a lot of room. The old ones are probably expendable.

If a disk or directory contains files that all have the same extension and you know for sure you want to delete them all, you can avoid the *Are you sure* question by specifying all files (*) plus the extension (rather than *.*). For example, type del *.doc instead of del *.*. Doing this can shave a second or two off the deletion, but be sure you know what you're doing.

Delete (Del or Erase)

Deletes files. Type the command as either
del or erase. The command form is:
del *file-specification* /p
file-specification is the drive, path,
filename, and extension of the file to delete.
You can use wildcards to delete a group of
files at once.
/p causes MS-DOS to prompt before
deleting each file with a message like this:
C:\OLDSTUFF\ANTIQUE.DOC,
Delete (Y/N)?
Press Y to delete the file, N to skip it and go
on to the next file (if any) that matches the
file specification you typed.

Delete

Type:	To:
C:\OLDSTUFF>del *.*	Delete all files in the OLDSTUFF directory
C:\NEWSTUFF>del *.bak	Delete all BAK files in the current directory
C:\DONTKNOW>del *.* /p	Delete the files in the DONTKNOW directory, prompting for confirmation before each is deleted

I Know I Put It Somewhere: Directory

Directory (Dir)

Displays a list of files on the specified disk or in the specified directory. The command can be modified with numerous switches, the most common of which are shown here. For a complete list, refer to the online MS-DOS Help. The basic command form is:

```
dir [file-specification] /a[attributes] /o[sort-order] /s /b /l
    /p /w
```

file-specification is the drive, path, filename, and extension. You can include wildcards to list groups of files.

/a[attributes] lists files with the specified attribute: H for hidden, S for system, D for directories, A for archive, or R for read-only. See the text for details.

/o[sort-order] sorts files in the order specified: N by name, E by extension, D by date and time, S by size, G by type (directories first), and C by compression ratio (DoubleSpaced drives only). See the text for details.

/s applies the command to the current directory and all its subdirectories, displaying all files in all relevant directories that match the file specification.

/b produces a bare listing—filenames and extensions only.

/l (that's a lowercase *L*) shows the directory listing using lowercase characters.

/p pauses after each screenful; very useful with long directories.

/w lists files and directories in wide format—five columns across the screen.

The Directory command, like Delete, has been a part of MS-DOS since the beginning. Unlike Delete, however, Directory has grown and changed during its long lifetime. At its simplest, Directory is one of the easiest commands to use and is certainly one of the first two or three every MS-DOS user learns. Everyone at some time has used this command:

```
C:\>dir a:
```

to list the files on the disk in drive A.

Such a command, as you well know, produces a display like the one shown in the screen below.

Easy enough, right? Ah, but there's more to Directory, far more.

Over the years, as MS-DOS grew to be so much more than it once was, Directory received periodic brain boosts to help it provide more useful information about the files that lie at the heart of everything you do with a computer. These days, Directory not only looks at a disk or directory and lists the files it finds there, it can also help locate strays, sort related files, display them selectively by attribute, tell you how compactly they're stored on a DoubleSpaced drive, and even (when you're really SICK of capital letters) display its output in lowercase.

```
C:\>dir a:

 Volume in drive A is JOES CAFE
 Volume Serial Number is 3E5F-10DE
 Directory of A:\

HOTSPUD  DOC     10,152 08-17-93  12:11p
BURGER   DOC     13,312 09-08-93   9:24a
TATER    TXT         64 09-08-93  10:47a
APPLE    PIE      6,869 09-02-93   6:20a
        4 file(s)       30,397 bytes
                     1,425,920 bytes free

C:\>
```

PRINTING A DIRECTORY LISTING

Printed directory listings can be pretty useful in helping you keep track of files, especially those on your floppy disks. To produce such a list, use the MS-DOS redirection symbol (>) to route the output of a Directory command to your printer. A full listing can be had by typing the command as:

```
dir [file-specification] > prn
```

For an abbreviated version that lists filenames and extensions only, try:

```
dir [file-specification] /b > prn
```

file-specification here, of course, refers to drive letter, or path, or a combination of drive, path, filename, and extension. Remember, too, that if you print to a laser printer, you might have to take the printer offline and press the formfeed button to tell the printer to eject the printed page.

One of the most useful of Directory's switches, the one that locates wayward files, is /s. This switch causes Directory to search through the current directory and all subdirectories for the file or files you specify. You can even search your entire hard disk from any directory by specifying the root directory as part of the command, like this:

```
C:\LOW\LOWER\LOWEST>dir \findme.txt /s
```

Try this switch, especially when time is short and you really, really need that file. Assuming that the file actually exists, you'll find your spirits soaring as you say, "Aha! Gotcha, you little..."

The only Directory switches that are likely to confuse you are the /a and /o switches, both of which can be customized further than most MS-DOS switches can. As described in the quick reference card for this command, /a[*attribute*] displays only the files that have (or lack) the attribute or attributes you specify. (Put a minus sign in front of an *attribute* to display files that do *not* have that attribute.) This is your ticket to viewing hidden and system files that otherwise don't appear in a directory listing—especially useful when Remove Directory tells you you're trying to delete a nonempty directory but a plain Directory command insists there isn't anything there. When you display files by attribute, these are the ways you specify what you want to see:

- Use /ah to show hidden files; use /a-h to show nonhidden files (which is the default, anyway).

- Use /as to show system files; use /a-s to show nonsystem files (again, the default).

- Use /ad to show directories but no files; use /a-d to show files but no directories. The former can be useful when you want to see what kinds of directories you've got on your disk.

- Use /aa to show files that haven't been archived; use /a-a to show files that have been archived. These are helpful when you want to see what all needs backing up (with MSBackup) or copying (with Xcopy), both of which can use the archive attribute to decide what to copy.

- Use /ar to show read-only files; use /a-r to list files that are not read-only. MS-DOS shows both, but doesn't distinguish between them, in a normal directory listing.

- Use any combination of the above to produce a listing that includes more than one attribute. For example, dir c:\myfiles /ahr shows all hidden and read-only files in the directory MYFILES.

The sort-order switch, /o, is very similar to /a but sorts the directory listing in different ways:

- To sort alphabetically by name (filename, that is): Use /on to sort from A to Z; use /o-n to sort from Z to A.

- To sort alphabetically by extension (basically, the file's last name): Use /oe to sort from A to Z; use /o-e to sort from Z to A.

- To sort by size: Use /os to sort from smallest to largest; use /o-s to sort from largest to smallest.

- To sort by date and time (this is a combo that groups by date and, within date, by time): Use /od to sort from oldest to most recent; use /o–d to sort from most recent to oldest.

- To group directories and files separately: Use /og to list directories first; use /o–g to list directories last.

- To sort files on a DoubleSpaced drive by compression ratio: Use /oc to sort from lowest to highest ratio; use /o–c to sort from highest to lowest.

And now, here are some examples to exercise this most flexible of MS-DOS commands:

Directory

Type:	To:
C:\OVERHERE>dir	See a listing of the current directory, OVERHERE.
C:\>dir a: /p	Display a list of files on the disk in drive A, pausing after each screenful.
C:\>dir \dos /w	Produce a wide (five-column) listing of the files in the \DOS directory.
C:\BIGDIR>dir *.doc /on /p	List all DOC files in the BIGDIR directory, sorting them alphabetically by filename.
C:\PERSONAL>dir /ahr	List all files in the PERSONAL directory that have the hidden and read-only attributes.
C:\>dir /ogn /w	List all files and directories in the root directory of drive C, grouping directories ahead of files and listing both directories and files alphabetically by name.

POWER PLAY

Overriding MS-DOS

This is something of an advanced topic, but if you're comfortable with editing your AUTOEXEC.BAT file, you can use a command called Set to define your own default format for directory listings. You do this by setting a variable called DIRCMD. For example, if you want a normal directory listing (on your system) to be shown with directories listed first (/og) and a built-in pause after each screenful, include the following command in AUTOEXEC.BAT:

```
set dircmd=/og /p
```

After you set your own default, you can also override that default by preceding the switch to override with a minus sign. For example, to tell MS-DOS you don't want directories listed first, you could type:

```
C:\>dir /o-g
```

If you didn't want the pause for some reason, you would type:

```
C:\>dir /-p
```

Same or Different? File Compare

File Compare (Fc)

Compares two files to determine whether they are the same or different. The command includes a number of switches, but if the details don't matter and all you need to know is whether the files are the same, the basic command form is pretty simple:

    fc /a /c file1 file2

/a abbreviates the output (which can be voluminous and hard to decipher) by displaying only the first and last matching lines wherever the command encounters differences in the files.

/c tells the command to ignore differences between uppercase and lowercase, essentially treating *RAM* and *ram* as equals.

file1 is the first file to compare. Include a drive and path if the file is not in the current directory.

file2 is the second file to compare. Include a drive and path here too if *file2* is not in the current directory—even if the file has the same path as *file1*.

The File Compare command, abbreviated (and typed) fc, compares the contents of two files to determine whether they are the same or different. File Compare can perform either ASCII (text) or binary (program) comparisons. Binary is mostly for people—especially programmers—who have to know exactly where and how two files differ. It's doubtful you'll ever need this, especially because you have to know hexadecimal or at least have a hexadecimal ASCII table available if you want to make sense of the output.

Even in an ASCII comparison, however, the output of this command can be tremendously confusing, especially if the files differ in a significant number of places. That's because File Compare displays a lot of information: the first matching line in each file, the last matching line in each file, and the lines that differ. If the details don't matter, however, and all you want to know is whether two files are the same, File Compare can come in handy. Just run the command, like this:

    C:\>fc a:newfile.doc a:oldfile.doc

and watch for the result. If the files are identical, you'll see:

    Comparing files NEWFILE.DOC and OLDFILE.DOC
    FC: no differences encountered

But expect a screenful of hullabaloo if the files differ.

Where Did I Write That? Find

Find is the bloodhound you can set on the trail of some text you know you saved somewhere, in some file. Comparable to the Search command in your word processor, Find sniffs through the contents of a file, looking for the text you tell it to locate. Like the hound, Find might not be necessary very often, but when you need it, it sure can save time.

Find

Finds every occurrence of specified text (called a string) in the file or files you specify. The basic command form is:

    find /n /i "string" file1
    file2...fileN

/n tells Find to show the line number of each line that contains the string you specify. This is useful in ASCII files, where each line ends in a carriage return.

/i tells Find to ignore differences between uppercase and lowercase.

file1, file2,...fileN are the files to search. You can include different drives and paths if necessary.

For the most part, Find is simple to use. You can set it to work on either format-ted or unformatted files, but the results are much cleaner when the files are the unformatted (ASCII) variety. Formatting, remember, is represented in the file by special program codes that produce beeps and odd characters on the screen. They won't cause Find to choke, but you might very well end up hearing those beeps and seeing peculiar results, including those unusual characters and unexpected line breaks.

The most important thing to remember about Find is not to get too carried away with it: While it is smarter than some MS-DOS commands, it's not really in the same class as the average Ph.D. You can use the /i switch to tell it to ignore differences between uppercase and lowercase, and that's all to the good. How-ever, Find is extremely literal, and it treats carriage returns as "real" charac-ters—just as real as *A*, *B*, and *C*. What that means to you is that Find does not know enough to be able to ignore a carriage return when it appears between two consecutive words you tell it to locate. That is, if you tell Find to locate "dark and stormy night" with a command like this:

```
C:\>find "dark and stormy night" gothic.doc
```

it will consider this a match:

```
On that dark and stormy night in October, while the wind
whistled through
```

but not this:

```
A scream cut through the frigid air on that dark[carriage return]
and stormy night in October.
```

Basically, if you use Find, it's important to remember that you can outsmart yourself if you try to make the search too complex. The best way to use Find is to ignore leading and trailing spaces and instead have it search for some unique or nearly unique combination of characters within a word. Here are some examples that show how to use Find:

Find	
Type:	**To:**
C:\>find /i "heart" courage.txt anatomy.txt	Find every occurrence of *heart*, in any combination of uppercase and lowercase, in the files COURAGE.TXT and ANATOMY.TXT. Notice that omitting spaces before and after the search string means that Find would consider *heartfelt*, *heartily*, and *heartache* valid matches.
C:\>find /n /i "contract" legal.txt	Display (with its line number) each line in LEGAL.TXT that contains *contract* in either uppercase or lowercase. Once again, note that spaces are omitted, so the search would also find *subcontractor* and *contractual*. On the whole, though, it's better to get too many matches than too few.

Find is unusual among MS-DOS commands in be-ing able to take input (in this case, the contents of a file) and "strain" it to produce the output you seek. Because of this ability, Find is what's known as a *filter* command. There are two other filter com-mands in MS-DOS: Sort, which sorts the lines of a file alphabetically or numerically; and More, which acts a lot like a /p switch in that it pauses output at the end of every screenful. For more information on these com-mands, as well as full details on Find, refer to the MS-DOS online Help.

Relocation Time: Move

New in version 6, the Move command is the long-awaited answer to the Directory-Copy-Delete sequence that, since version 1, was the only way to move files from one disk or directory to another. (Yes, this was a bit of shortsightedness on the part of MS-DOS, but let bygones be bygones.)

You can use Move to do any of the following:

- Move a single file from one place to another. If you do this and specify the destination as the same disk and directory you're moving from, Move assumes you just want to rename the file.

- Move a set of files from one or more disks or directories to a single destination disk or directory.

- Move a group of files specified with wildcards to a single destination disk or directory.

- Rename a directory by specifying its old name as the "file" to be moved and its new name as the "destination." You cannot, however, sneak a change in the directory tree past the Move command. That is, you cannot move a directory from one branch to another, nor can you move it from one level of a branch to a higher or lower level in the same branch. Sorry.

Move
Moves one or more files from one disk or directory to another. The basic command form is:
move /y *file1*[,*file2*]...[,*fileN*] *destination*
/y causes Move to create a new destination directory (if it doesn't already exist) without prompting for confirmation as it usually does.
file1, *file2*,...*fileN* are the files to be moved. You can use wildcards to specify a group of related files. If you specify more than one file or group of files to move, be sure to separate them with commas.
destination is the disk or directory to move the file or files to.

Move is simple to use and tells you what it's doing with a message like this:

```
c:\smart\moves.doc => c:\notsmart\moves.doc
```

Move can create a new directory and then move files to it. If you try this, however, it's important to remember that Move will create a new directory *only* *if* you are moving more than one file. For example, you might use the following command in an attempt to move CHECK.TXT to a new subdirectory, MATE:

```
C:\>move a:check.txt \mate\
```

In fact, the command causes Move to *rename* the file from CHECK to MATE, even though you might have thought you were being clever by including backslashes to define a path. On the other hand, this:

```
C:\>move knight,queen,bishop mate
```

works just fine because you specify multiple files to move. In this case, Move can assume that the destination is a directory. If the directory doesn't exist, Move will ask whether you want to create it.

In form and format, Move is a lot like Copy. It does, however, differ in two important ways: First, Move relocates rather than duplicates files. Second, Move does not allow you to combine several files into one. To combine files and then relocate them, you'll have to use Copy first and then Move. In version 6.2, Move provides more protection for existing files than it did in version 6.0: If one or more files with the same name and extension exist at the destination, Move prompts before overwriting any of them with a Yes/No/All choice like that described earlier for Copy.

Here are some ways to use the Move command:

Move

Type:	To:
C:\ACTIVE>move oldfile.doc c:\storage	Move OLDFILE.DOC from the current directory, ACTIVE, to the STORAGE directory.
C:\>move \up\stock?.doc \down	Move all DOC files with a six-character filename starting with STOCK from the UP directory to the DOWN directory. Poor soul.
C:\>move \oldname \newname	Rename the OLDNAME directory to NEWNAME. (Unless you use the MS-DOS Shell, this is the only way in MS-DOS to rename a directory; the Rename command works only with files.)

A Rose by Any Other Name: Rename

Another very simple command, Rename simply changes a file's name. You can change the filename, the extension, or both. The file must remain in the same directory, however, so you can't change either the drive or any part of the path. MS-DOS decrees there will be no clever "moving" of files here by changing the drive or path; for that kind of work, you now have Move.

Rename is so simple to use, all you need (if anything more) are the few examples in the table on the following page that show how it's done.

Rename (Ren)

Changes the name of a file. Type the command as either ren or rename. The command form is:

    ren oldname newname

oldname is the current name of the file. You can include a drive and path, and you can use wildcards for any part of the name or extension. If you use wildcards, the characters represented by the wildcards are identical in both the old and new names.

newname is the name you want to give the file. Do not include a drive or path here. If you do, Rename displays *Invalid parameter* and returns to the command prompt.

Rename	
Type:	**To:**
C:\CHANGE>ren pearls.doc oysters.doc	Change the name of PEARLS.DOC in the CHANGE directory to OYSTERS.DOC.
C:\>ren \change\pearls.doc oysters.doc	Do the same as above, but from a different directory.
C:\ROME>ren nero.* fiddle.*	Rename all files named NERO in the ROME directory to FIDDLE, keeping all the original extensions.

Show Me: Type

Type

Displays the contents of a file onscreen. The command form is:

type *filename*

filename is the name of the file to display. You can specify a drive and path, but you cannot use wildcards. To control scrolling of a long file, use More, as described in the text.

The Type command is your MS-DOS version of a show-me button. Its one and only job: to display the contents of a file onscreen. Type is a quick and useful way to see what any unformatted file contains, especially because you can tack a More command on the end to give yourself push-button control over scrolling. This command, for example:

```
C:\>type c:\dos\readme.txt | more
```

displays screen after screen (after screen) of the MS-DOS file README.TXT. Thanks to the More command on the end, scrolling pauses after each screenful. To continue, all you do is press a key. To quit after a screenful or two, press Ctrl+Break. When you reach the end of the file, Type goes away, to come again another day.

There are only two things to remember about Type:

- First, you can't use it with wildcards to display sets of documents. That is, you can't type a command such as:

```
C:\>type a:*.txt | more
```

to display a set of text files on the disk in drive A. Nope, if you want to see them all, either combine them with Copy (recommended only if you don't mind turning many files into one) or use the Type command separately for each one (a conservative approach).

- Second, use Type primarily to display *unformatted* (ASCII text) files. Although you can use Type with some formatted documents, such as those your word processor creates, other types of documents, such as spreadsheets, drawings, and bit maps, are stored and coded in a way that makes them about as readable as hieroglyphs. Program files, of course, are out of the question unless you're bored and want something weird to look at for a while.

That said, here are the two most common uses of Type:

Type	
Type (no pun intended):	**To:**
C:\>type a:smallfry.txt	Display a short file named SMALLFRY.TXT stored on the disk in drive A.
C:\>type \bigstuff\whale.txt ¦ more	Display a long file named WHALE.TXT that's stored in the BIGSTUFF directory. Notice the More command tacked on the end to control scrolling.

One Fell Swoop: Xcopy

Xcopy is to Copy what a jet is to a biplane: newer, bigger, and better. How so? Well, first of all, there's nothing wrong with Copy. Copy is great for duplicating one file or many files— as long as they are all on the same disk or in the same directory. Aha, and right. Xcopy can work its way deep into a directory tree to do its job. With Xcopy, you can:

- Copy all or just selected files from a directory and all its subdirectories.

Xcopy

Copies files from one or more directories. Xcopy can be used to duplicate directory trees or to copy files selectively. The command form is as follows (lots of switches, but they're not hard to use):

```
xcopy source destination /a /m /d:date /p /s /e /v /w
```

source is the drive, path, and file specification of the files to copy.

destination is the drive or path to which you want to copy the files. To duplicate a directory tree exactly, give *destination* the same directory name as the name of the top-level directory you are copying. Follow the destination name with a backslash, like this:

```
C:\>xcopy \clone a:\clone\
```

/a and **/m** copy files that have their archive attributes set, meaning they have been created or changed but not yet backed up. /a leaves the archive setting on the original as is; /m turns off the setting on the original (just as MSBackup does), a signal that the file has been backed up. If you back up files regularly and you want to use /a or /m, opt for /a so that your Xcopied files won't be left out of your next backup.

/d:date copies all matching files that were created or modified on or after the date you specify as *date*. When typing a date, use the same format that MS-DOS displays when you use the Date command. (Type **date** at the command prompt to see the format.)

/p causes Xcopy to prompt for confirmation before copying each file.

/s applies your Xcopy command to all nonempty subdirectories of the directory you're copying.

/e applies your Xcopy command to all *empty* subdirectories of the directory you're copying. Use /e in combination with /s to duplicate a directory tree exactly.

/v verifies each copy to ensure accuracy. You probably don't need this; Xcopy is reliable.

/w causes Xcopy to wait until you press a key before it starts copying files.

- Duplicate an entire branch of the directory tree on another disk, up to and including empty subdirectories.

- Pick and choose among files, copying only those that have changed, or only those created or modified on or after a date you specify.

In version 6.2, Xcopy prompts before overwriting existing files, just as Copy does. If you don't have version 6.2, remember to check filenames on the destination with the Directory command.

Sound good? It is. Xcopy is so good, in fact, that if you habitually use directories, it should come to mind as soon as or sooner than Copy when you need to duplicate files. Xcopy is so polite that if it can't tell whether the destination you specify is a filename or a directory name, it asks. If the directory you specify as a destination doesn't exist, Xcopy creates it. Whenever you want to copy a set of files—and it would be helpful to duplicate the directories they came from—think Xcopy.

If Xcopy is so great, is there any time you should not use it? Yes. When you want to copy all the files on a startup disk or any other disk that contains hidden or system files. Xcopy does not copy either hidden or system files, so they'd be left behind. If you're copying a directory with either of these types of files, use either Diskcopy (if you're copying a floppy disk) or System (if you're copying the MS-DOS system files).

POWER PLAY

Shape Up Your Backup

Although MSBackup is the utility of choice for backups, you can use Xcopy to perform a "quick-and-dirty" backup that also duplicates a directory tree in the process. Here's how:

1. First, use the Directory command with the /a and /s switches to check on all files in the branch of the directory you want to back up. Your command will look something like this:

```
C:\>dir \branch /s /aa
```

The end of the directory listing that results will show the total number of files listed and the total number of bytes they occupy. If

the number of bytes shows that all the files will fit on the destination floppy, you're in business.

2. Xcopy those files with a command like this:

```
C:\>xcopy \branch a: /s /a /e
```

The /s and /a switches copy all files in BRANCH and all its subdirectories that have changed since the last backup. Xcopy duplicates the directory structure of BRANCH exactly, including, thanks to the /e switch, any empty subdirectories it might contain. (You can, of course, leave out the /e switch if the empty directories are unimportant.)

Now for some examples:

Xcopy

Type:	To:
C:\>xcopy \movies a:\movies\ /s /e	Copy the MOVIES directory, all files, and all subdirectories, even empty ones, to duplicate the directory structure exactly on the disk in drive A. If the MOVIES directory doesn't exist on the disk in drive A, Xcopy creates it. (Note: If you omit the backslash after MOVIES in the destination path, Xcopy asks whether the destination is a directory or a filename.)
C:\DUCKS>xcopy *.qwk a: /s	Copy all QWK files in the DUCKS directory and its subdirectories to the disk in drive A.
C:\POPCORN>xcopy a:*.doc /d:8-14-93	Copy to the current directory, POPCORN, all DOC files in the root directory of the disk in drive A that were created or modified on or after 8/14/93.
C:\BEES>xcopy *.hny a: /a /s	Copy all new or changed HNY files in the BEES directory and all its subdirectories to the disk in drive A. This is a quick backup that preserves the directory structure in the copy.

More About Hardware

You Mean There's More?

Actually, there's *lots* more. But you don't have to understand auto engineering to drive a car, and you don't have to understand electronics to drive a computer. So, sad to say, if you want the real nitty-gritty, you're going to have to look elsewhere. (If you're interested, there are some nice, big books on hardware... really big...in the 800-page range.)

This chapter actually takes you a little bit beyond the "average user's" familiarity with hardware. Here, you'll take a look at some details you really ought to know in order to understand a few of the more exotic but sometimes necessary MS-DOS commands: those that deal more with the machine than they do with your data. Because those commands cozy up to the hardware, they tend to include switches that ask you to know some computer jargon—device driver, baud, data bit, and things like that. When you first encounter these terms, they look pretty forbidding, but if you take it easy, they soon become intelligible. Just remind yourself that whatever a human invented, another human (that's you) can understand.

This chapter covers three main types of hardware: the display and keyboard (most of which you've already seen), device drivers (all of which help MS-DOS use mice and other add-ons to your system), and ports (two of which can be pretty important to you). Once you're familiar with these components, you can appreciate the rest of the chapter, which explores hardware-related MS-DOS commands.

Taking the CON

If you've been working your way through this book, you already know that MS-DOS has a single name for the display and the keyboard: CON (for *console*). You also know that the keyboard is your main input device and the display is your main output device, and the reason MS-DOS can use one name for both devices is that they're pretty much two halves of a whole: Things go in one and come out the other, with little chance that you or MS-DOS will confuse the two.

That's about all you need to know concerning the CON device. Easy, isn't it? For CON-related commands that you should know, refer to the later, alphabetically arranged descriptions of ANSI.SYS, Clear Screen, Device, Mode (the display), and Mode (the keyboard).

Next up, devices and their drivers.

Not Exactly *Car and Driver,* But ...

When you think of *driver,* what comes to mind? A car? A golf club? Where computers are involved, what should come to mind is a device driver, a very special kind of program that mediates between MS-DOS and a specific hardware device on your system. Essentially, a device driver "drives" the hardware it's designed to work with—for example, a mouse, a joystick, a printer, a modem, or the keyboard.

Ah, you think. But isn't driving the hardware the job MS-DOS is supposed to do? Sure. And it does. But there are two qualifications to make here. First, MS-DOS does not have built-in awareness of all the many kinds of devices people can attach to their systems. It does not, for example, look for and instinctively know how to use a mouse. Second, even among devices of the same kind, variations can be significant. On the surface, the different makes and models of these various devices work the same. Inside, however, where MS-DOS hangs out—and where small differences can be crucial—they can be vastly different. For instance, as anyone who's fussed with printers can tell you, printer A and printer B—though they're both dot-matrix printers or both laser printers—can nevertheless be so different that each must have its own printer driver to interpret codes and produce documents correctly.

To keep from overburdening MS-DOS with the details of each and every make, model, and type of hardware in existence (an impossible job anyway), Microsoft provides the operating system with a basic set of device drivers; these drivers can handle the standard system devices:

- CON, for the keyboard and display.

Once you've got input and output down cold, you can glide right by the abbreviation *I/O* when you see it in reference to computers, as in "I/O ports" or "I/O device." It's no big deal. I/O stands for Input/Output and refers to any program or device that performs either or both of those functions. True, the programs and devices can quickly get mind-bogglingly complicated, but leave that for programmers. The real point is that I/O, like many other hardware-related terms, might look technical, but it's really not that hard to understand.

POWER PLAY

What, Exactly, Is a "Device"?

It's natural to think of *device* as referring to something touchable and "plug-in-able," but not all devices (as MS-DOS defines them) are as easily recognizable as a mouse or a printer. Extended and expanded memory, for example, are considered installable devices by MS-DOS (because they're driven by HIMEM.SYS and EMM386.EXE). Network connections are installable devices too, and because networks are enormously complex, such "devices" are driven by all kinds of programs that define not only who your computer can talk to, but when, where, and how, as well.

If you want to see what kinds of drivers MS-DOS recognizes for your computer, use the Mem command, described in the next chapter. Type:

```
C:\>mem /d /p
```

The resulting list will identify all programs currently in memory. Default device drivers, such as CON, COM1, and LPT1, are listed as system device drivers. Installed device drivers have names such as XMSXXXX0 and MS$MOUSE and are identified as follows:

```
Installed Device=device-name
```

- COM1 through COM4, for a maximum of four serial ports (normally used for modems and mice, but also for printers).

- LPT1 through LPT3, for a maximum of three parallel ports (normally used for printers).

- NUL, for an odd "device" called the *bit bucket* that takes output and sends it to oblivion. (Useless as it may seem, NUL comes in handy to programmers and advanced MS-DOS users as a means of getting rid of unwanted program output, such as comments and messages.)

- CLOCK$, for the system timekeeper. Leave this alone.

To identify devices to MS-DOS, you must know how to edit your CONFIG.SYS file. If that's new territory for you, read the chapter "Make a File with Edit," at the end of this section.

These basic MS-DOS devices are sort of like the staples you keep in your pantry—the flour and salt and so on. But you need a little more to turn out a chocolate cake. Where hardware is concerned, the extras you need are known as *installable device drivers*. Installable device drivers are programs that roll in at startup, as either additions to or replacements for the default MS-DOS drivers. From that point on, the drivers handle the special needs of specific devices, working with MS-DOS to turn all your devices into a working system.

Only a few MS-DOS commands deal specifically with devices and device drivers, and only three are significant to you: Device and Devicehigh, which load device drivers into memory so MS-DOS can use them; and MSCDEX, which enables MS-DOS to use a CD-ROM drive and to recognize it by drive letter. These are

AUX, PRN

For the most part, AUX and PRN are synonyms for the first serial port and the first parallel port. Therefore, if you see AUX or PRN, assume it means COM1 or LPT1 unless you know that your system is different.

153

commands you really should know about if you plan to add new hardware to your system.

Ports of Call

And finally, you arrive at ports. But forget tropical breezes and cool drinks with little paper umbrellas in them. What you're visiting here are those weird-looking plugs on the back of your computer, the ones with elaborate patterns of prongs and holes. Compared to your household plugs and receptacles, these were designed by Salvador Dali.

A port is, in 20 words or less: a channel through which a computer sends or receives information. That's it. A port is, therefore, less a plug than it is a transfer point, a connection. True, the transfer and the connection are always to a cable, but that's the way computers operate. The cable is merely the carrier; the port does the work (thanks to the aforementioned prongs and holes).

Serial vs. Parallel

Aside from connections for the keyboard and display, there are two basic kinds of ports your computer can be equipped with: serial and parallel. When you use one of these ports, you have one main concern: What kind is it? This is important. Serial ports transfer information bit by bit: dit, dot, dot, dit, dit, that kind of thing. Parallel ports transfer bits in bunches, 8 bits per bunch, over a (parallel) set of wires. Serial and parallel ports are not the easiest things in the world to distinguish, but you can learn to spot the clues, as shown in the photograph. (If you want to check your printer to see whether it's serial or parallel, check the connection at the printer end, not the one at the computer end—after turning the computer and printer off, of course.)

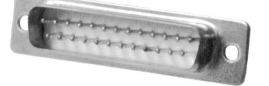

Serial connector

Parallel connector

MS-DOS can work with up to three parallel ports (which, remember, it calls LPT1, LPT2, and LPT3) and up to four serial ports (COM1, COM2, COM3, and COM4). But even though MS-DOS can recognize all these ports, you don't necessarily have all or even some of each kind. What does that mean? It means that MS-DOS provides a three-car/four-truck garage, but the Mercedes and pickups don't come with the territory. You have to buy those, and how many you buy depends on what you're going to use your computer for.

Most computers are equipped with at least one parallel port and one or two serial ports (and probably a game port for a joystick). These ports are usually on circuit boards inserted inside the machine. From outside the computer, you can't see the boards themselves; what you see are the sockets that form the boards' connections to the outside world—the ports. Inside the box, your computer has what are called expansion slots, partly visible as oblong, metal-faced openings on the back of the computer. In these slots, you can install additional circuit boards, including more parallel and serial ports—if you need them. For example, if you need both a modem and a mouse, which are serial devices, you obviously need two serial ports. (Internal modems do not, however, require a serial port.) If you want two parallel printers—say, a dot-matrix printer for color and a laser printer for high-quality output—you need two parallel ports. Get the picture? One port for each serial or parallel device. Extra ports are fine if you have them, but they won't be used until you attach something to them.

Serial Ports à la Mode

Parallel ports are easy to use: They're basically plug and go. Serial ports can be a different matter because they insist on being told how to behave. Serial ports are meant primarily for communicating with another computer although they are also used for mice, printers, and certain other devices. They have to be told how quickly to transfer information, as well as how to indicate which bits in the stream represent data, timing bits, and "end-of-character" signals (all of which are needed to let the device on the receiving end know how to tell one bit from the other).

Most of the time, you can use the setup software that comes with your modem or other serial device to arrange matters between MS-DOS and your serial port. Sometimes, however, you'll have to give those instructions yourself—when you set up a serial printer, for example. Specifically, you have to tell MS-DOS about the following:

- Baud: The rate of data transfer. MS-DOS supports rates from 110 through 19,200 baud.

- Parity: The form of error checking used to verify that transmitted characters are sent and received correctly. Error checking is based on the value of a special bit (called a *parity bit*) that can accompany each transmitted character. MS-DOS supports five forms of error checking: none (no parity bit), even, odd, mark, and space.

- Data bits: The number of consecutive bits (usually 7 or 8) used to represent one character.

- Stop bits: The number of "bits" (actually, timing signals) used to separate one character from the next. Usually, 1 stop bit is used.

POWER PLAY

Of Bits and Baud

If you want to be PC correct, you should use the term *bits per second* rather than *baud* in referring to your modem. Why? Technically, *baud* refers to the number of events (changes) that occur in a signal in one second. Each signal change—for example, from low to high frequency—is supposed to equal one bit. These days, because modems are extremely sophisticated, they are capable of encoding 4 or more bits in each signal change. (Don't ask how, at least not here, because it's really complicated.) The point is that a 9600 "baud" modem isn't really operating at 9600 baud. Because each signal change actually represents 4 bits, the modem is operating at 2400 baud (2400 signal changes per second), but the effective transfer speed is 9600 bits per second. The upshot is, for accuracy, you should refer to your modem's transfer speed in bits per second. (Unless you're truly talking about the number of signal changes per second, which no one else does.)

MS-DOS provides one command—Mode—that you use in three ways to control your serial and parallel ports. You use Mode to:

- Set printer output—control the number of lines per inch and characters per line on a parallel printer.

- Configure the serial port—set up a serial port for action.

- Redirect printing—tell MS-DOS to use a serial printer. (This command must come after you use Mode to configure the serial port. No similar requirements are needed by parallel printers.)

All three commands are described in the following alphabetically arranged descriptions of device-related commands.

Circuit boards aren't usually difficult to install, but to install one, you must open the computer and work with its innards. If that makes you uncomfortable, ask your dealer to do it for you. If you want to try, work carefully. Turn off the computer before you open it. Get rid of any static on your body by touching some metal object. Handle the circuit board by the edges only, and keep all screws you remove in a small container close at hand. If you drop a screw inside the machine (not hard to do because they're very small), *do not* try to be clever and suck it out with a magnetic screwdriver. (Use a pair of tweezers instead.) *Follow the instructions* that come with the board. And finally, although you must be careful in all other respects, once you're sure the board is lined up correctly, don't be afraid to apply some firm pressure to the board when you press it into place. Usually, circuit boards don't slide into position, they pop.

ANSI.SYS: More Control

ANSI.SYS (pronounced "ansee-dot-sis") looks like a file-name and extension, so it comes as no surprise to find out that's exactly what it is. ANSI.SYS is a device driver, shipped with MS-DOS, that can give you considerably more control over your screen and keyboard than MS-DOS normally provides. When you use ANSI.SYS, MS-DOS follows ANSI's instructions rather than those for the default CON device it normally turns to at startup. In order to gain access to any capabilities of ANSI.SYS, however, you must tell MS-DOS that you want to use ANSI.SYS instead of CON. And you do this by identifying ANSI.SYS to MS-DOS as a device in your CONFIG.SYS file.

After you've loaded ANSI.SYS, you can use it, as described later under "Mode: Control the Keyboard," to control the number of lines displayed onscreen. This capability is useful enough that it's built into some MS-DOS programs. For example, if you use the online MS-DOS Help, you can start Help with a /h switch that automatically sets your screen to the highest number of lines it's capable of displaying—50 lines per screen on a VGA or better display.

ANSI.SYS
Replaces the default keyboard and display driver with a more sophisticated version that requires about 4 KB of memory. To be usable, ANSI.SYS must be identified to MS-DOS at startup in your CONFIG.SYS file. The command is:
`DEVICE=C:\DOS\ANSI.SYS`
to load ANSI.SYS into conventional memory, or:
`DEVICEHIGH=C:\DOS\ANSI.SYS`
to load ANSI.SYS into upper memory if enough is available. (Be sure to substitute the name of your MS-DOS directory if it's not C:\DOS.) If MS-DOS cannot load ANSI.SYS into upper memory, the program will be loaded into conventional memory instead.

POWER PLAY

Beyond the Fringe

If you really put ANSI.SYS to work, you can use it to display all kinds of things onscreen, and you can even use it to redefine keys on your keyboard. This kind of tinkering, though, walks pretty close to programming because you have to pack some fairly cryptic instructions into strings of characters known as escape sequences. Once you define your escape sequences, ANSI.SYS can use the instructions in them to control the keyboard or the display. This side of ANSI.SYS's personality is really beyond the scope of this book, but you might be interested to see what an escape sequence looks like. Here's a fun one that uses the Prompt command to display the standard command prompt (pg) in bold yellow on blue but returns to normal (white on black) for all typed and displayed text:

```
C:\>prompt $e[1;33;44m$p$g$e[0m
```

Hmmm.... Well, you can try this if you like, but before you do, be sure to install ANSI.SYS as described in the text. Otherwise, this Prompt command won't work. To return your command prompt to normal, type:

```
C:\>prompt $p$g
```

Cls: A Clean Slate

Clear Screen clears the screen for you. That's all it does, but it sure comes in handy when you've got a lot of commands and their output scattered over your onscreen workspace. Whenever you want a fresh start, use Clear Screen.

Clear Screen (Cls)

Clears the screen, returning the command prompt to the upper left corner.

The command form is:

```
cls
```

No more need be said.

Device: Load Drivers into Conventional Memory

Device

Loads installable device drivers into memory at startup. Device can be used only in CONFIG.SYS. You must include a separate Device command for each device driver you want to load. Basically, all a Device command does is point MS-DOS to the location of the device driver you want to use. The command form is shown below. The all-uppercase format is used because it is typical of the way CONFIG.SYS commands are typed; you can use lowercase if you want:

> DEVICE=[*DRIVE:*][*PATH*]*FILENAME*
> [*DRIVER-CONTROLS*]

drive, *path*, and *filename* specify the location and name of the device driver to load.

driver-controls represents any parameters and switches, required or optional, that you want to specify to control the behavior of the device driver. The actual parameters and switches you use depend entirely on the device driver you are loading. See the examples at the top of the facing page.

The Device command identifies a non-native (installable) device driver to MS-DOS and loads the driver into conventional memory at startup. If you add a mouse or other device to your system, you might very well find that the device's installation program adds a Device command to your CONFIG.SYS file to enable MS-DOS to detect and use the new hardware.

On many systems, Device appears several times in CONFIG.SYS because every installable device driver you want to use must be loaded separately with its own Device command. MS-DOS itself supports the following installable device drivers you might want or need to use. The sample commands shown in the table on the facing page assume that all drivers are in your \DOS directory; if necessary, replace DOS with the name of your own MS-DOS directory. All drivers listed are described in this chapter and the next; for details on switches used in the samples, refer to the descriptions of the drivers themselves.

If your system has free upper memory (which you can check for by typing mem), MemMaker can inspect your CONFIG.SYS file and change Device commands to Devicehigh commands in order to use that upper memory for some or all of the drivers currently being loaded into conventional memory. The Devicehigh command itself is discussed in the next chapter.

Installable Device Drivers, Courtesy of MS-DOS

Device Driver	Function	Sample Command for CONFIG.SYS
ANSI.SYS	Provides extended control over the screen and the keyboard.	DEVICE=C:\DOS\ANSI.SYS
EMM386.EXE	Enables use of upper memory and provides simulated expanded memory to programs that need it. Invaluable on 80386 or better systems.	DEVICE=C:\DOS\EMM386.EXE RAM
HIMEM.SYS	Enables use of extended memory and allows MS-DOS to be loaded into the high memory area. Invaluable on systems with an 80286 or better processor with at least 350 KB of extended memory.	DEVICE=C:\DOS\HIMEM.SYS
RAMDRIVE.SYS	Creates a simulated disk drive in memory. Very fast, very nice to have if your system has memory to spare.	DEVICE=C:\DOS\RAMDRIVE.SYS 1024 /E

Mode: Control the Display

As you can see from this and the following descriptions, Mode is a command with many faces. Although it's not among the most often used MS-DOS commands, Mode can be either valuable (as when changing the display) or necessary (as when setting up a serial port for printing or communications). This particular form of Mode lets you control the number of characters and lines displayed on the screen.

If you've added ANSI.SYS to your CONFIG.SYS file, 43-line mode can be really useful when you're scanning directories or using Type to display files. Check it out. If you like 43-line mode, you can create two small batch files to activate this Mode command with simple two-character commands. See the chapter "Make a File with Edit," later in this section, for details.

Mode (for the display)

Sets the number of characters per line and lines per screen. You can set the characters per line at any time. To set the number of lines per screen, however, you must have loaded ANSI.SYS from your CONFIG.SYS file. The command form is:

```
mode con cols=x lines=x
```

con is the name of the display. You must include this.

cols=x sets the number of characters per line. You can specify x as either 40 or 80 (the default).

lines=x sets the number of lines per screen. If you have an EGA display, you can specify x as either 25 (the default) or 43. If you have a VGA or better display, you can also specify 50. To use this form of the command, remember that you must have ANSI.SYS loaded.

Mode: Control the Keyboard

Mode (for the keyboard)

Sets the typematic (repeat) rate of the keyboard, which governs the speed at which keystrokes repeat and the waiting period before a keypress begins repeating. The command form is:

```
mode con rate=x delay=x
```

con is the name of the keyboard. You must include this.

rate=x sets the speed at which a key repeats when pressed and held down. You can specify x as any value from 1 (the slowest) through 32 (the fastest). The default is 20 or 21 on most keyboards. To use 32, you should have fingers as light as butterflies dancing on air.

delay=x sets the amount of time MS-DOS waits before repeating a key when you hold it down. You can specify x as 1 (for 0.25 second), 2 (for 0.50 second), 3 (for 0.75 second), or 4 (for 1.0 second). The default is 2. If you use 1, especially in combination with a high repeat rate, you're really off to the races.

This is the Mode command you use basically to control the touch of your keyboard. This form of Mode needs little explanation and no description beyond what you see on the quick reference card.

Mode: Set Printer Output

To control printer output, Mode sets the number of characters per line and lines per inch you can print. You probably don't need this, because your applications will do the job a lot better. Still, setting printer lines to 132 characters (if you have an IBM-compatible or Epson-compatible printer) can be useful, especially if you use the MS-DOS Editor a lot and tend to type more than 80 characters before pressing Enter to end a line. Use this when printing ASCII files only.

Mode (for printer output)

Sets characters per line and lines per inch on an IBM-compatible or Epson-compatible printer. This command does not work with laser printers. The command form is:

```
mode lptn cols=x lines=x
```

lptn is the name of the port to which the printer is connected. You can specify n as 1 (for LPT1), 2 (for LPT2), or 3 (for LPT3).

cols=x specifies the number of characters (columns) per line. You can specify x as 80 (the default) or 132.

lines=x sets the number of lines per inch. You can specify x as 6 (the default) or 8.

If you check up on Mode in the online MS-DOS Help, you'll see that this command form also includes a retry switch, which tells MS-DOS whether to try and try again if the printer doesn't respond. By default, Mode does not retry. Leave it that way. Setting retries can cause problems, especially if you use a network.

Mode: Set Up a Serial Port

This form of Mode is probably the most confusing, yet it can turn out to be the simplest to use. Why? It's confusing because this is where you encounter *baud*, *parity*, and all those other exotic communications terms. It's also simple because when you configure a serial port—that is, set it up to communicate via modem or with a printer—you shouldn't have to figure out a darn thing; somebody else should tell you all the settings you need. Besides which, if you're setting up to communicate via modem, you most likely have a communications program that can do all the work for you. And if you're setting up a serial

Mode (for a COM port)

Configures a serial (COM) port for use with a modem, printer, or other serial device. For all settings, see your instruction manual for the values you need to use. You can omit any of the following values if the default is the setting you need. The command form is:

    mode comn baud=b parity=p data=d stop=s retry=r

comn is the name of the serial port you are setting up. You can specify *n* as 1 (for COM1), 2 (for COM2), 3 (for COM3), or 4 (for COM4).

baud=b sets the transmission rate. You can specify *b* as 110, 115, 300, 600, 1200, 2400, 4800, 9600, or 19200. (19200 is not supported on all systems.) If you prefer, abbreviate these values (respectively) as 11, 15, 30, 60, 12, 24, 48, 96, or 19.

parity=p sets the type of error checking. You can specify *p* as n (for none), e (for even), o (for odd), m (for mark), or s (for space).

data=d sets the number of bits used to represent one character. You can specify *d* as 5, 6, 7, or 8. The default is 7.

stop=s sets the number of "bits" used to separate characters. You can specify *s* as 1, 1.5, or 2. The default is 2 for a transmission rate of 110, 1 for all other speeds.

retry=r is for setting up a serial printer and defines the type of action MS-DOS takes if the printer does not respond. You can specify *r* as n (for none, the default), e (for error), b (for busy), p (for "keep trying"), or r (for ready). Avoid this switch unless your documentation tells you to include it.

printer, your printer manual should give you the exact settings you need. The manual should even show you how to type the Mode command and how to put it and the next form of the Mode command in your AUTOEXEC.BAT file.

This form of Mode is included here in large part so that you don't feel you're working in the dark if you ever have to use it. Here's a sample of the two commands you need in order to set up a serial printer. (Use your own settings, of course.)

```
mode com2 baud=96 parity=n data=8
mode lpt1=com2
```

Mode: Redirect Printing

Mode (redirect printing to a serial port)

Sends printer output destined for a parallel port (which MS-DOS assumes) to a previously configured serial port. The command form is:

```
mode lptn=comn
```

lptn is the name of the parallel port to redirect (probably LPT1). You can specify n as 1 (for LPT1), 2 (for LPT2), or 3 (for LPT3).

comn is the serial port to be used for printing. You can specify n as 1 (for COM1), 2 (for COM2), 3 (for COM3), or 4 (for COM4).

This form of the Mode command is needed only if you are setting up a serial printer. MS-DOS, remember, assumes you have a parallel printer connected to LPT1. That's not always the case, however. You could be using LPT2 or LPT3 as your printer port. If you're using a serial printer, you have to go the extra mile and tell MS-DOS not only which parallel port to use, but to which serial port the printer is connected. This is called redirecting output from a parallel port to a serial port. (A small piece of trivia that might interest you.)

Assuming you know which parallel port you're using and which serial port your printer is connected to, the rest is easy. Just use the parallel=serial form of Mode shown on the quick reference card, and the rest is a piece of cake. If you have only one printer, and it's a serial model, you'll probably want to include this command, as well as the Mode command that configures the serial port, in your AUTOEXEC.BAT file. Your printer's documentation should tell you all you need to know.

If, for some reason, you want to stop redirecting printing during a session with MS-DOS, type the Mode command with the parallel port but no serial port. For example, to stop redirecting LPT1 to a COM port, type:

```
C:\>mode lpt1
```

Zap. It's done.

Print: Hard Copy

The Print command does exactly what it says: It prints files. You can use Print with any ASCII file, and you can "line up" a set of files for printing by sending them to what is called a queue. (A printer queue is similar to a line of people at a checkout counter.) When a queue exists, Print prints the files in order, one after the other.

Although Print can be useful, you're normally much better off turning to the printing-related commands in your applications rather than to the MS-DOS Print command. Why is this? Because the printing-related commands in your applications are specifically designed to handle the types of documents you create in those applications. For example, a spreadsheet is a potentially enormous grid of rectangular cells—like the bricks in a wall—that contain numbers, formulas, and so on. If you try to print such a document with Print, MS-DOS doesn't know what to do about aligning all those cells, and it most certainly doesn't know anything about performing the calculations you build into the document. The result, if it's even readable, is often mush. The spreadsheet program, on the other hand, knows exactly how to line everything up, apply italics or boldfacing or underlining where you want it, and print and calculate the values you want on your printout. The result is beautiful.

Print does come in handy, however, when you want a quick way to print an ASCII file and you don't care about ornamentation. If all you want is something readable, feed Print an ASCII file, and something readable is what you'll get, very quickly. Print is, therefore, a much faster way to get hard copy of files such as the README.TXT file or plain-text files that you receive via a communications program. All you do is command MS-DOS to print, and print it will.

When you use Print, you actually load a small program into memory (where it remains for the duration of your MS-DOS session). This program gives MS-DOS a limited—very limited—form of multitasking, in the sense that Print can be printing at the same time you're pounding away at some other task, such as formatting disks or even using your word processor to write the next chapter of your Great American Novel. This feature sounds slick and, in fact, is pretty impressive when you realize that MS-DOS manages the trick by periodically turning the processor's attention (for small fractions of a second) to printing until the job is done. There is a down side to all this, however, and it's one you should remember: Printing while you're doing other work slows down both printing and the work you're doing. And on a not-so-fast computer, this slowdown can be anywhere from significant to excruciating.

Print is used in either of two forms, as shown on the quick reference cards accompanying this description. The first form defines the way Print is to operate. It can be used only when you first use Print, which stands to reason: After the

Print (print files)

This form of the Print command allows you to specify the files you want printed. The basic command form is:

```
print file-specification /t
```

file-specification is the drive, path, filename, and extension of the file or files to print. You can include multiple files, even from different drives and paths, by separating them with spaces. You can also use wildcards to specify a group of related files.
/t removes all files from the print queue.

Print (define print characteristics)

Available only the first time the Print command is used during the current session, the following switches allow you to define which printer port you want to use and the size of the queue you want Print to manage. The basic command form is:

```
print /d:device /q:size
```

/d:device tells Print the name of the port connecting the computer to the printer you want to use. Print assumes LPT1 (a parallel printer connected to the first parallel port). You can specify device as LPT2 or LPT3 for a parallel printer, or as COM1, COM2, COM3, or COM4 for a serial printer. If used, /d:device must precede any filenames on the command line. (For a serial printer, you have to use the Mode command ahead of time to set up the port for use with the printer; refer to the description of Mode, for a COM port, for information about this task.) For example, type:

```
C:\>print /d:lpt2
```

to use the printer connected to the second parallel port.
/q:size specifies the size of the print queue. Print assumes a maximum queue size of 10 files. You can specify from 4 through 32 files.

first Print command, the program is in memory, where you can't unload it or change it. You can define several Print characteristics, but most are on the exotic side. One switch, for example, defines the amount of time available for Print to transmit a single character to the printer. And you don't specify that time in something as easy to understand as seconds. You specify the amount of time in terms of ticks of the computer's internal timer. Although these switches can help fine-tune Print's activities, you don't really need any more than the /d and /q switches described here. For that matter, you really don't even need /d because the first time you use Print, it prompts for the port to use (if no port is specified) with this message:

```
Name of list device [PRN]:
```

By default, PRN is the same as LPT1, which is the printer port generally used for parallel printers. If LPT1 is the correct port, press Enter. If you want to use a printer connected to a different port, specify the port (LPT2 or LPT3 for a parallel printer; COM1, COM2, COM3, or COM4 for a serial printer). Print responds:

```
Resident part of PRINT installed
```

You're off. From here on, use Print whenever you want during the current session. Because the program is already in memory, Print will remember where to send all your print jobs.

The second, and far more often used, form of the Print command is the one you use to control actual print jobs. That one, as you can see, is simple. You tell Print what to print, and press Enter. Bingo. The file or files are added to the queue. To cancel (empty) the queue, use the /t switch. Here, the only surprise you'll encounter occurs if you cancel the queue while a file is being printed. Printing most likely will continue for at least a short time because your printer is empty-ing its buffer—the place it warehouses transmitted characters that are waiting to be printed. Characters are transmitted very quickly, and the buffer in some printers can hold a lot of text, so you might end up several pages down the road by the time your printer finally gets the message that you want to terminate.

Here are some examples:

Print

Type:	To:
C:\>print /d:lpt2	Tell Print to use the printer connected to LPT2.
C:\>print /d:lpt2 c:\myfile.txt	Tell Print to use the printer connected to LPT2 and, in the same command, to print the file MYFILE.TXT. (Notice that the /d switch must come before the filename.)
C:\>print a:alls a:well b:that.nds well	Print four files, ALLS and WELL on drive A, THAT.NDS on drive B, and WELL in the current directory (the root of drive C).

Print's Very Own IQ Test for You

If you look up Print in the online MS-DOS Help, you'll see two additional switches that control the print queue: /c and /p. These switches can drive you batty if you try to use both in a single command to add some files to the queue at the same time you're trying to remove others. The /c and /p switches work as follows (+ means the file is added to the queue, – means the file is removed from the queue):

```
print /c file1 file2 file3 /p file4 file5 file6 /c file7 file8...

print /p fileA fileB fileC /c fileD fileE fileF /p fileG fileH...
```
NOTE: Each queue entry (drive, directory, subdirectories, and filenames) must 64 charactors or less.

See? If you need to play around with a print queue, your best approach, even though it means more than one command, is to cancel the existing queue and then reenter the Print command, specifying the files you want to print. Of course, no one's going to arrest you for using /c and /p. If that's your preference, have fun.

RAMDRIVE.SYS: Virtually Instant Disk Access

If you have a computer with 2 MB or more of RAM, RAMDRIVE.SYS is almost a necessity. What does it do? It creates what's called a *RAM drive*, or *virtual disk drive*—that is, it sets aside the amount of memory you specify so that MS-DOS can use that memory as if it were an incredibly fast disk drive—fast because the "disk" in memory eliminates the need for MS-DOS to go out and look for information on a physical disk. And no matter how fast a disk drive is, accessing infor-mation in a RAM drive is much faster, especially on a high-powered computer.

RAMDRIVE.SYS

Creates a RAM drive in memory that can be used as if it were a real disk drive. To create a RAM drive, you add a Device or Devicehigh command to CONFIG.SYS. RAMDRIVE.SYS allows you to specify sector and directory sizes, but you don't need those parameters for normal use. The following basic command form should do nicely:

`DEVICE=C:\DOS\RAMDRIVE.SYS [SIZE] /E /A`

C:\DOS\RAMDRIVE.SYS is the drive, path, and filename of the device driver. Substitute your own MS-DOS directory name if RAMDRIVE.SYS is in a directory other than \DOS.

SIZE sets the size, in kilobytes, of the RAM drive. You can specify any size from 4 through 32767 (huge!); a happy medium is somewhere in the 1024 (1 MB) to 2048 (2 MB) range. If you don't specify a size, MS-DOS creates a 64-KB RAM drive—really too small to be useful.

/E creates the RAM drive in extended memory. Use this if your computer has extended, but no expanded, memory. Be sure to include either this switch or /a to avoid having MS-DOS try to create the RAM disk in conventional memory.

/A creates the RAM drive in expanded memory. Use this if your computer has available more expanded memory than extended memory. Expanded memory tends to be slower than extended, so if you have a choice, use the /e switch instead. For more about extended and expanded memory, refer to the next chapter.

After you create a RAM drive, you use it just as if it were the real thing: Save files on it, run Directory on it, even DoubleSpace it, if you want. (You can't, however, format it.) A single line in CONFIG.SYS is all you need to create a RAM drive. MS-DOS will assign the new "drive" its own letter, and away you go. And how do you find out the drive letter for the RAM drives? Watch the screen during startup while CONFIG.SYS is processed. You'll see a line like this:

```
Microsoft RAMDrive version 3.07 virtual disk D:
```

Here, drive letter D has been assigned to the RAM drive.

There are really only two drawbacks to using a RAM drive, but both can be significant, so read on before deciding that a RAM drive is better than a new Ferrari:

- First, information stored on a RAM drive exists in memory only, and you know what happens to information in memory when you shut down or reboot the computer. Poof. If you use a RAM drive for data, you absolutely must remember to save all that data before shutting down. This won't be a problem if you're working from an application, because all self-respecting applications refuse to quit if they're in charge of any unsaved documents. But if you're working from the command line, always remember to save your data on a real disk. This point can't be overemphasized or overstated. Forget to save your work a few times, and you'll see why.

POWER PLAY

Making a Clean Sweep

Many programs save temporary files on disk as they're working and then delete these files when you finish up and exit. These programs usually look for a special directory for their temporary files. The location of the directory is controlled by the TEMP environment variable.

But what happens when these guests are abandoned on your disk? Sometimes program problems occur, and temporary files become stranded on the disk. Because a RAM drive empties automatically when you shut down, it's the perfect spot for

temporary files. To tell your programs to store temporary files on the RAM drive, you can use a com-mand called Set. For example, if your RAM drive is assigned drive letter D, just add the line:

```
SET TEMP=D:\
```

to AUTOEXEC.BAT. All programs that use the TEMP environment variable will now save their temporary files on your RAM drive. When you shut down for the day, those files are guaranteed to disappear.

- Second, a RAM drive does make the memory you commit to it unavailable for other uses for the remainder of your MS-DOS session. If you have plenty of extended memory (at least a megabyte or two), that's a perfect home for a RAM drive. Somewhat less desirable, but still useful, is committing expanded memory to a RAM drive (not as efficient). The least desirable option, and one you should consider only if having a RAM drive outweighs the loss, is to put the beast in conventional memory. This choice can eat up a lot of conventional memory and, quite possibly, make the pool of available memory too small for your other programs to run, so think carefully before doing this. It's rarely an attractive option.

If you have extended or expanded memory to spare—and you're the careful type—try using a RAM drive. You'll love it.

SmartDrive: Memory like an Elephant

SmartDrive (Smartdrv)

Creates a disk cache in extended memory. The basic command form that 6.2 Setup places in your AUTOEXEC.BAT file is a simple:

```
c:\dos\smartdrv.exe /x
```

You can, however, modify the command with several options, among them:

```
c:\dos\smartdrv.exe /x [drive+] [drive-]
```

/x turns off write caching for all drives. Use this if you want to be sure information is never stored in the cache before being written to disk.

drive+ turns on both read and write caching for the drive you specify; *drive–* turns off both read and write caching for the drive you specify. To turn on read caching only, just specify *drive* without a plus or minus sign.

After you've started the cache, you can use the /x and *drive+* and *drive–* switches to control caching for individual drives. To see the status of your cache, use another switch, /s, at the command prompt by typing:

```
C:\>smartdrv /s
```

Equally important, to force all cached information to be written to disk, use SmartDrive's /c switch, like this:

```
C:\>smartdrv /c
```

If your computer has enough extended memory, MS-DOS uses SmartDrive to create a disk cache for you during setup. A disk cache is a section of memory reserved for holding information read from disk. The point of having such a thing: So that MS-DOS can search memory, rather than go out to a physical disk, when you tell it you want to work with a file or part of a file that has recently been accessed.

As with a RAM drive, a disk cache is a means of using available memory to avoid time-consuming disk accesses. Superficially, a disk cache doesn't sound like a big deal; after all, once you've used a file, how many times do you use it again and again? In actuality, though, you'll find that a cache helps quite a lot, as you can see from the following SmartDrive report.

The number of "hits" represents the number of times MS-DOS was able to find information it needed in the cache, rather than having to access the disk physically to get the information:

```
C:\>smartdrv /s
Microsoft SMARTDrive Disk Cache version 5.0
Copyright 1991,1993 Microsoft Corp.

Room for     256 elements of   8,192 bytes each
There have been   51,361 cache hits
    and    5,184 cache misses

Cache size:  2,097,152 bytes
Cache size while running Windows:  2,097,152 bytes

              Disk Caching Status
drive   read cache   write cache   buffering

  A:       yes          no           no
  B:       yes          no           no
  C:       yes          no           no
Write behind data will be committed before command prompt returns.

For help, type "Smartdrv /?".

C:\>
```

Version 6.2 Setup does *not* turn write-caching off if SmartDrive is already in memory or if your AUTO-EXEC.BAT file contains a SmartDrive command. To check on write-caching, type *smartdrv /s* at the command prompt. To turn write-caching off, add the /x switch to the command in your AUTO-EXEC.BAT file. (For help with editing the file, refer to "Make a File with Edit," later in this section.)

Notice that this report tells you not only about read caches, it also refers to write caches and write-behind data. What's that? SmartDrive is able to cache both information read from disk (read cache) and information that's destined for disk storage (write cache). When you use write caching, SmartDrive places information you want to save in the cache, waiting for a time when the disk is idle to do the actual job of storing the data.

Write caching, too, can speed up your system, but there's a drawback that you don't get with read caching: Information can be lost. This is obviously not just bad—it's very bad. So SmartDrive acts to avoid such problems when it can. Before the computer reboots when you press Ctrl+Alt+Del, SmartDrive automatically writes all cached information to disk. In version 6.2 of MS-DOS, Setup also adds SmartDrive to your AUTOEXEC.BAT file with write-caching turned off (with the /x switch), so you must deliberately enable this feature if you want it. In addition (as you can see from the report), Smart-Drive also writes—"commits"—all cached information to disk as each command completes and before MS-DOS redisplays the command prompt. This protects you from losing cached data by shutting down before SmartDrive can empty the write cache. SmartDrive can't, however, anticipate when the power will go off or when you'll push the reset button, but to help you in these instances, it provides the /c switch described on the quick reference card. Use it.

POWER PLAY

Caching a CD-ROM Drive

By default, SmartDrive read caches your floppy drives and your hard disk. If you have version 6.2 of MS-DOS, SmartDrive can also cache CD-ROM drives, but only if your CONFIG.SYS names a device driver for the CD-ROM drive and you've used the MSCDEX command to enable the drive and link it to a drive letter. The command form you need in CONFIG.SYS looks something like this:

```
DEVICE=C:\DIR\DRIVER /D:ID
```

where *dir* and *driver* point to the directory, filename, and extension of the CD-ROM driver (which your documentation should tell you about), and *id* is a "signature" assigned as an identifying label for the drive. The *id* part of the command takes the form MSCD000 for the first CD-ROM drive, MSCD001 for the second, and so on. So, for example, if you have a CD-ROM drive with a driver named CDROM.SYS in the CD directory,

the Device command you'd put in your CONFIG.SYS file would look something like this:

```
DEVICE=C:\CD\CDROM.SYS
  /D:MSCD000
```

That done, you could then enable the drive by typing the following at the command prompt or by putting it in AUTOEXEC.BAT:

```
C:\>mscdex /d:mscd000 /l:g
```

This command assigns drive letter G to the CD-ROM drive known to MS-DOS as MSCD000.

To enable read caching for the CD-ROM drive, you would then use the command:

```
C:\>smartdrv g
```

If you need help with any of these commands, refer to the online MS-DOS Help, your CD-ROM's documentation, or both.

More About Memory

How Much Do You Need to Know?

Memory management, like disk compression, is a really important feature in recent versions of MS-DOS. Of course, MemMaker (introduced in version 6.0 of MS-DOS) can do all the memory management for you: If your system works fine as is and MS-DOS is merely your springboard to applications, you don't really have to understand anything more about memory than how to type memmaker—no need to learn the nitty-gritty details. You won't really appreciate the memory-management capabilities of version 6.2 of MS-DOS, but that's all right. If you really want to understand memory, however, this chapter will exercise your mind a bit. You'll encounter a few somewhat hairy details about memory and memory-related commands, so if you find you're getting in over your head, feel free to stop or skip the chapter until you think you're ready for it. Do, however, read up on MemMaker in Section 4; you won't regret it.

Memory Is Made of This

Have you ever been confused by references to EMS, XMS, UMBs, HMA, RAM, ROM, and all that other memory-related alphabet soup? Don't worry, you're not alone. Really. Memory is one of the trickier parts of computers to understand, but it's not impossible, nor do you have to absorb vast quantities of information. To prove it, take a show-and-tell approach to understanding memory. The show is on the next page.

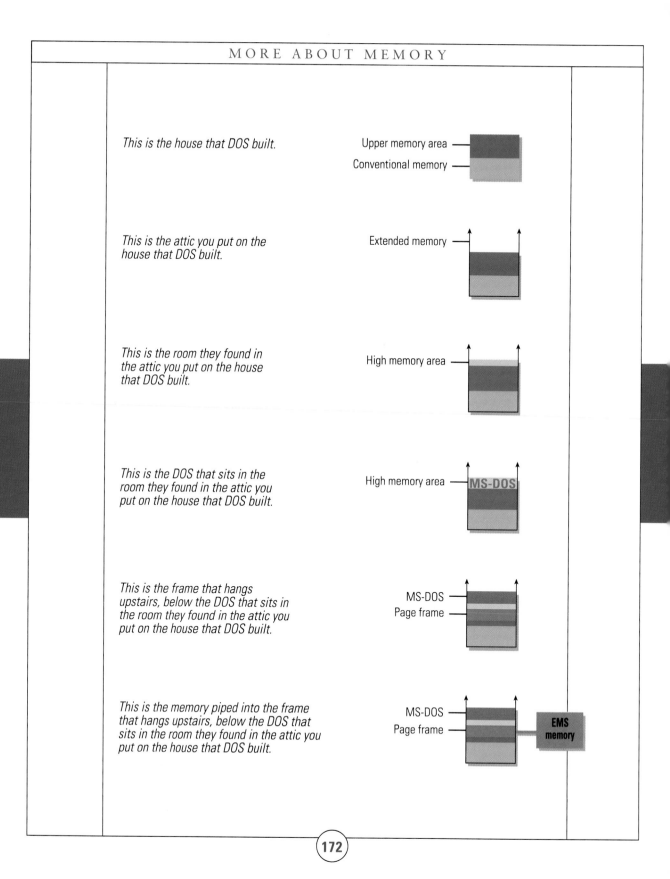

This is the house that DOS built.

Upper memory area
Conventional memory

This is the attic you put on the house that DOS built.

Extended memory

This is the room they found in the attic you put on the house that DOS built.

High memory area

This is the DOS that sits in the room they found in the attic you put on the house that DOS built.

High memory area — MS-DOS

This is the frame that hangs upstairs, below the DOS that sits in the room they found in the attic you put on the house that DOS built.

MS-DOS
Page frame

This is the memory piped into the frame that hangs upstairs, below the DOS that sits in the room they found in the attic you put on the house that DOS built.

MS-DOS
Page frame
EMS memory

Now here's the tell.

About Memory

To begin with, memory is hardware. It's chips that contain millions of tiny "cells," each of which can hold one binary digit, or bit. Bits are pumped into and out of these cells by the processor and are handled in groups of eight. Eight bits, you'll recall, make up one byte. And, of course, bytes are the foundation of all computer activity. Essentially, then, you can think of the bits moving through a memory chip as comparable to people marching in a drill team or a parade, only in this parade everyone moves in groups of eight.

Functionally, and of far more practical importance to you, however, memory is storage. There are two basic types of memory, RAM (random access memory) and ROM (read-only memory). Of these, RAM is really the only type of memory that counts where your work is concerned, because RAM is what holds your programs, your data, and—usually—MS-DOS itself. (MS-DOS does come in a ROM-based form but is much more common as the RAM-based, stored-on-disk form you installed from your upgrade disk or disks.)

Conventional and Upper Memory

MS-DOS was born to live in a 1-MB house—no more, although when it was young, it could do with less. That's the way MS-DOS was originally designed, and in order for newer versions to remain compatible with older ones, that's the way MS-DOS has remained. Now, the 1 MB of memory that MS-DOS could use was originally divided into two sections: a lower floor including 640 KB of what's called conventional memory and an upstairs of 384 KB of what's called upper, or reserved, memory. (This division, arbitrary though it sounds, is actually based on the fact that the 8088 processor, for which MS-DOS was originally created, liked to think in 64-KB units of memory, known as segments. But that's beside the point.)

Conventional memory is basically handed over to MS-DOS and to applications and their data, no strings attached. Thus, any program designed to run with MS-DOS can use any available portion of that 640 KB of conventional memory without any problems at all (except when there's not enough

How does 640 KB plus 384 KB equal 1 MB? Remember that computers think in 2s and powers of 2. A kilobyte is the power of 2 that's closest to 1000, and that happens to be 1024 bytes (2 to the 10th power). Now, 1 million in the decimal system is 1000 times 1000. A megabyte, in the world of 2s, is 1024 times 1024. Therefore, a megabyte (1 MB) is actually 1024 kilobytes. And, of course, 640 KB plus 384 KB equals 1024 KB. Confused? Trust your computer.

Not enough room to run that game? If a program refuses to start because it says your computer doesn't have enough memory, try restarting and requesting an alternative startup. A clean boot (press F5 when you see the message *Starting MS-DOS*) won't load MS-DOS out of the way in high memory, but it will give you the least amount of program overhead and just might give your program enough memory to camp in. If a clean boot doesn't work, try an interactive boot (F8 rather than F5) and say "yes" only to the bare essentials (CONFIG.SYS lines that begin with DOS=, lines that include HIMEM.SYS and EMM386.EXE, and AUTOEXEC.BAT lines that set the search path and command prompt). If your program is *not* installed on a DoubleSpaced drive, you can gain an additional 40+ KB of memory by requesting a clean boot minus DoubleSpace (Ctrl+F5) or an interactive boot minus DoubleSpace (Ctrl+F8). These options, however, make it impossible for you to use a DoubleSpaced drive until you reboot.

room, which you'll get to next). Upper memory, in contrast, was held in reserve for hardware—for example, to give video a place to store images destined for the screen.

As it turned out, this division of 1 MB of RAM into 640 KB of conventional memory and 384 KB of upper memory didn't anticipate the way in which application programs would grow in size and power as people began to want their computers to do more and more. Within a few years, actually, programs grew to the point that they began to crowd and jostle each other in conventional memory, grabbing for whatever memory they could get, like shoppers on the twenty-fourth of December. At the same time, the 384 KB of upper memory ended up being largely unused. Something had to give, and the first something to go was the 640-KB limit. This is when extended (XMS) and expanded (EMS) memory entered the picture.

Extended and Expanded Memory

Extended memory and expanded memory are the two ways in which you can add more RAM to your computer. Basically, you can think of extended memory as sitting directly on top of the 1-MB pile that MS-DOS uses, whereas expanded memory sits more off to the side, as shown in the illustration on page 172. Both extended and expanded memory are normally out of reach as far as MS-DOS is concerned. The key word here, though, is *normally*. Special programs within MS-DOS can make both types of memory available to you. The two types are, however, made available in very different ways.

To provide you with extended memory, MS-DOS relies on a part of itself called HIMEM.SYS, which is known as an extended memory manager. HIMEM.SYS is something of a "superDOS" in the sense that it can reach up, up, and way above the head of "kentDOS." It's been given this power so that it can control extended memory and keep programs from fighting over who gets what and so that it can make a home for MS-DOS itself in the special segment of extended memory called the HMA (more about the HMA later). If your computer has an 80286 or better processor and 1 MB of RAM, you've probably got 350 KB or so of extended memory. If your computer has more than 1 MB of RAM, you probably have a lot more than 350 KB of extended memory.

Once HIMEM.SYS makes extended memory available, programs such as Microsoft Windows and Windows-based applications happily gobble up as much as you can give them. And even if you don't use such programs, you can make good use of extended memory within MS-DOS by handing it over to a RAM drive, which is memory you tell MS-DOS to use as if it were a very fast disk drive, or to a SMARTDRV.EXE cache. (Oh, sorry...a cache is a section of memory in which SMARTDRV.EXE temporarily warehouses information read

XMS

(No clever pronunciations here, just plain "eks-em-ess"). Short for Extended Memory Specification, a set of "rules" that govern how extended memory is used. MS-DOS version 6.2 uses XMS version 3.0. (Yes, rules come in versions too.)

EMS

(Just plain "ee-em-ess.") Short for Expanded Memory Specification, a set of "rules" that govern how expanded memory is used. You often see this as LIM-EMS after the companies that developed the specification: Lotus, Intel, and Microsoft. MS-DOS version 6.2 uses EMS version 4.

from disk. Using a cache can speed up your work because MS-DOS can search the cache for files you've already used rather than having to go out to disk time and time again.)

As for expanded memory, that's another way of providing programs with more than the 640 KB of running space MS-DOS normally offers. Whereas extended memory works pretty much like an information warehouse, expanded memory works more like a slide carousel. (You know. Click. "That's the Grand Canyon. Harry stuck his thumb in front of the lens again." Click. "That's Ralphie chasing a cougar." Click. "That's the cougar chasing Ralphie." Click....)

When a program uses expanded memory, the information stored there is slipped, as needed, into and out of a reserved section in upper memory called a *page frame*. The page frame is about 64 KB in size and, like the screen used for showing slides, is used to "show" that information to the requesting program. In the case of expanded memory, that information is moved around in blocks called pages (analogous to your slides). Expanded memory is handled by the MS-DOS program EMM386.EXE, which is known as an expanded memory manager (EMM). EMM386.EXE also moonlights as a provider of the UMBs you'll find out about shortly.

When EMM386.EXE is at work, it provides expanded memory to programs that need it (which are also the only ones that can use it) by turning extended memory into simulated expanded memory—simulated in the sense that expanded memory was originally designed to be installed in a computer as a bank of memory chips controlled by their own expanded memory manager. With EMM386.EXE, you can essentially use your computer's extended memory as either extended or expanded memory. In the real world—in your work with MS-DOS—expanded memory can be used to create a RAM drive, but for the most part it should be considered a potential resource for programs that need expanded memory and cannot use extended memory.

Upper Memory and UMBs

UMBs sound like they ought to contain little green people. Obviously, they're far less sensational, but they're also far more useful. (At least until little green people arrive to prove their utility.) As already mentioned, upper memory is the 384 KB of memory originally reserved for use by video and other hardware. This area of RAM is inhabited by some programs, but for the most part, it remains empty. The empty spaces, or regions, are basically vacant sections between inhabited areas. UMBs (upper memory blocks) are just blocks of space within a region.

What can you do with UMBs? Well, you don't do anything with them, at least not directly. What you can do, however—with the Devicehigh and Loadhigh commands, described briefly later in this chapter—is fill them with device drivers (programs that manage devices you add to your system) and with memory-resident software (including part of the program named DBLSPACE.BIN that controls use of DoubleSpaced drives). Why do this? To free up the conventional memory these programs would otherwise occupy—sometimes dozens of kilo-bytes of K. And as everyone knows, you can never have too much conventional memory.

Room with a View: The HMA

And finally, you get to the high-memory area, or HMA. This is a magical little 64-KB block of memory that sits just above the 1-MB boundary on a computer that contains extended memory. How can memory be magical? Well, MS-DOS should no more be able to see the HMA than you can see the top of your head. (Without the mirror, silly....)

What's so special about the HMA? It's an extra 64 KB of memory that MS-DOS—plain and unadorned MS-DOS—can use without any help, even though the HMA exists *beyond* the 1-MB boundary that MS-DOS presumably cannot peer over. The technical sleight of hand involved is clever in its own right, but there's a practical advantage to the HMA: You can use it to hold part of MS-DOS itself. And that is a big deal. Big enough that a lot of people rushed to upgrade to MS-DOS version 5.0, in which this feature first appeared. Big enough that in version 6.0, which kicks in further memory optimization with MemMaker, MS-DOS can free up more conventional memory than was possible with any previous version. And all you need in order to use this HMA are HIMEM.SYS and the command called (appropriately enough) Dos.

As you can see, memory is a rather complex topic. MS-DOS includes a number of special programs and commands that help you make the most of your computer's memory. Among them are HIMEM.SYS and EMM386.EXE, as well as RAMDRIVE.SYS, SMARTDRV.EXE, and the Dos, Device, Devicehigh, Loadhigh, and Mem commands. All of these are described either here or in the preceding chapter (RAMDRIVE and SMARTDRV), but to really use them well, you also have to know how to make them work together. To see them as a group, refer to "Do It Yourself or Do It with MemMaker," in Section 4.

If you DoubleSpace your hard disk, you'll find that version 6.2 of MS-DOS can push Double-Space upstairs, into the HMA. Version 6.0 can't do this. The benefit to you: another 10+ KB of free conven-tional memory. On a memory-hungry system (and whose isn't?), that's like getting a free dessert with your free lunch.

Dos: Load MS-DOS High

Dos

Loads part of MS-DOS into the HMA and also opens a pipeline to upper memory so that device drivers and memory-resident programs can be loaded into upper memory. Simple as it is to use, the Dos command does insist on appearing only in CONFIG.SYS. You can load MS-DOS high and enable use of UMBs in a single command, as follows:

```
DOS=HIGH,UMB
```

Or you can load MS-DOS high and enable UMBs using separate Dos commands:

```
DOS=HIGH
DOS=UMB
```

The Dos command can appear anywhere in CONFIG.SYS after the line that loads HIMEM.SYS. The easiest way to add it to the file is by running the redoubtable MemMaker, described in Section 4.

It's said that good things come in small packages. Well, judging by the number of letters in its name, Dos is small package, indeed. But the benefits Dos brings are large. One of the key additions to version 5 of MS-DOS, this command handles two big jobs: It loads MS-DOS into the HMA if the HMA is available, and it opens the door to loading device drivers and memory-resident programs into upper memory. And both of these features, as you now know, help make as much conventional memory as possible available for other programs to use. The Dos command is a memory conservationist's dream.

As you can see from the reference card for this command, Dos is also simplicity personified. It does, however, make a few demands—demands that have to do with memory and are non-negotiable, so pay attention:

- Your computer must have an 80286 or better processor.

- You can use a Dos command only in CONFIG.SYS. It won't work from the command line.

- If you want to load MS-DOS into the HMA, you must include a command in CONFIG.SYS that loads an extended memory manager. On any MS-DOS system, HIMEM.SYS works perfectly. (You can, however, use a different extended memory manager if you have one.) Assuming that you want to use HIMEM.SYS and that it is in your \DOS directory, the command you include in CONFIG.SYS looks like this:

```
DEVICE=C:\DOS\HIMEM.SYS
```

- If you want to use UMBs, you must *follow* the line that loads your extended memory manager with a line that loads an *expanded* memory manager. For this, EMM386.EXE will work fine on any MS-DOS system with an 80386 or better processor. (Again, you can substitute an alternative expanded memory manager if you have one.) Assuming that you want to use EMM386.EXE and that it is in your \DOS directory, the command you include in CONFIG.SYS looks like this:

```
DEVICE=C:\DOS\EMM386.EXE
```

For more on HIMEM.SYS and EMM386.EXE, refer to the descriptions of these commands later in this chapter. To help you pull it all together, this is what the

Dos-related commands in your CONFIG.SYS file should look like when you load MS-DOS into the HMA and you enable UMBs:

```
DEVICE=C:\DOS\HIMEM.SYS
DEVICE=C:\DOS\EMM386.EXE
DOS=HIGH,UMB
```

For help with editing your CONFIG.SYS file and using memory-related commands as a group, refer to "Make a File with Edit," the next chapter, and "Do It Yourself or Do It with MemMaker," in Section 4.

Devicehigh: Fill UMBs with Device Drivers

Devicehigh

Loads device drivers into UMBs if they are available. The command form is shown below. The all-uppercase format is used because it is typical of the way CONFIG.SYS commands are typed; you can use lowercase if you want:

DEVICEHIGH=[*DRIVE:*][*PATH*] *FILENAME*[*DRIVER-CONTROLS*]

DRIVE, *path*, and *filename* specify the location and name of the device driver to load.

DRIVER-CONTROLS represents any parameters and switches, required or optional, that you want to specify to control the behavior of the device driver. The actual parameters and switches you use depend entirely on the device driver you are loading. See the examples in the description of the Device command.

The Devicehigh command serves exactly the same function as the Device command, with one big difference: Instead of loading a device driver into conventional memory, Devicehigh tries to load the device driver into upper memory instead. Using Devicehigh is simple, and you don't even have to worry about how much upper memory is available: If Devicehigh can't load a particular driver into upper memory, it loads the driver into conventional memory instead.

The easiest and most effective way to use Devicehigh is to let MemMaker tinker with CONFIG.SYS for you, as described in "Do It Yourself or Do It with MemMaker," in Section 4. If you want to put Devicehigh to work yourself, you have to know how to edit CONFIG.SYS, and you have to pay attention to certain basic requirements:

- If you are using Devicehigh with the MS-DOS memory managers (HIMEM.SYS and EMM386.EXE), your system needs an 80386 or better processor and at least 350 KB of extended memory.

- You must precede any Devicehigh commands in CONFIG.SYS with Device (not Devicehigh) commands that load HIMEM.SYS and EMM386.EXE, plus a Dos command that enables use of UMBs. The commands look something like this:

```
DEVICE=C:\DOS\HIMEM.SYS
DEVICE=C:\DOS\EMM386.EXE NOEMS
DOS=HIGH,UMB
```

You can use the Dos command (again in CONFIG.SYS only) to deliberately turn off use of the HMA and UMBs with the command:

DOS=LOW,NOUMB

or two separate commands:

DOS=LOW
DOS=UMB

But these are the MS-DOS defaults anyway, so using Dos to avoid use of the HMA and UMBs really does nothing more than pound the point home.

Let MemMaker do the job for you. It's really much easier, especially because MemMaker has an edge over you: It can watch as programs are loaded to determine exactly how much memory they need. If you let MemMaker take over, it uses a fancy form of Devicehigh, like this:

```
DEVICEHIGH /L:REGION1[,MINSIZE1];REGION2[,MINSIZE2]...;
    REGIONn[,MINSIZEn] /S=DRIVER [DRIVER-CONTROLS]
```

The command form is shown here just to raise your eyebrows and let you see how clever MemMaker is. You can use the same form if you want—all the details are in the online MS-DOS Help for Devicehigh. Of course, you'll have to do some thinking and planning. And if you're not a real do-it-yourself type, don't forget about the last time you tried to work on the plumbing...or was it the wiring...or maybe the car. MemMaker has its advantages.

EMM386.EXE: Open the Door to Expanded Memory and UMBs

EMM386.EXE

Enables MS-DOS to provide simulated expanded memory to programs that need it. EMM386.EXE also performs the valuable job of enabling the use of UMBs for loading device drivers and memory-resident programs. EMM386.EXE is a device driver and must be loaded with a Device command in CONFIG.SYS in order to be useful. The following line shows the basic command and the switches most often used. The all-uppercase format is used because it is typical of the way CONFIG.SYS commands are typed:

```
DEVICE=C:\DOS\EMM386.EXE RAM NOEMS HIGHSCAN
```

C:\DOS\EMM386.EXE is the drive, path, and filename of EMM386.EXE. Substitute the name of your MS-DOS directory if it is not DOS.

RAM tells EMM386.EXE to provide both UMBs and expanded memory (as needed). Include this switch if you need both. Do not use this switch with the NOEMS switch.

NOEMS tells EMM386.EXE to provide UMBs but no expanded memory. Include this switch if none of your programs use expanded memory. (Check their documentation if you suspect they might.)

HIGHSCAN tells EMM386.EXE to be as aggressive as possible in seeking out available UMBs for use. Note the troubleshooting tip on this page, however.

As you can see from the quick reference card, EMM386.EXE is the MS-DOS device driver that provides simulated expanded memory to programs that need it and—more important—enables the use of UMBs for holding device drivers and memory-resident programs. (To load device drivers into upper memory, you use the Devicehigh command; to load memory-resident programs into upper memory, you use Loadhigh.) True to its name, however, EMM386.EXE works only on computers with 80386 or better processors. It also requires at least 350 KB of extended memory, although this amount is typical on any current system with 1 MB of RAM.

Because EMM386.EXE is a memory-management device driver, it must be loaded into memory with a Device (not Devicehigh) command in CONFIG.SYS. The easiest way to get this done, and done right, is to use MemMaker, as

HIGHSCAN OR BYE, SCAN? The HIGHSCAN switch can free up a little more memory, but it might cause some computers to hang or behave oddly. If this happens, perform a clean boot, remove the HIGHSCAN switch, and then reboot your computer.

described in "Do It Yourself or Do It with MemMaker," in Section 4. This is particularly true because EMM386.EXE includes a number of exotic parameters and switches, most of which—thankfully—are needed only in very special circumstances.

Where EMM386.EXE is concerned, the bottom line (as accountants and politicians like to say) is this: If you have a computer with at least 1 MB of RAM and an 80386 or better processor and you don't use any other program that provides expanded memory and UMBs, do use EMM386.EXE. And if you're at all uncomfortable working with CONFIG.SYS, let MemMaker handle the job. It's easy and effective because MemMaker not only handles EMM386.EXE for you, it also analyzes your device drivers and memory-resident software and adjusts CONFIG.SYS to make the best use of UMBs it can figure out.

HIMEM.SYS: Open the Door to Extended Memory and the HMA

HIMEM.SYS is the anchor that keeps all memory above 640 KB in your system tied down and available for use. Without HIMEM.SYS, you can't use extended memory or the HMA. Without access to extended memory, you can't use EMM386.EXE to get at expanded memory or UMBs. See? Without HIMEM.SYS, your brainy computer has no more smarts than a basic 640-KB unit.

So what's the catch, right? HIMEM.SYS looks easy enough to stick in CONFIG.SYS, and it is. Well, there are two sort-of catches:

- HIMEM.SYS works only on 80286 or better systems.

- HIMEM.SYS requires at least 350 KB of extended memory to play with.

Now, you might ask why these are "sort-of" catches and not the real McCoys. Well, first of all, it's pretty hard to find a late-model computer that isn't based on at least an 80386 processor. So catch number 1 really applies only to machines

---

HIMEM.SYS

Enables use of extended memory and the HMA on an 80286 or better system. A device driver, HIMEM.SYS must be loaded with a Device (not Devicehigh) command in CONFIG.SYS. MemMaker can add the command to CONFIG.SYS for you, but so that you know what's what, here's the basic command:

`DEVICE=C:\DOS\HIMEM.SYS`

C:\DOS\HIMEM.SYS is the drive, path, and filename of HIMEM.SYS. Substitute the name of your MS-DOS directory if it is not \DOS. HIMEM.SYS includes a number of optional switches (for special circumstances). For information about these switches, refer to the MS-DOS online Help for HIMEM.SYS.

in the PC and PC/XT class, and if you have either of those types of computer, you really don't need version 6.2 of MS-DOS to begin with. Neither a PC nor a PC/XT can make use of the best features of version 6.2. Catch number 2 is the same kind of deal: Most recent computers have at least 1 MB of RAM, of which 384 KB is almost surely extended memory. Therefore, if you have a computer with an 80286 processor (or better) and 1 MB of RAM, HIMEM.SYS is almost certainly for you. And it's a feature of MS-DOS you really ought to take advantage of because even if your machine has a limited amount of RAM, version 6.2 can free dozens more kilobytes of conventional memory by loading not only MS-DOS but part of DoubleSpace into the HMA.

HIMEM.SYS sounds like the dream device driver, and so it actually is. There is, however, one thing to note about it—or, more specifically, one difference to note between HIMEM.SYS and EMM386.EXE. HIMEM.SYS works on systems with an 80286 or better processor; EMM386.EXE works on systems with an 80386 or better processor. There's a difference of one processor generation between the two. If your computer has an 80386 or better processor, you obviously have nothing to worry about. If your computer has an 80286 processor, however, you need to know that HIMEM.SYS will gladly make extended memory and the HMA available to you, but to gain access to expanded memory and UMBs, you'll have to find a third-party 80286-based program (such as QRAM from Quarterdeck Office Systems) that works with HIMEM.SYS to make these memory options available to you. For advice on this, consult your local software dealer.

Bottom line again: If you have the right computer, use HIMEM.SYS. Better yet, take it easy—let MemMaker put it to work for you.

Loadhigh: Fill UMBs with Programs

Loadhigh (Lh)

Loads memory-resident programs into available upper memory. The command form is:

lh *program* [*program-options*]

program is the drive, path, and filename of the program to load into upper memory.

program-options represents any parameters, switches, or other options you type when starting the program. The example using Print in the table on page 183 shows one such use of program options.

Loadhigh does for memory-resident programs what Devicehigh does for device drivers: It loads them into available upper memory, far from the madding crowd in conventional memory. Loadhigh is actually the fifth and alphabetically last member of the memory-optimizing quintet in MS-DOS, the others being HIMEM.SYS, EMM386.EXE, Dos, and Devicehigh. Working together, especially under the initial direction of MemMaker, these device drivers and commands can free up considerable amounts of conventional memory—80 to 100 KB or even more, depending on how your system is set up and what programs you normally run.

If you're an experienced MS-DOS user, you probably know about batch files—collections of MS-DOS commands that you save in files with the extension BAT. You can then run a "batch" of commands as a group, rather than typing them individually. Batch files, with the exception of AUTOEXEC.BAT, are beyond the scope of this book. If you know how to construct and use them, however, do be aware that you can use Loadhigh from within any batch file, not just AUTOEXEC.BAT.

Unlike its companions, however, Loadhigh works from the command line or from AUTOEXEC.BAT, rather than from CONFIG.SYS. The reason for this is simple: AUTOEXEC.BAT handles programs; CONFIG.SYS handles hardware. In addition to being competent, Loadhigh is smart. It doesn't bomb out on you if you say, "Load this program into upper memory" but Loadhigh can't find enough room for the program in a UMB. It loads the program into conventional memory instead. Government should be so quietly efficient.

Of course, the fact that Loadhigh can use UMBs doesn't give you the ability to toss everything but your data into upper memory. Loadhigh, you must remember, works with memory-resident, or TSR (terminate-and-stay-resident), programs. These are programs, such as MS-DOS's own Print and Doskey, that sit on the sidelines of memory like bench warmers on a baseball or football team. Where most programs, such as your word processor, stay in memory only as long as you are using them, TSR programs (once started) stay in memory whether or not you're using them. When they're not active, they sit quietly, waiting to be called. When you call them, they do their work and then retire to the sidelines until you need them again; there they stay until the current session with MS-DOS concludes or, if they understand such commands, until you send them to the showers by unloading them.

If you use memory-resident software, you have two easy ways to put Loadhigh to work:

- If the program is one that you use all the time, add its name to your AUTOEXEC.BAT file and then run MemMaker. If MemMaker finds that the program can fit into upper memory, it will give the program a Loadhigh command for you. (If you need help changing AUTOEXEC.BAT, refer to the next chapter, "Make a File with Edit.")

- If the program is one that you use occasionally, type the Loadhigh command at the command prompt. Here's an example using Doskey:

```
C:\>lh doskey
```

Then you can see, with the Mem command (described next), whether the program is in upper memory, like this:

```
C:\>mem /d /p
```

Search the list of programs in the section of Mem's report headed *Upper Memory Detail*. If the program is listed there, it's in upper memory.

Here are some examples of Loadhigh commands:

Loadhigh	
Type:	**To:**
C:\>lh doskey	Load the Doskey command recorder into upper memory. This is really useful and saves a lot of typing.
C:\>lh print /d:lpt2	Load Print into upper memory, at the same time specifying that you want it to send its output to the printer attached to LPT2.

Mem: Check Up on Memory

Given that MS-DOS is capable of doing all kinds of helpful things to make memory use more efficient on your computer, it stands to reason there must be a way for you to see and admire what MS-DOS is doing. (And also, of course, to check on how much of what type of memory is available for use—a not-so-minor detail.) Your peephole into that swirling mass of electronic thought is the Mem command. With Mem, you can:

- See how much memory, and what types of memory, your computer has.

- See how much of each type of installed memory is used, and how much remains free.

- See how big available blocks of conventional and upper memory are, so you can cram even more stuff in.

- Satisfy yourself that MS-DOS is sitting in the HMA.

- See where and how programs and device drivers are loaded into conventional and upper memory.

The output of a typical Mem command varies according to the way you've set up your system. For example, you don't see a report on extended memory unless your system has more than 640 KB of RAM; you don't see a report on expanded memory unless you enabled expanded memory with EMM386.EXE (or a comparable program);

Mem

Displays various reports on memory and how it is being used. The command form is:

mem /c /d /f /m *program* /p

/c (or /classify) lists the programs currently loaded into conventional and upper memory (if available), gives the size of each program, and summarizes memory use with a report much like the one shown in text.

/d produces an extremely detailed report showing all programs, device drivers, and areas of free memory in conventional and upper memory (if available). This report is interesting but probably far more detailed than you need. If you try it, also use the /p switch. The report is very long.

/f shows the amounts of conventional and upper memory that are currently free for use. If you use this switch, you'll see upper memory separated into regions. Let MemMaker handle these for you.

/m *program* shows memory use for the program or device driver you specify as *program*. Like /d, this is a switch you probably don't need.

/p pauses the report after each screenful. You might need this with the /c switch; you definitely need it with /d.

and you don't see a report on upper memory unless you've used both EMM386.EXE (or a comparable program) and the DOS=UMB command. All these are details, however. To help you see what Mem produces, here's a pretty typical report for a computer after optimization with MemMaker:

```
C:\>mem

Memory Type        Total  =   Used  +    Free

Conventional        640K       35K       605K
Upper               155K       95K        60K
Reserved            128K      128K         0K
Extended (XMS)    7,269K    3,293K     3,976K

Total memory      8,192K    3,552K     4,641K

Total under 1 MB    795K      130K       665K

Largest executable program size    604K  (618,944 bytes)
Largest free upper memory block      60K  (61,136 bytes)
MS-DOS is resident in the high memory area.

C:\>
```

By now, you should be familiar enough with the terms to understand most, if not all, of this report. Working from the top, you can see that Mem is telling you how much conventional, upper, and extended memory the system contains. The only part of this that might confuse you is the information about reserved memory. The 128 KB shown is memory that's off-limits. (If you've upgraded from version 6.0 of MS-DOS, you might recall seeing this called Adapter RAM/ROM instead.)

The remainder of the report summarizes the types of memory in the system, showing how much is used, how much is free, and how large a program can still be loaded and run (largest executable program size). Most of the time, you'll probably just use Mem to satisfy your curiosity. If you reach the point that you want to start making decisions about which programs to load where, Mem is your starting point for sure.

Just think what psychiatrists could do with a Mem command. Scary, isn't it? Here are some examples of typical Mem commands:

Memory

Type:	To:
C:\>mem	See a report like the one shown in text
C:\>mem /c	See the names and sizes of programs loaded into conventional and upper memory
C:\>mem /d /p	See the whole enchilada—a complete report of programs loaded into memory (pausing after each screenful)
C:\>mem /f	See how much free memory is available
C:\>mem /m doskey	See how much memory Doskey is using

If you've updated from MS-DOS version 6.0 to version 6.2, you're probably pleasantly surprised to see that Mem now inserts commas in large numbers—no more counting digits and inserting mental commas to figure out that 8388608 is really 8,388,608 bytes. If you've upgraded from version 5, this report is probably an even more pleasant surprise: Mem now knows how to display decimal numbers, so you no longer have to wrack your brain figuring out the decimal equivalents of hexadecimal values.

Make a File with Edit

Edit, You're No Word Processor

But that's OK. Edit isn't meant to be a replacement for a full-fledged word processor. It lacks the whiz-bang formatting, page-layout, graphics, hyphenation, spell-checking, annotation, you-name-it-we've-got-it features of today's word processors. What's it good for then? For creating, changing, saving, and printing unformatted text (ASCII) files. And what are text files good for? Well, if you want to bang out a quick fan letter to Elvis, Edit is all you need. If you want to write a Basic program or create the world's most elaborate batch file, Edit is just the ticket for that too....

But presumably you're not interested in becoming the nerd of the nineties, so think of Edit simply as the program you need when you want to make changes to AUTOEXEC.BAT and CONFIG.SYS or when you want to read or print text files, such as the README.TXT file shipped on your version 6.2 disk or disks. (Printing this file, by the way, is strongly recommended.) Basically, Edit is a handy, cheap (as in free), and easy-to-use tool for working with unformatted text files.

POWER PLAY

Batch Applies to More Than Cookies

In this chapter, you'll see a number of references to batch files. What are they? They're collections of MS-DOS commands that you put together and save as a file with the extension BAT.

MS-DOS recognizes BAT as a valid extension for an executable file—one containing instructions to be carried out—so when you "run" the file by typing its name at the command

(continued)

continued

prompt, MS-DOS carries out all the commands in the file, beginning to end. It's automation in action.

Experienced MS-DOS users often concoct batch files when they want to save a series of commands they use regularly. This simple set of commands, for example, could be a batch file:

```
cls
dir a: /w
pause
format a: /q
```

Do you see what this does? The first command (cls) clears the screen. The second (dir a: /w) displays a wide listing of the files on the disk in drive A. The third (pause) is a command you haven't seen in this book, but basically what it does is tell MS-DOS to stop until you press a key to continue (or press Ctrl+Break to cancel the batch file). The fourth command (format a: /q) formats the disk in drive A (unless you already pressed the Ctrl+Break combination).

As you can see, by saving commands in a batch file, you can eliminate the need to type those commands, one after the other, each time you want to perform a particular job with MS-DOS. What this example doesn't show, however, is that batch files can get complex because MS-DOS lets you control execution within a batch file. You can, for example, use a command called Choice that prompts for input; you can then send MS-DOS to one set of commands or another within the batch file, depending on what you

type. You can also use "logic" commands, such as If, that carry out one set of instructions if a condition is true, another set of instructions if a condition is not true. All this, unfortunately, is well beyond the scope of this book, but if you're interested, most larger, intermediate-level books on MS-DOS initiate you into the batch file club.

To end this, here's a piece of trivia you might enjoy: The term *batch* comes from days of old, when computers handled jobs in batches—sets of operations that ran without human interaction. Thus, when you ran a batch job, you would give the computer the instructions and data it needed, set it going, and wait for the job to be completed. No peeking, and certainly no "Hey, wait—cancel that and start over." Version 6.0 of MS-DOS turned this definition of *batch* somewhat on its ear by introducing the Choice command as a means of making batch files interactive. Version 6.2 stretches the definition even further by allowing you to step through a batch file, just as you can step through CONFIG.SYS and AUTOEXEC.BAT when you press F8 for an interactive boot. To request interactive execution of a batch file, you run it with a command like this:

```
C:\>command /y /c myfile.bat
```

For more on this and other batch-related commands, refer to the topics "Command" and "Batch Commands" in the online MS-DOS Help.

Touring Edit

Edit is a full-screen, menu-based text editor, which means that, unlike a traditional MS-DOS command, it lets you work in a (fairly) colorful onscreen window like this one:

The command that starts Edit takes the following basic form:

    edit [*path*][*filename*][.*ext*]

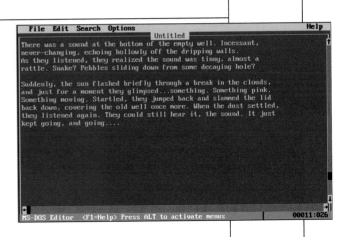

- Type just the command name, edit, to start the editor and begin creating a new file.

- Include a path, filename, and extension to do either of the following:

  - Open an existing file.

  - Assign a name to a new file-to-be. Doing this "pre-assigns" a name to a new file. If you don't want to do this, just start Edit, create your file, and name it when you want with the Save As command (described later).

A First Look

When you start Edit without specifying a filename, you see an opening screen with a number of new and possibly strange features, the most important of which are labeled and described in the illustration below. In the middle of the screen is a large message that offers to show you Edit's Survival Guide. If you accept the offer, the screen divides, as shown on the next page.

> If you specify the name of a file, be sure to include a drive and path if the file is not in the current directory. Also, remember to include the extension if the file has one. Edit, unlike application programs, does not search for a default extension; and this difference can trip you up because you're probably not accustomed to including the extension when you open or create a document file.

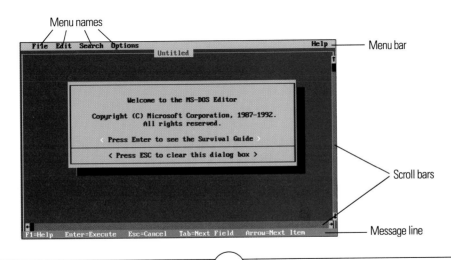

Menu names

Menu bar

Scroll bars

Message line

187

Above the editing window, labeled *Untitled*, is a second window that contains the *Survival Guide* you asked for:

The Help window can be really useful while you're becoming familiar with Edit. Ever thoughtful, Edit even allows you to keep both windows open and change their sizes as you work in one or the other:

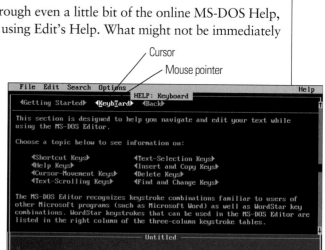

```
 File  Edit  Search  Options                                          Help
                       HELP: Survival Guide
Using the MS-DOS Editor:

   ▪ To activate the MS-DOS Editor menu bar, press Alt.
   ▪ To activate menus and commands, press the highlighted letter.
   ▪ To move between menus and commands, use the direction keys.
   ▪ To get help on a selected menu, command, or dialog box, press F1.
   ▪ To exit Help, press Esc.

Browsing the MS-DOS Editor Help system:

   ▪ To select one of the following topics, press the Tab key or the first
     letter of the topic. Then press the Enter key to see information on:

   ◄Getting Started►   Loading and using the MS-DOS Editor and the
                       MS-DOS Editor Help system
   ◄Keyboard►          Editing and navigating text and MS-DOS Editor Help

Tip: These topics are also available from the Help menu.
                            ─ Untitled ─
<F1=Help> <F6=Window> <Esc=Cancel> <Ctrl+F1=Next> <Alt+F1=Back>
```

- To move between windows with the mouse, just click in the window you want.

- To move between windows with the keyboard, press F6.

- To change the size of a window with the mouse, place the mouse pointer (actually a "mouse rectangle" in Edit) on the horizontal line across the top of the editing window and drag up or down.

- To change the size of a window with the keyboard, press Alt+Plus to expand the current window (the one containing the cursor); press Alt+Minus to make it smaller. Use the Plus and Minus keys on the numeric keypad (with NumLock either on or off). It's easier than holding down Alt and Shift and then pressing Plus in the top row of the keyboard to expand the current window.

> To get rid of Edit's Help window at any time, press Esc.

Help at Hand

If you've worked your way through even a little bit of the online MS-DOS Help, you'll have no problems at all using Edit's Help. What might not be immediately obvious, however, is that you don't have to start from the Survival Guide. If you take a look at the illustrations, you'll see that Edit offers five menus and that the one at the far right of the screen is called Help. Any time you want help:

1. Point to Help and press the left mouse button, or press Alt+H.

Cursor

Mouse pointer

```
 File  Edit  Search  Options                                          Help
                       HELP: Keyboard
 ◄Getting Started►  ◄Keyboard►  ◄Back►

This section is designed to help you navigate and edit your text while
using the MS-DOS Editor.

Choose a topic below to see information on:

   ◄Shortcut Keys►           ◄Text-Selection Keys►
   ◄Help Keys►               ◄Insert and Copy Keys►
   ◄Cursor-Movement Keys►    ◄Delete Keys►
   ◄Text-Scrolling Keys►     ◄Find and Change Keys►

The MS-DOS Editor recognizes keystroke combinations familiar to users of
other Microsoft programs (such as Microsoft Word) as well as WordStar key
combinations. WordStar keystrokes that can be used in the MS-DOS Editor are
listed in the right column of the three-column keystroke tables.
                            ─ Untitled ─

<F1=Help> <F6=Window> <Esc=Cancel> <Ctrl+F1=Next> <Alt+F1=Back>
```

2. Choose the Help category you want by pointing to the category and pressing the left mouse button. If you have no mouse, type the highlighted letter in the category name or use the arrow keys to highlight the name and then press Enter.

3. Once in a particular Help category, navigate the same way you do in the online MS-DOS Help: Click anywhere between the bright left and right arrowheads with your mouse, or use the Tab key to select any topic shown between arrowheads and then press Enter.

About Those Menus

As you no doubt know, menus are the way most full-screen, graphically oriented programs let you choose commands. Edit offers four menus other than Help: File, Edit, Search, and Options. Basically:

- The File menu includes the commands you need to start a new file (New), open an existing file (Open), save the file you're working on (Save), save and name the file you're working on (Save As), print all or part of the file you're working on (Print), and quit the editor (Exit).

- The Edit menu lets you remove selected text from a file (Cut), duplicate selected text (Copy), insert cut or copied text (Paste), or send selected text into the ozone (Clear).

- The Search menu helps you search a file for a particular string of characters (Find), repeat a search (Repeat Last Find), or both find and change a string of characters wherever they occur in the file (Change).

- The Options menu lets you customize colors and other settings (Display) and, if necessary, tell Edit where to find its Help file, EDIT.HLP, if the file is not in the current search path (Help Path).

You'll find out a little more about these commands in the rest of the chapter. And, of course, you can always use Help.

Entering Text

Practically everyone who uses a computer has used a word processor of some kind, so the basics of using Edit should be so self-evident they're laughable. Type, and the words you type appear onscreen. Backspace, and characters disappear one by one. Press Enter, and the cursor moves to a new line....

Aha. The Enter key. This is something you do need to know about, because Edit doesn't work the same way a word processor works. When you type a letter or some other document in a word processor, you know that the program takes care of line lengths for you. When a line gets too long, the program automatically moves to a new line. This is called wordwrap, and it's characteristic of word-oriented applications. Edit, as already mentioned, is not a word processor. Edit is a line-oriented program, which means that you must press Enter to create line breaks. If you don't remember to press Enter, Edit allows you to ramble for 255 characters and then suddenly stops as if it had hit a brick wall. At that point, you can decide either to press Enter right then and there—at the end of this humongous 255-character line—or (more sensibly) to back up 175 characters and *then* press Enter (to give yourself a normal 80-character line).

To create a file, use the following keys:

(Really) Basic File-Editing Keys

Use:	To:
↵ Enter	End a line... ...and start a new one.
Tab ↦	Indent a line 8 spaces. (If you like your tabs smaller or larger, use the Display command on the Options menu to change the default.)
← Backspace	Delete a character or a tab to the left of the cursor. (If more than one character is selected, as described on the facing page, delete all selected text.)
7 Home , ↵ Enter & ↑	Insert a line above the current line.
Delete	Delete the character above (at) the cursor. (If more than one character is selected, as described on the facing page, delete all selected text.)
Insert	Alternate between the default insert mode (which inserts characters into a line) and overtype mode (which replaces existing characters). You can easily tell which mode is in effect: In insert mode, the cursor is a blinking underline; in overtype mode, the cursor changes to a blinking rectangle.

Editing Text

You know that entering text is but the first step in your journey to a completed document. There's editing involved too, and that means moving around, selecting, and changing text.

To get around in a document, you can simply use the left, right, up, and down arrows, but Edit also gives you a surprising number of ways to jump around. Some additional ways to get around in a document are shown in the table at the top of the facing page:

Edit: Moving the Cursor

Use:	To:
← or →	Move left or right one character.
↑ or ↓	Move up or down one line.
Ctrl + ← or Ctrl + →	Move left or right one word.
Home	Move the cursor to the beginning of the current line (the first character if the line is indented).
End	Move the cursor to the last character of the current line.

Once you've positioned the cursor where you want it, you can insert new text simply by typing. (Be sure you haven't toggled to overtype mode with the Ins key.) You can also delete characters, beginning with the one at the cursor position, by pressing the Del key.

If you want, you can also replace or remove an entire block of text, from one word to several lines' worth. To do this, however, you must first *select* the text to act upon, and for that, you use the following keys:

Edit: Selecting Text

Use:	To:
⇧ Shift + ← or ⇧ Shift + →	Select one character to the left or right. Hold down Shift and press the left or right arrow key successive times to select more characters.
⇧ Shift + Ctrl + ← or ⇧ Shift + Ctrl + →	Select one word to the left or right. Hold down Shift and Ctrl and press the left or right arrow key successive times to select more words.
⇧ Shift + ↓	Select the *current* line and, at the same time, move the cursor to the line below the selected line. If the cursor is not at the beginning of the line, the following line is selected as well.
⇧ Shift + ↑	Select the line above the current line and, at the same time, move the cursor to the beginning of the selected line. If the cursor is not at the beginning of the line, the current line is selected as well.

Using the Clipboard

Edit comes with a special feature called the Clipboard. If you're a Microsoft Windows user, you're probably already aware that the Windows Clipboard is a place where you can store information that you want to reuse. Edit's Clipboard is much the same—it's a temporary way station for text you want to use somewhere else in your document. You can use the Clipboard for three tasks, widely known as cutting, copying, and pasting:

- Cutting is removing selected text but saving it on the Clipboard for use somewhere else in your document. To cut text, select it and either choose Cut from the Edit menu or press Shift+Del.

- Copying is duplicating selected text by copying it to the Clipboard. Copy text when you want to use that text somewhere else in the document but don't want to remove (cut) it from its current location. To copy text, select it and either choose Copy from the Edit menu or press Ctrl+Ins.

- Pasting, which applies to either cut or copied text, inserts the contents of the Clipboard into your document at the location of the cursor. To paste text into a document, cut or copy it to the Clipboard, move the cursor to where you want the text to appear, and then either choose Paste from the Edit menu or press Shift+Ins.

Saving Your File

After you go to the bother of creating or changing a file, you no doubt want to keep it on disk. Saving is easy enough, as long as you understand the difference between Save and Save As:

- Save stores a file on disk under its current name. If you're creating a file, haven't yet named it, and attempt to use Save, Edit displays a message (called a dialog box) asking for a name, as shown here:

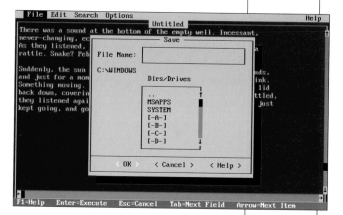

Type the name. (Don't forget the extension.) If you want to save to a different drive or directory, tab to the Dirs/Drives box and use the mouse or the up and down arrow keys to highlight what you want. To choose a different drive, press End and then use the up arrow key. (Drives are at the end of the list; End takes you directly to them.) Press Enter to change the drive or directory.

- Save As lets you assign a filename (and extension) to a file. You can use Save As either to save a new file for the first time or to save a file under a different name. When you choose Save As, Edit displays a dialog box very much like the one shown in the description of the Save command. Fill in the blanks as described.

Practice Sessions

All right, what you haven't learned about Edit by now, you should be able to figure out really easily. The remainder of this chapter shows you a few interesting ways to use Edit. First, take a look at how you can customize your Edit screen. If you want to follow along on your computer:

1. Start the machine, if necessary, and start Edit by typing:

   ```
   C:\>edit
   ```

2. Press Esc to get rid of Edit's offer to show you the Survival Guide.

3. Press Alt and then O to open the Options menu, shown at right:

4. Press Enter to choose the high-lighted command, Display. The Display dialog box appears, shown below.

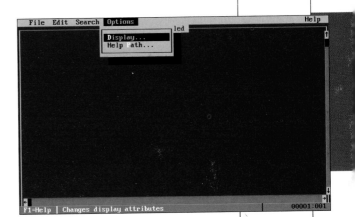

This is where you can set screen colors, turn the scroll bars on or off, and tell Edit how large you want your tabs to be. Go ahead and try it. For example, use the arrow keys to set the foreground color (your text) to blue. Press Tab, and use the arrow keys to set the background color (the window area) to cyan.

Notice that the box to the left of the color choices changes as you highlight one color after the other. Now, tab again and press the Spacebar to turn off scroll bars.

Tab once more and type 5 to set tabs to five spaces. Press Enter, and this is what you've got:

```
 File  Edit  Search  Options                                      Help
                         ▐Untitled▌
Well, it's not the prettiest screen in the world, but...




MS-DOS Editor   <F1=Help> Press ALT to activate menus        00001:05B
```

5. Use the Display command again to reset the defaults: white foreground, blue background, scroll bars on, and 8 spaces for tabs. Fun, yes?

All right, now for some serious stuff. Previous chapters have mentioned that you sometimes have to edit AUTOEXEC.BAT and CONFIG.SYS. You know now how to move around in a file, add and change text, and save. Here's how to load and take a look at these files:

1. Press Alt+F to open the File menu. Press O to choose the Open command. This is what you see:

```
 File  Edit  Search  Options                                      Help
                         Untitled
                       ─ Open ─
   File Name: █.TXT

   C:\WINDOWS
                         Files                    Dirs/Drives

      BOOTLOG.TXT
      MSWRKGRP.TXT                                 ..
      NETID.TXT                                    MSAPPS
      SETUP.TXT                                    SYSTEM
                                                   [-A-]
                                                   [-B-]
                                                   [-C-]
                                                   [-D-]
                                                   [-E-]


        < OK >          < Cancel >        < Help >

F1=Help   Enter=Execute   Esc=Cancel   Tab=Next Field   Arrow=Next Item
```

Notice that Edit proposes TXT as the default extension. That is, indeed, the extension it goes looking for by default. You must still, however, type an extension—even TXT—when you save or open a file in the MS-DOS Editor.

2. In this case, you want to take a look at AUTOEXEC.BAT or CONFIG.SYS. Tell Edit to open AUTOEXEC.BAT (generally easier than CONFIG.SYS to understand). In the File Name box, which should contain the cursor, type:

```
c:\autoexec.bat
```

The drive and path aren't necessary if the root directory of drive C is the current directory, but what the heck. Include them anyway, just to be sure you specify the correct location. Press Enter. A second or two later, AUTOEXEC.BAT appears in the editing window. Don't do anything to it. You're just looking.

3. To put AUTOEXEC.BAT back to bed and prepare for the next exercise, press Alt, F, and N to tell Edit you've finished with this file and want to work with a new one. Because you haven't made any changes to AUTOEXEC.BAT, the screen clears without a hitch.

As a final exercise, edit your CONFIG.SYS file to load ANSI.SYS, and then create two small batch files that shift your screen between 25-line mode and 43-line mode. Here's what to do:

1. Use the Open command on the File menu (Alt, F, O), type c:\config.sys, and press Enter to open your CONFIG.SYS file.

2. After the file has appeared, scan it to see whether it contains the line DEVICE=C:\DOS\ANSI.SYS. If it does, you don't have to make any changes, so just save the file again. If the line doesn't appear, press Ctrl+End to move the cursor to the end of the file. Type:

```
DEVICE=C:\DOS\ANSI.SYS
```

(Substitute the name of your MS-DOS directory if it is not \DOS.)

3. All right, now save the changed file: Press Alt, F, and S.

4. To create the first of your batch files, press Alt, F, and N to prepare for a new file. Now type:

```
@echo off
mode con lines=43
cls
```

The line @echo off at the beginning keeps the lines of your batch file from being displayed as the batch file runs. You know what the other commands do.

5. All right, save the file. Press Alt, F, and A (the Save As command), and type:

```
c:\43.bat
```

when Edit asks for a filename.

6. Now, create the batch file that will return your screen to the default 25-line mode. Press Alt, F, and N, and then type:

```
@echo off
mode con lines=25
cls
```

7. You're done. Press Alt, F, and A, and save the file as c:\25.bat.

8. To quit Edit, press Alt, F, and X.

If you changed your CONFIG.SYS and created these two batch files, you can put everything to work by restarting your computer (so that the new command in CONFIG.SYS will take effect). Afterward, to switch to 43-line mode, simply type:

```
C:\>43
```

To change back to 25-line mode, type:

```
C:\>25
```

Have fun.

If you followed the example that changed your CONFIG.SYS, you'll be glad to know you're not stuck with ANSI.SYS forever. To get rid of it, edit your CONFIG.SYS file again. Either select and delete the line or, if you think you might have a use for ANSI.SYS later on, place the cursor at the beginning of the line and then type a semicolon (;). The ; character tells MS-DOS to ignore the command. Using a semicolon is a nice way of neutralizing CONFIG.SYS commands (some of which can be pretty complex) without actually deleting them from the file.

4 Special Effects

Physical Fitness with ScanDisk and Defrag

Disk Aerobics

If you'd never in your life exercised anything more than the finger that controls your TV remote, you wouldn't jump into a fitness program without first making sure you could handle the strain. Where your computer is concerned, you should have the same basic consideration for your disk drives—those mechanical marvels that work harder than most parts of the system, yet carry the responsibility of ensuring that all your programs and data remain safe, sound, and sacrosanct.

MS-DOS, in version 6.2, gives you two tools (three if you count the now obsolete Check Disk) to examine, repair, and otherwise keep your disk drives in fine fettle. Whether you're interested in a routine checkup or a complete physical, ScanDisk and Defrag are there when you need them—ready to check out your disk drives for reliability (Scan-Disk) and to optimize storage on them for efficient performance (Defrag).

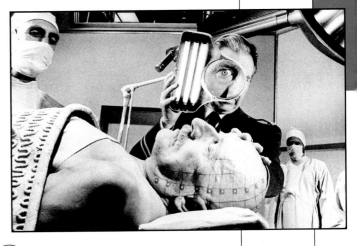

Concern for the health of your disk drives is particularly important if you're planning to use DoubleSpace. Of all the parts of MS-DOS, Double-Space is the one that exercises your disk drives the hardest, so it's important for you to understand that disk reliability, clean file storage, and disk compression go hand in hand. In fact, version 6.2 of DoubleSpace considers both ScanDisk and Defrag so important that it runs them automatically while compressing a disk. The reason: to provide an extra measure of protection for your data and to guarantee that DoubleSpace works only with neatly organized disks that can handle the load.

ScanDisk, Defrag, and File Storage

Although you don't have to know anything at all about disk storage in order to use ScanDisk and Defrag, this is one part of using MS-DOS in which it helps to know at least the basics—specifically, it helps to know about bad clusters on disks and about file fragmentation.

Bad Clusters

Bad spots, which ScanDisk calls "bad clusters," are parts of the disk surface that contain areas (sectors) that are physically not reliable enough to hold either your programs or your data. Why are these sectors bad? Sometimes because the disk has been damaged at that particular location or has worn out over time. Other times, the spot was flawed when the disk was made. Regardless of the reason, ScanDisk considers these spots too risky to hold information and refuses to let MS-DOS store information in them.

Now, before you get all excited, note that bad sectors are not necessarily an indication that a disk is unusable. Many reliable disks, including hard disks, function truly and well despite a few bad sectors here and there. After all, nothing's perfect. Is your skin absolutely flawless? Didn't think so.

What you do have to know, however, is that if ScanDisk reports that a disk has a large number of bad clusters, you have to take the report seriously. Such a report definitely indicates that a disk is flawed and very likely unreliable. If the disk is a floppy, throw it out so that you don't mistakenly use it later on to hold a valuable file. If the disk is a hard disk, back up your important files and run ScanDisk everyday. If the disk gets worse, take it to your dealer. Although you probably won't like hearing this, your dealer will most likely tell you to replace the disk.

Do not attempt to run DoubleSpace on a disk with a lot of bad clusters just because you want to cram a little bit more data on it or because you'd like to get a little more use out of it.

File Fragmentation

Aside from detecting bad spots, ScanDisk can also examine the way files are actually stored on a disk. When it does this, it looks at many aspects of file storage, including misplaced file segments and a condition known as file fragmentation. Errors in file storage are matters that you leave to ScanDisk, both for finding and for fixing. File fragmentation, however, is something you use ScanDisk to find and Defrag to fix.

In order to understand file fragmentation and what it means to you, you have to know a little about how files are stored on disk and how MS-DOS can unfailingly find exactly the file you want when you want it. A key term here is *clusters*. You've learned that MS-DOS divides a disk into tracks and sectors. A cluster is nothing more than a bunch of sectors—two, four, maybe more—that MS-DOS treats as a unit when storing your files. You don't ever have to think about clusters in your day-to-day dealings with your system, but the way that MS-DOS stores information in clusters is directly related to file fragmentation.

File fragmentation occurs naturally over time as MS-DOS saves and deletes files. To picture fragmentation and how it happens, imagine a newly formatted disk, floppy or hard. MS-DOS "sees" storage on this disk as a chain of clusters rather like a train of empty tank cars waiting to be filled. When you tell MS-DOS to save a file on this disk, what does it do? It goes out, takes a look, says to itself "wow, space galore," and pops the file into the first available clusters on the disk. The result is just like using the first few tank cars in the train to hold the milk from 5000 cows.

Time passes, and you save other files on the disk. The storage space fills up—here, with a file that needs 5 clusters, there with a file that needs 25. Until the disk is full, MS-DOS can go on pouring your files into one cluster after the other without a hitch, just as if it were pouring the milk from different-sized cow herds into successive tank cars. But you don't always *add* files to a disk. You *delete* them, too. And what happens then? Each time you delete a file, a "hole" opens up—a hole that matches the number and position of the clusters formerly used to hold that file. Over time, holes open up here and there on the disk.

MS-DOS, economical soul that it is, recycles those holes by filling them with new files you save. But because files vary in size, MS-DOS can't always find a hole that's the exact size of a new file it's saving. So MS-DOS saves different portions of the file in different holes (clusters or groups of clusters), some of which can be far apart on the disk surface. On a busy, well-used disk, more and more files are broken apart over time and stored in discontinuous sets of clusters. That's fragmentation.

In and of itself, fragmentation is not dangerous: MS-DOS is a most reliable recordkeeper, and barring storage problems caused by a faulty disk or a badly behaved program, it can always find the pieces of a file, no matter how fragmented the file is. Fragmentation can affect you, however, if you find that your disk is working overtime and taking longer to find files or, in version 6.2, if you try to run DoubleSpace and it tells you the disk is too fragmented to compress.

Now, with that background firmly in place, it's on to ScanDisk and Defrag.

Checkup and Repair with ScanDisk

You use ScanDisk whenever you want to check on file storage, fragmentation, or physical bad spots on a disk. ScanDisk works on both DoubleSpaced and uncompressed hard and floppy disks, as well as on RAM drives and memory cards. It does not work on CD-ROM, network, or Interlnk drives.

Basically, ScanDisk performs a two-part disk checkup: It looks for problems with file storage, and then, if you choose, it charges into a surface scan. The file-storage checkup is quick. The surface scan takes longer because it involves a thorough check for bad clusters.

POWER PLAY

Bad Clusters, Good Information?

When ScanDisk encounters a bad cluster, it often finds that one or more of the sectors in the cluster (usually 512-byte chunks) are damaged, rather than the entire cluster. To safeguard the information in that cluster, ScanDisk moves as much information as it can to another, completely reliable cluster. Unfortunately, however, ScanDisk cannot always recover the information occupying the actual bad sector(s) within the cluster. When ScanDisk can't recover information, it replaces that part of the file with zeros. Thus, after ScanDisk reports that it has patched a bad spot on your disk, you might find that a file contains zeros where it used to contain information. If ScanDisk replaces part of a program file, you'll probably have to reinstall the program. If it replaces part of a data file, you'll have to rely on your own memory or a backup copy to repair the damage. Whatever you do, don't blame ScanDisk. The disk itself was flawed.

Checkup

During the file-storage check, you'll see that ScanDisk checks some pretty exotic-sounding places:

- On a non-DoubleSpaced disk, it checks out the media descriptor, file allocation tables, directory structure (ah, that at least sounds familiar), and the file system. While ScanDisk is doing all this checking, you see a screen like this one:

```
Microsoft ScanDisk

ScanDisk is now checking the following areas of drive C:
    √    Media descriptor
    √    File allocation tables
    »    Directory structure
         File system
         Surface scan




   < Pause >    < More Info >    < Exit >

C:\DOS
```

- On a DoubleSpaced disk, the checkup list gets longer, in part because the program recommends checking two drives: the noncompressed "host" of the compressed drive and the actual compressed drive. (For more on this, refer to the chapter "Grow Your Disks with DoubleSpace.") During the

check of the compressed drive, ScanDisk surveys a number of items even more exotic-sounding than those it looks at on an uncompressed drive. These include, but are not limited to, a DoubleSpace file header, DoubleSpace file allocation table, compression structure, and volume signatures. During a check of a DoubleSpaced drive, ScanDisk shows you this:

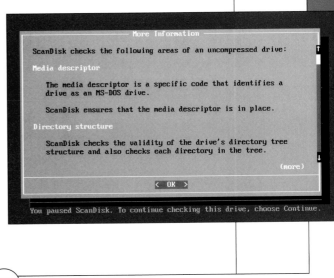

Whew! As you can see, there's a lot going on. Relax and don't worry.

Oh, if you're the curious type and you want to know at least a little about these lists, take advantage of the buttons marked Pause and More Info (shown in the earlier illustrations). While ScanDisk is running:

1. Press P or click the Pause button to stop the action for a while. (This is actually optional when you want information, but choosing Pause seems like the polite thing to do.)

2. Press M or click More Info. When you do, ScanDisk displays a More Information box that describes what the program is currently doing:

3. When you've seen enough, press Enter or click OK to return to the main screen.

4. If you paused ScanDisk, press C or click Continue to let ScanDisk get on with the job.

Problem Found (and what to do about it)

Your relationship with ScanDisk will mostly be as smooth as sailing on a calm sea, especially if you use high-quality disks. Squalls and tempests do arise, however, so you shouldn't be too surprised (if not exactly delighted) to find that someday ScanDisk does tell you it found a problem during a check of file storage or during a surface scan. If the problem emerges while ScanDisk is checking storage, the culprit is generally some "glitch" that caused an error in the way the file's storage locations on disk were noted in one of the master indexes (FAT and others) that MS-DOS and DoubleSpace use to save and retrieve files accurately. If the problem comes to light during a surface scan, part of the disk surface itself is either damaged or close enough to failure that it shouldn't be used for storage.

Disk errors of any kind make most people uncomfortable enough to rate a fairly detailed explanation, so here goes.

Storage Errors

Your first indication of trouble in River City comes as ScanDisk is ticking off the various items it checks during a look at file storage. If it encounters a problem in any of these areas, it displays a message telling you what's wrong and giving you a choice of options, including asking for More Info, as shown in the screen at right:

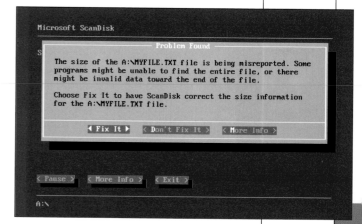

Because disk errors can be serious, make it a habit to choose More Info in these situations. You'll get quite a bit of background information that can help you decide what to do next. For example, the More Info screen that appears when you choose it from the above screen looks like this:

What now? Well, chances are you want to fix the problem, so here's what you do next:

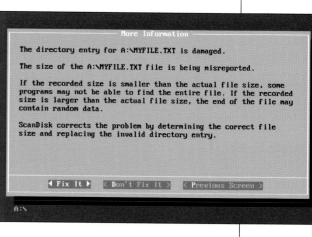

1. If you see a Fix It button, choose it. If, as happens when ScanDisk finds lost clusters, you see Save and Delete buttons, use the instructions from the More Info box to choose whichever is more appropriate.

2. The first time you choose to fix a problem during a scan, ScanDisk asks whether you want to create an Undo disk, as shown here:

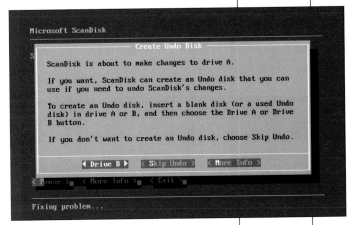

This isn't a bad idea. Even though creating the Undo disk adds a little time to the fix-it process, the disk itself gives you a way to put things back as they were if the repair turns out to be worse than the ailment (resulting, for example, in lost data or a program that misbehaves).

3. If you choose to create an Undo disk, place a blank floppy disk (or a previously used Undo disk) in drive A or B. Choose the button labeled with the drive containing your Undo disk (for example, the button labeled *Drive B* in the screen above).

4. From this point on, ScanDisk takes over and makes any necessary repairs.

5. At the end of the process, ScanDisk by default asks whether you want to continue into a surface scan. Consider doing this if ScanDisk has been fixing errors. Better safe than sorry.

6. When everything's done, surface scan and all, ScanDisk reports on all the problems it found and fixed on the disk:

Notice the buttons at the bottom of the screen. Choose the More Info button to find out what kinds of errors ScanDisk fixed, and how.

7. Optional, but recommended (especially for a hard disk): Choose the View Log button to see a log file detailing all the errors and fixes ScanDisk performed for that disk. After you've scanned the log, choose the Save Log button to store a copy in the root directory of your hard disk. (If the log already exists, choose Append to add to it or choose Overwrite to replace the old log with the new one.)

8. Exit ScanDisk.

If any of the fixes affected program files or valuable data files, run the program(s) and take a look at the data files immediately. If you encounter any problems:

- Either replace the file with an undamaged copy from an original program disk or a backup disk.

- Or use the Undo disk immediately to back out of the changes. Remember, however, that you can use this disk *only* if you have not changed the disk that you repaired in any way. If you're going to use the Undo disk, do it right away. This is important.

Finally, if you were good and chose the More Info button as ScanDisk fixed errors, you've probably got some other recommendations from ScanDisk to follow up on. Do so. For example, if ScanDisk found lost clusters—little orphans unattached to any other files on the disk—the More Info screen told you that those clusters could be gathered into a file with a name such as FILE0000.CHK. The screen also told you that if you decided to save those clusters you should use the Type command to see what kind of information was in them and use Delete to get rid of FILE0000.CHK if the information is useless (probably) or unusable (likely).

Hot Patching

And now what happens if ScanDisk finds no problems with your file storage *but* you continue on to a surface scan and it finds one or more bad spots on a disk? Again, it asks if you want to fix them. If you say "I do," ScanDisk swings into a process known as hot patching or hot fixing, which sounds a little like resurfacing a street or a roof. Actually, it involves moving all recoverable information out of the damaged cluster and then marking the cluster as "bad" (literally). What happens? Well, you see pretty much the same types of messages you do when ScanDisk fixes storage errors, but the order in which they appear differs slightly. Here is how it goes:

1. First, you see a message, briefly displayed, that tells you ScanDisk is *gathering information it needs to safeguard the contents* of the drive.

2. This message is quickly followed by a Problem Found dialog box that, like the one shown earlier, gives you a choice of fixing, not fixing, or getting More Info. Once again, opt for More Info. Your disk's at stake, after all, and when ScanDisk fixes bad clusters, there's some extra incentive: The More Info screen is the only way you're going to find out which files are affected by the damage.

Because some storage errors cause problems in more than one of the areas ScanDisk checks, don't be surprised if your one problem produces one or more additional Problem Found dialog boxes. Your disk isn't necessarily going to pot. It's much more likely that ScanDisk is simply being thorough and fixing everything related to a single—and not always serious—storage problem. Choose the More Info button for each error, make note of any instructions you find there, and continue.

3. When you choose More Info, you see a message like this:

   Make note of the directory and filename. If ScanDisk finds more than one bad cluster in its surface scan, make note of every directory and filename it tells you about in the More Information dialog box.

4. After you check out More Info, choose Fix It to fix the problem or (unlikely) Don't Fix It to ignore the situation.

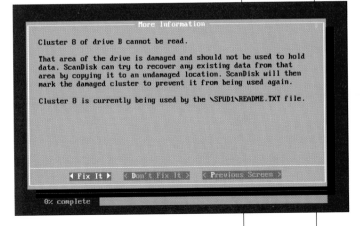

5. If you've chosen Fix It for the first time, ScanDisk asks whether you want to create an Undo disk. Patching the disk being scanned will take longer if you choose to create an Undo disk, but the disk itself will be good, if temporary, insurance. Remember, the Undo disk must be a blank floppy or a used Undo disk that fits in either drive A or drive B.

6. When all patching is complete, ScanDisk displays a message that tells you three important things: to back up the disk as quickly as possible, to run ScanDisk often (until your confidence is restored), and to have the drive checked if more errors occur. To finish up, ScanDisk then displays a message telling you how many bad clusters were patched.

7. Once again, before you leave thinking all's now right with the world, choose the View Log button at the bottom of the ending screen. If the disk you scanned is your hard disk, choose the Save Log button. Later on, you might find the log useful in comparing where, how, and to what extent your hard disk seems to be encountering problems.

If you chose to create an Undo disk, check the file or files that occupied bad clusters right after ScanDisk finishes fixing your disk. If the affected file is a program file, run the program. If the affected file is a data file, try to load the file into the application that created it. If you have any problems, replace the file with a new, undamaged copy (either from an original program disk or from a backup disk). If replacing the file is out of the question, use the Undo disk to restore the patched disk to its former state, but remember you must do so immediately. As soon as you change the repaired disk's files or directories—even with so small a change as saving or deleting a 10-byte file—your Undo disk will be unusable.

CLOSE THOSE FILES

Do not run ScanDisk on a disk that has any open files. In addition, avoid running ScanDisk from any active program or from Microsoft Windows or (if you use it) the MS-DOS Shell when the Task Swapper is active. For ScanDisk to do its work properly—meaning without risk of data loss—the disk you check must be unchanging, and all files on it must be neatly closed and put away. The only time you can ignore this warning is when you use the /c switch, described in the text. As a rule of thumb, however, make it a habit to run ScanDisk only when you're not running other programs, and only from the MS-DOS (not Windows, not MS-DOS Shell) command prompt.

Undoing hot patching means that ScanDisk completely restores the earlier state of the disk. In other words, bad clusters regain their reputations as reliable data holders. Make the Undo disk if you want, but think before using it.

207

Now. Knowing how ScanDisk works, how do you start this miraculous program? In any of several ways, depending on what you want to accomplish.

For a Complete Checkup

To give a disk a complete physical, including a surface scan, use the following form of the ScanDisk command:

```
scandisk [drive:] /s
```

drive is the letter of the drive you want to check. You can specify more than one drive if you want by separating drive letters with spaces (scandisk a: c:), or you can omit the drive letter if you want to check the current drive (scandisk).

/s (or /surface) tells ScanDisk to swing right into a surface scan as soon as it finishes checking file storage (which is always the first part of a disk scan).

By default, if you don't include the /s switch, ScanDisk stops after checking file storage and asks whether you also want a surface scan:

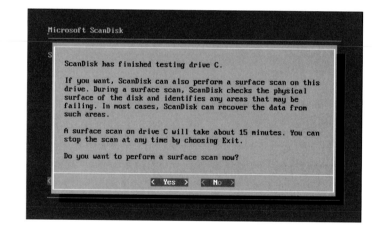

Do request a surface scan if you've never performed a complete scan on a disk, especially your hard disk. By default (meaning if you don't use the /autofix switch described in the next section), ScanDisk also asks what to do if it finds storage errors on the disk. If you read the previous pages, you know what to do.

For Repair Work on Files and Directories

The easiest way to go about repairing storage errors is to let ScanDisk prompt for guidance. If you prefer, however, you can use one of three other options—the /all, /autofix, and /nosave switches—to control how ScanDisk goes about its repair work. The command form is as follows:

```
scandisk [drive:] /all /autofix /nosave
```

If you want ScanDisk to patch bad clusters with a minimum of prompting, use the /s switch with the /autofix switch described in the next part of this chapter. Normally, /autofix fixes file-related errors. When used with /s, however, it causes ScanDisk to assume you want bad clusters patched, too. Bear in mind, however, that if you use /s and /autofix, ScanDisk will not give you the option of choosing the More Info button to find out what files occupy the bad clusters, and you will therefore not know which of your files might contain strings of zeros in place of information ScanDisk was unable to recover from badly damaged sectors. Your choice: speed or thoroughness.

drive is, as usual, the drive to scan and repair. You can, if you choose, specify more than one drive by separating the drive specifications with spaces. If you specify more than one drive in the same command, ScanDisk pauses after checking storage on the first disk and asks whether you want to continue with a surface scan. Whatever decision you make about a surface scan then applies to all other disks you specified. After checking each disk, ScanDisk displays a report and waits until you choose the Next Drive button at the bottom of the screen before moving on to the next.

/all, which you can type as /al, applies the scan and repair to all nonremovable drives (hard disks and RAM drives) on the computer. If you want to scan both floppy and hard disks, specify the drive letters instead of using this switch.

/autofix, which you can type as /au, tells ScanDisk to fix storage errors without prompting. When you use this switch, ScanDisk just forges ahead and presents you with a done deal at the end. If it finds errors it will, however, pause to ask whether you want to create an Undo disk.

/nosave, which you can (yuk) type as /nosa, tells ScanDisk to delete lost clusters instead of saving them in a FILE000.CHK file. This switch is a timesaver, but using it does mean that you don't have a chance to look at the contents of any lost clusters ScanDisk finds. (The loss is usually not particularly significant.)

When you repair errors, remember that ScanDisk does allow you to create an Undo disk, which you can use in the event that you have to reverse the repairs it makes. Also remember, however, that as soon as you change anything about the files stored on the disk you repaired, your Undo disk is history.

To put an Undo disk to work, however, this is the form of the ScanDisk command you need:

```
scandisk /undo [drive:]
```

where *drive* is the drive—either A or B—containing the Undo disk. Follow the instructions ScanDisk displays.

For a Quick Checkup

After you've checked a disk thoroughly, there's no need to spend large amounts of time checking it again and again. It does help, however, to be able to give that disk a "quick and dirty" scan every so often to be sure it's still functioning just fine and that no storage problems have crept in. To do this, you use ScanDisk in the form:

```
scandisk [drive:] /checkonly
```

Here, *drive* is, again, the letter (followed by a colon) of the drive containing the disk to scan. Omit the drive letter if you want to scan the current drive, or include multiple drives by separating their designations with spaces. The /checkonly switch, which can also be entered as /ch, tells ScanDisk to check out file storage and directories, but not to fix any errors it finds.

The /checkonly switch essentially tells ScanDisk to carry out the first part of the checkup described earlier. Because it's a good way to keep yourself current on the state of your disks, consider adding the command to your AUTOEXEC.BAT file so that your boot disk is automatically checked whenever you start or restart the computer. If you add this command to AUTOEXEC.BAT, the command looks like this:

```
scandisk /ch
```

When you run ScanDisk with the /checkonly switch, the program reports errors but doesn't automatically fix them or prompt for instructions on what to do with them. If ScanDisk does find errors, rerun the command either in its simplest form (scandisk [*drive*:]) or with the /s switch.

Checking for Fragmentation

And now you come to fragmentation, which will serve nicely as a lead-in to Defrag. To check for file fragmentation, use ScanDisk in the form:

```
scandisk /f file-specification
```

where *file-specification* represents the drive, path, filename, and extension of the file or files you want to check. You can use wildcards with this switch to check a group of files in a particular directory. You cannot use wildcards to check an entire disk—check one directory at a time.

When you check a disk for fragmentation, ScanDisk does not display its usual colorful self. True to its MS-DOS (and Check Disk) ancestry, it displays its results in the same way Directory, Mem, and other MS-DOS commands do— as text output, as shown here:

```
C:\>scandisk /f *.*
COMMAND.COM contains 6 noncontiguous blocks.
```

If none of the files you specified are fragmented, ScanDisk tells you that:

```
All specified file(s) are contiguous.
```

in which case, you have nothing to worry about. If you do find that a lot of files on a disk are fragmented, however, especially if DoubleSpace tells you the disk is too fragmented to compress, then it's on to Defrag.

If you use the /checkonly switch to check more than one disk, watch the screen. You'll have to choose the Next Drive button to continue when ScanDisk finishes checking each disk.

If you're going to use MemMaker to optimize memory use on your system, add the ScanDisk command to AUTOEXEC.BAT after you've run MemMaker. You'll shorten the amount of time MemMaker takes. (Remember that Mem-Maker reboots your system a couple of times.) Besides, when you run Mem-Maker, it's a good idea to disable all but the necessary commands in AUTOEXEC.BAT. Some commands, especially those that run other batch files, can cause problems for MemMaker.

POWER PLAY

Custom Control

This part of the chapter is really for experienced computer users who understand a fair amount about MS-DOS file storage and are comfortable editing startup files. If you fall in that category, take note of ScanDisk's /custom switch, which works with a file named SCANDISK.INI to let you customize the way disk scans are performed—even from within a batch file. SCANDISK.INI is a long file, filled with comments that explain how it is put together and how you can change settings to control the way ScanDisk works when you use the /custom switch. Here's what part of the file looks like:

```
# SCANDISK.INI
#
# This file contains settings you can use to customize the ScanDisk program.
#
# -------------------------------------------------------------------
# The [ENVIRONMENT] section contains the following settings, which
# determine general aspects of ScanDisk's behavior:
#
# Display      Configures ScanDisk to run with a particular type of
#              display. The default display type is Auto (ScanDisk
#              adjusts to the current display).
#
# Mouse        Enables or disables mouse support. The default value is On.
#
# ScanTimeOut  Determines whether ScanDisk should detect disk timeouts
#              while performing a surface scan. The default value is On.
#
# NumPasses    Determines how many times ScanDisk should check each
#              cluster during a surface scan. The default value is 1.
#
# LabelCheck   Determines whether ScanDisk should check volume labels
#              for invalid characters.  The default is Off.
#
[ENVIRONMENT]
   Display     = Auto   # Auto, Mono, Color, Off
```

To modify SCANDISK.INI, load it into the MS-DOS Editor (or another text editor). As you can see from the sample, the file contains numerous comments, so read through it before you start tangling with the details. When you're ready, edit the section headed [CUSTOM], changing the default settings to those you want. For example, if you want ScanDisk always to add to an existing log, and you don't want it to prompt for an Undo disk, you would change the following lines from this:

```
    SaveLog     = Off          ;Off, Append, Overwrite
    Undo        = Prompt       ;Prompt, Never
```

to this:

```
    SaveLog     = Append       ;Off, Append, Overwrite
    Undo        = Never        ;Prompt, Never
```

Save the edited file when you're done.

To make ScanDisk use your chosen settings, use it with the /custom switch (which you can shorten to /cu), either from the command prompt or from within a batch file:

```
    scandisk /custom
```

When you run Check Disk, you see a report ending with a suggestion that you use ScanDisk instead of Check Disk. This is good advice if you're concerned about the shape your disk is in, but don't let this message make you think Check Disk has been outlawed. It's still a fast and easy way to find out how much space you have on a disk.

Getting in Shape with Defrag

Defrag, which started life as a Symantec/Peter Norton utility, has one job to do: optimize physical disk storage. That means arranging files neatly on a disk, head to tail, end to end. Like ScanDisk, Defrag should never be used when Microsoft Windows or the MS-DOS Shell's Task Swapper is running, and for the same reason—possible loss of data. Enough said about that.

Although Defrag in action resembles the surface-scanning part of ScanDisk, Defrag is a lot more like MSBackup and other windowed MS-DOS utilities in the sense that it lets you choose what you want to do from menus of commands. Although you can use a number of command line options and switches to tell Defrag how to run, the easiest way to use this utility is to stick to a very basic command form:

```
defrag [drive:]
```

drive being the drive that you want to optimize. Omit a drive letter if you want to defragment the current drive.

When you start Defrag, it begins by taking a few seconds to check your computer's memory. If you didn't specify a drive to defragment, the program then asks you to choose a drive, as shown here:

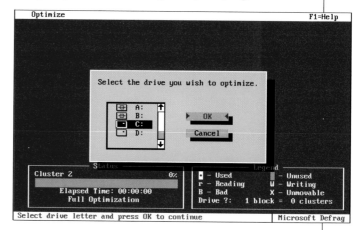

Next (assume a non-DoubleSpaced drive here) Defrag goes to the disk, reads and analyzes its file-storage information, and then presents you with one of three recommendations:

> **Defrag is mostly for uncompressed drives. If you specify a compressed drive—a floppy, for example—Defrag won't choke, it will hand the task over to DoubleSpace. You're in no danger if you accidentally tell Defrag to optimize a compressed drive, but don't be surprised to see Defrag tell you it's subcontracting the job.**

- If the drive is in fine shape, Defrag tells you *No optimization necessary*.

- If the drive needs some cleanup, but not a lot, Defrag recommends that you *Unfragment Files Only*.

- If the drive could use a lot of TLC, Defrag suggests a *Full Optimization*.

All right, no optimization is easy to understand, but what's the difference between unfragmenting files only and a full optimization?

Half a Loaf or the Whole Thing?

Unfragmenting files is very fast and is essentially the same as choosing half a loaf. A full optimization takes much longer, but you end up with the disk equivalent of a complete makeover.

When it unfragments files, Defrag consolidates fragmented files, but it doesn't do all the fine-tuning that you get with a full optimization. You end up with gaps between files, and with your directories untouched, but that's OK. If Defrag determines that a disk needs unfragmenting only, go with the flow and accept the recommendation. It's fast and effective.

When it performs a full optimization, Defrag not only consolidates fragmented files, it physically moves directories to the front (beginning of disk storage) and moves all gaps between files to the back (end of disk storage) to minimize the amount of work and head movement required of your disk drive. Because so much happens, a full optimization can take a long time, as in hours. If a disk needs full optimization, you're well advised to do it, but wait until a time you won't be needing the computer for a while. It's always a good idea to optimize a badly fragmented disk, but this doesn't fall into the "emergency" category. "Soon" will do fine.

Everything Else You Need to Know About Defrag

It's not much, and what you need you can easily get from Defrag's online help, which you can request either by clicking F1=Help at the top of the screen or by pressing F1.

To choose a topic, highlight it and press Enter, or point to it and press the right mouse button.

And what about Defrag's one and only other menu, Optimize? That one's easy, too.

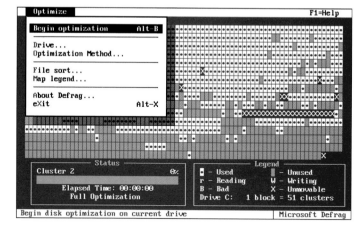

The first option, Begin Optimization, starts the defragmenting process. You don't need this if you accept Defrag's recommendation after it analyzes your disk's storage:

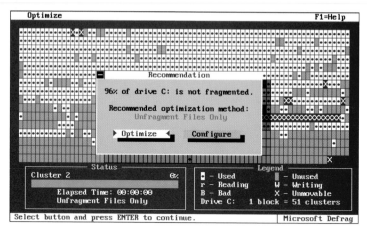

By the way, if you choose to defragment a DoubleSpaced drive, you'll find that Defrag opens the Optimize menu with the highlight on Begin Optimization when DoubleSpace finishes working with the compressed drive. You don't want to begin anything at this point, so choose eXit instead. The important work already happened—when Defrag temporarily returned you to MS-DOS with the message:

```
Please wait
Now starting the DoubleSpace program
to defragment your compressed drive
```

That's when DoubleSpace picked up the ball, defragmented and remounted the drive, and then returned you to Defrag. Clever and cooperative programs, they are.

The rest of the options on the Optimize menu are:

- Drive, which lets you choose a drive to optimize (if you change your mind about the one you specified or want to optimize another).

- Optimization Method, which lets you choose between a full optimization and unfragmenting files only. (This really applies only to disks needing full optimization.)

- File Sort, which lets you decide how you want filenames sorted within each directory. (The File Sort criteria are shown at right.) Bear in mind, however, that this option simply lets you choose how to sort filenames. It does not affect the way files are physically positioned on the disk.

- Map Legend, which tells you pretty much the same things you see in the lower right corner of the Defrag window.

- About Defrag, which displays copyright information.

- Exit, which leaves Defrag.

Oh, yes. You'd probably like to have a clear view of what Defrag looks like when it's working. Here it is:

This book can't show it, but this is a lively display because Defrag moves those clusters around to show you what's going on. The effect is not unlike watching one of those speeded-up movies of a house being built or, maybe, the activity in an anthill. Enjoy it. After all, your computer won't be usable for a while anyway....

Foil the Bad Guys with Anti-Virus and Vsafe

Viruses vs. Bugs

When the disease of the month starts floating around your school or office, everyone begins to talk about "the virus" or "the bug" that's going around. Viruses and bugs both live in computer terminology too. If you've read one or two newspaper or newsmagazine articles about viruses of the computer kind, you know that they're "bad" programs that can somehow infect the machines with which they come in contact. But if you're going to talk about computers, viruses, and the people who get their kicks from infecting helpless hard disks, you've got to be clear on the difference between a virus and a bug. They're very different things, even though both conjure mental images of crawly critters.

A virus, as the magazines say, is a bad program. It's one that is deliberately created, has a particular name associated with it, and is designed to be sneaky and probably antisocial as well. A bug, by contrast, is far from deliberate. It's an error in a program that causes a miscalculation in a spreadsheet, or it's faulty code that causes your database to lock up. A bug is nameless; it was never meant to be. However, a bug, like a virus, can range in effect from irritating to potentially destructive. The big difference is that a bug is accidental. A virus is not. Bugs should be reported to the program's developers. Viruses should be shot down with Microsoft Anti-Virus and its companion, Vsafe.

217

Too Much Hype, or Too Much Risk?

In theory, someone could create a good virus, something that would roam the promised "information superhighway," seeking out and destroying bad viruses. In real life, viruses are not so noble. Some, admittedly, are designed by their creators to be harmless, "fun" things that do nothing worse than play pranks—displaying, for example, extremely literate messages of the "ha ha, gotcha" variety. Viruses of this type, electronic graffiti, are nuisances that reflect badly on their designers' upbringing and social skills. Other viruses, however, are darker and more dangerous. These are the viruses that attack programs and hard disks. Many destroy data, damage (corrupt) program files so that they will no longer run, or interfere with the operation of the computer. In extreme instances, some

such viruses alter critical startup information on a hard disk or even reformat the disk, destroying everything stored on it. Here, see for yourself:

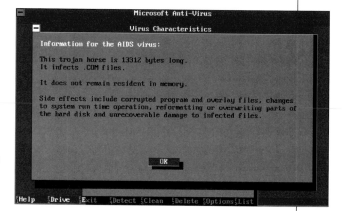

Cute, isn't it?

But knowing that some viruses are really menacing is only part of being educated about this subject. The other part is knowing how much

you are truly at risk. This is sometimes difficult to determine, but your computing habits play a big role, just as your living habits play a large role in your present and future health. If, for example, your computer never connects via modem to another computer, you never install anything but shrink-wrapped, bought-and-paid-for software, and you never move programs from one computer to another, then the chance of infecting your computer is very small. The chance does still exist, because viruses can invade legitimate software too, but the risk of infection is remote.

On the other hand, if you freely exchange programs with your friends, gladly accept bootleg software (shame on you), and connect to all kinds of other systems, your chances of infection are much greater. Why? Because viruses attach themselves to program files in order to infect disks and move from one computer to another, and the more you encounter programs that have traveled around, the greater your likelihood of encountering a virus. If you connect to large online services and networks, you don't have much to worry about because these are carefully monitored for viruses, but the same isn't always true of smaller bulletin boards and is probably not true of the friend with whom you telecommunicate every evening.

Generally speaking, then, you can evaluate your own chances of infection by taking a look at how you transfer programs, and with whom. Face it. The parallel between virus-free computing and virus-free living is striking. But, of course, even the most careful person can get the flu, and even the most carefully managed computer can pick up a virus. To check for and deal with viruses that might already be hidden on a disk, you use Microsoft Anti-Virus; to guard against future infection, Vsafe is it.

The Virus Hunter: Microsoft Anti-Virus

Microsoft Anti-Virus is the Sherlock Holmes of virus protection. Turn it loose on your hard disk (or on any new floppy disks), and Anti-Virus will track down and destroy any of hundreds of known viruses. Anti-Virus works by detecting changes in program files. In keeping with its Holmesian nature, it can even search for evidence of so-called Stealth viruses—extremely sneaky viruses that infect program files without seeming to make any changes to them.

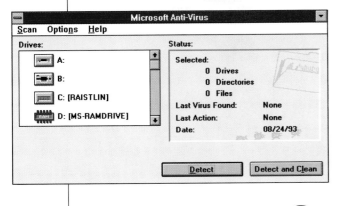

Version 6 of MS-DOS supports two forms of the Anti-Virus program: one that runs under MS-DOS and one that runs under Microsoft Windows. The two versions are almost identical, but given Windows' greater graphics talent, the Windows-based version of Anti-Virus is prettier, as you can see by comparing their opening screens.

To avoid confusion, the text from this point on will call the MS-DOS–based version just plain Anti-Virus and will call the Windows-based version Windows Anti-Virus.

> **Microsoft Anti-Virus is controlled by several files in your \DOS directory. If you use the MS-DOS version of Anti-Virus, the files you need start with letters *MSAV*. If you use the Windows version of Anti-Virus, the files start with the letters *MWAV*.**

Starting Anti-Virus

• To start Anti-Virus (for MS-DOS) from the
command line, type:

    C:\>msav

• To start Windows Anti-Virus:
    1. Open the Microsoft Tools program group.
    2. Double-click the Anti-Virus icon.

Note that you cannot run Windows Anti-Virus unless
you chose to install it when you ran MS-DOS Setup.
If you did install the program and you try to start it
by typing the name of its program file, MWAV.EXE,
at the command prompt, all you get is a copyright
notice and a message telling you *This program
requires Microsoft Windows*.

Starting Up and Getting Around

As you can see from the quick reference card, starting either version of the program is simple and needs little explanation. Like the other windowed utilities shipped with MS-DOS, both Anti-Virus and Windows Anti-Virus offer online Help. If you want to immerse yourself in the intricacies of antivirus operations, help in either version of the program is a great way to get started. That, plus the information in the virus list, can quickly make you comfortable with the idea of antivirus programs, if not their targets.

To get help:

• With Anti-Virus, press F1.

• With Windows Anti-Virus, open the Help menu or press F1.

If you're using Anti-Virus, take note of the dark bar along the bottom of the window. You'll see different messages appear here, including lists of "speed keys" that can make your work with Anti-Virus faster and easier. Although the bar lists key names, it's also sensitive to mouse actions, so if you have a mouse, you can point to the "key" you want and press the left mouse button instead of manually pressing the key on the keyboard. The numbers correspond to function keys: 1 means F1, 2 means F2, and so on.

As you can see in the earlier illustration, the opening window lists keys that get help (F1), select a drive (F2), quit the program (F3), and so on. The only ones that might give you pause are F7, possibly F8, and F9. Here's what they do:

• F7 deletes special checklist files in which Anti-Virus and Windows Anti-Virus save information about file sizes, dates, times, and other attributes to defend your system against unknown viruses. You'll find more about these checklist files in the later discussion "Setting Virus Traps."

• F8 displays a dialog box in which you can set various options for virus checking. These options also are discussed in "Setting Virus Traps."

• F9 opens the Virus List window. Use this to see the names of some known viruses and read about the kinds of damage they do.

As you use Anti-Virus, you'll note that the contents of this bar change according to what you're doing. During a virus scan, the bar tells you what's going on.

When you select one of the buttons in the window, the bar tells you what that button does. When you're using Anti-Virus Help, the list shows the keys you use in maneuvering through Help. Refer to this bar often as you use Anti-Virus.

(If you use Windows Anti-Virus, you don't have such a communicative bar, but don't feel shortchanged. Everything you need is on the menus at the top of the window.)

Search, or Search and Destroy

Once you get Anti-Virus or Windows Anti-Virus started and you're comfortable working in their windows, how do you go about getting them to deal with any viruses that might be on your disk? Basically, using either Anti-Virus or Windows Anti-Virus is a simple matter of choosing a disk and then indicating

whether you want merely to search for viruses (Detect) or to both search for and destroy (Detect And Clean) any viruses found on the disk. Here's what you do:

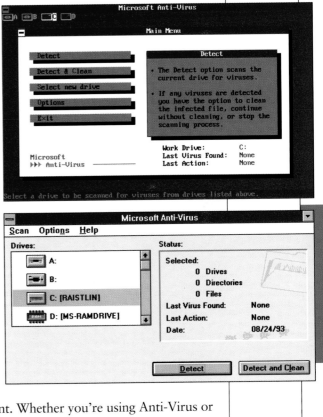

1. If necessary, choose the disk you want to search for viruses.

   • If you're using Anti-Virus, press F2 to display a list of drives at the top of the screen. Then, if you have a mouse, click on the drive you want; if you don't have a mouse, use either the Tab key or the right and left arrow keys to highlight the drive you want, and press Enter.

   • If you're using Windows Anti-Virus, just click the drive you want in the Drives list box. You can select more than one drive simply by clicking whichever others you want to scan.

2. Choose the type of operation you want. Whether you're using Anti-Virus or Windows Anti-Virus:

   • Choose the Detect button to search for but not eliminate viruses from the disk. (If you're using Anti-Virus, take the fast route and just press F4.)

- Choose the Detect And Clean button to both search for and destroy viruses. (If you're using Anti-Virus, press F5.)

As the scan progresses, both Anti-Virus and Windows Anti-Virus keep you informed of progress by showing you "gas gauges" that indicate how much of the scan is complete:

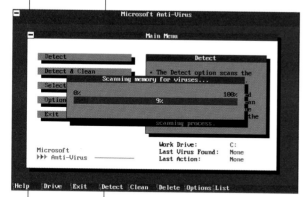

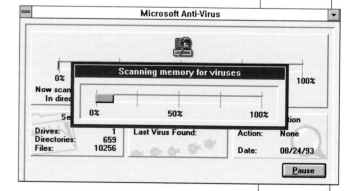

When the virus scan is complete, both antivirus programs produce a report showing you how many disks and files were scanned, how many infected files were found and, of those, how many were cleaned:

Command-Line Options

Anti-Virus is easy to start from the MS-DOS command prompt, but you can also choose to elaborate on your command with any of numerous switches. The following command form shows the switches you're most likely to find interesting. For a complete list, request the online MS-DOS Help for Msav.

```
msav [drive:] /s /c /r /p /f
```

drive is the drive containing the disk you want to check. If you omit *drive*, Anti-Virus checks the disk in the current drive. Specifying a drive does not, however, initiate a virus check. For that, also include either /s or /c.

POWER PLAY

For (the many) Windows Users Only

If you've used Windows and Windows-based applications for a while, you probably know about a feature called drag-and-drop. When you use drag-and-drop, you select something—for example, a filename or a block of text—drag it somewhere with the mouse, and drop the selection at the new location. Happily, Windows Anti-Virus lets you apply drag-and-drop to virus scanning as a quick means of checking a file for infection.

To use drag-and-drop scanning, do the following:

1. Open the Windows File Manager. (Windows Anti-Virus does not have to be running at the time.)

2. Open two windows; you'll probably want to tile them so that you can easily see filenames in each.

3. In one window, display your \DOS directory and scroll until the filename MWAV.EXE is showing. In the other window,

display the name of the file you want to scan.

4. Select the name of the file to be scanned, drag it to *mwav.exe* in the \DOS window, and release the mouse button to "drop" the file onto *mwav.exe*.

At this point, if Windows is set up to request confirmation for mouse operations, it displays a message asking *Are you sure you want to start MWAV.EXE by using FILENAME.EXT as the initial file?* Odd as this question looks, click Yes.

Windows Anti-Virus now starts, runs through its usual memory check, and then scans the file you dropped onto it. Drag-and-drop scanning is as simple as that. Do note, however, that you can use this method to scan only one file at a time. Although Windows allows you to select, drag, and drop multiple files when you move or copy them, Windows Anti-Virus scans only the first file you drop on it. If you select more than one file, it ignores the rest.

When you start Anti-Virus with switches that plunge you directly into a virus scan from the command line, be aware that when the scan is complete, Anti-Virus will bounce you back to the command prompt. This sudden exit might be disconcerting because it doesn't happen when you perform the same type of search after starting Anti-Virus with a simple msav command. Remember the difference. Consider it part of Anti-Virus's charm or something.

/s searches for viruses but does not remove any that are found. If you use /s, you can't use /c.

/c cleans—it searches for viruses and removes any that are found. Don't use /c with /s. They're mutually exclusive.

/r tells Anti-Virus to create a report named MSAV.RPT, which it saves in the root directory of the disk you scan. This report records the date and time of the virus search and lists the number of viruses in the boot sector and in your files that were found and removed. (The boot sector is a critical portion of a system disk; it contains a program that loads MS-DOS into memory at startup. Not surprisingly, the boot sector is the target of many destructive viruses.) The report is saved as an unformatted text file, so you can easily display it with the Type command or print it with Print or Copy (copy msav.rpt > prn). This is what a typical report (for a clean disk) looks like:

```
C:\>type msav.rpt
Microsoft Anti-Virus.
Virus search report for date: 08-11-93, Time 16:16:11.


Total boot sector viruses    FOUND   : 0
Total boot sector viruses    REMOVED: 0

Total Files                  CHECKED: 473
Total File viruses           FOUND   : 0
Total File viruses           REMOVED: 0


END OF REPORT.
C:\>
```

The /p and /f switches cause Anti-Virus to behave as if it were *not* a program designed to run in a window. /p initiates a virus search on either the drive you specify or the current drive (if you don't specify a drive) and ends with a report just like the one illustrated for the /r switch. Anti-Virus does not, however, save the report on disk, so if you want a recorded history of virus searches, include the /r switch in your command, like this.

```
C:\>msav d: /p /r
```

When you use /p, Anti-Virus displays the name of each file it scans for viruses. The name appears only briefly because the scan is conducted so quickly. If you're not interested in seeing filenames, add the /f switch to your command, like this:

```
C:\>msav /p /f
```

This tells Anti-Virus to run its scan but not bother you with the name of each file it looks at.

Use the /r switch if you want to keep a record of your virus searches, especially those performed on your hard disk. To avoid having new reports overwrite older ones, rename existing reports—for example, MSAV.001, MSAV.002, and so on—before running Anti-Virus with the /r switch.

If you use the /p switch, there will be a time during which Anti-Virus displays the message *Scanning memory for viruses...* but doesn't otherwise seem to be doing anything. Don't start wondering if Anti-Virus is broken. It's not. It's just busy and isn't paying any attention to you. Soon enough, Anti-Virus will launch into scanning files for viruses, and then you'll see a nice, constantly changing line that displays the name of each file on the disk as Anti-Virus scans it.

Setting Virus Traps

Both Anti-Virus and Windows Anti-Virus are easy to use and, because they do whatever cleanup is required, actually require little help from you. Once you know your way around these programs, however, you might want to fine-tune their behavior with the various Options settings. To see what these settings are:

- With Anti-Virus, press F8.

- With Windows Anti-Virus, open the Options menu and choose the Set Options command.

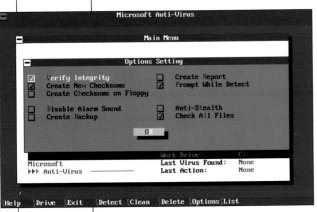

At first glance, these settings don't look very inviting, but then they're not meant to be warm and fuzzy. Just take them one by one, and you'll be all right. And if you want, you can ignore them altogether because the most useful options are already turned on for you by default.

Here, briefly, is the lowdown on what the settings are and what they do:

- Verify Integrity: On by default, this setting verifies whether a program file has changed since the last time you scanned the disk. To determine whether changes have occurred, the program uses information it records in a checklist file named CHKLIST.MS. You should leave this setting turned on.

- Create New Checksums: On by default, this setting calculates and saves a value called a checksum that's based on the actual bytes that make up a program file. The values calculated are stored in the checklist file and are useful in defending your system against viruses that Anti-Virus and Windows Anti-Virus don't automatically look for and recognize. Leave this on too.

- Create Checksums on Floppies: Off by default, this setting tells the antivirus program to calculate checksums for floppies. You probably don't need this.

- Disable Alarm Sound: Off by default, this setting seems backwards in the sense that turning it *on* means turning *off* the warning bell that the antivirus program sounds whenever it encounters a possible virus. Leave the setting turned off.

- Create Backup: Off by default, this setting makes a backup copy of an infected file before cleaning it. The backup is given the extension VIR. If you choose to create such potentially hazardous files, be sure to use them only if the risk of infection is less than the risk of losing the program.

- Create Report (Anti-Virus only): Off by default, this option can be turned on to create a virus scan report (the same report produced by the /r switch you use from the command line). The report, remember, produces a text file named MSAV.RPT that essentially provides "hard copy" of the report you see after a virus scan.

- Prompt While Detect: On by default, this setting causes Anti-Virus and Windows Anti-Virus to display a Verify Error or a Virus Found warning when it encounters a possible virus during a Detect scan. Both warnings are described later. Leave this option turned on. To be sure that it works properly and gives you all possible options, leave the Verify Integrity and (in Windows Anti-Virus) the Wipe Deleted Files settings turned on too.

- Anti-Stealth: Off by default, this option should be turned on if your system holds valuable programs and data or is at risk of being infected by viruses. The Anti-Stealth option enables Anti-Virus and Windows Anti-Virus to carry out an extra-sensitive search for Stealth-type viruses, which might otherwise evade detection. If you turn this on, be sure that Verify Integrity is turned on too.

- Check All Files: On by default, this option causes Anti-Virus and Windows Anti-Virus to check every file on the disk. Turning this option off limits the scan to executable (program) files. Because a complete check that covers every file on the disk can take quite a while, you might want to turn off this option after you've initially scanned the entire disk. If you do turn off the Check All Files option, leave Create New Checksums turned on to provide an added bit of protection for the disk, and be sure to scan floppies thoroughly before installing new software.

- Wipe Deleted Files (Windows Anti-Virus only): Off by default, this option enables Windows Anti-Virus to kill viruses so that they are not merely dead but *really* (most sincerely) dead. Normally, if Windows Anti-Virus finds a virus, it displays a Virus Found dialog box in which one of the choices is Delete. If you choose Delete, the file is deleted but not completely cleared from the disk. If you turn on Wipe Deleted Files, on the other hand, the option changes to Wipe, which tells Windows Anti-Virus to overwrite every cluster of the infected file, eliminating all trace of it on the disk. This option should lay even the zombies to rest.

Intruder Alerts

And what happens if Anti-Virus or Windows Anti-Virus actually finds what it thinks is an intruder? That depends.

If you're running a *detect* scan rather than a detect-and-clean scan and the problem is a known virus, Anti-Virus displays a message and suggests what to do about it. If the same thing happens with Windows Anti-Virus, you see a Virus Found dialog box that lets you choose whether to Clean (remove) the virus from the file, Stop the scan, Delete (replaced by Wipe if you turned on Wipe Deleted Files) the file from the disk, or Continue without doing anything.

If—again—you're running a detect scan and the problem represents a change in a program file (which Anti-Virus and Windows Anti-Virus figure out by comparing a file's current vital statistics against those recorded in the checklist file), you hear an alarm and see a Verify Error warning like the one below:

What to do?
Choose Update
if the file has
legitimately
changed—if, for
example, you
replaced an old
program file with
a newer version.
Choose Delete if
you can't account
for the change and
you want to delete
the file. (This but-

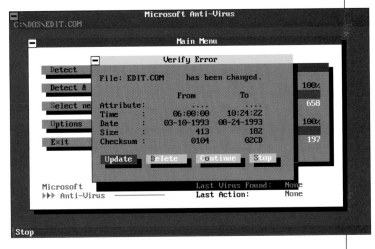

ton appears if there's a change in either the file's size or checksum, both of which are good indicators of virus activity.) Choose Continue if you want to continue the scan without doing anything to the suspect file. Or choose Stop to end the virus scan.

A fourth option, Repair, appears in the Verify Error message if Anti-Virus or Windows Anti-Virus detects that a file's date or time has changed but the rest of the file's records appear to be just fine. If you see a Repair option, choose it if you want to return the date and time to their original settings (meaning those that the program detected during an earlier scan).

POWER PLAY

Shut Up, Anti-Virus, I Know What I'm Doing

Although antivirus programs are great protectors, there *is* one time when you might—no, you surely will—wish they were a little less enthusiastic. That time comes after you upgrade to a newer version of a program you've been using (even MS-DOS). The reason? An upgrade usually means lots of new but changed files, bearing the same names as the older files you've been using. Right. The next time you run the antivirus program, it's going to be ring, ring, alarm, alarm, as the program dutifully tells you of each and every changed file. To avoid having to respond to one such "virus catch" after the other, do the following before upgrading software:

1. Run Anti-Virus or Windows Anti-Virus before upgrading to be sure that your system is clean.

2. After the check, if you're using Anti-Virus, press F7. If you're using Windows Anti-Virus, choose Delete CHKLIST files from the Scan menu. This little act deletes the antivirus program's "memory" of what the old program files are supposed to be like.

3. Install the upgrade. If you want to be extra careful, run a virus scan on each floppy disk before installation.

4. After the upgrade, run Anti-Virus or Windows Anti-Virus again, this time to create new checklist files for the system. This is your protection for the future.

The Stalker: Vsafe

Anti-Virus and Windows Anti-Virus are like the antibiotics that get rid of infections in your system. Vsafe is more like a vaccine that you use to prevent infection in the first place. Once you know your system is virus free, you might want to run Vsafe to keep it that way.

Starting Vsafe

A memory-resident utility, Vsafe sits in about 23 KB of memory—out of the mainstream but watching your system for signs of unauthorized activity, including attempts to format the hard disk or to change an executable (program) file. If it detects anything untoward, Vsafe warns you and asks what you want to do. The warning and your options are described a little later.

1. To start Vsafe, type its name:

   `C:\>vsafe`

2. To open a pop-up window and modify Vsafe settings, press Alt+V and type the number of the setting you want to change. Press Esc to close the window.

3. To remove Vsafe from memory, open the pop-up window and press Alt+U. (You can't stop Vsafe with Alt+U from the command prompt.)

The hotkey (Alt+V) shown on the screen is a special key combination that allows you to open a small pop-up window in which you can set or change monitoring options.

To change an option:

1. Press Alt+V to open the pop-up window.

2. Type the number of the option you want to change.

3. Press Esc. This closes the pop-up window and carries out any changes you made, but it does not shut down Vsafe. The program remains safely in memory until you press Alt+V to reopen the window and then press Alt+U to unload the program.

As you can see from the Xs in the On column in the illustration at right, some options are turned on by default, whereas others are turned off. The default settings enable Vsafe to monitor the most vulnerable parts of your system. The others enhance monitoring, but some can make Vsafe overly protective to the point that you spend a lot of time telling it that nothing's wrong. This is especially true of option 3,

Vsafe includes a number of command line switches you can use to control the way it behaves, but the easiest way to start it is simply to skip the switches and type its name:

`C:\>vsafe`

When it loads, Vsafe tells you that it's up and running with a message:

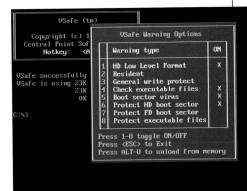

General Write Protect, which tells Vsafe to warn you anytime a program attempts to write to disk. The following table describes each of these warning signals:

Vsafe Options		
Option #	Option Name	Description
1	HD Low Level Format	Warns of an attempt to format the hard disk. This is turned on by default because of the obvious damage that can occur.
2	Resident	Warns of an attempt by a program to remain in memory. This is turned off by default. Don't turn it on if you expect to be loading all kinds of memory-resident software.
3	General Write Protect	Warns of program attempts to write to disk. This is off by default and probably should remain off.
4	Check Executable Files	Tells Vsafe to check all executable (program) files MS-DOS opens. This option is turned on by default, and you should probably leave it on.
5	Boot Sector Virus	Checks all disks for viruses hidden in the boot sector, a special section that tells whether the disk is bootable. Leave this turned on.
6	Protect HD Boot Sector	Warns of attempts to change the boot sector or partition table of the hard disk, both of which are essential for a hard disk to remain both usable and bootable. Leave this turned on too.
7	Protect FD Boot Sector	Warns of attempts to change the boot sector of a floppy disk. This is off by default and probably unnecessary for most computer work.
8	Protect Executable Files	Warns of attempts to modify executable (program) files. This is off by default and can probably stay off.

If you want, you can start Vsafe and turn certain options on or off at the same time with the following command format:

Viruses being rejected by VSafe

```
vsafe /option+ /option-
```

Type a slash, the option number, and a plus to turn a particular option on; a slash, the option number, and a minus to turn an option off.

Messages from Vsafe

If Vsafe detects possible virus activity, it warns you with a ringing sound and displays a boxed message that flashes *Vsafe Warning* in red above a brief description of the problem and some labeled "buttons" asking what you want to do. These buttons are:

- Stop. Choose this if Vsafe warns you about a program you are trying to run. It might tell you, for example, that the file has been changed or that the program is attempting to stay in memory. Choosing Stop prevents the program from loading and, possibly, freeing a virus to damage your system.

- Continue. Choose this if you're pretty sure Vsafe is just being overly protective and you want to continue on your way. Read the warning first, though, and think the situation through.

- Boot. Choose this to reboot the system and thus ensure that you have a "clean" working environment.

- Update. Choose this if a file has changed, you know it's healthy, and you want Vsafe to update its internal record to let the file "pass" the next time you use it.

Vsafe and Windows

Although you start and control Vsafe from the MS-DOS command prompt, you can enable the program to send you warnings while you're using Windows. The trick here is to start a second program, called the Vsafe Manager, that keeps an open line to Vsafe while Windows is running. To use the Vsafe Manager, make either of two small changes in the way Windows runs. Here are your options, both easy. Check them out and decide which you prefer.

- You can choose to change a special file named WIN.INI, which sets up (initializes) Windows at startup in much the same way that AUTOEXEC.BAT sets up MS-DOS. Here's what to do:

    1. Use the MS-DOS Editor to open WIN.INI. The file should be in your Windows directory.

    2. Near the top of the file, change the line that reads load= to:

        ```
        load=mwavtsr.exe
        ```

        If your load= line is already occupied, move the cursor to the end of the line, type a comma, and then type:

        ```
        mwavtsr.exe
        ```

    3. Save the file and close the editor. You're done.

- You can add the Vsafe Manager to your Windows Startup program group. This is what to do:

    1. Start Windows if necessary. Open the Startup group, and then minimize it (not really essential, but helpful).

2. Open the File Manager and resize its window so that you can see the minimized Startup group icon.

3. In the File Manager window, display your \DOS directory and scroll to the file MWAVTSR.EXE.

4. Click on MWAVTSR.EXE to select it, drag it to the Startup group icon, and drop it there. Close the File Manager window. You don't need it anymore.

5. Restore the Startup group window. You'll see the Vsafe Manager icon, a doctor's bag, sitting there. As a final step, click the Vsafe Manager icon to select it, and choose Properties from the File menu. Click the check box to the left of Run Minimized. Now the Vsafe Manager will run as an icon whenever you use Windows.

If you use either of these approaches to activate the Vsafe Manager, be aware that it will work only if Vsafe has been started previously from the MS-DOS command prompt. That is, you cannot start Windows, jump out to an MS-DOS prompt, start Vsafe, and then return to Windows. The procedure must always be: Start Vsafe, and then start Windows (to load the Vsafe Manager).

Sleep Better at Night with Backup

Back Up Doesn't Mean Reverse

Q: Why were floppy disks invented?

A: So you could back up your hard disk.

Lies, you say, and rightfully so, but there's an element of truth here nonetheless. All it takes is one encounter with an uncooperative hard disk to learn just how much you've come to rely on its always being there—ready, willing, and most of all able to work. Of course the possibility of a broken hard disk isn't the only reason to back up your files. There's always the chance you might delete some important files and not realize, until too late, that you still needed them.

Backups don't always have to mean gloom and doom, either. Look at the bright side: It's easy, over time, to fill a hard disk with files. Surely you don't need immediate access to all those data files you created back in 1988. Wouldn't it be nice to store them on floppies and free up the space that they're taking on your hard disk? After all, one of the reasons DoubleSpace was put into MS-DOS version 6.0 was simply to help people find more storage space. So if you look at all the reasons for doing them, backups make a lot of sense.

Through version 5 of MS-DOS, the process of backing up and (if need be) restoring files to a hard disk wasn't the easiest or most entertaining way to spend your time. Backup did,indeed, work, but it wasn't fun. Beginning with version 6.0, MS-DOS began to offer you a new and improved Backup that is not only smarter than "old" Backup, but easier to use and more flex- ible. This new Backup, like the antivirus utility, comes in two forms: one for MS-DOS and one for Microsoft Windows (MSBACKUP.EXE for MS-DOS and MWBACKUP.EXE for Windows).

Back up routinely— it might save your neck.

Understanding Backups

No doubt, you're just itching to start backing up your hard disk, but leave that for a few minutes. Take some time to find out what backups are all about— work before play and all that. To begin with, what does it mean to do a backup? Well, that one's easy. Backing up means making copies of files on another disk. Most of the time, you back up so that you have a "spare" you can turn to in case the working copy of a file is lost or damaged, but backing up is also a good way of archiving files that change from day to day. By keeping backups, you ensure that you always have at least a recent version of the file so that you don't have to rebuild the file from scratch if it is lost or damaged.

Knowing what a backup is, all you need is a basic understanding of how Backup works. Here, the Product Support folks at Microsoft have found that some people run into a little difficulty. In truth, Backup isn't the easiest of MS-DOS utilities to understand, but it isn't that hard either. Mostly, the new concepts you need to cement in your head are these:

- Setup files
- Backup types

Set Yourself Up with Setup Files

A setup file is a special file, with the extension SET, in which Backup keeps a record of the files you select for backup. Also included in this record are the settings for certain choices you make, such as whether you want the backed up data compressed on the target disk, whether you want to be prompted with a beep, and whether you want to protect the backed-up data with a password.

Saving those optional settings can be very useful, but practically speaking, the principle value of a setup file is as an aid in remembering which files you've backed up as a group. Thanks to setup files, you don't have to think back and wonder whether you backed up BIRDS and BEASTS together or separately. Nor do you have to remember whether you included both the LION and the LAMB directories when you backed up BEASTS. Backup lets you save the selections for each group of files in a different setup file, and Backup displays the names of your setup files when you request a backup, so you don't ever have to keep track of which files you back up together. (Of course, if you don't want to bother with all this, you don't have to; Backup automatically creates and saves a setup file named DEFAULT.SET and is perfectly happy to use that file to keep track of all your backups.)

Setup files, then, free you from having to remember what you backed up, and how. That's easy enough. Now what about backup types? Well, backing up is more than just plain copying (which Copy and Xcopy can do perfectly well), and if you take backups seriously, there will come a time when you want to back up different sets of files in different ways. That's where backup types come in.

How Do I Back Up? Let Me Count the Ways

Whether you use the MS-DOS form of Backup (MSBackup) or the Windows version (Windows Backup), you can choose either a full or a partial backup. The reason you have a choice here is that, ideally, backing up is not a one-shot deal. To do it right, you should set up a backup schedule, and that means performing periodic backups, like this:

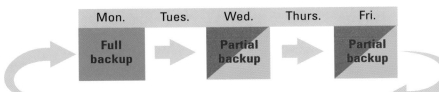

Because backing up is a cyclical endeavor, it's plain to see that full and partial backups can save both time and floppy disk space:

- A full backup archives every single file in a given group of files. It's equivalent to buying the complete *Encyclopaedia Britannica*.

- A partial backup is what you need when you want to archive only those files within a set that are new or changed since the last backup. It's quicker than a full backup (and cheaper in terms of disk space)—somewhat like adding the *Book of the Year* for, say, 1990 through 1993 to your *Encyclopaedia Britannica*.

Once you perform a full backup, which you should do the first time you archive a set of files and at the beginning of each backup cycle, you can then go on to choose the kind of partial backup you want for the in-between times. For this, you have two additional choices, incremental and differential (which sound rather like car transmissions). Both incremental and differential backups act only on new or changed files, but they differ subtly, based on the way they treat a little signal called the archive bit, or the archive flag. (Be patient, there *is* a reason for all this.)

What a Difference a Bit Makes

The archive bit is a tiny part of every file's directory entry and, as befits the two-state nature of a single bit, it can be either turned on or turned off. If you've used the Attribute command or the /a switch of the Directory command, you've seen the tracks of the archive bit. Suppose, for example, you type this command:

```
C:\>attrib myfile.doc
```

MS-DOS responds with something like this:

```
A          C:\MYFILE.DOC
```

That *A* tells you that the archive bit is turned on. So what? Well, small though it is, the archive bit is used and appreciated by certain programs, including Backup and Xcopy. When these programs archive files, they check the archive bit of each file in the backup set. If the bit is turned on for a particular file, the programs assume that the file is either new or changed. If the bit is turned off, they assume that the file has already been archived.

And how does all this affect you? Simple. Backup (or Xcopy or numerous other programs) can use the archive bit to do some smart copying. It can use the state of the archive bit not only to "decide" whether a file has been backed up already, but also to decide whether the file needs backing up again. Here's how the archive bit works in Backup:

- A full backup copies all the files in the backup set and turns off each file's archive bit.

- An incremental backup copies all files in the backup set that have their archive bit turned on, and then it turns off the archive bit for each one.

- A differential backup copies the same files as an incremental backup but leaves the archive bit turned on.

To picture how this works, imagine you have a group of files sitting in a directory. Some are waving flags labeled "Copy Me," others aren't. You start your backup cycle with a full backup:

> When you set up your own backup strategy, don't try to mix and match incremental and differential backups; you'll more than likely end up with a confused mess. Start each backup cycle with a full backup, but then stick with either incremental or differential backups until it's time to perform another full backup.

- Every file, whether it's waving a flag or not, gets copied to your backup disk. In addition, each file that had a flag comes out of the backup empty-handed.

Time goes by—a day, a week, it doesn't matter. In that time, some of those original files have been changed, and new files have been added to the directory. Now, only new and changed files are waving flags. A sufficient number of files have changed, however, that it's time for a partial backup. The full backup copied every file, so all you need to copy this time are the flag-wavers:

- If you choose an incremental backup, only the files waving flags get copied. All of them lose their flags in the process.

- If you choose a differential backup, again only the files waving flags get copied, but they get to keep their flags and continue waving them around.

The image of a bunch of files clutching flags is pretty ludicrous, but think now about what happens the *next* time you archive these files. So far, you've backed up all files in the directory and, whether you chose an incremental or a differential second backup, you've copied all new or changed files, too. And so more time passes, and you're ready for your third backup.

If you chose an incremental backup last time, the only files with flags are those that are new or have changed since the last backup. Because the flags get taken away at each incremental backup, you know that any files now waving flags are different from the files you last backed up. Therefore, an incremental backup is just the ticket for archiving new files at each backup *and* for archiving files for which you want to track *changes* from one backup to the next. An incremental backup is what you need if you tend to use a lot of different files, or if you need to keep copies of files that evolve over time—for example, a contract you're negotiating, a report you're writing, or a database you're developing or updating.

On the other hand, if you chose a differential backup last time, remember that you copied some files and left them to continue waving their flags around. Because they still have their flags, Backup will assume that they need archiving again—whether or not the files have actually changed. Doing another differential backup therefore means you'll be copying the same files again, even if they're no different now than they were at the last backup. Seems a little odd to keep copying the same files...or is it? Not really. If you work with the same files day after day, a differential backup is just right for keeping one complete set of files (your full backup set) *plus* one separate set that comprises all the new files as well as any that have changed at any time since the last full backup. A differential backup is appropriate when you don't have to worry about archiving successive versions of your files as you change them.

The following rules summarize what you need to know about backups in general; from there on, it's time for the specifics.

MSBackup and Windows Backup both come with their own online Help for you to browse. This chapter covers the basics of understanding and using a backup program. For specifics on either version, however, do remember that online Help is there if you need it.

THE BACKUP RULES OF THUMB

- Do a full backup the first time you back up a set of files and at the beginning of each new backup cycle (weekly, monthly, or whatever).

- Do incremental backups between full backups if you work with a lot of different files and you want to be able to archive different versions of files that change over time.

- Do differential backups between full backups if you work with the same files over and over and want to keep only two backup sets—one complete set and one set of new or changed files.

Starting Backup

If you're using MSBackup, you start the backup program from the MS-DOS command prompt. The easiest and fastest way to get to MSBackup is simply to type:

```
C:\>msbackup
```

If you're using Windows Backup, you doubtless already know that you start it from Windows. You'll find it in the Microsoft Tools program group in Program Manager, along with Windows Anti-Virus and Windows Undelete. To start Windows Backup:

When you're a pro at using MSBackup, you might want to use the command in the form:

```
msbackup
```
setup-file

where *setup-file* lets you start MSBackup and specify the setup file you want to use.

1. Start Windows if necessary.

2. Open the Microsoft Tools program group.

3. Double-click on the Backup icon.

First Time Out

The first time you use either MSBackup or Windows Backup, you don't jump straight into the backup program. In order to be sure that your backups proceed smoothly and accurately, both versions of Backup start out by configuring themselves to work with the floppy disk drives on your computer. When you start MSBackup, you don't have much choice about configuring because your only options are to configure or quit, as shown in the screens at the top of the facing page.

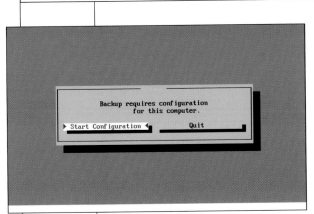

Windows Backup is a little less binary about the matter but still insistent, and for good reason: It won't back up to anything but the hard disk on your system until you've configured it to work with your other drives.

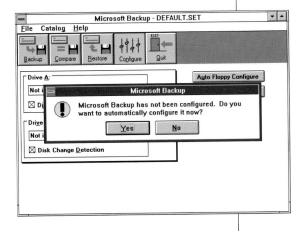

With either version of the program, the main task of configuration involves a procedure called a compatibility test, in which Backup performs a smallish backup of your \DOS directory. It takes a few minutes, but when it's over, Backup is ready to go.

The configuration process is similar in MSBackup and Windows Backup, although the MSBackup version begins with some hardware checks that Windows Backup doesn't need. The screens you see during this part of the MSBackup configuration might be confusing, but don't let them worry you. Press Enter whenever the program stops and waits for a response, choose the drive on which you want to run the compatibility test, and step ahead with confidence.

As for the configuration itself, you'll notice a fair amount of activity when either MSBackup or Windows Backup works through the process. You can basically just let either form of Backup do what it needs to do, but:

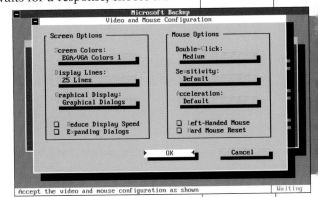

- A lot of messages appear. Read them before you go on to the next stage.

- Verify selections when you're asked to. If you're using MSBackup, tab to the drive you want to test and press the Spacebar when MSBackup asks you to select a drive.

- Feed the computer disks when necessary, and press a key or mouse button when Backup asks.

Beyond this, sit back and watch the show.

To start the configuration process:

- With MSBackup, press Enter when Start Configuration is highlighted (which it is by default).
- With Windows Backup, click Yes (the default) or press Enter.

The Real Thing

Now you're ready for the real thing. Once you've got an idea of what backups are all about, actually using MSBackup or Windows Backup is relatively easy. The process is very similar in both versions of the program. Both give you three main choices related to backups:

- Backup itself, which as you now know well, copies valuable files to another disk. You'll probably use floppies, but if you have one, you can also use another hard disk or a removable hard disk cartridge. If you have access to one, you can also back up to a network drive. You cannot, however, back up to tape drives.

- Compare, which compares backups with the originals to verify that the copies are accurate.

- Restore, which reverses the backup operation by copying files from the backup disk to your hard disk.

POWER PLAY

Configuring at Other Times

In addition to Backup, Compare, and Restore, both MSBackup and Windows Backup include a fourth choice: Configure. The compatibility test that runs when you first use MSBackup or Windows Backup configures the backup program to work with your existing hardware. If you add, remove, or change drives or if you want to use a different drive for backups, use the Configure option. If you're using MSBackup, you also use the Configure option to change display or mouse settings. The following steps walk you through the basics of configuring MSBackup and Windows Backup to work with a new or changed drive. Refer to online Help for more details.

1. Start MSBackup or Windows Backup.

2. Choose Configure from the program's opening screen.

3. To identify the new drive or drives to Backup, do the following:

   - If you're using MSBackup, choose Backup Devices from the Configure dialog box. Choose Auto Config from the Backup Devices dialog box to

Backing Up Is Nice to Do

So now you've configured MSBackup or
Windows Backup to work with your
computer. Now, each time you start the
program (and in the case of MSBackup,
choose Backup from the opening screen),
you see one of the screens shown here:

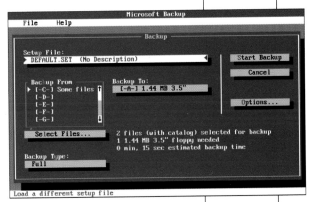

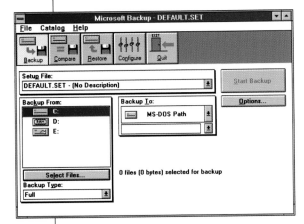

If you read through all that
boring stuff at the beginning of this
chapter, the options on the screen
should be almost self-explanatory.
Here, as you can see above and at
left, both MSBackup and Windows
Backup let you select the setup file
to use and the type of backup you
want, in addition to the more
obvious selections: what files you want to back up, what drive they're on, and
what drive they're going to.

tell MSBackup to automatically configure itself to work with your floppy
drives. This should work fine if your computer is completely IBM PC
compatible. If Auto Config doesn't work, choose the button for the drive
in question, and choose an appropriate description in the Drive X Configuration box that appears next. Choose OK in the Drive X Configuration box and the Backup Devices box when you're done. When the
Configure screen reappears, choose Compatibility Test to run a test
backup on the drive. When everything's done, choose Save to save the
new configuration.

– If you're using Windows Backup, click Auto Floppy Configure to have
Windows Backup automatically configure your floppy drives for you.
Again, this should work fine if your computer is completely IBM PC compatible. If Auto Floppy Configure doesn't work, open the drop-down list
box for the drive in question and choose the description that matches the
drive. Click Compatibility Test to run a test backup on the drive. That's
all you do until you quit Windows Backup. At that time, be sure to check
the Save Configuration box in the Exit Backup dialog box. You can then
quit, knowing that Windows Backup will save the changes you made.

The rest of this section describes the steps you take for a typical first-time backup.

Step 1: Look at the Backup From list. If the drive you want to back up from is not selected, choose the drive:

- With the mouse, simply point and click.

- With the keyboard (and MSBackup), press Tab until a dark highlight is in the Backup From list, and then use the up or down arrow key to highlight the drive you want.

Step 2: Choose Select Files, either with the mouse or with the Tab key. When you choose the Select Files button, Backup spends a few seconds reading disk information into memory and then opens a rather involved secondary window.

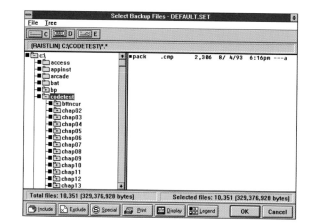

The main part of either screen will be a relatively familiar sight if you've used either Windows File Manager or the MS-DOS Shell. On the left, you see a diagram listing the directories on the current drive. On the right, you see a list of files in the current directory. These two "panes" are where you select the files to back up.

OUTSMART YOURSELF?

You *can* sneak around the initial configuration testing with both MSBackup and Windows Backup, but there's no point in doing so. If you try to outsmart MSBackup, your only backup destinations will be a 360-KB drive A and the MS-DOS Path, which is a directory on your hard disk. If you try to outsmart Windows Backup, you see only MS-DOS Path in your Backup To list, and this defaults to the \DOS directory on your hard disk. Remember, neither backup program will properly recognize the floppy drives on your system until configured to work with those drives. If you skipped the initial configuration, go back to the section "First Time Out," on page 238.

If you've DoubleSpaced your hard disk, Backup will show two drive letters for your single hard disk, so don't be surprised if you see two letters, such as C and H. This is normal. Depending on how you set up disk compression, either drive letter can contain data files. You can back up from a DoubleSpaced drive, but before you do, you might want to read up on compressed drives in the chapter "Grow Your Disks with DoubleSpace." Knowing a bit more about your DoubleSpaced drive is not critical, but it won't hurt, either.

POWER PLAY

Button It Up

When you work in the Select Backup Files window, you can use the three buttons labeled Include, Exclude, and Special to fine-tune your file-selection process.

Include and Exclude, which produce virtually identical dialog boxes, allow you to use wildcard characters to specify groups of files you always want to include or exclude from a backup. You can use these buttons, for example, to ensure that all files with the DOC extension are included in the backup or to exclude all files with the BAK or TMP extension.

- With MSBackup, type the path and
  file specification you want to include
  or exclude. Check the Include All
  Subdirectories box to extend the
  inclusion/exclusion to all subdirectories of the directory you specified.
  Choose OK, and when the Select

  Backup Files window reappears, you'll see all filenames that match your
  specification selected or deselected accordingly. To edit your list of included
  or excluded files, choose Edit Include/Exclude List. Select the item you want
  to edit, and then choose Edit to modify the selection, press Del=Delete to
  remove it, or press Ins=Copy to duplicate it. Choose OK to make the change.

- With Windows Backup, type the path
  and file specification, and choose
  Include or Exclude as appropriate.
  Check the Include All Subdirectories
  box to extend the inclusion/exclusion
  to all subdirectories of the directory
  you specified. Choose Add to add the
  file specification to the Include/Ex-
  clude List at the bottom of the dialog
  box. To edit the list, select the item to
  edit. Choose Add to duplicate it in the
  list, choose Delete to remove it.

If you want to fine-tune your backup even further, you can use the Special button to open the Special Selections dialog box, which lets you apply a number of
different criteria to your backup.

(continued)

continued

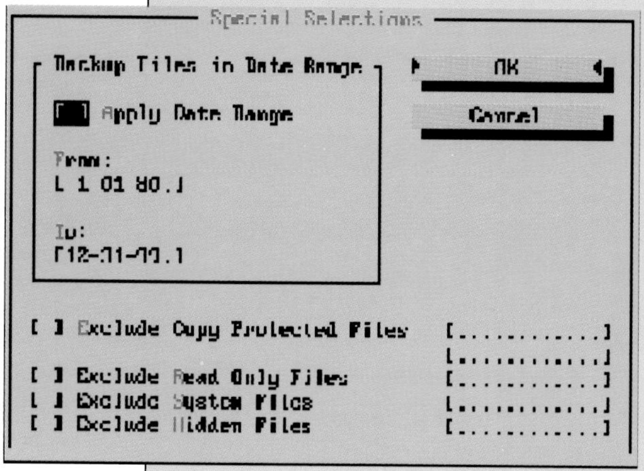

Special Selections

Backup Files in Date Range
☐ Apply Range
From:
1/ 1/80
To:
12/31/99

☐ Exclude Copy Protected Files:

☐ Exclude Read-Only Files
☐ Exclude System Files
☐ Exclude Hidden Files

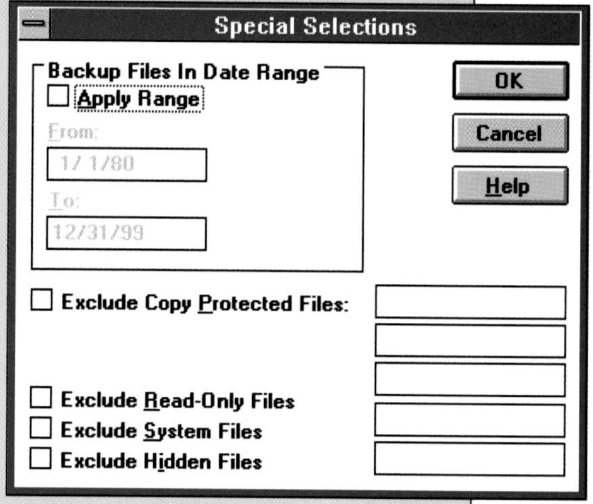

OK
Cancel
Help

As you can see, this lets you customize the backup so that it includes files created or modified within a certain range of dates. It also lets you automatically exclude copy-protected, read-only, hidden, and system files. Click OK when you're done.

Step 3: Scroll around. To see different directory names, scroll up or down through the list in the left pane. To see different filenames, scroll up or down through the list in the right pane. Both backup programs respond to the mouse, if you have one, and you can scroll around easily with the scroll bars. If you use the keyboard with MSBackup, use Tab to move the highlight from the left pane to the right, Shift+Tab to move from the right pane to the left. Use the PgUp and PgDn keys to scroll one screenful at a time in either pane, and use the up and down arrows to move the highlight from one list item to the next.

Step 4: Make your selections. If you have a mouse, make your selections simply by pointing and either double-clicking with the *left* mouse button or by clicking with the *right* mouse button. Either works. To select all the files in a directory, point to the directory name in the left pane and click with the right mouse button or double-click with the left mouse button. If you're using the keyboard with MSBackup, press the Spacebar to select either files or directories. In MSBackup, a check mark appears to the left of each selected filename; in Windows Backup, the filename changes to red and a square block also appears to the left of the filename.

Choose OK to return to the main Backup window. Now you're ready to fine-tune the backup and set it running.

Step 5: Choose the drive you're going to back up to. If the drive you want isn't showing, you can see a list of recognized drives and drive capacities by clicking the Backup To list. (If you're using the keyboard with MSBackup, use Tab to move the highlight to the Backup To button and press the Spacebar to see the available drives.)

Step 6: Choose the backup type. If you're backing up files for the first time, you'll want the default selection, Full, in the Backup Type list. If you're doing a partial backup, open this list and select either an incremental or a differential backup.

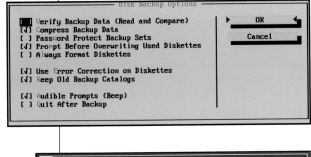

Step 7: Check out your options. At this point, you've really done all you have to do to prepare for a backup, but if this is your first tour through MSBackup or Windows Backup, choose Options and take a moment to view the available options.

These are the settings, mentioned earlier in the chapter, that you can use to "customize" your backups. Whatever options you choose here are stored in the setup file, so choosing them once applies them to all successive backups made from that particular setup file (which you'll get to shortly). As you can see, the most useful options are preselected for you. You can see descriptions of the others in the online Help. If you look at the tips in the margins of this chapter, you'll also find references to two notable options, Always Format Diskettes and Keep Old Backup Catalogs.

Step 8: Back up. Starting the backup process is the easiest choice of all: Choose Start Backup. Anticlimactic as this description seems, choosing Start Backup sets MSBackup or Windows Backup in motion and ends with all the files you selected backed up from the drive you specified to one or more disks in the drive you targeted. Along the way, you'll be prompted to insert additional target disks as they are needed.

Step 9: Save your setup. Before you leave Backup for greener pastures, there's one last item to look at: the Setup File box. By default, MSBackup and Windows Backup keep a list of your backup files and backup settings in the file named DEFAULT.SET. This is fine if you back up the same files all the time, but if you concoct different backup procedures for different sets of files, you can save time

> The Backup option Always Format Diskettes sounds like a good thing, but it isn't necessarily what you want. Both backup programs automatically format unformatted disks; what this option does is tell MSBackup or Windows Backup to format every backup disk you use. Chances are you don't want this. It adds time to the backup, and even if you use a backup disk that already contains files, you don't have to reformat the disk because MSBackup and Windows Backup both tell you that the disk has files on it and ask whether you want to overwrite the existing information.

and effort by recording your file selections and backup choices in different setup files. It's easy:

1. Choose the Save Setup As command from the File menu.

2. In the dialog box that appears, type a name for the setup file. (Make it a standard MS-DOS filename, please, and let MSBackup or Windows Backup assign the extension.) Optionally, fill in the Description box with up to 30 characters that describe the backup set.

```
┌─────────────────────────────────────────────────────┐
│ ▬              Save Setup File                       │
├─────────────────────────────────────────────────────┤
│ Dir:    c:\windows                        ┌────────┐ │
│ File Name:                                │   OK   │ │
│ ┌──────────────────┐                      └────────┘ │
│ │ INVENT.SET       │                      ┌────────┐ │
│ └──────────────────┘                      │ Cancel │ │
│ Description:                              └────────┘ │
│ ┌──────────────────────────────────────┐ ┌────────┐ │
│ │ Mousetraps, anti-grav, etc.          │ │  Help  │ │
│ └──────────────────────────────────────┘ └────────┘ │
│ Files:                 Directories:                  │
│ ┌──────────┐           [..]                          │
│ │default.set│          [lmouse]                       │
│ │          │           [msapps]                       │
│ │          │           [msmail]                       │
│ │          │           [system]                       │
│ │          │           [-a-]                          │
│ │          │           [-b-]                          │
│ │          │           [-c-]                          │
│ └──────────┘                                          │
└─────────────────────────────────────────────────────┘
```

3. If you want, use the Directories box to choose a directory other than the default \DOS directory in which to save the setup file.

4. Choose OK to save the file.

Three Days or Weeks or Months Later

And now, what about later backups? Do you do anything different? Well, not really a whole lot, but:

- If you saved your file selections and settings in a setup file, start off by opening the setup file you need. Choose the file from the Setup File list. If the filename isn't displayed, use the Open Setup command on the File menu to find the file. If you make any changes to your setup file, save the changes with the Save Setup command, also on the File menu.

- If you want to change your file selections, use the Select Files button to make your changes.

- If you want to perform a different type of backup—for example, incremental instead of full, or vice versa—choose the backup type you want.

Comparing Oranges and Oranges

Most of the time, you'll use MSBackup or Windows Backup just to safeguard your important files. On occasion, however, you might want to compare the backup of a file to the original—perhaps to verify that you've backed up the most recent version or simply to verify that the backup was copied accurately. For those times, you use the Compare option in MSBackup and Windows Backup. Once you've walked through a backup, Compare is a snap...except for one small detail: the backup set catalog. Backup set catalogs need a little explanation, so it's time for a small, somewhat dizzying, digression here.

Both MSBackup and Windows Backup keep records of prior backups in two sets of files called master catalogs and backup set catalogs (also rather confusingly known as catalog files). Here's how backup recordkeeping works. When you back up a set of files, MSBackup and Windows Backup save those filenames and your backup settings in a setup file. That setup file is named DEFAULT.SET unless you save your filenames and settings in a different SET file by using the Save As command on the program's File menu. That's not the end of it, though.

In addition to this SET file, MSBackup and Windows Backup also create a detailed record that includes not only a list of the files you backed up and the type of backup you performed, but the directory structure of your source disk and the original locations of those backed-up files. This is all information that MSBackup and Windows Backup use when you tell them to restore files to the disk from which they were backed up. *This* record is saved as a backup set catalog, a file with the extension FUL (for full backup), INC (for incremental), or DIF (for differential).

Now (deep breath), in addition to the setup file and the backup set catalog, MSBackup and Windows Backup also create a master catalog with the extension CAT. This master catalog contains a record of all the backup set catalogs (FUL, INC, and DIF) for each setup (SET) file you use and for each full backup cycle. By default, master catalogs are stored on your hard disk, in your \DOS directory.

Well that's about a thousand words, give or take a few, so here's a picture to help explain them all:

Setup file

```
INVENT.SET

GETMICE.DOC
ANTIGRAV.UFO
NOSMOG.CAR
PEGASUS.PET
NOBREAK.EGG

OPTIONS:
SOUND BEEP
COMPRESS FILES
```

Master catalog

```
INVENT.CAT

BACKUP1.FUL
BACKUP1A.INC
BACKUP1B.INC
```

Master catalog

```
INVENT.CAT

BACKUP2.FUL
BACKUP2A.INC
BACKUP2B.INC
```

When you're working in the Backup window, you might want to turn off the Keep Old Backup Catalogs option to save disk space. If you leave this option turned on, MSBackup and Windows Backup keep saving old catalogs, which eventually become about as useful as those stacks of magazines you keep (the ones that are turning a little yellow with age but that you're convinced you'll sort through one day). If you turn off Keep Old Backup Catalogs, MSBackup and Windows Backup keep only the catalogs for the current backup cycle—a neater arrangement and probably adequate, unless you really need catalogs that go back through more than one backup cycle.

POWER PLAY

What a Weird Filename

Although the diagram at the bottom of the previous page showing backup set catalogs identifies them merely as BACKUP1.FUL, BACKUP1A.INC, and so on, MSBackup and Windows Backup (in real life) assign some rather cryptic names to backup set catalogs. Once you know how to decipher them, though, the names are quite meaningful. Here's an example:

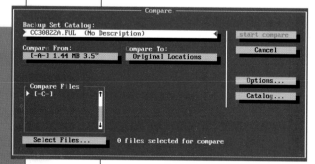

First drive that was backed up ⌐

Day of the backup ⌐

Type of backup performed: FUL=full DIF=differential INC=incremental

C C 3 0 8 2 2 A . F U L

Last drive that was backed up ⌐

└ Sequence order of backup

└ Month of the backup (August)

└ Last digit in year of the backup (1993)

Now, how does all this relate to comparing backups? You choose the backup set catalog containing the file or files you want to compare, and then you choose the actual file(s) to compare.

From the illustrations, you can see that much of the Compare window is similar to the Backup window. To compare backup files with originals, you:

1. Choose Compare from the menu on the opening screen.

2. Select the backup set catalog you need from the Backup Set Catalog list. If you choose a master catalog, you can choose files to compare from any list of files contained in its backup set catalogs. If you choose a backup set catalog, you can compare only the files contained in that catalog.

3. Select the drive containing the backup disk, the drive to compare from.

4. Select the file or files to compare.

5. Choose the drive containing the files to which you want to compare the backups. If you open the Compare To list, you'll see that you can compare backups not only to their original locations, but to files on other drives or in other directories (which makes Compare kind of like a graphical File Compare command).

6. Choose Start Compare to get the comparison going. At the end of the comparison, MSBackup and Windows Backup display a report on what they found.

Restoring to Refill the Same or a Different Tree

And now you come to the last part of MSBackup and Windows Backup, the Restore option, which returns backed-up files either to their original locations or to alternate locations you can specify. Even if you've never seen it before, the Restore window should look really familiar.

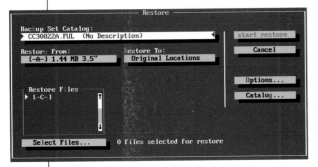

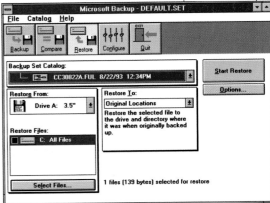

The only real difference between this and the Compare window is the replacement of *Compare* with *Restore*. Here's how to go about restoring files. The process is virtually identical to comparing them:

1. Choose Restore from the menu on the opening screen.

2. Select the catalog you need from the Backup Set Catalog list. If you choose a master catalog, you can choose to restore files from any list contained in its backup set catalogs. If you choose a backup set catalog, you can restore only the files contained in that catalog.

3. Select the drive containing the backup disk, the drive to restore from.

4. Select the file or files to restore.

5. Choose the drive and directory to which you want to restore files. Here, as in Compare, you can specify not only the original location, but other drives or other directories. If you choose to restore files to other drives or directories, however, take one added step.

6. Choose Options and turn on Prompt Before Creating Directories and Prompt Before Overwriting Files (called Prompt Before Overwriting Existing Files in MSBackup). Both of these options will help you protect your existing directory tree and the files in it.

7. Choose Start Restore to begin filling out the branches of your specified directory tree.

The end.

Go Back in Time with Undelete

The Great Mistake

You're busy. You're in a hurry. You type del *.doc without noticing that the current directory is MUSTKEEP. You press Enter. Your hard disk purrs into action and a few seconds later, it's done. All your DOC files are gone from MUSTKEEP. A second after that, you blink dazedly at the command prompt, whack your forehead, and bellow, "I thought I was in the GOTTA-GO directory! What did I just do???"

Sound familiar? Every longtime computer user has just such a tale to tell, and it's the accumulation of those tales, with their sad accompaniment of mournful wails and gnashing teeth, that prompted the inclusion of Undelete in MS-DOS. Undelete—the command for people who (sometimes) act first and think later.

Undelete first appeared in version 5 of MS-DOS. Welcome as it was then, Undelete in version 6 is even better. The new, easier-to-use Undelete can be virtually foolproof, and it comes in two forms, one for MS-DOS and another for Microsoft Windows. Under MS-DOS, Undelete looks and acts like other

commands you run from the command prompt. The Windows-based version is much prettier, but it does basically the same job as its command line cousin.

To use Undelete confidently and well, all you have to do is remember that it serves two closely related functions, one of which is to protect the integrity of deleted files so that Undelete can recover them completely.

- Delete protection is the part of Undelete that safeguards deleted files. You can use either of two protection resources, Delete Tracker or Delete Sentry. When you turn on delete protection, Undelete runs as a memory-resident program, watching for deletions and recording information that will help you recover any files you mistakenly send to oblivion. You don't absolutely have to use delete protection, but it's worth the small amount of memory it consumes (roughly 10 KB to 15 KB), especially because you can unload Undelete if you need the memory it's using.

- After you turn on delete protection you can, of course, use Undelete to recover deleted files. Remember, though: Its effectiveness at recovering files depends a great deal on whether you enabled delete protection.

Now, on to the details.

About Delete Protection

Delete protection is, simply, a matter of turning the job of managing information about deleted files over to Undelete. When you do this, you provide yourself with a level of security that makes it unnecessary to rely only on the file-storage information recorded by MS-DOS—information that can quickly be overwritten and thus make the file unrecoverable by any means.

Providing yourself with delete protection is a simple matter. All you have to do is load Undelete each time you use your computer (or at least whenever you're planning to do some serious deleting) and tell it what type of delete protection you want. You can choose either of two varieties, Delete Sentry or Delete Tracker:

- When you use Delete Sentry, Undelete sets up a hidden directory named SENTRY in which it saves the actual contents of all deleted files. Because the files still exist in the SENTRY directory, they remain completely recoverable. Using Delete Sentry is the most effective method of protecting deleted files. It does, however, require some storage space (typically 7 percent) on your hard disk. If you use Delete Sentry, you can almost always recover deleted files, but you must remember the "almost always" part. It's true that your files do remain intact in the SENTRY directory, but bear in mind that this directory is not endlessly expandable. That means it fills up over time, and when it gets full, Undelete starts getting rid of the oldest files in the directory. And when Undelete gets rid of the files, they're really gone.

- When you use Delete Tracker, Undelete records information about deleted files in a special file of its own. This file, named PCTRACKR.DEL, contains directory and file-storage information related to each deleted file. The trick here is that MS-DOS doesn't erase information in a deleted file—it merely makes a note to itself that the area on disk that has been used to store the file is now free to store other information. In a sense, you can think of PCTRACKR.DEL as a secondary, guarded copy of the MS-DOS file-storage

information, a copy that Undelete can use to recover files—at least until MS-DOS uses their storage locations on disk to hold other files you save. Using Delete Tracker is more effective than relying on MS-DOS alone, but because this method does not protect the actual contents of a file, it is less effective than using Delete Sentry. As you'll see later, Delete Tracker does require some space on the disk, but not as much as Delete Sentry.

And now you come to a rather signi-ficant fork in the road: How you actually start delete protection on your computer depends on whether you're using the MS-DOS version of Undelete or the Windows version. Because the MS-DOS and Windows versions of Undelete look wildly different, they're covered separately in the rest of this chapter. The topics are organized as follows:

Delete Sentry or Delete Tracker: Choose one. You don't know when you might need some protection.

- Configuring Delete Protection
  - Delete Protection with MS-DOS Undelete
  - Delete Protection with Windows Undelete
- Recovering Deleted Files
  - Recovering Files with MS-DOS Undelete
  - Recovering Files with Windows Undelete

Configuring Delete Protection

When you start delete protection with Windows Undelete, it adds the Undelete command you need to your AUTOEXEC.BAT file; as a result, delete protection is automatically launched whenever you start or restart your computer. If you're using MS-DOS, your Undelete doesn't do this, so you should give some serious consideration to adding an Undelete command to AUTOEXEC.BAT as well.

Is there anything else you need to know? Only this: The first time you use delete protection, Undelete creates a file named UNDELETE.INI in your \DOS directory. This file contains the settings it is currently using—the drives you've protected, the type of protection, and so on. The next time you start Undelete, it refers to UNDELETE.INI and sets itself up to run the same way. Nice touch.

Delete Protection with MS-DOS Undelete

To start delete protection, either from the command prompt or with a command in AUTOEXEC.BAT, you can use a simple:

```
undelete /load
```

The /load switch tells Undelete to start Sentry protection for your hard disk and to use its default settings for such matters as the amount of disk space it reserves and the length of time it monitors files before purging them from your SENTRY directory. This is probably the only form of the command you need, but if you want to protect more than your hard disk or use Delete Tracker instead of Delete Sentry, you can use either of the following forms of the command instead:

```
undelete /sdrive
```

or:

```
undelete /tdrive[-files]
```

/sdrive applies Delete Sentry protection to the drive or drives you specify as drive. To include several drives in the same command, repeat the /s and use a space to separate the switches—for example:

```
C:\>undelete /sc /sa
```

/tdrive applies Delete Tracker protection to the drive you specify as drive. If you want, you can also specify a number from 1 through 999 for files, to tell Delete Tracker how many entries to include in its PCTRACKR.DEL file. You can include several drives in the same command here too. For example:

```
C:\>undelete /tc /ta-30 /tb
```

If you omit files, by the way, Undelete uses the following values:

Undelete: Delete Tracker Default Values		
Disk Capacity	**Number of Files**	**Size of PCTRACKR.DEL**
360 KB	25	5 KB
720 KB	50	9 KB
1.2 MB, 1.44 MB	75	14 KB
20 MB	101	18 KB
32 MB	202	36 KB
Larger than 32 MB	303	55 KB

After you start delete protection, you can use three additional switches to check on and control Undelete:

```
undelete /unload /status /purge[drive]
```

/unload removes Undelete from memory. Using this switch frees about 13 KB of memory, but you must remember that unloading Undelete also means that delete protection will no longer be in effect.

/status produces a report on Undelete and the method of protection currently in effect. The report looks something like this:

```
UNDELETE - A delete protection facility
Copyright (C) 1987-1993 Central Point Software, Inc.
All rights reserved.


Delete Protection Method is Delete Sentry.
Enabled for drives : C
```

/purge[drive] purges the SENTRY directory for the drive you specify as *drive*. If you don't specify a drive, Undelete searches the current drive. Use /purge with caution. Once the command is carried out, all the deleted files in your SENTRY directory will be gone for good. If you think you want to purge the file, first review its contents, as described in the section "Recovering Files with MS-DOS Undelete," beginning on page 258.

Delete Protection with Windows Undelete

If you're using Windows Undelete, you do the following to start Undelete and turn on delete protection:

1. Open the Microsoft Tools program group.

2. Double-click the Undelete icon.

3. Choose Configure Delete Protection from the Options menu.

   If this is your first exposure to Undelete, click each of the options. As you do, the description in the shadowed box to the right will tell you about the option you selected. When you finish, click the option you want (only one is active at a time) and click OK.

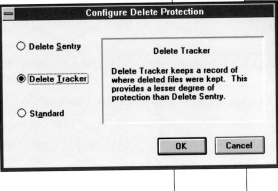

4. If you chose Standard, meaning no delete protection, that's it. If you chose either Delete Sentry or Delete Tracker, however, a second dialog box appears.

- For Delete Sentry, most of the default settings in the dialog box are probably adequate. Use the Drives button to extend protection to other drives. You might also want to change the settings for the length of time files are to stay in the SENTRY directory or the amount of space you want to set aside for deleted files. By default, Delete Sentry includes all files (*.*) under its protective wing except for files with the extensions listed in the Exclude box. These settings

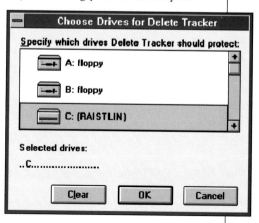

are probably fine, but you can modify either the include or the exclude list if you want. When you finish, click OK. If you are configuring delete protection for the first time, Undelete will tell you that it can change your AUTOEXEC.BAT file. Then, whether you're doing this for the first or the fifteenth time, Undelete ends the session by reminding you to reboot your computer to have the changes take effect.

- If you chose Delete Tracker, the second dialog box you see, as shown at right, is much simpler.

  Here, all you do is identify the drives to be affected by deletion tracking. Click one or more drives to select them. If you change your mind (or if, at a later time, you want to disable

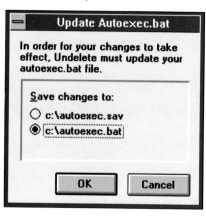

protection for a drive), either click the selected drive again or choose the Clear button at the bottom of the dialog box. When you finish and click OK, you'll see a message telling you to reboot the computer. If you're configuring deletion tracking for the first time, Windows Undelete will precede this message with an offer to change AUTOEXEC.BAT for you.

Recovering Deleted Files

Of course, the whole idea of using delete protection—or any feature of the Undelete command—is to recover files you deleted by mistake. You don't have to understand exactly how Undelete works in order to use it, but to avoid frustration (as in "What do you mean you *can't* recover that file?"), you should know a little about how MS-DOS deletes files and how its behavior relates to delete protection and file recovery.

Basically, you need to know how MS-DOS uses a little something called the file allocation table, or FAT, to record file-storage information. If you've read earlier chapters of this book, you know that MS-DOS doesn't place files on disk as long, continuous strings of bytes. It stores files in equal-size compartments known as clusters. Sometimes clusters containing the pieces of a single file are physically all over the map on a well-used disk, especially a hard disk. Now, it's true that only programmers really need the inside scoop on clusters, but it certainly helps to know that MS-DOS locates clusters by number and that it uses a file's directory entry and the FAT to record the numbers of the clusters occupied by the file. So how does all this relate to deletions?

When you delete a file, MS-DOS doesn't actually go out to the disk and physically clean out all the clusters in which the file is stored. Instead, MS-DOS marks the file's directory entry and FAT entries as available for reuse. Even this information isn't actually removed, however, so although the file is gone in your mind, enough traces of it remain on disk for a file-recovery program such as Undelete to trace and restore the file's directory entry and FAT entry and thus restore the file to its rightful place. But two key factors determine how well a file can be recovered:

- What you did between the time you deleted the file and the time you realized you had to get it back

- What type of delete protection, if any, you had in place when the file was deleted

If you don't use delete protection, the only way you can get a file back is by using the information that MS-DOS recorded in the file's directory entry and the FAT. If you delete a file, immediately realize you made a mistake, and immediately use Undelete, you should have no problem recovering the file. However, if you have changed the state of the disk—for example, by saving another file—your deleted file might not be recoverable. The reason: MS-DOS might have overwritten the file's directory entry, some or all of its FAT entries, and even some of the clusters containing the actual file contents. And once overwritten, information cannot be recovered. Not at all, not ever.

If you were using Delete Tracker at the time you deleted the file, your chances of recovery are better than if you were relying only on MS-DOS: Undelete can refer to the PCTRACKR.DEL file to find the information it needs to restore the file. Here too, however, the file might not be fully recoverable if you've saved another file and MS-DOS has used clusters belonging to the deleted file to store the recently saved file.

If you were using Delete Sentry to protect the file, you should be in fine shape, unless you deleted the file so long ago that Undelete has purged it from the SENTRY directory. If the file hasn't been purged, however, it's fully recoverable because its contents are safely tucked away in the SENTRY directory.

Enough theory; onward to practice. If you have both MS-DOS Undelete and Windows Undelete, you should read both of the following sections. Windows Undelete makes file recovery easy and quick, but it undeletes only files judged to be in Perfect, Excellent, or Good condition. To recover files that are in Poor or Destroyed condition, you must use MS-DOS Undelete.

Recovering Files with MS-DOS Undelete

To recover deleted files with MS-DOS Undelete, you use the following command form:

```
undelete[file-specification] /ds /dt /dos /all /list
```

file-specification is the drive, path, filename, and extension of the file or files you want to recover. You can use wildcards to undelete a group of files. If you omit a file specification, Undelete assumes all files in the current directory.

/ds undeletes files protected by Delete Sentry, prompting for confirmation before recovering each file from the SENTRY directory.

Undeleting Files with MS-DOS Undelete

- Remember to include a drive and path if the file or files to undelete are not in the current directory. Doing this will save you from the shock of seeing *No entries found* when you know that you did, indeed, delete the file you're trying to recover.

- When you use the /ds and /dt switches, bear in mind that the *only* files you'll see listed are those that match your file specification and have the type of protection you specified. That is, /ds lists only files protected by Delete Sentry; /dt lists only files protected by Delete Tracker.

- When you use the /dos switch, you see all files that match your file specification—in the records kept by MS-DOS (which include nearly all your files).

/dt undeletes files protected by Delete Tracker, also prompting for confirmation before recovering each one.

/dos undeletes files using the information kept by MS-DOS, again prompting for confirmation. When you use this switch, Undelete displays a question mark in place of the first character in the name of each deleted file. If you choose to undelete the file, you'll be asked to type a character to replace the question mark. The whole thing looks like this:

```
Using the MS-DOS directory method.

    ?EST1              18  8-22-93 10:35a  ...A  Undelete (Y/N)?y
    Please type the first character for ?EST1   .  : t


File successfully undeleted.
```

/all undeletes files without prompting for confirmation before recovering each. When you use the /all switch, Undelete uses the SENTRY directory if it is available. If there is no SENTRY directory, it uses deletion tracking. If that is not available either, Undelete turns to MS-DOS. If it has to use the MS-DOS file-storage records, Undelete replaces the missing first character of each filename with a number sign (#). If this produces a duplicate filename, it then tries each of the following characters, in order: #%&0123456789ABCDEFGHIJKLM NOPQRSTUVWXYZ. If you use the /all switch and end up with filenames starting with # or some other character, use the MS-DOS Rename command to correct the filenames. For example:

```
C:\>ren #aved.doc saved.doc
```

/list produces a list of deleted files but does not recover any of them. The list you see depends on the file specification you provide (of course) and on whether you use the /ds, /dt, or /dos switch.

Now, with all that under your belt, you're probably itching for a demonstration. The illustration here shows what Undelete looks like when you specify the /ds switch:

As you can see, Undelete displays quite a bit of information. Even though the /ds switch was specified in the command that produced this output, you can see that Undelete runs through its repertoire, reporting not only on the SENTRY directory but on

> **If you don't use the /ds, /dt, and /dos switches in your command, Undelete first tries the SENTRY directory if it exists, then the deletion-tracking file, and finally the MS-DOS records. If you don't know how a deleted file was protected, this is the way to try to find it.**

```
C:\>undelete /ds

UNDELETE - A delete protection facility
Copyright (C) 1987-1993 Central Point Software, Inc.
All rights reserved.

Directory: C:\
File Specifications: *.*

    Delete Sentry control file contains     1 deleted files.

    Deletion-tracking file contains     0 deleted files.
    Of those,     0 files have all clusters available,
                  0 files have some clusters available,
                  0 files have no clusters available.

    MS-DOS directory contains     1 deleted files.
    Of those,     0 files may be recovered.

Using the Delete Sentry method.

    NEWFILE  DOC     54928  8-04-93  6:20a  ...A  Deleted: 8-24-93  7:19p
This file can be 100% undeleted. Undelete (Y/N)?
```

the deletion-tracking file (nonexistent in this example) and the MS-DOS directory information (which here tells you that the single deleted file that Undelete found through MS-DOS can't be recovered). Interesting as these items are, however, the real point of Undelete shows at the end of the display—specifically, in the line that says *This file can be 100% undeleted. Undelete (Y/N)?* If you ever have to recover a file, this will be a most welcome message. And even though the display isn't very colorful, when a needed file is at stake, who cares?

Beyond this, remember only that when you type a file specification you must think about how Undelete will respond to it. Above all, remember to include a drive and path if the file was not deleted from the current directory. If you're in, say, the SUN directory and the file you want to undelete was stored in the STARS directory, typing undelete eclipse.doc will net you *No entries found*— a discouraging message at the least, and a potential shock if the file was especially valuable.

POWER PLAY

What About Directories?

The MS-DOS version of Undelete has some strengths you don't find in Windows Undelete, but it also has a single great weakness. MS-DOS Undelete can recover even badly damaged files, which Windows Undelete cannot do, but as counterpoint to that, you must remember that MS-DOS Undelete normally can't recover the contents of a deleted directory. The *only* time you can "trick" Undelete into recovering files in a deleted directory is when you've had the deleted directory and its files under Sentry protection. To try to recover the directory and its files, do the following:

1. Re-create the deleted directory. That is, if you deleted TENTS and all the files in it, use the Make Directory command to make a new TENTS directory,

in exactly the same part of the directory tree it inhabited before.

2. Use Undelete and specify the newly re-created directory as part of the file specification. For example, to recover all deleted files in TENTS, type undelete \tents*.* as your command.

This should cause Undelete to find and display the files in your TENTS directory. It won't display any subdirectories of TENTS, but if you re-create those subdirectories, you should be able to recover their files as well by entering a separate Undelete command for each—for example, undelete \tents\camps*.* and so on.

If you tend to use Deltree with gay abandon, let Delete Sentry be your conscience and your guide.

Recovering Files with Windows Undelete

Windows Undelete, as you can see from the illustrations, is far livelier looking than MS-DOS Undelete. It's also stronger in one respect: It can recover deleted directories as well as deleted files. If you delete a directory, with or without subdirectories, and you have to recover it, use Windows Undelete right away, and follow this simple process:

1. Undelete the directory.

2. Display that directory.

3. Undelete the files you want to recover.

If the directory contained subdirectories with additional files you want to recover, follow the same three steps for each subdirectory.

Do note, however, that Windows Undelete can't recover all deleted files. Any that it finds in Poor or Destroyed condition are beyond its reach. Your only recourse for files in such bad shape is MS-DOS Undelete. And even then, complete recovery is far from guaranteed. Beyond this basic warning, recovering files or directories with Windows Undelete is easy. First, however, a look at the Undelete window (shown above).

Here are the high points:

- The list taking up most of the window is, of course, a list of deleted files in the current directory. Notice that Undelete tells you what condition the files are in. Remember that Undelete can't recover files that are in Poor or Destroyed condition. Because of this, even though such files are listed in the window, they're "grayed out" and can't be selected.

- The notes at the bottom of the window tell you about the currently selected file: where it came from, how it was protected, and so on.

- The row of large buttons labeled Undelete, Drive/Dir, and so on are fast alternatives to choosing commands from the File menu. Here, briefly, is what these buttons do:

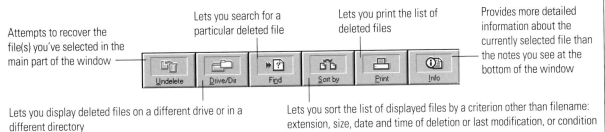

Attempts to recover the file(s) you've selected in the main part of the window

Lets you search for a particular deleted file

Lets you print the list of deleted files

Provides more detailed information about the currently selected file than the notes you see at the bottom of the window

Lets you display deleted files on a different drive or in a different directory

Lets you sort the list of displayed files by a criterion other than filename: extension, size, date and time of deletion or last modification, or condition

When you click the Find button, you see a dialog box like this one:

Notice that not only can you provide a file specification in this dialog box, you can—happily—even tell Windows Undelete to search the files you specify for specific text. Do remember to include a drive and path, however; by default, Find searches every deleted file on the current disk—not those displayed in the Undelete window alone. Choose the Groups button in this dialog box if you want Windows Undelete to search for deleted files associated with particular applications, such as Windows Notepad or Microsoft Word for Windows.

Find Deleted Files

File specification:
`*.*`

Containing:

☒ Ignore case
☐ Whole word

OK
Cancel
Groups...

Deleted files found: 0
Search drive: C:

Now, about undeleting files. That's the easy part, provided the files are in reasonably good condition:

1. Use the Drive/Dir button to display deleted files for the drive and directory you want to work with.

2. By pointing and clicking, select one or more files to undelete. Windows Undelete will highlight each one as you go. Click a selected file again to unselect it.

3. Choose the Undelete button. (Or, if you prefer, press Alt+U or choose Undelete from the File menu.) If the file was protected by MS-DOS, Windows Undelete will ask you to provide the first letter of the filename before it continues, like this:

Enter First Character

The first letter of this file was destroyed by MS-DOS. Please type in the new first letter.
? HARON.DOC
All normal characters are valid.

OK   Cancel

That's all there is to it. Just remember the other buttons in the window if you ever have to search for a deleted file or you want to narrow the search by scanning files for specific text.

Undelete. There you have it. May you seldom have to use it.

Transfer Files with Interlnk

Ten-Dollar Network Anyone?

So you finally got that laptop computer. Or your business grew to the point that you needed another machine. Or maybe you bought a small computer for the kids so they wouldn't hog yours and clog its hard disk with games and school-work. For whatever reason, you ended up with two computers. More comput-ers, more fun, right? Are you also having lots of fun copying files to floppies so that you can move them from one machine to the other? Or have you, perhaps, been tearing out your hair over file transfer because the two computers have different-size floppy drives? Well, relief is here. Buy a ten-dollar cable, and

in minutes you and MS-DOS can create a miniature network all your own—a network in which you can shuttle files from one computer to the other and, if you want, even use one com-puter to run programs installed on the other.

Sounds good, doesn't it? But it's not too good to be true. Oh, there *is* a catch, of course: The comput-ers have to be relatively close to-gether, say within about 6 feet of each other. But otherwise, all you need is the cable and MS-DOS. As Ross Perot might say, "It's that simple."

What's in a Name?

The part of MS-DOS you use for transferring files between computers is actually a trio of programs named Interlnk, INTERLNK.EXE, and Intersvr (short for Interlnk server). These three programs work closely together, to the extent that you can't use one without the others. To help you figure out what's what, this chapter uses *file transfer* to refer to the entire file-transfer feature, *Interlnk* (no little *i*) for the file-transfer command. That said, get ready to use file transfer, the feature.

As mentioned, file transfer is a three-part harmony in which each piece has a vital role to play. Here are the pieces and what they do:

- INTERLNK.EXE is a device driver that enables a computer to use files stored on another computer. Like all installable device drivers, INTERLNK.EXE must be loaded into memory at startup, with a command in your CONFIG.SYS file. More about this later.

- Interlnk is the program you run on the *client*, the computer that is going to use files stored on another computer.

- Intersvr is the program you run on the *server*, the computer that is going to share files with the client.

A Little Net Speak

If you haven't experienced the joys of working on a network, you might find the terms *client* and *server* a little confusing, so here's a brief explanation.

A network, as you undoubtedly know, is a bunch of computers that are connected so that they can communicate with one another: transfer electronic mail, share files, and so on. To complicate matters, networks come in different types. For example, there are *peer-to-peer* networks in which all computers are "equals," able to share their resources with any other computers in the network. Another type of network, known as a *client/server* network, consists of one or more central computers (servers) to which other computers (clients) connect when they need to use shared files, printers, and other resources. In a client/server network, the server provides, and the client receives. This is basically the way file transfer works in MS-DOS, and that's why the computer that provides files is called the server and the computer that receives files is called the client.

Getting Back to That Cable

Before you can do anything about transferring files, you must, of course, have a means of linking your computers. Either of the following will work:

- A free serial port on each computer, plus a 7-wire, null modem cable to connect the two machines

> About that name, Interlnk. It's not a typo. It's pure MS-DOS: an eight-character filename assigned to a feature that could have used just one more letter. Sometimes those filename limits can be just a bit constricting....

- A free parallel port on each computer, plus a bidirectional parallel cable to connect the two

Whoa, there! What's that?

Well, this stuff sounds technical, but don't worry. First of all, most computers these days come with one or two serial and parallel ports installed, so the chances are pretty good that your computers already have available ports. If you don't know how to check for these, take a look at the back of your computer; the ports should be marked. If they're not, start Microsoft Diagnostics by typing **msd**. If you're looking for serial ports, choose COM Ports on the opening screen. If you're looking for parallel ports, choose LPT Ports instead.

As for the cables, they're easy too. A null modem cable is basically a serial cable with a twist. In it, two wires—the sending and receiving wires—are crossed so that the wire used to transmit by one computer is used to receive by the other, and vice versa. Similarly, a bidirectional parallel cable is simply a parallel cable that can transfer information in both directions. Although their names make these cables sound all serious and technically complex, you should have little trouble getting one. All you have to do is take a trip to your local computer store. A null modem cable of the type that was used for the testing in this book is relatively easy to find and should cost you about ten dollars. A bidirectional parallel cable might be a little harder to locate, but a hardware dealer or a printer store should be able to help you out.

Once you've got the cable you need, just plug each end into an appropriate port on each of your computers. Now you're ready to set up file transfer itself.

Setting Up

Although file transfer is very easy to use once you've set it up, it does involve setting up three programs, so you'll probably welcome a little hand-holding the first time around. All you really need is to know what steps to take and when. Here they are in brief—for full descriptions, see the upcoming descriptions of Interlnk, INTERLNK.EXE, and Intersvr.

1. Set up the server—the computer that will be supplying files. If version 6 of MS-DOS is installed on the server, all you have to do is run the Intersvr program on it with the following command:

   ```
   C:\>intersvr
   ```

   If the server is running an earlier version of MS-DOS, however, you'll have to transfer the files you need to it first. The easiest way to do this is to resort to floppy disks and manually transfer the Interlnk and Intersvr files. If you're comfortable with computers, however, you can use the Intersvr remote copy command, described later.

2. Set up the client—the computer that will be receiving files. The first time you use file transfer, this involves modifying CONFIG.SYS and rebooting the computer to install the INTERLNK.EXE device driver. Basically, this just involves adding a Device command line to CONFIG.SYS:

```
DEVICE=C:\DOS\INTERLNK.EXE
```

(If your MS-DOS files are in a directory other than \DOS, you use your directory name instead, but you know that. For more details, refer to the description of INTERLNK.EXE.)

3. After you install INTERLNK.EXE on the client and reboot the computer, set up the client for file transfer by running the Interlnk command. The basic command is a simple:

```
C:\>interlnk
```

You can, however, expand this command to specify particular drives on the client and server computers. Details coming up.

Transferring Files

After you've set up the software, you can transfer files from the server to the client with ease. The procedure is simple and very similar to the procedure outlined for setting up:

1. Start Intersvr on the server computer. When you start Intersvr, a full-screen display appears. In the middle of the display is a box (shown at right) listing the drives and printers you can use from the client computer.

```
This Computer      Other Computer
  (Server)            (Client)

A:               equals  C:
B:               equals  D:
C: (505Mb)       equals  E:
D: (4Mb)         equals  Not Connected
LPT1:            equals  LPT2:
LPT2:            equals  LPT3:
LPT3:            equals  Not Connected
```

2. Run Interlnk on the client. When you do, you see a display very similar to the one produced by Intersvr but (as shown below) with a list of drive letters on your computer that are redirected (roughly, linked) to drives on the server.

```
C:\>interlnk
    Port=COM1
    This Computer      Other Computer
      (Client)            (Server)

    E:        equals  A:
    F:        equals  B:
    G:        equals  C:
    LPT2:     equals  LPT1:
C:\>
```

If Intersvr is not running on the server when you boot the client computer or try to start Interlnk, you'll see the message *Connection NOT established*. Horrifying as this sounds, all it means is that Interlnk sought but did not find its partner Intersvr. To patch things up, run Intersvr on the server, and then run Interlnk again.

At first, this display looks a little confusing, but just take it easy and all will be clear. The display is telling you what drive letter on the client (*This Computer*) you should use to access a particular drive on the server (*Other Computer*). For example, if Interlnk tells you that drive letter M on the client equals drive C on the server, all you have to do to access files on the server's drive C is pretend that it's really drive M on the client. To get a directory listing of the server's drive C, for instance, you would either:

– Change the current drive (on the client) to M and then use Dir:

```
M:\>dir
```

– Or request a directory listing for drive M:

```
C:\>dir m:
```

This might all sound a little dizzying, but once you've accessed a server drive, you'll agree it's really a piece of cake.

3. To quit and return to having two independently functioning computers, press Alt+F4 on the server. When you use file transfer, your server computer is literally the slave of the client computer and cannot be used for anything but providing files. When you quit by pressing Alt+F4, you break the connection, end your transfer session, and return your server to full functionality.

A Closer Look at INTERLNK.EXE

INTERLNK.EXE is the device driver that enables the client computer to use the Interlnk command to access files on the server. As already mentioned, you install INTERLNK.EXE with a Device command in CONFIG.SYS. When you first install it, you'll need to reboot your computer to load the driver. (MS-DOS reads device drivers into memory only at startup.)

When you edit your CONFIG.SYS file to install INTERLNK.EXE, a simple:

```
DEVICE=C:\DOS\INTERLNK.EXE
```

should be fine for most systems. Be sure, however, to add the command *after* (below) any other CONFIG.SYS commands that assign drive letters—for example, place INTERLNK.EXE below a Device command that creates a RAM drive.

By default, INTERLNK.EXE loads into upper memory—if, that is, you configured MS-DOS to use UMBs and if there's enough room available. By default, INTERLNK.EXE requires a fairly hefty 8 KB to 9 KB of memory because it scans all available ports, assuming you'll want to use them all. If you don't need all of INTERLNK.EXE's capabilities, however, you can cut its appetite for RAM with three optional switches:

- /com, which eliminates scanning parallel ports for the file-transfer connection. For example, if you're using a null (serial) modem cable, you can use the command:

```
DEVICE=C:\DOS\INTERLNK.EXE /COM
```

- /lpt, which eliminates scanning serial ports for the file-transfer connection. For example, if you're using a bidirectional (parallel) cable, you can use the command:

```
DEVICE=C:\DOS\INTERLNK.EXE /LPT
```

- /noprinter, which eliminates support for using a printer connected to the server. For example:

```
DEVICE=C:\DOS\INTERLNK.EXE /NOPRINTER
```

The device driver also includes a number of other switches. If you're interested in them, or if you use Microsoft Windows, refer to the online MS-DOS Help for INTERLNK.EXE.

When you want to add a Device command for INTERLNK.EXE to your CONFIG.SYS file, take a moment to check out one other item: the highest drive letter that MS-DOS will recognize on your system. By default, MS-DOS recognizes one letter more than the highest drive letter on your system. As you saw earlier, however, MS-DOS needs some spare letters on the client so that it can use them as "aliases" for the actual drives on the server. The command you need to check (or add) is called Lastdrive, and it has a really simple form:

```
lastdrive=letter
```

where *letter*, which can be any letter through Z, specifies the highest drive letter MS-DOS will recognize.

When you check the Lastdrive command in your CONFIG.SYS, be sure that it specifies a drive letter high enough to accommodate all the drives on the client—including RAM drives, CD-ROM drives, and host drives for DoubleSpace—and still leaves enough spare letters to cover the drives you're going to use on the server.

SERIAL MICE AND WINDOWS

If you use a serial mouse with Microsoft Windows, use either the /com switch or the /lpt switch to tell INTERLNK.EXE to skip the serial port your mouse is using. If you connect your computers through serial ports, include the /com switch and tack on the number of the port to which you're attaching the cable. For example:

```
DEVICE=C:\DOS\INTERLNK.EXE /COM2
```

If you connect through parallel ports, just add the /lpt switch to be sure that INTERLNK.EXE does not scan your serial ports:

```
DEVICE=C:\DOS\INTERLNK.EXE /LPT
```

For more information, refer to the MS-DOS online Help for INTERLNK.EXE.

A Closer Look at Interlnk and Intersvr

Interlnk and Intersvr are the matching halves, the yin and yang, of file transfer under MS-DOS. Interlnk always runs on the client computer; Intersvr always runs on the server. Both programs run reliably if you start them with the simplest possible commands:

```
C:\>intersvr
```

on the server and:

```
C:\>interlnk
```

on the client.

Both commands do, however, take some optional parameters and switches, so here's a closer look at ways you can enhance each one.

For Intersvr, the enhanced (though still not complete) form of the basic command is as follows:

```
intersvr [drive:] /x=drive: /rcopy
```

drive specifies a particular drive on the server that you want to make available for file sharing. If you don't specify a drive, Intersvr shares all drives on the computer. You can specify more than one drive in a single command by separating the letters with spaces, like so:

```
C:>intersvr a: c:
```

/x excludes the drive you specify as *drive* from being shared. For example, if you don't want to share drive D, the command would be:

```
C:\>intersvr /x=d:
```

/rcopy, which stands for remote copy, should be needed (if ever) only the first time you use Intersvr on a new server, and then only if the server is not running version 6 of MS-DOS. What /rcopy does is transfer the files you need from the client to the server—necessary because these files did not appear before version 6.0. Basically, then, you need /rcopy only if your server is running a version from 3.0 through 5.0 of MS-DOS. To transfer the files via remote copy, do the following:

1. Cable the computers together if necessary.

2. On the *client* computer (which must be running MS-DOS 6.0 or 6.2), type:

```
C:\>intersvr /rcopy
```

When you do this, a remote-copy display appears on the client screen, as shown here:

```
                        InterInk Remote Installation



 Interlnk will copy its program files to another computer that is connected
 to this one by a 7-wire null-modem cable.

 Before continuing, make sure the cable connects the two computers' serial
 ports.


 Specify the serial port of the other computer, and then press ENTER:

                          ┌─────────┐
                          │  COM1   │
                          │  COM2   │
                          └─────────┘



Enter=Continue    F3=Exit              │
```

Choose the serial port that connects the computers, press Enter, and Intersvr will walk you through the process of transferring the files. This will involve typing a few odd-looking MS-DOS commands, but don't worry. Follow the instructions and everything will be fine.

Now, what about the other star of the show, Interlnk? Its command form is extremely simple:

```
interlnk [client:]=[server:]
```

client is a specific drive letter that you want to use on the client to refer to a particular drive on the server. If you use this form of the command, be sure that the letter you choose is a valid—and available—drive letter on the client computer. And note that the parameters are optional. Accepting the default assignments that the device driver makes is a very safe way to go.

server, of course, is the letter of the drive on the server that you want to equate with the drive letter you specify as *client*. Be sure that the *server* drive actually exists and is listed in the display shown when you start Intersvr on the server.

For example, suppose you are very fond of typing the letter *X* and decide you want to use *X* to refer to the server's drive C. Start Interlnk by typing:

```
C:\>interlnk x:=c:
```

To break the link, type the command again, this time leaving out the server drive:

```
C:\>interlnk x:=
```

At any time after starting Interlnk, you can also check on the current status of drive assignments with the command:

```
C:\>interlnk
```

Grow Your Disks with DoubleSpace

The Dynamic Duo

Everyone who's heard about version 6 of MS-DOS has likely heard about DoubleSpace, the disk-compression utility that pulls scores of megabytes of extra storage out of a hard disk with the élan of a magician pulling a rabbit out of a hat.

How does DoubleSpace do such a thing? Basically, it turns one disk into two— a normal uncompressed drive and a second compressed drive that often holds twice as much as it should be able to. Details follow, but before you get to them there's a little matter to take care of: rumors.

Rumor Central and Peace of Mind

Perhaps you've heard that DoubleSpace in version 6.0 is not completely reliable—that it can sometimes cause problems on a hard disk, up to and including loss of data. Is there truth to these rumors? Partial truth, but not nearly what the stories would indicate. Some of the problems actually result from user error, but others don't.

On a computer with a normal, healthy hard disk, DoubleSpace in both versions 6.0 and 6.2 of MS-DOS is safe, reliable, and effective. With some hard disks, however, DoubleSpace can be too demanding a drill sergeant. It works a hard disk…well, hard. And some disks, for various reasons, cannot handle the stress. They falter. Is DoubleSpace the problem? Not really. In most cases, it's merely the last straw on the camel's back.

To bring peace of mind to the doubters of the world, DoubleSpace in version 6.2 includes several safety features not found in version 6.0—features that the

MS-DOS people at Microsoft like to equate with a "passenger-side airbag and antilock brakes." The main additions are:

- A data-protection program called DoubleGuard
- A more rigorous setup process that relies on ScanDisk to verify the reliability of a drive about to undergo compression
- The ability to uncompress a DoubleSpaced drive

In version 6.2, DoubleSpace does everything it can to protect your data. If you still mistrust it, however, there's only one thing for you to do: Don't use DoubleSpace. MS-DOS will work fine on your computer, but you will be missing the advantages of disk compression. In the end, it's really your choice.

How Does It Work?

DoubleSpace is what's technically known as a disk-compression utility. There's a lot of magic behind DoubleSpace, but as already mentioned, DoubleSpace essentially works by splitting one drive into two drives, one compressed and the other uncompressed. But that still doesn't explain how compression works, does it? Well, take a look at compression itself. What does it mean? What's being compressed, the disk itself? Of course not. DoubleSpace compresses files. When you use compression on a disk, you make it possible for DoubleSpace to save files on the disk in a special shrunken format. Think of it this way. Suppose you wanted to pack a dozen inflated balloons into a shoebox. The obvious thing to do is deflate the balloons.

That's basically what DoubleSpace does: It lets the "air" out of files so that they take up less room on the disk. When DoubleSpace compresses a file, the file normally shrinks to about half its former size. Once it's been shrunk, the file then requires half the disk storage it needed previously. The net result, then, is that your free disk space "grows" by the same amount your file shrank.

Luckily, you don't have to know any more about how compression happens than you have to know how a magic cookie could make Alice small in Wonderland. You can still enjoy the result, and where DoubleSpace is concerned, once you understand that it makes files smaller, you understand the basics of disk compression. All you need from this point on are a few more details that help define the terms you encounter when you use DoubleSpace.

The File That Acts Like a Disk

Although a DoubleSpaced disk is split into compressed and uncompressed portions, the disk is still, of course, a single piece of hardware. But to MS-DOS, the split is so complete that the compressed and uncompressed portions are even known by different drive letters.

For example, if you compress your entire hard disk, drive C, you end up with two drive letters that refer to it: C for the compressed portion and another letter, usually *H*, for the uncompressed portion. If you want a listing of the files on drive C, you type:

```
C:\>dir
```

If you want a listing of the files on drive H, you type:

```
C:\>dir h:
```

Now, how do these two parts of the disk differ? Well, here's where things get a little metaphysical. The uncompressed portion of the drive is reserved for files that cannot (or ought not) be compressed, among them your MS-DOS system files, a SENTRY directory if you use delete protection, and a Windows swap file (which Windows uses while it's "swapping" active files in and out of memory).

The uncompressed portion is also the home of the compressed disk. What? Exactly so. In fact, the uncompressed part of the disk is known as the host of the compressed drive. When you compress a disk, DoubleSpace creates, unknown to you and unseen by the world, a special file on the uncompressed (host) drive. This file is called a compressed volume file, or CVF, and it usually has the name DBLSPACE.000. Now, this CVF can be huge. It can, in fact, take up most of the physical disk space on the host. For example, if you request a directory listing of a DBLSPACE file, you see something like this:

```
Volume in drive H is HOST_FOR_C
Volume Serial Number is 1B15-4674
Directory of H:\

DBLSPACE 000 118,468,096 08-29-93   5:22p
        1 file(s)  118,468,096 bytes
                     2,557,952 bytes free
```

Some whopping file, isn't it? Why is it so big? Because the CVF is where DoubleSpace actually stores all the files you save on the compressed disk. The CVF—the hidden file named DBLSPACE.000— essentially becomes the compressed disk.

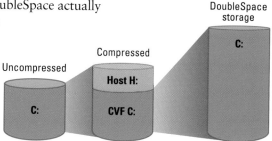

DoubleSpace storage

Compressed

Uncompressed

But what's the point of the CVF? Why does Double-Space have to put files in another file? The point is that a compressed file is not usable in its shrunken form. Before a program can work with it, the file must be fattened up again. That's the job DoubleSpace handles, and that's why it uses a CVF to hold compressed files.

DoubleSpace shrinks and expands files "on the fly," as they're being moved to and from memory and the disk. Essentially, DoubleSpace acts as their guardian. When a program calls for a particular file, DoubleSpace searches the CVF, finds and uncompresses the file, and passes the now-usable file to the rest of MS-DOS. Its work temporarily over (where that file is concerned), DoubleSpace then settles down and waits for its charge to come home, at which time it recompresses the file and puts it back into the CVF fold.

Teaching MS-DOS to Read Compressed Disks

Given a basic understanding of compression and the CVF, is there more you need to know? A little more. You have to know about DBLSPACE.BIN and DBLSPACE.INI. The relationships between these two files and DBLSPACE.000 are close to the point of entanglement, but located at the heart of disk compression is DBLSPACE.BIN.

DBLSPACE.BIN is the brains of the operation. Without it, you have no DoubleSpace. Not only that, you have no access to DoubleSpaced drives. An add-on to MS-DOS itself, DBLSPACE.BIN is what enables MS-DOS proper to access and use any hard or floppy disks you compress with DoubleSpace. This file is so important that it is loaded very early in the startup process—even before CONFIG.SYS is processed. DBLSPACE.BIN is stored, with the hidden, system, and read-only attributes, in the root directory of your startup hard disk and (once you've installed DoubleSpace) on every bootable floppy you create. Do not delete this file.

And what about DBLSPACE.INI? This is an initialization file that tells DoubleSpace how to set itself up. In version 6.2, you can—carefully—edit DBLSPACE.INI to control certain aspects of DoubleSpace behavior. You can,

On some disks, you'll find the CVF named DBLSPACE.001, DBLSPACE.002, and so on. Regardless of the number in the extension, remain aware that this file represents the disk's CVF. Note also that the CVF is assigned the hidden, system, and read-only attributes to keep it safe from inadvertent deletion. Do not ever attempt to work directly with a DBLSPACE.000 (or 001 or 002...) file. In particular, do not delete such a file. You could lose all the information stored on your compressed drive. A word to the wise.

If you need all the memory your computer can possibly provide, remember that, with version 6.2, you can boot without loading DoubleSpace into memory by pressing either Ctrl+F5 for a clean boot or Ctrl+F8 for an interactive boot. Remember too, however, that when you boot without DoubleSpace, you can't use compressed drives.

for example, edit DBLSPACE.INI to turn off DoubleGuard (the data-protection program) or to prevent DoubleSpace from automatically mounting compressed floppies (that is, cancel its ability to recognize compressed floppies). Unless you're an advanced or confident user, however, your best bet is to ignore DBLSPACE.INI. Be glad it's there, but leave it alone.

DoubleGuard

No, this doesn't improve your personal aura, nor do you buy it as a stick, roll-on, or aerosol spray. New in version 6.2, DoubleGuard is a data-protection program that sits in your computer's memory. It works by enabling Double-Space to run periodic checks on itself. These checks let DoubleSpace verify—within the contents of the memory entrusted to it—that all is well with your data and that a wayward program has not caused problems that could damage information.

If DoubleGuard detects a problem, it will halt the computer to protect the data in its care. You can turn off DoubleGuard either from the command line or from DBLSPACE.INI. Doing so will speed up your system and release more memory, but you should do this only after running all your programs to verify that none of them conflict with DoubleSpace. Even then, be aware that disabling Double-Guard means that your compressed files will have a little less protection.

Running DoubleSpace Setup

Now that you're versed in "double-talk," you can get to the fun part: using it. Although you can just jump in and get started, you might want to do a little preparation, to save time later:

- Inventory the files on your disk and delete any that you no longer want. (Come on, *everybody's* got at least some of those hanging around.) This is especially important if your disk is full or if you plan to hand the whole disk over to DoubleSpace, as described later. Give DoubleSpace some room to maneuver, and do yourself a favor by not bothering to compress files you don't care about to begin with.

- If you've got some valuable files on the disk, back them up. DoubleSpace setup offers you this option, but if you back up ahead of time, you can back up only your important files. It's another winner, timewise.

One other item to note: DoubleSpace can take a long time to compress a hard disk. Be sure to run DoubleSpace Setup when you can spare the computer for an hour or more. That said, when you're ready to go, start out with a simple:

```
C:\>dblspace
```

As you can see from the initial setup screen, you'll need to run DoubleSpace Setup before you can play around with compressed drives. Setup configures your system for disk compression and, not incidentally, compresses your hard disk. Until you run through this setup program, you can't use DoubleSpace as a utility to compress a removable disk,

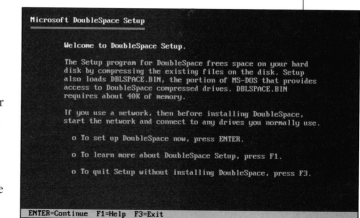

such as a floppy. After the setup is complete, however, DoubleSpace lets you manage any compressed or compressible disks when and as you choose.

Compressing vs. Creating

When you run DoubleSpace Setup for the first time (or, in version 6.2, after uncompressing all compressed drives on your system), you start off by choosing either an Express Setup or a Custom Setup. An Express Setup compresses your entire C drive, essentially handing over all but a few megabytes to the CVF. A Custom Setup lets you choose between compressing the hard disk of your choice (if you have more than one) and creating a new compressed drive. Hmmm…what's the difference?

When you create a new compressed drive, you tell DoubleSpace to leave existing files on the disk alone and simply turn whatever free space remains into a compressed drive. When you compress an existing disk, you compress all the files on it (except the uncompressible ones, such as those needed to boot MS-DOS). The following table will help you weigh the alternatives:

Compressing vs. Creating: Pros and Cons

Compress Existing Disk	Create New Compressed Disk
Preferable if the disk is full	Possibly preferable if the disk contains a lot of free space
Time-consuming	Much faster than compressing an entire disk and all the files on it
Compressed drive retains the current drive letter (such as *C*), and the host is assigned a new, higher drive letter (such as *H*)	Compressed drive is assigned a new drive letter, and the host retains the current (old) drive letter
Not easily reversible in version 6.0; not an issue in version 6.2	Compressed drive can be deleted and space can be recovered—in version 6.0, this was an advantage; in version 6.2, it's not an issue

In version 6.0, a significant difference existed between creating a new compressed drive and compressing your existing drive: You could delete the new compressed drive if you wanted to. In version 6.2, the difference no longer applies because DoubleSpace now lets you uncompress any drive you want. Safety, safety…

When you make your choice and tell DoubleSpace to get started, it begins (in version 6.2) by running ScanDisk to verify that the drive is reliable and can handle compression.

When ScanDisk is finished (assuming that it finds your hard disk reliable), DoubleSpace creates a DBLSPACE.INI file for you and reboots the computer. When the DoubleSpace window returns, you see the upper screen.

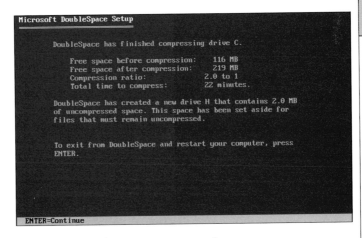

```
Microsoft DoubleSpace Setup

   DoubleSpace is now compressing drive C.

   Start time:              11:05:19pm
   Current time:            11:16:27pm
   Estimated finish time:   11:38pm

   Time left:               About 22 minutes.

   Currently compressing:   C:\DOS\DBLSPACE.BIN


                            29% complete


Compressing Files...
```

From here on in, there's nothing for you to do but watch. Or take a nap. Or go have dinner. When compression is complete, DoubleSpace defragments the newly compressed drive and then resizes

```
Microsoft DoubleSpace Setup

   DoubleSpace has finished compressing drive C.

      Free space before compression:    116 MB
      Free space after compression:     219 MB
      Compression ratio:                2.0 to 1
      Total time to compress:           22 minutes.

   DoubleSpace has created a new drive H that contains 2.0 MB
   of uncompressed space. This space has been set aside for
   files that must remain uncompressed.


   To exit from DoubleSpace and restart your computer, press
   ENTER.




ENTER=Continue
```

the newly created CVF. When it's all over, you see a welcome report (as shown in the lower screen).

Isn't it grand!

NO 6.2?

Well…if you have version 6.0 and want to be sure your disk can safely be compressed, you'll have to rely on a third-party utility, such as Norton Disk Doctor, to perform a disk scan for you. If your hard disk is old or has caused problems before, either skip DoubleSpace or invest in a program that can check the disk for you. And don't forget to back up all important files before you run DoubleSpace Setup.

DoubleSpace Options

After you've run through the DoubleSpace initiation rite and compressed your hard disk, you can use DoubleSpace as a utility for managing compressed disks and for compressing entire disks or creating new compressed disks.

Fine, but does this mean you have to treat compressed disks differently from uncompressed ones? Well, mostly not. But there are some operations, formatting in particular, that are directly related to file storage, and for these, you generally work through DoubleSpace rather than using the traditional MS-DOS commands. The following sections walk you through the highlights of using Double-Space both from the command prompt and from the DoubleSpace window. Some tasks, such as altering compression ratios, are not covered here. For information on those tasks (or on any commands described here, for that matter), use DoubleSpace help. You can get help in either of two ways:

- From the MS-DOS command prompt, type:

```
C:\>help dblspace
```

    for a guide to command line switches and parameters, as well as notes, tips, and examples regarding ways to use DoubleSpace.

- From within the DoubleSpace window, press F1 to open a Help menu. Wander through the topics as you would in any other windowed Help file.

Mounting and Unmounting

Is there a horse involved here? What's mounting got to do with compressed disks? Obviously, there's no horse. Mounting and unmounting refer to the days of tape storage in which large reels of tape had to be carried to and then mounted on tape drives (not the neat little cassette drives of today, either).

DoubleSpace, by default, mounts your hard disk in order to make it and your compressed drive available for use. In version 6.2, DoubleSpace also automatically mounts compressed floppy disks by default, so you really don't ever have to worry about mounting or unmounting them. Just use them and be happy.

There might come a time, however, when you have to mount a disk because DoubleSpace doesn't recognize it as a compressed drive. If you have version 6.2, this is unlikely to happen, but if you have version 6.0, you'll use the Mount option regularly with your floppies. Regardless of your reason for doing it, mounting and unmounting disks is easy:

- From the DoubleSpace window, choose Mount to mount a compressed disk; choose Unmount to unmount one. (You probably won't have much use for

Unmount—DoubleSpace does that automatically when you remove a compressed floppy and switch to an uncompressed one.)

- From the command prompt, mount a disk with the command form:

    ```
    dblspace /mount drive:
    ```

and unmount one with the command form:

    ```
    dblspace /unmount drive:
    ```

In both cases, *drive* is the drive containing the disk in question.

Formatting a Compressed Disk

When you want to format a compressed disk:

- From the DoubleSpace window, choose Format from the Drive menu.

- From the command prompt, use the command form:

    ```
    dblspace /format drive:
    ```

    Once again, *drive* is the drive containing the disk to format. Abbreviate the /format switch as /for if you want.

When you format a compressed disk, be aware that such a format is irreversible and that formatting does not return a disk to its original uncompressed state. Formatting a compressed disk merely clears out the CVF and all the files in it, essentially leaving you (or your disk) holding an empty bag.

Deleting a Compressed Drive

In your work with DoubleSpace, don't confuse deleting with uncompressing. When you delete a compressed drive, you remove the CVF and everything in it. Deleting a compressed floppy or a new drive you created on a hard disk essentially returns the disk to its former, uncompressed state—minus all the files formerly held in the CVF. Deleting is not, therefore, the same as uncompressing, which restores all compressed files to their original, precompression bulk. In fact, DoubleSpace won't allow you to delete the CVF on a fully compressed startup hard disk.

If you decide you want to delete a compressed drive:

- From the DoubleSpace window, select the drive and choose Delete from the Drive menu.

- From the command prompt, use the command form:

    ```
    dblspace /delete drive:
    ```

    where *drive* is the drive containing the disk on which you want to delete the CVF. You can abbreviate this switch as /del if you prefer.

> If you're using version 6.0, don't forget that you have to mount the floppy before you can format it.

Compressing Another Disk

You can choose to compress another disk or create a new compressed drive, and you can do so either from the DoubleSpace window or from the command prompt. Before you choose to compress a disk, either floppy or hard, be sure that it is formatted and that it contains enough free space. (See the MS-DOS online Help for the free space required by each type of disk.)

To compress another disk (hard disk, RAM drive, or floppy):

- From the DoubleSpace window, choose Existing Drive from the Compress menu. When you press Enter, DoubleSpace will scan all drives (including RAM drives) on your system for compressible disks. Choose the drive you want from the list DoubleSpace displays.

- From the command prompt, use the command form:

```
dblspace /compress drive:
```

drive, of course, is the letter of the drive containing the disk you want to compress. You can abbreviate the switch as /com.

To create a new compressed drive (hard disk or RAM drive only, no floppies):

- From the DoubleSpace window, choose Create New Drive from the Compress menu. When you choose this option, DoubleSpace lists the uncompressed hard disks and RAM drives on your system, as well as uncompressed host drives if they contain available space.

- From the command prompt, use the command form:

```
dblspace /create drive:
```

where *drive* again refers to the drive containing the disk to compress. Abbreviate the switch as /cr if you want.

Defragmenting

Compressed drives, even though they're handled by DoubleSpace, need defragmenting every now and then, just as uncompressed drives do. When you "defrag" a compressed drive, you move all free space in the CVF to the end of the file. Use the following procedure:

- From the DoubleSpace window, select the drive and choose Defragment from the Tools menu.

- From the command prompt, use the command form:

```
dblspace /defragment [drive:]
```

where *drive* is the letter of the drive to defragment. If you omit a drive, the command defragments the current drive—assuming it's compressed, of course. You can abbreviate the switch as /def.

Checking a Compressed Disk

In version 6.2, the easiest and best way to check a compressed disk is to run ScanDisk. If you try to use DoubleSpace's /chkdsk switch, implemented in version 6.0, you simply see this message:

```
C:\>dblspace /chkdsk
The DoubleSpace CHKDSK command has been superseded by Microsoft
ScanDisk.

To check drive X, quit DoubleSpace and then type SCANDISK X: at the
command prompt.
```

If you're using version 6.0, however, you still use DoubleSpace Chkdsk, as follows:

- From the DoubleSpace window, choose Chkdsk from the Tools menu.

- From the command prompt, use the command form:

```
dblspace /chkdsk /f [drive:]
```

/f fixes storage errors if any are found. *drive* is, of course, the drive to check. You can omit *drive* if you want to check the disk in the current drive.

Finding Out What's What

If you're working with DoubleSpace from the DoubleSpace window, it's easy to see which drives, especially floppies, are compressed and which are not. It's staring you right in the face—except when the basic screen is overlaid by a command's report or dialog box.

From the MS-DOS command prompt, however, seeing which drives are compressed isn't quite as simple. But there's an easy way to find out:

```
c:\>dblspace /list
```

Your disk drives blink on for a moment or two, and when the command is done, you see something like this:

And what if you want to catch up on the statistics for a particular drive?

```
C:\>dblspace /list
Drive  Type                       Total Free  Total Size  CVF Filename
-----  ----                       ----------  ----------  ------------
  A    Compressed floppy disk        2.04 MB     2.49 MB  H:\DBLSPACE.000
  B    Floppy drive                  1.15 MB     1.16 MB
  C    Compressed hard drive       114.56 MB   194.84 MB  I:\DBLSPACE.000
  D    Available for DoubleSpace
  E    Available for DoubleSpace
  F    Available for DoubleSpace
  G    Available for DoubleSpace
  H    Floppy drive                  0.03 MB     1.39 MB
  I    Local hard drive              2.34 MB   115.37 MB
  J    Local RAMDrive                1.99 MB     1.99 MB

DoubleGuard safety checking is enabled.
Automounting is enabled for drive(s) AB

C:\>
```

That's easy too—from the DoubleSpace window or from the command prompt.

- From the DoubleSpace window, select the drive that interests you, and then choose Info from the Drive menu, and this is what you see:

- From the command prompt, use the command form:

      dblspace /info [*drive*:]

where, once again, *drive* is...right, you've got it. Omit *drive*? That's right, you'll get the stats for the current drive.

```
 Drive  Compress  Tools  Help

                                                 Free          Total
                        ┌─── Compressed Drive Information ───┐
                        │ Compressed drive C is stored on uncompressed drive I │
                        │ in the file I:\DBLSPACE.000.                          │
                        │                                                       │
                        │   Space used:              80.28 MB                   │
                        │   Compression ratio:        1.5 to 1                  │
                        │                                                       │
                        │   Space free:             114.56 MB                   │
                        │   Est. compression ratio:   2.0 to 1                  │
                        │   Fragmentation:                0%                     │
                        │                                                       │
                        │   Total space:            194.84 MB                   │
                        │                                                       │
                        │  < OK >   < Size >   < Ratio >   < Help >             │
                        └───────────────────────────────────────────────────────┘

 DoubleSpace    F1=Help  ALT=Menu Bar  ↓=Next Item  ↑=Previous Item
```

Controlling DoubleSpace

DoubleSpace includes a number of options you can use to control its behavior. As mentioned earlier in this chapter, the key to most of this is DBLSPACE.INI. Most of the options listed in DBLSPACE.INI, however, are for advanced users. For example, one (/HOST) lets you change the drive letter assigned to the host of a compressed drive. Another (/MAXFILEFRAGMENTS) lets you set the allowable limit on fragmentation, and another (/MAXREMOVABLEDRIVES) sets the maximum number of removable drives that DoubleSpace can use.

Two DoubleSpace options, however, are useful to the less advanced; both are controllable either from the command line or from DBLSPACE.INI. They are /AUTOMOUNT, which specifies whether you want floppy drives automatically mounted, and /DOUBLEGUARD, which determines whether DoubleGuard watches over your data.

To control automatic mounting from the command line, use the command form:

      dblspace /automount=*value*

To affect all floppy drives, specify *value* as 0 to prevent automatic mounting, or 1 to enable automatic mounting. If you want to be more selective, specify *value* as one or more drive letters to enable automatic mounting of the specified drive(s) only. For example:

      C:\>dblspace /automount=a

enables automatic mounting for drive A only.

For more information about the options controlled from within DBLSPACE.INI, consult MS-DOS online Help. The fastest way to get to this information is to use the Find command on Help's Search menu and specify dblspace.ini as the text to search for.

To control whether DoubleGuard goes on duty, use the command form:

```
dblspace /doubleguard=value
```

Specify *value* as 0 to disable DoubleGuard; specify *value* as 1 to enable Double-Guard protection. (The recommended setting is the default, 1, which enables protection.)

When you use either of these options from the command line, your computer pauses for a few seconds, and then DoubleSpace sends you a message of acknowledgment:

```
DBLSPACE.INI has been modified.

For this change to take effect, you must restart your computer.
```

As you can see, DoubleSpace has taken the initiative and done for you what the next part of this section describes: edit DBLSPACE.INI.

Although you can edit your DBLSPACE.INI file, you really should do so only if you understand disk compression and how it works with your computer and your software. If you fall into that group, here's how to go about editing the file.

For safety's sake, first make a backup copy of your existing DBLSPACE.INI. The file is in the root directory of the *host* of your compressed startup drive and has the system, hidden, and read-only attributes, so to make the copy:

1. Change to the appropriate drive and directory and remove the attributes with the command:

```
I:\>attrib -s -h -r dblspace.ini
```

2. Now you can use the Copy command to duplicate the file. Give the copy a name such as DBLSPACE.AAA or DBLSPACE.ZZZ. Don't use the extension 001, 002, 003, or the like. For example:

```
I:\>copy dblspace.ini dblspace.aaa
```

To edit the file:

1. Start the MS-DOS Editor and open the file with the following command (note the current drive shown in the prompt):

```
I:\>edit dblspace.ini
```

2. Make the changes you want. For example, to enable automatic mounting of floppies for drive A only, edit the AutoMount line to read:

```
AutoMount=A
```

SWITCH-HITTING?

If you add the **SWITCHES** option to **DBLSPACE.INI** and then uninstall version 6.2, you might see an error message telling you that **DBLSPACE.INI** contains an invalid **SWITCHES** setting. If this happens, use the **MS-DOS Editor** to edit the file and remove the **SWITCHES** line. Close and save the file. Then edit **CONFIG.SYS** and add the **SWITCHES** setting(s) you need. Finally, close and save **CONFIG.SYS**, and reboot the computer. Your problem should be solved.

3. Save the file by pressing Alt, F, X and then pressing Enter when Edit asks whether you want to save the changes. (This is why you had to remove the file's attributes earlier.)

4. Use the Attribute command again, this time to restore the hidden, system, and read-only attributes to the changed file:

```
I:>attrib +s +h +r dblspace.ini
```

5. Reboot the computer to have the changes take effect.

Going Back to SingleSpace

In version 6.2, you can uncompress any drive you compressed as long as there's enough free space for uncompression to work. If the disk is too full, Double-Space tells you so with a message like the one in the screen at right. Uncompressing works on drives that are entirely compressed and on those containing a compressed drive that you created. It also works on both hard disks and floppies. When you uncompress, you essentially back out of compression the same way you got in—that is, you uncompress one or more drives on the system. During the process, DoubleSpace uncompresses all the files on the disk,

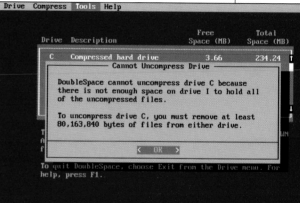

possibly stopping to defragment the disk, resize the CVF, or both along the way. If you uncompress all mounted compressed disks on your system, DoubleSpace goes even further. When the last disk is uncompressed, DoubleSpace removes the compression program itself, DBLSPACE.BIN, so that your computer no longer recognizes compressed drives at all.

The process of uncompressing a drive can take as long as (or longer than) the process of compressing one, so be sure to undertake this step only when you can spare your computer for an hour or more. To uncompress a drive:

- From the DoubleSpace window, select the drive to uncompress and choose Uncompress from the Tools menu.

- From the command prompt, use the command form:

```
dblspace /uncompress [drive:]
```

where *drive* is the drive to be uncompressed. If *drive* is omitted, DoubleSpace uncompresses the current drive.

If you choose **Uncompress** from the **DoubleSpace Tools** menu and you're uncompressing drive C, **DoubleSpace** starts off by suggesting you back up the drive before continuing. Do yourself a favor and back up important files before starting **DoubleSpace**.

The first thing DoubleSpace does when it uncompresses a disk is to run ScanDisk—both the file-storage portion and the surface scan—on the compressed and uncompressed portions of the disk to be sure the disk can handle its return to "normality." As you can imagine, this is a lengthy process. Although you *can* choose to exit the surface scan when ScanDisk begins checking your *compressed* drive, think twice about doing this, especially if you're uncompressing your primary hard disk or a disk containing valuable files. Investing a few extra minutes in seeing things through will ensure that DoubleSpace won't try to use bad sectors to hold data it uncompresses.

When DoubleSpace swings into the uncompression part of its routine, you see a familiar-looking display with a "gas gauge" telling you how far along the process has gone. At the bottom of the screen, you see the message *Shrinking compressed drive...*, which is quickly followed by *Uncompressing files...*. Get used to it. You'll be staring at the latter message for quite some time if you uncompress a hard disk that contains a lot of data.

In addition, at some point while you're uncompressing a disk, remember that you might see DoubleSpace stop uncompressing to defragment both your uncompressed and compressed drives. It does this to give itself some real, physical disk space to work in. (Don't forget that compressed files grow as they're uncompressed; DoubleSpace has a lot of juggling to do here.) During defragmenting, you'll see the Defrag screen appear while your uncompressed drive is being defragmented. Later, you'll see:

```
Please wait
Now starting the DoubleSpace program
to defragment your compressed drive
```

when Defrag hands the job of defragmenting the compressed drive over to DoubleSpace.

When the job is done, DoubleSpace removes the drive letter assigned to the compressed drive: It's as if DoubleSpace had never touched the disk. If you removed compression from the system altogether by uncompressing the last mounted compressed drive, DoubleSpace ends the show by removing DBLSPACE.INI and DBLSPACE.000 and by rebooting the computer without loading DOUBLESPACE.BIN into memory. Virgin, if crowded, territory once again.

So that's DoubleSpace. How to do, how to undo, and how to work with compressed drives. Don't forget to clean house once in a while. Even a compressed drive eventually gets full.

If you request a directory listing of a floppy disk you've uncompressed, you might find a file named READTHIS.TXT. This is just a file that DoubleSpace places on every compressed floppy to tell you that the disk has been compressed. This is now a lie. Delete the file.

Do It Yourself or Do It with MemMaker

RAM Cram

RAM cram. Sounds like some kind of college fraternity thing, doesn't it? Or maybe some kind of football scramble invented in Los Angeles. Actually, such images aren't all that far off. Or at least they're not if they make you think of lots of people pushing, shoving, and jostling for room in a small area—a phone booth, a VW bug, or the unintended landing zone of a ball-carrying athlete. The whole idea of RAM cram is crowding. Competition for space. Overpopulation. Specifically, overpopulation of that valuable piece of real estate called your computer's conventional memory.

So how crammed is your RAM? Do your programs have room to stretch out, or do you find yourself loading this program and unloading that one in order to give RAMbeau the memory it needs to run quickly and well?

Give Me RAM, Lots of RAM

First things first. Don't blame your programs for wanting RAM. They and their memory needs are what people have asked for. People like bells and whistles—great graphics, desktop publishing, task switching; word processors and spreadsheets that do everything but think. But all those capabilities require RAM, sometimes a lot of RAM. So where is a program to find it, and how is MS-DOS supposed to provide it? Obviously, your wallet is the first target. No computer can use memory that isn't there, so if you want to run large, sophisticated applications and entertainment programs, you have to give your computer the brains to work with such software. You have to install the memory.

And what about after you install the memory? Well, if you read or scanned the chapter "More About Memory," in Section 3, you know that MS-DOS was born to run in 640 KB of conventional memory. That was a lot of memory in the mid-1980s, but 640 KB today doesn't buy nearly the computing whizbang that it did in those early days. Today, many programs demand not only their (large) share of your computer's 640 KB of conventional memory, but some additional amount of extended or expanded memory too. Given that fact, your job then becomes a matter of helping MS-DOS set up and manage the memory in your computer to the best of its ability, taking into account the way your system is set up and the kinds of programs you use. For most people, that means...

Running MemMaker

MemMaker, which appeared in version 6.0 of MS-DOS, is a program that automates the process of optimizing memory use in your computer. In order to use MemMaker, all you need is an 80386 or better computer with at least 1 MB of RAM (standard on most systems these days). Tinkering with memory use, however, is not always easy, nor is it much fun in a lot of cases, especially where device drivers and memory-resident programs are concerned. In version 5, in fact, optimizing memory use was really a job for knowledgeable and advanced users: Make a mistake and load a program into the wrong part of memory, and you could hang the system but good. There'd be no way of recovering from the error short of restarting with a bootable floppy (which, of course, you would have to have prepared ahead of time, anticipating that your experiments just might go awry).

Now, the thing about optimizing memory is that it is desirable on a multitude of computers—not on those of advanced users alone. People who don't worship

POWER PLAY

Dèjá Vu

In order to understand some of the background information in this chapter, you need to understand what the upper memory area is. Briefly, it's an underused, often sparsely populated 384-KB area of memory that sits just above your computer's 640 KB of conventional memory. In versions 5 and 6 of MS-DOS, free portions of upper memory can be used to hold device drivers and memory-resident programs on any 80386 or better computer with 1 MB or more of RAM. The benefit to you: more conventional memory for your applications and data to use.

Because you have version 6 of MS-DOS, you can use MemMaker to automate the process of modifying your CONFIG.SYS and AUTOEXEC.BAT files. The result: MS-DOS loads device drivers and programs into upper memory as efficiently as possible at startup.

For a more detailed description of memory, refer to the earlier chapter "More About Memory."

these machines can benefit from effective memory use, too. But because they don't bother to learn all the ins and outs, tricks and traps, they need some help. That's MemMaker, a clever program that runs through a series of steps. It:

1. Reboots your system and "watches" as device drivers and memory-resident programs are loaded at startup.

2. Evaluates alternatives (sometimes thousands of them) to determine how those device drivers and memory-resident programs can be loaded to make the most efficient use of available memory.

3. Makes the necessary changes to your CONFIG.SYS file and your AUTOEXEC.BAT file.

4. Again restarts the system to test the optimized setup. At this point, MemMaker also asks you to watch for any evidence of problems. If no problems occur, it...

5. Saves your old configuration (just in case you have to undo its changes), displays a report showing before and after statistics for available memory, and exits stage right when you press Enter.

When you run MemMaker, it takes over, and you might feel as though you put your computer on autopilot. It pauses only when it asks a few simple questions at the beginning and, later, when it asks you to press a key. Before you start MemMaker, however, take care of a few small tasks.

POWER PLAY

A Small Matter You Might Want to Handle

If your AUTOEXEC.BAT file ends by starting a program, such as Microsoft Windows or a word processor, you might want to use the MS-DOS Editor to disable the command temporarily. Each time MemMaker reboots the system, you'll have to quit the program anyway, and it's a lot easier to simply keep the command from being carried out to begin with. Making this change in AUTOEXEC.BAT isn't difficult:

1. Type edit c:\autoexec.bat to start the editor and open the file.

2. Search the end of AUTOEXEC.BAT for the line that names the program MS-DOS usually starts for you. For example, the line starting Microsoft Windows will be:

   ```
   win
   ```

   The line starting your word processor might look something like this:

   ```
   word
   ```

3. To disable the command, move the cursor to the beginning of the line and type rem, followed by a space. This word (actually a batch command, short for *remark*) tells MS-DOS to ignore the line. Your altered command will look something like this:

   ```
   rem win
   ```

4. Press Alt, F, X, and Enter to save the changed file.

First, mentally review your inventory of programs. Early in the game, MemMaker will ask whether any of your programs require expanded memory, and your answer will determine how MemMaker alters your startup configuration. Although MemMaker won't mind waiting while you figure out whether any of your programs need expanded memory, you'll probably feel more comfortable knowing the answer ahead of time. Consult your program manuals if you don't know whether your programs use expanded memory.

This research taken care of, head for the computer and, if you're running Microsoft Windows, quit. Don't run MemMaker while Windows is running.

The Easy Way

Running MemMaker is really a piece of cake. You don't have to know anything about it or how it works. If you're at all apprehensive, don't be. MemMaker is safe. Even if something goes wrong during the optimization process, you can always undo all changes and restore your system to exactly the same condition it was in before you ran MemMaker. In a nutshell, all you do to run the program is type:

```
C:\>memmaker
```

and press Enter whenever MemMaker asks you to. The rest is practically automatic. If you're getting too confused, you can even tell MemMaker to slow

down and display help by pressing the F1 key. When you do, a small window will open, as shown here:

Notice the small up and down arrowheads in the screen. Those arrowheads tell you whether there's more help information above or below the windowful you're looking at. Press the PgUp key to scroll up, the PgDn key to scroll down.

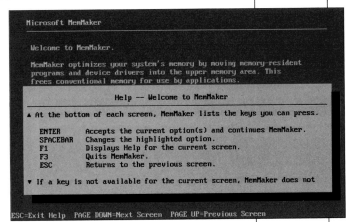

The series of steps and screens starting on page 292 walks you through a typical MemMaker setup—one in which you choose Express Setup to let MemMaker make all the decisions for you. This method takes a conservative approach to memory optimization and works fine for practically everyone. Choose Express Setup if any of these descriptions fit you:

- You generally leave installation, troubleshooting, and fine-tuning either to your program-installation software or to someone else, such as Uncle Jack.

- You'll be perfectly happy with any increase in memory you can get—that is, you're not interested in going the extra mile to collect every possible byte of free memory you can find. Typically, Express Setup increases the available memory by 10 KB or more—sometimes by a lot more—and most people find that's just fine.

- You don't want to have to decide which device drivers and memory-resident programs to load into upper memory.

- You use Microsoft Windows and Windows-based applications only—that is, you don't run MS-DOS applications with Windows.

There are, however, two situations in which you might want to go a little bit further and choose Custom Setup rather than Express Setup: if you run Microsoft Windows *and* you run MS-DOS applications from Windows, or if your display relies on an EGA or a VGA (but not a Super VGA). If either or both of these descriptions fit your computer and the way you use it, scan the next part of this chapter, "A Little More Control," before pressing on with MemMaker.

That said, take a look at MemMaker in action:

1. When you start Mem-Maker by typing its name at the command prompt, it opens with a screenful of information, as shown above. Take the time to read it. When you're ready, press Enter to continue.

2. The next screen Mem-Maker displays asks whether you want an Express Setup or a Custom Setup. Express Setup is selected by default, so press Enter again to approve the choice.

3. Now you see a screen asking you whether you use programs that need expanded memory: Answer Yes or No, depending on your needs.

4. Now MemMaker briefly checks whether you have Microsoft Windows installed on your hard disk. After the

```
Microsoft MemMaker

  Welcome to MemMaker.

  MemMaker optimizes your system's memory by moving memory-resident
  programs and device drivers into the upper memory area. This
  frees conventional memory for use by applications.

  After you run MemMaker, your computer's memory will remain
  optimized until you add or remove memory-resident programs or
  device drivers. For an optimum memory configuration, run MemMaker
  again after making any such changes.

  MemMaker displays options as highlighted text. (For example, you
  can change the "Continue" option below.) To cycle through the
  available options, press SPACEBAR. When MemMaker displays the
  option you want, press ENTER.

  For help while you are running MemMaker, press F1.

                    Continue or Exit? Continue
ENTER=Accept Selection  SPACEBAR=Change Selection  F1=Help  F3=Exit
```

```
Microsoft MemMaker

  There are two ways to run MemMaker:

  Express Setup optimizes your computer's memory automatically.

  Custom Setup gives you more control over the changes that
  MemMaker makes to your system files. Choose Custom Setup
  if you are an experienced user.

              Use Express or Custom Setup? Express Setup




ENTER=Accept Selection  SPACEBAR=Change Selection  F1=Help  F3=Exit
```

```
Microsoft MemMaker

  If you use any programs that require expanded memory (EMS), answer
  Yes to the following question. Answering Yes makes expanded memory
  available, but might not free as much conventional memory.

  If none of your programs need expanded memory, answer No to the
  following question. Answering No makes expanded memory unavailable,
  but can free more conventional memory.

  If you are not sure whether your programs require expanded memory,
  answer No. If you later discover that a program needs expanded
  memory, run MemMaker again and answer Yes to this question.

  Do you use any programs that need expanded memory (EMS)? No

ENTER=Accept Selection  SPACEBAR=Change Selection  F1=Help  F3=Exit
```

check for Windows, MemMaker tells you it will restart the computer (for the first time), as shown in the screen at right. Remove any floppy disks from your drives and press Enter. The computer goes through a complete startup, as it does when you turn it on. During this phase, watch your startup messages so you can remember what a typical startup looks like. You don't have to memorize anything—just pay attention. You'll see why in a moment.

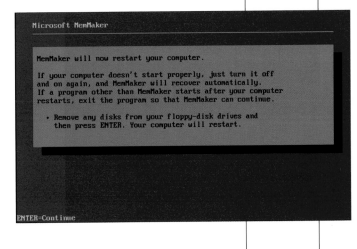

```
Microsoft MemMaker

MemMaker will now restart your computer.

If your computer doesn't start properly, just turn it off
and on again, and MemMaker will recover automatically.
If a program other than MemMaker starts after your computer
restarts, exit the program so that MemMaker can continue.

    • Remove any disks from your floppy-disk drives and
      then press ENTER. Your computer will restart.

ENTER=Continue
```

5. When MemMaker restarts, it watches how device drivers and programs are loaded. (You don't see any of this happening.) It then moves on to tell you that it's evaluating different ways to optimize memory and ends by modifying CONFIG.SYS and AUTOEXEC.BAT. Next it tells you it will once again restart the computer—this time, to test the new configuration.

```
Microsoft MemMaker

MemMaker will now restart your computer to test the new memory
configuration.

While your computer is restarting, watch your screen carefully.
Note any unusual messages or problems. If your computer doesn't
start properly, just turn it off and on again, and MemMaker
will recover automatically.

    • Remove any disks from your floppy-disk drives and
      then press ENTER. Your computer will restart.

ENTER=Continue
```

Notice that MemMaker tells you to watch the startup and make note of unusual messages or "problems," meaning any indications that a device driver or program is not loading or starting correctly. Now you see why you were told to watch startup. Press Enter to reboot once again.

6. This time, MemMaker returns to tell you that device drivers and programs are running in upper memory. It also asks you to press Enter ("choose Yes") if your system appears to be working properly.

```
Microsoft MemMaker

Your computer has just restarted with its new memory configuration.
Some or all of your device drivers and memory-resident programs
are now running in upper memory.

If your system appears to be working properly, choose "Yes."
If you noticed any unusual messages when your computer started,
or if your system is not working properly, choose "No."

Does your system appear to be working properly? Yes

ENTER=Accept Selection  SPACEBAR=Change Selection  F1=Help  F3=Exit
```

Assuming that it is and that you press Enter, you see one final message, as shown at right.

Not bad for an investment of about 5 minutes. This illustration shows the results on a real computer that gained almost 91 KB of conventional memory through MemMaker. Chances are that your computer won't gain as much because most of the effect in the illustration came about by loading

```
Microsoft MemMaker

MemMaker has finished optimizing your system's memory. The following
table summarizes the memory use (in bytes) on your system:

                              Before        After
  Memory Type                 MemMaker      MemMaker      Change

  Free conventional memory:   519,936       610,848       90,912

  Upper memory:
    Used by programs                0        94,048       94,048
    Reserved for Windows            0             0            0
    Reserved for EMS                0             0            0
    Free                            0        31,840

  Expanded memory:             Disabled      Disabled

Your original CONFIG.SYS and AUTOEXEC.BAT files have been saved
as CONFIG.UMB and AUTOEXEC.UMB.  If MemMaker changed your Windows
SYSTEM.INI file, the original file was saved as SYSTEM.UMB.

ENTER=Exit   ESC=Undo changes
```

BEST OF BOTH WORLDS

If you run MemMaker and find that a program or a device driver doesn't work properly when loaded into upper memory, don't fight it. Rerun MemMaker, but choose a custom setup this time. MemMaker then displays a list of options: Tell it you want to be able to determine which programs and device drivers are loaded into upper memory. When MemMaker asks about your problem program, tell it to continue loading the program into conventional memory. MemMaker will omit that program from consideration but will once again optimize all the other device drivers and memory-resident programs in CONFIG.SYS and AUTOEXEC.BAT. You'll end up having the best of both worlds.

```
Microsoft MemMaker

You have specified that you want to undo the changes MemMaker made
to your system files.

When you started MemMaker, it made backup copies of your CONFIG.SYS
and AUTOEXEC.BAT files (and, if necessary, your Windows SYSTEM.INI
file).  MemMaker restores these files by replacing the current files
with the backup copies it made earlier.  If the files have changed
since MemMaker made the backup copies, those changes will be lost
when you restore the original files.

  · To restore your original system files now, press ENTER.

  · To cancel, press ESC.

  a
  SYSTEM.INI file, the original file was saved as SYSTEM.UMB.

ENTER=Restore Files   ESC=Cancel
```

memory-hungry networking software into upper memory. If you do use a network at the office, however, you can see how much you might stand to gain from running MemMaker. And even under everyday circumstances, MemMaker can easily gain you an extra 10 KB, 20 KB, or more of usable conventional memory.

If your system did not seem to start properly, don't panic. Notice the message on the last line of the screen at the top of this page: *ESC=Undo changes*. If your computer had problems rebooting, press Esc. MemMaker will display the message shown at left. Go ahead and press Enter. Everything will be back as it was in a few seconds.

A Little More Control

That's basically MemMaker. There are, however, a few circumstances in which you might want to go a little bit beyond the basics and opt for Custom Setup. This option lets you decide whether MemMaker should take a number of different factors into account when determining the optimum setup for your computer. Although Custom

Setup is usually best left to experienced users, consider choosing it if either of the following describes your situation:

```
Microsoft MemMaker

                    o
               Advanced Options


Specify which drivers and TSRs to include in optimization?    No
Scan the upper memory area aggressively?                      No
Optimize upper memory for use with Windows?                   No
Use monochrome region (B000-B7FF) for running programs?       No
Keep current EMM386 memory exclusions and inclusions?         Yes
Move Extended BIOS Data Area from conventional to upper memory? Yes



To select a different option, press the UP ARROW or DOWN ARROW key.
To accept all the settings and continue, press ENTER.




ENTER=Accept All  SPACEBAR=Change Selection  F1=Help  F3=Exit
```

- You use Microsoft Windows, *and* you use MS-DOS–based applications with Windows.

- You have an EGA or a VGA (but not a Super VGA) display.

If either shoe fits, choose Custom Setup. MemMaker asks you to choose the options you want to control by displaying a list (as shown above):

- If you use Microsoft Windows and you run MS-DOS–based applications from Windows, press the down arrow key until the highlighted response is the *No* to the right of the question *Optimize upper memory for use with Windows?* Press the Spacebar to change the answer to *Yes*.

- If you have an EGA or a VGA display, press the down arrow key until the highlighted response is the *No* to the right of the question *Use monochrome region (B000-B7FF) for running programs?* Press the Spacebar to change the answer to *Yes*.

When you're finished, press Enter to accept the list of options and responses. MemMaker will now swing into action. If it finds Windows on your hard disk, it will ask you to confirm your Windows directory; otherwise, the rest of your memory optimization will be as described earlier.

> On some computers, choosing to use the monochrome region can cause difficulties. If you make this choice and you notice problems when MemMaker reboots the system, press Esc at the end when MemMaker gives you the option of choosing to undo all changes.

For Advanced Users

If you're an advanced user, the information in this section can help you use MemMaker to fine-tune your system. Use the information if you understand how your system is put together and if you're comfortable with editing CONFIG.SYS and AUTOEXEC.BAT. If you're not at that level of familiarity with your machine, take a rain check. The book will be waiting when you're ready.

Clean Sweep

If you and your computer have been together for a long time, there's a chance that your CONFIG.SYS and AUTOEXEC.BAT files contain commands for loading device drivers and memory-resident software that you don't really need or that you don't use very often. If that's the case, think about cleaning out those files before you run MemMaker. MemMaker is smart, but it's not smart enough to know what you want and what you don't. When it optimizes your CONFIG.SYS and AUTOEXEC.BAT files, it works with whatever it finds in those files.

If you're comfortable with editing files *and* you understand your system well enough to know which device drivers or memory-resident software you can safely remove, try starting your memory optimization process by cleaning up CONFIG.SYS and AUTOEXEC.BAT. For safety's sake, make a backup copy of the original files and give them names such as CONFIG.111 and AUTOEXEC.111. (Don't use BAK or DAT as an extension.) When you're editing the files themselves, don't delete any lines. Instead:

- Insert a semicolon at the beginning of each command in CONFIG.SYS that you want to disable, like this:

```
;DEVICE=C:\DOS\RAMDRIVE.SYS 1024 /E
```

- Insert rem and a space at the beginning of each command in AUTOEXEC.BAT that you want to disable, like this:

```
rem doskey
```

Doing this keeps the commands easily recoverable, yet it also puts them out of the way when you optimize memory use. Later on, you can make any command fully usable once more just by removing the semicolon or rem at the beginning.

Fine-Tuning

If you're an advanced user, really familiar with your system, you might also want to consider optimizing the load order of your device drivers and memory-resident programs so that the largest ones are loaded first. An easy way to do this is to use MemMaker to gather some statistics for you. To do this:

1. Run MemMaker and reboot your system.

2. When the computer restarts, find a file named MEMMAKER.STS in your MS-DOS directory. This file, created by MemMaker, contains information about the memory requirements of each of the device drivers and memory-resident programs in your CONFIG.SYS and AUTOEXEC.BAT files.

3. Print the file with the following command:

```
C:\>copy c:\dos\memmaker.sts prn
```

POWER PLAY

Order Please

If you decide to fine-tune your CONFIG.SYS file, be sure you understand how the HIMEM.SYS, EMM386.EXE, and Dos commands interact. In particular, be sure HIMEM.SYS and EMM386.EXE appear in the following order in CONFIG.SYS:

```
DEVICE=C:\DOS\HIMEM.SYS
DEVICE=C:\DOS\EMM386.EXE options
```

The reason these commands must appear in the order shown is that HIMEM.SYS opens the door to memory use beyond 1 MB. Until MS-DOS loads HIMEM.SYS, it is unable to handle extended memory, expanded memory, or UMBs (which, if you want the gory details, depend on the remapping of memory locations above 1 MB into memory locations between 640 KB and 1 MB). Basically, then, you can assume that no extra memory whatsoever is available until HIMEM.SYS is loaded. And only after it is loaded can EMM386.EXE be brought into play to handle simulated expanded

memory or—more to the point here—UMBs. Note that you must use either EMM386.EXE's NOEMS option or the RAM option to create UMBs.

The Dos command is a bit of a stinker in that it actually can appear anywhere in CONFIG.SYS and still work correctly. That is, you can include your DOS=HIGH,UMB command at the very beginning of CONFIG.SYS, even before HIMEM.SYS and EMM386.EXE make their respective appearances, and still manage to load MS-DOS into high memory and gain a pipeline to UMBs.

Because humans don't think like MS-DOS, however, you'll probably find your CONFIG.SYS file much easier to follow and understand if you arrange the commands in the order that reflects the way they're carried out. To wit:

```
DEVICE=C:\DOS\HIMEM.SYS
DEVICE=C:\DOS\EMM386.EXE options
DOS=HIGH,UMB
```

4. The section you're interested in is headed *[SizeData]*. A typical entry looks like this:

```
Command=C:\DOS\ANSI.SYS
Line=15
FinalSize=4256
MaxSize=9072
FinalUpperSizes=0
MaxUpperSizes=0
ProgramType=DEVICE
```

The specific line you want is *MaxSize*, which tells you the maximum amount of memory the device driver or program requires when loading into memory. (This is not always the same as the driver's or program's file size.)

5. Using the data from MaxSize as a guide, arrange the lines in CONFIG.SYS and AUTOEXEC.BAT so that the drivers and programs requiring the most memory are loaded first.

6. Run MemMaker again or, if you prefer, tinker with the Devicehigh and Loadhigh commands on your own.

Customizing Startup

Having It Your Way

You've done it the MS-DOS way so far; now it's time to have it your way. Here, in the last chapter of this section, you get to the ice cream on the pie. You get to have some fun with startup and make your computer a little more truly your own.

Have you ever wished you could do a little more to control MS-DOS at startup? Maybe boot the system cleanly so your favorite game doesn't tell you "not enough memory," or boot with the system optimized for either your spreadsheet (which likes expanded memory) or your word processor (which likes extended memory). Or maybe just make life a little easier for yourself and the others who use the computer— so that, instead of having to teach everyone the Change Directory command, you could just present them with this little menu:

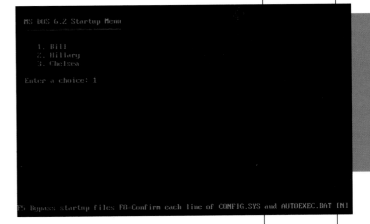

They enter a choice, and presto, they pop straightaway into their own document directories and most-used programs.

That's what customizing startup is all about, and with version 6 of MS-DOS, you've got three ways to go about it, one easy way, a second that requires exercise of at least a few brain cells, and a third that's more advanced and demanding than the other two.

The Easy Way

The easy way to customize startup is a matter of remembering two keys in version 6.0, four in version 6.2. These are the keys, introduced early in this book, that you can press when the screen displays the message *Starting MS-DOS* to choose either a clean boot or an interactive boot:

- F5, in versions 6.0 and 6.2, produces a clean boot that bypasses CONFIG.SYS and AUTOEXEC.BAT.

- F8, in versions 6.0 and 6.2, produces an interactive boot, a clever means of customizing your system by walking through your CONFIG.SYS commands and letting you choose those that you want to execute. In version 6.2, F8 is even more useful than in version 6.0 because it also steps through your AUTOEXEC.BAT file. (Version 6.0 just gives you a Yes/No choice as to whether you want the entire AUTOEXEC.BAT file processed.)

- Ctrl+F5, in version 6.2 only, produces a clean boot just as F5 does, but does not load the 30-odd kilobytes of DBLSPACE.BIN that give you access to DoubleSpaced drives. Of course, leaving DBLSPACE.BIN out of memory also means that you cut off your ability to access compressed drives, so this is an option to consider only in certain circumstances—for example, when you're settling down to use a single program, such as a graphics-intensive game, that requires large amounts of memory *and* is stored on an uncompressed drive.

- Ctrl+F8, in version 6.2 only, produces an interactive boot and, again, leaves DBLSPACE.BIN on the shelf. Use this if you're comfortable with your system's setup and you understand enough about what you want to do to know which CONFIG.SYS and AUTOEXEC.BAT commands you need to run in order to start MS-DOS with the system configured the way you and your programs want it.

The F5 and F8 keys were, at first, intended more to save people from their own good intentions than to provide a way to customize the computer. They were included in MS-DOS primarily to give advanced users a way to get around a broken CONFIG.SYS file without having to reinstall MS-DOS. Ctrl+F5 and Ctrl+F8 were added in version 6.2 to give people a quick way to increase available memory, although at the expense of being able to access any DoubleSpaced drives.

As it turns out, however, the interactive boot options provide anyone with a quick-and-dirty means of "customizing." If you know what you want to do,

---

If you're using F8 or Ctrl+F8 to step through an interactive boot and you reach a point at which you want to either carry out or bypass all remaining commands in CONFIG.SYS, AUTOEXEC.BAT, or both, you don't have to continue tapping Y or N like a rat in a lab experiment. Press Esc to carry out all remaining commands; press F5 to bypass them all.

POWER PLAY

Expletive Deleted

The F5 and F8 keystrokes were included in version 6.0 of MS-DOS more as protective devices than as "customization" options. Not incidentally, they also kept the air clear in more than a few cases. Until version 6.0 came along, changes to CONFIG.SYS could sometimes cause serious problems because tinkering with CONFIG.SYS commands, especially those involving memory, could cause your computer to "hang" at startup and leave you up the proverbial creek. Why did this happen? Well, think about it.

It's a conundrum of the first order, or at least it was until version 6.0. Previously, if your computer did hang, your only option was to boot from a system-formatted floppy. Of course, booting from the floppy

assumed that you'd taken the advice in your MS-DOS book seriously and had actually created such a disk in the first place—before you plunged elbow-deep into changing CONFIG.SYS.

With MS-DOS version 6.0, the F5 and F8 keys brought this Franken-stein tale to a happy end. You can bypass your CONFIG.SYS and AUTOEXEC.BAT files entirely (with F5) or in part (with F8) by pressing the appropriate key when this message appears onscreen:

```
Starting MS-DOS...
```

Now, if your computer hangs because of a mess you made in CONFIG.SYS, all you have to do is reboot with either the clean or the interactive option.

you can step through the commands in CONFIG.SYS and AUTOEXEC.BAT, signaling Yes or No to each, in order to start the computer and tailor it roughly to your preferences. For example, each time you start up, you can press F8 or Ctrl+F8 and then proceed to choose (assuming that these commands are part of your startup already) whether you want to create a RAM drive, whether you want to load Doskey, whether you want to load ANSI.SYS, and so on. If you make a mistake, of course, you'll have to reboot and try again.

The Middle Road

The second way of customizing startup is really just a variation on the foregoing Yes/No approach. In this, you take advantage of a well-placed question mark or two to turn CONFIG.SYS into a file you can step through selectively even if you don't choose an interactive boot. Using the question mark is as easy as pressing a key, as long as you don't mind editing CONFIG.SYS. You can add a question mark to most any command in CONFIG.SYS, and wherever you add one of these inquisitive beasts, MS-DOS will stop and prompt for a Y or N as it's processing CONFIG.SYS.

Although the commands you're most likely to tinker with are Device and Devicehigh commands that load device drivers, you can use the question mark with other CONFIG.SYS commands too. One really useful one (with no possible complications or ramifications) is the Numlock command, which lets you choose whether to turn off the NumLock key at startup. This small but mighty command is a great addition to MS-DOS for people who forget to check NumLock before pounding the cursor-movement keys on the numeric keypad and then end up staring at a string of 4s, 8s, 6s, or 2s on the screen. It's also an excellent way to get started using the question mark.

To see how the question mark is used, let's begin by taking a look at a simple CONFIG.SYS without question marks. (If you can't make heads or tails of it, refer to "Deciphering CONFIG.SYS," below.)

```
DEVICE=C:\DOS\HIMEM.SYS
DEVICE=C:\DOS\EMM386.EXE NOEMS
DOS=HIGH,UMB
NUMLOCK=OFF
SHELL=C:\DOS\COMMAND.COM C:\DOS\ /P
DEVICEHIGH=C:\DOS\SETVER.EXE
DEVICEHIGH=C:\DOS\DBLSPACE.SYS /MOVE
BUFFERS=30
FILES=30
LASTDRIVE=Z
```

POWER PLAY

Deciphering CONFIG.SYS

If you haven't modified your CON-FIG.SYS file, most of the sample file above probably resembles your own CONFIG.SYS file (as you'd see it if you used the Type command or the MS-DOS Editor). If you're still having a hard time figuring out what those commands mean, here's a quick line-by-line rundown.

The first line loads HIMEM.SYS, the MS-DOS extended memory manager.

The second line loads EMM386.EXE, the program that allows MS-DOS to simulate expanded memory for programs that need it and that also paves the way for use of UMBs. The NOEMS switch shown here tells

EMM386.EXE that the computer in question doesn't need expanded memory, so the command as it's shown really gives EMM386.EXE just one job: providing upper memory to programs that can use it.

The DOS line loads MS-DOS into the high memory area; the UMB part of the command maintains an active "line" to upper memory so that MS-DOS can use UMBs.

The NUMLOCK line turns the NumLock key off at startup. You can, if you want, make this command NUMLOCK=ON if you want to be sure NumLock is always on at startup (but it usually is turned on by default anyway, so there's not much point to the ON setting).

The SHELL line tells MS-DOS where to find the part of itself called the command interpreter. Strange as it seems, MS-DOS needs this command. Why? Because it's so selfless that it sometimes allows other programs to take over part of the memory it's using and thus overwrite some of its own instructions. When that happens, MS-DOS uses the Shell command to refresh its memory about where to find the parts of itself that were overwritten. (Seems like self-immolation, doesn't it? But that's MS-DOS for you.)

The first DEVICEHIGH command loads the Setver program into (notice) upper memory. Setver is a program that sets up a table of fake MS-DOS version numbers in memory, with one fake version

number corresponding to a specific application. When a program isn't designed to recognize the version of MS-DOS you're using, you can use Setver to "fool" the program into thinking it's using a different version of MS-DOS. Don't monkey with this command unless you're told to.

The second DEVICEHIGH command loads DBLSPACE.SYS. This program determines where in memory DBLSPACE.BIN will end up: high or low. (Read up on Double-Space if this one has you confused.)

The BUFFERS line tells MS-DOS to set up 30 buffers—portions of memory—for temporarily holding information read from or about to be written to disk. Generally, you should change the Buffers setting only if the documentation for an application tells you to.

The FILES line tells MS-DOS that the maximum number of files it can have open at one time is 30. Again, this is a setting you should change only if the documentation for an application recommends a higher setting.

The LASTDRIVE line sets the highest drive letter MS-DOS can recognize. This is a setting you can play with relatively freely, as long as you don't go below M or N, especially on a system with DoubleSpaced drives.

With the exception of Numlock, you should consider most of this CONFIG.SYS file off-limits to the question mark for the simple reason that these commands have important jobs to do. There is one command, however, that you might want to consider modifying: the command that loads EMM386.EXE.

Suppose you wanted to change this CONFIG.SYS so that you could choose between using expanded memory and using extended memory at startup. Where different memory types are concerned, remember that one type of program prefers expanded memory, which is provided by EMM386's RAM switch; another prefers extended memory, which is provided by EMM386's NOEMS switch. If you have programs of both types, such a startup option could be useful. Both the RAM and NOEMS switches enable EMM386.EXE to provide support for upper memory, so the only difference between using expanded memory and using extended memory is the name of the switch.

Here's how you would change the file to have MS-DOS prompt before carrying out a command. Notice that the question mark is used with Numlock and two EMM386.EXE commands. To make the changes more visible, they're shown in magenta.

```
DEVICE=C:\DOS\HIMEM.SYS
DEVICE?=C:\DOS\EMM386.EXE RAM
DEVICE?=C:\DOS\EMM386.EXE NOEMS
DOS=HIGH,UMB
NUMLOCK?=OFF
SHELL=C:\DOS\COMMAND.COM C:\DOS\ /P
DEVICEHIGH=C:\DOS\SETVER.EXE
DEVICEHIGH=C:\DOS\DBLSPACE.SYS /MOVE
BUFFERS=30
FILES=30
LASTDRIVE=Z
```

From now on, every time you boot the system, you'll see a prompt when MS-DOS reaches each of your "questionable" commands:

```
DEVICE=C:\DOS\EMM386.EXE RAM [Y,N]?
DEVICE=C:\DOS\EMM386.EXE NOEMS [Y,N]?
NUMLOCK=OFF [Y,N]?
```

When MS-DOS gets to the EMM386.EXE commands, answer Y and then N to load the RAM version of the command that initiates both expanded memory and upper

If you like to use RAM drives, the question mark can be a really useful means of controlling when a RAM drive is created and how large it is. To give yourself the option of creating RAM drives of different sizes, you could include the following commands in CONFIG.SYS. (These examples assume that you have at least 1 MB of extended memory to spare; for more details on RAM drives, refer to the chapter "More About Hardware," in Section 3.)

```
DEVICE?=C:\DOS\RAMDRIVE.SYS 512 /E
DEVICE?=C:\DOS\RAMDRIVE.SYS 1024 /E
```

The first command gives you the option of creating a 512-KB RAM drive; the second gives you the option of creating a much larger, 1-MB, RAM drive.

POWER PLAY

Don't Get Carried Away

Although the question mark is a terrific help in giving you some options in CONFIG.SYS, use it sparingly, and only if you understand what you're doing. In addition, if you use the question mark to allow yourself to enable or disable access to extended, expanded, or upper memory, be sure to check the rest of the commands in your CONFIG.SYS file so that you don't cut off the type of memory needed by a different command. Devicehigh will load device drivers into conventional memory if upper memory is not available; other commands, such as a Device command that creates a RAM drive in expanded memory, will simply refuse to execute if no expanded memory is available. But the result of your work will be messy, and your system won't function the way you want it to. Besides, when you're using computers,

messy will eventually get you into trouble. Be logical. Be consistent. Be right.

Furthermore, bear in mind that the question mark doesn't work in AUTOEXEC.BAT, so this "middle road" to customization is really most appropriate when you want to control hardware setup.

There are ways to link options in CONFIG.SYS to sets of commands in AUTOEXEC.BAT, but they involve some understanding of batch files and batch commands. In particular, they involve the batch commands If and Choice, both of which stick at least their toes into programming waters.

If you want to tie CONFIG.SYS and AUTOEXEC.BAT into a neat, interactive bundle, the way to do so is with the menus described next.

memory, or answer N and then Y to load the NOEMS version of the command that initiates extended memory and upper memory. (You wouldn't, of course, answer Y to both or N to both, but you knew that....) Press Y in response to the NumLock prompt, and the little light on the NumLock key blinks off. Press N, and the light stays on.

The Not-Especially-Easy Way

And now you come to the cleanest, nicest way of giving yourself some startup options: menus. These are fun to use, and there's a foolproof example for you to try a little later, under the heading "A Little Practice for You." But wade through some of the murky prose first so that you know what you're doing if you try this out on your own machine.

Startup menus—like menus at restaurants, in Microsoft Windows, or in online Help—are lists of choices. When you choose from a menu, you tell the menu-bearing program, "This is what I want." Now, in programs such as Windows and online Help, creating menus requires a lot of thought, a lot of work, and a lot of programming skill. In version 6 of MS-DOS, creating a startup menu requires only that you understand a few easy-to-use commands. Ready?

First of all, here's a reminder of what a menu looks like. This one's a little more realistic than the one shown at the beginning of the chapter:

```
MS-DOS 6.2 Startup Menu

    1. GAMES
    2. WORDS
    3. NUMBERS

Enter a choice: 1








F5=Bypass startup files F8=Confirm each line of CONFIG.SYS and AUTOEXEC.BAT [N]
```

The Basic Ingredients

Where do you create a startup menu for an operating system? In CONFIG.SYS, of course. (Well, maybe not "of course," but it's a purely logical choice, as you'll see.) And how does a startup menu work? A lot like menus in restaurants where dishes are listed and called for by number. You know, "I'll have the number three with chicken tacos, please," or "I'll have number seven, eggs over easy, wheat toast, and hash browns." True, MS-DOS menus aren't nearly so appetizing, but they can be just as gratifying, and a lot less fattening.

The basic parts of an MS-DOS menu are known as *configuration blocks* and *block headers*. A configuration block is simply the startup equivalent of the foods that make up your edible number three or number seven menu selection:

Selection Number 3 (edible)	Selection Number 3 (startup)
Two tacos (beef, chicken)	DEVICE=C:\DOS\EMM386.EXE NOEMS
Rice	LASTDRIVE=M
Beans	NUMLOCK=OFF
Salad	DEVICEHIGH=C:\DOS\ANSI.SYS

A block header is simply the name (or number) you associate with the contents of the configuration block. This name or number is what appears on the startup menu, so it's more or less the link that helps MS-DOS make the connection between your choice on the menu and the commands in the configuration block that choice represents. Here, if this is starting to give you a headache, a diagram might help:

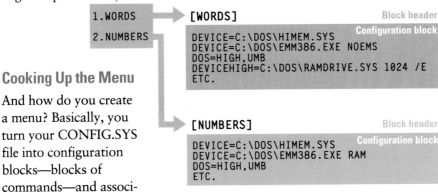

Cooking Up the Menu

And how do you create a menu? Basically, you turn your CONFIG.SYS file into configuration blocks—blocks of commands—and associate each block with a block header that becomes the name of a menu item. At the top of your CONFIG.SYS file, you define the menu with any of five menu-related commands, three of which are probably all you need for a simple startup menu. Here's what the menu section of a simple CONFIG.SYS file would look like:

```
[MENU]
MENUITEM=GAMES
MENUITEM=WORDS
MENUITEM=NUMBERS
```

[MENU] is a block header that tells MS-DOS you're defining a menu. You must include this header. MenuItem is the command that defines a menu choice. It takes the form:

```
menuitem=blockname[,menu-text]
```

blockname is the name you assign to a configuration block. The name can be up to 70 characters long, but it can't contain spaces or any of the following characters:

```
/ \ , ; = [ ]
```

For most menus, a short, descriptive name (such as *WORDS*) is all you need, especially because you can use the *menu-text* option to describe the menu selection in detail.

menu-text is whatever text you want MS-DOS to display for the selection on the startup menu. If you don't include *menu-text*, MS-DOS displays the *blockname* to describe the selection. If you use *menu-text*, you can run on for up to 70 characters; there are no "illegal" characters in this option.

The MenuItem commands in the foregoing example do not include any menu text, so your startup menu would use the block names like this:

```
MS-DOS 6.2 Startup Menu


   1. GAMES
   2. WORDS
   3. NUMBERS


Enter a choice: 1
```

If, on the other hand, you included menu text, like this:

```
MENUITEM=GAMES,The Game Wizard - Guardian of the Realm
MENUITEM=WORDS,This is my favorite word processor
MENUITEM=NUMBERS,This is my trusty spreadsheet
```

the startup menu would display:

```
MS-DOS 6.2 Startup Menu


   1. The Game Wizard - Guardian of the Realm
   2. This is my favorite word processor
   3. This is my trusty spreadsheet


Enter a choice: 1
```

You get the idea. Notice, however, that menu text is displayed the same way you typed it, uppercase and lowercase (and any spelling errors too).

Connecting to Configuration Blocks

All right, menus seem easy enough to set up, and so they are. The next step, however, requires thought on your part. Uh-huh. Mindwork. And unfortunately, no one can help you with it because this is where you put together the configuration blocks that define your customized startup options. The basic form is simple enough, as you can see in the illustration on the facing page.

The diagram shows a complete CONFIG.SYS file, building on the menu blocks you've already seen. Now it includes different configuration blocks that contain the sets of commands MS-DOS would carry out for each menu choice.

Do you see what happens? If the owner of this hypothetical computer chooses GAMES at startup, MS-DOS goes to the block labeled [GAMES] and carries out the HIMEM.SYS and DOS commands. If the owner chooses WORDS, MS-DOS goes to the block labeled [WORDS] and carries out those commands instead. And if the owner chooses NUMBERS, MS-DOS goes to the block labeled [NUMBERS] and follows the instructions there.

But, you say, what about that block labeled [COMMON]? That's not defined as a menu option. You're quite right, but fear not. COMMON is the name of a block that MS-DOS recognizes automatically. You use it to hold commands that you want carried out no matter which menu choice you select—that is, the commands in the [COMMON] block are *common* to all startup options.

Notice that the [COMMON] block appears at the end of CONFIG.SYS here. A [COMMON] block can appear anywhere in CONFIG.SYS and still work all right, but as your MS-DOS documentation will tell you, the end of CONFIG.SYS is a good place to put it. Why? Because a [COMMON] block at the end gives application programs a place to put any commands they need to add to CONFIG.SYS for themselves.

```
[MENU]
MENUITEM=GAMES
MENUITEM=WORDS
MENUITEM=NUMBERS

[GAMES]
DEVICE=C:\DOS\HIMEM.SYS
DOS=HIGH

[WORDS]
DEVICE=C:\DOS\HIMEM.SYS
DEVICE=C:\DOS\EMM386.EXE NOEMS
DOS=HIGH,UMB
NUMLOCK=OFF
DEVICE=C:\DOS\RAMDRIVE.SYS 1024 /E

[NUMBERS]
DEVICE=C:\DOS\HIMEM.SYS
DEVICE=C:\DOS\EMM386.EXE RAM
DOS=HIGH,UMB
NUMLOCK=ON
DEVICEHIGH=C:\DOS\ANSI.SYS

[COMMON]
SHELL=C:\DOS\COMMAND.COM C:\DOS\ /P
DEVICEHIGH=C:\DOS\SETVER.EXE
DEVICEHIGH=C:\DOS\DBLSPACE.SYS /MOVE
BUFFERS=30
LASTDRIVE=Z
```

Adding a Little Garnish

If you were to put together a menu with what you've learned so far, you'd have a no-frills startup menu. How about adding a little color? And while you're at it, how about giving MS-DOS a little initiative so you don't have to watch startup every time? It's easy, and this is the fun part.

To add color, you use the MenuColor command. Like all menu commands, it goes in CONFIG.SYS. The command is simple:

    menucolor=*text*[,*background*]

text is the color that you want for displaying words; *background* is the color you want the background of the screen to be. The defaults are what you normally see with MS-DOS: white text, black background. But come on, that gets positively boring. Specify something else. All you have to do is choose numbers from the following table to tell MS-DOS which colors you want for text and background:

> On some displays, colors 8 through 15 blink on and off. If you choose one of these colors and end up with a psychedelic display, back down to colors 0 through 7.

Color Options with the MenuColor Command

Color Number	Color	Color Number	Color
0	Black	8	Gray
1	Blue	9	Bright blue
2	Green	10	Bright green (blazing green)
3	Cyan (blue-green, very nice)	11	Bright cyan
4	Red	12	Bright red
5	Magenta (purple)	13	Bright(!) magenta
6	Brown	14	Yellow
7	White (not what you want)	15	Bright white (this is it)

So, for example, if you want bright white characters on a blue background, include this in CONFIG.SYS:

```
MENUCOLOR=15,1
```

If you want bright white characters on cyan, the command would be:

```
MENUCOLOR=15,3
```

If you want green characters on (the default) black background, the command would be:

```
MENUCOLOR=2
```

Easy enough, right? And what about telling MS-DOS to babysit itself? That's easy too. You use the MenuDefault command to tell MS-DOS which menu choice to carry out if you don't make a selection within a certain amount of time. (Otherwise, MS-DOS will sit waiting for a choice all day, all month, all year....) The MenuDefault command looks like this:

```
menudefault=blockname[,timeout]
```

blockname is the name of the default configuration block—the one you want MS-DOS to go to if you don't make a selection; *timeout*, which you can freely omit, tells MS-DOS how long to wait for a choice before it carries out the default configuration block. In the sample CONFIG.SYS you've been following in this chapter, suppose you usually chose WORDS when you started up. You could tell MS-DOS to use WORDS if you don't make a choice within 5 seconds by putting this command in CONFIG.SYS:

```
MENUDEFAULT=WORDS,5
```

When you use the MenuDefault command, your startup screen changes slightly to show the time remaining until the default is carried out:

```
MS-DOS 6.2 Startup Menu
═══════════════════════


    1.  GAMES
    2.  WORDS
    3.  NUMBERS


Enter a choice: 2        Time remaining: 03
```

> The information in the rest of this chapter is really more advanced than anything else you've found in this book. Although you should get the hang of modifying your CONFIG.SYS and AUTOEXEC.BAT files with the explanations here, err on the side of caution: If you're even the least bit unsure about doing this, *don't*, at least not right now. Read your MS-DOS manual and read up on batch files first. You won't hurt anything by waiting a while before setting up your own multiple-configuration startup with a matching AUTOEXEC.BAT, and in the long run, you'll find it's much better to be safe than sorry. Oh, and if you do experiment, be sure to save backup copies of CONFIG.SYS and AUTOEXEC.BAT before starting. That way, you'll always have a nice, clean, unmodified version of each to go home to.

A Little Practice for You

And now for that promise of some hands-on practice for you. If you want to try out a menu on your own computer, there's a way to do it without compromising your system at all. What you're going to do is duplicate your CONFIG.SYS commands in each startup "option" you create. That way, no matter what choice you make from your startup menu, you'll know that your system will end up configured just as it always is. For safety's sake, you'll make a duplicate of your original CONFIG.SYS file at the outset. Here's what to do:

1. Change to the root directory of your startup drive, and type this:

   ```
   C:\>copy config.sys config.111
   ```

   CONFIG.111 is now your safety net, a backup copy of the original.

2. Start the MS-DOS Editor and open CONFIG.SYS.

3. If the cursor is not at the top of the screen, press Ctrl+Home to put it there. Press Enter to create a blank new line, and press the up arrow to position the cursor in the new line.

4. Type the following to create a menu. Feel free to change the text however you want, but be sure that whatever menu items you create match the block headers you later put in CONFIG.SYS. All right, here goes:

```
[MENU]
MENUITEM=ONE
MENUITEM=TWO
MENUCOLOR=15,3
MENUDEFAULT=ONE,5

[ONE]
```

5. Now move the cursor to the first character of the first command in your original CONFIG.SYS file. Press Ctrl+Shift+End to select the rest of the file.

6. Copy the selected text to the Clipboard by pressing Ctrl+Ins.

7. Press the down arrow to remove the selection highlight from the text you copied. Press Enter to create a blank line, type *[TWO]*, and then press Enter again.

8. Press Shift+Ins to insert a copy of your original CONFIG.SYS under this second block header. Press Ctrl+End to move to the line below the last copied line and type:

```
NUMLOCK=OFF
```

This will give you a way of seeing that MS-DOS is carrying out different sets of configuration commands when you choose options ONE and TWO—or whatever you named them. (If you had a NUMLOCK=OFF command in the CONFIG.SYS file, change the command in the copy to NUMLOCK=ON.)

9. Press Alt, F, X to quit the Editor. Press Enter when the Editor asks if you want to save the changed file.

That's it. You now have a startup menu and a multiple-configuration (more than one startup choice) CONFIG.SYS file. To test it, reboot the system a couple of times, and try out each of the startup options. As the system starts up, watch the light on the NumLock key. It will go off during one of the startups.

When you get tired of all this, here's how to return everything to normal:

1. Rename the sample file with the command:

```
C:\>ren config.sys config.tst
```

2. Recover your original CONFIG.SYS with the command:

```
C:\>ren config.111 config.sys
```

If you want to experiment with startup menus some more, keep CONFIG.TST and confine your modifications to the [TWO] block. That way, you can always boot with the untouched copy of CONFIG.SYS in block [ONE] if necessary. To test your modifications, rename your working CONFIG.SYS to CONFIG.111

again and rename CONFIG.TST to CONFIG.SYS. Do this, and your original copy of CONFIG.SYS will always remain as pure as the soap that floats.

Linking to AUTOEXEC.BAT

And now, to add one final touch: How to link startup options in a multiple-configuration CONFIG.SYS file to matching sets of commands in your AUTOEXEC.BAT file. First, perhaps you're wondering why you'd want to link CONFIG.SYS and AUTOEXEC.BAT to begin with. Well, take another look at the sample CONFIG.SYS file (diagram) on page 309. Notice that the [WORDS] block sets up the computer to run without expanded memory and with a RAM drive, whereas the [NUMBERS] block sets up the computer to run with expanded memory and no RAM drive.

If you're going to set up your computer for word processing, it stands to reason that you might be happy to have AUTOEXEC.BAT do some preparatory work for you—for example, set the search path to your \DOS and word processing directories and make WORDWORK the current directory. In contrast, when you set up for working with NUMBERS, you might want to set the path to your \DOS and finance-related directories, start Undelete with the Sentry option, and make FINANCE the current directory.

To do this, you need to know about a variable named CONFIG and a command named Goto. A variable is a generic name that you can use with the Set command to tell MS-DOS to associate that name with some particular information. For example:

```
C:\>set today=wednesday
```

tells MS-DOS that the generic name *today* should be associated with the specific day Wednesday. In and of themselves, variables aren't much use in everyday work with MS-DOS, but they can be quite helpful in controlling batch files. In particular, a variable named CONFIG is ideal for controlling AUTOEXEC.BAT. The reason: When you set up a multiple-configuration CONFIG.SYS file, MS-DOS automatically sets the CONFIG variable to the option you choose from your startup menu. That means that MS-DOS "remembers" which configuration you choose. Given the sample CONFIG.SYS in this chapter, for instance, MS-DOS would set CONFIG=WORDS if you chose the WORDS startup, CONFIG=GAMES if you chose the GAMES startup, and CONFIG=NUMBERS if you chose the NUMBERS startup.

Now, how does this help with AUTOEXEC.BAT? That's where the Goto command comes in. Goto, as its name implies, tells MS-DOS to "go to" a particular section of a batch file and to carry out the commands in that section, so if you think about it, Goto and the CONFIG variable give your AUTOEXEC.BAT the

equivalent of a block header. To use them, you simply add this line to
AUTOEXEC.BAT:

```
goto %config%
```

and then group your AUTOEXEC.BAT commands in the order you want them
carried out. (Yup, this is the hard part.) First, place the commands you always
want executed at the top of AUTOEXEC.BAT. Next, create a "block" for each
startup option. Begin each block with the name of the option (preceded by a
colon), fill the block with the commands you want carried out when that option
is chosen from the startup menu, and (important!) end each block with the
command goto end, like this:

> *:option*
> *command*
> *command*
> *command*
> goto end

At the very end of AUTOEXEC.BAT, add a one-word closing preceded by
a colon:

```
:end
```

To help you see how this file-bridging operation works, this illustration shows
an AUTOEXEC.BAT file that matches the earlier sample CONFIG.SYS. If you're going to try this kind of construction work on your own computer, study this blueprint carefully. In particular, make note of the Goto commands (all of them) and the block labels identifying different sections of the file. Be sure to use colons as shown here.

```
@echo off
c:\dos\smartdrv.exe
set prompt=$p$g
set temp=c:\temp
doskey
c:\dos\mouse
goto %config%
```
— Commands that are always carried out, regardless of startup chosen

```
:games
path=c:\;c:\dos;c:\games
cd \games
goto end
```
— Commands that are carried out only if *games* is chosen from the startup menu

```
:words
path=c:\;c:\dos;c:\wp
cd \wordstuff
goto end
```
— Commands that are carried out only if *words* is chosen from the startup menu

```
:numbers
path=c:\;c:\dos;c:\spread;c:\tax
undelete /sc
cd \finance
goto end
```
— Commands that are carried out only if *numbers* is chosen from the startup menu

```
:end
```
— A very important little word; don't forget it

And don't forget: Before you start modifying the AUTO-EXEC.BAT file, *make a backup copy with a name such as AUTOEXEC.111 so you'll have a clean version of AUTOEXEC.BAT that you can return to.*

Putting It on the Table

And that's that. After all your work to customize startup, do you want to know what happens? Sure, you do. Here's how startups with multiple-configuration CONFIG.SYS files and modified AUTOEXEC.BAT files proceed:

1. You boot the computer. After checking out the hardware and making itself at home in memory, MS-DOS looks for CONFIG.SYS.

2. MS-DOS reads CONFIG.SYS from disk, scans the file, and finds out that you want it to display a menu.

3. The menu displayed, MS-DOS then sits patiently and waits for you to make a choice by pressing a key. So you press a key.

4. Your keystroke firmly in hand, MS-DOS then looks down the blocks of commands in CONFIG.SYS until it finds the block associated with your menu choice.

5. It carries out the commands in that section of CONFIG.SYS, as well as those in the [COMMON] block, and ignores any commands in the file that are related to other menu choices.

6. When it finishes carrying out CONFIG.SYS, MS-DOS turns to the AUTO-EXEC.BAT file and romps through the remainder of your startup. First, it carries out all commands at the beginning of AUTOEXEC.BAT. When it finds the command goto %config%, it checks the CONFIG variable, finds out which startup option you chose, and then scans AUTOEXEC.BAT for a line that matches the setting. When it finds that line, MS-DOS goes directly to the first command beneath it and proceeds to carry out all commands until it reaches the command goto end. At this point, it skips everything else in AUTOEXEC.BAT and goes straight to the line that simply states :end.

The result: A computer with its hardware and device drivers, and MS-DOS itself, configured the way you want.

Windup

And here, except for the troubleshooting tips in the following chapter ("Real Questions, Real Answers") and the chapter on ASCII and IBM extended characters, you've reached the end of your close encounter with MS-DOS. You've followed a sometimes tortuous path, but if you've invested the time and attention asked of you in the first chapter, you should have learned all you need to know about MS-DOS—indeed, you should qualify as quite an expert by now. Perhaps you even had a little fun and feel like inves- tigating MS-DOS further.

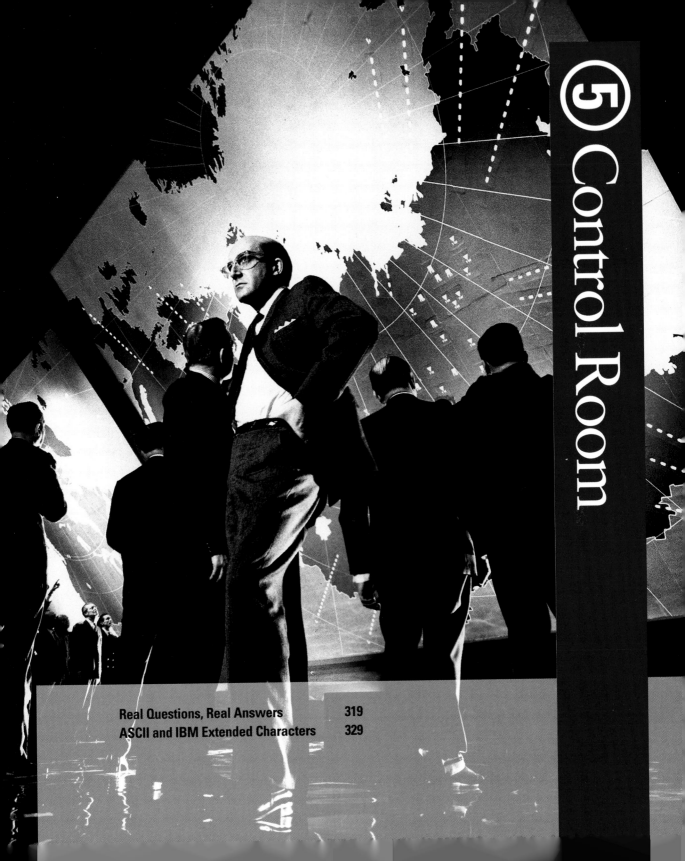

5 Control Room

Real Questions, Real Answers

What's So Real About Them?

The information presented in question-and-answer format here was supplied by a special group of people—the folks who, through Microsoft Product Support Services, help real people with real concerns about using MS-DOS. They're the people who, when asked "What would you like a non-expert's book about MS-DOS to cover?" enthusiastically responded with the information presented here. The rest of the chapter is theirs.

Q: I'm going to install DoubleSpace, but I'm a little worried. What if something goes wrong?

A: Version 6.2 of MS-DOS includes ScanDisk and other features that make DoubleSpace even safer to use than it was in version 6.0, so chances are excellent that nothing will go wrong, especially if you have a relatively new computer and have not experienced any problems with your hard disk in the past. If your hard disk is well used, defragment the disk ahead of time if you can.

If something does go wrong, just remember that troubleshooting a problem with compressed data is difficult and risky and might best be left to experienced support engineers. If you believe your compressed drive is corrupted and you're not comfortable trying to figure out what to do next, contact Microsoft Product Support Services.

Rule #1 when troubleshooting compressed drives is: Back up as soon as you can. If you can access some of your data but not all of it, back up what you can. If you're working with a damaged compressed drive, its reliability may deteriorate as you work to correct the problem.

Q: I am currently using a third-party disk-compression software package and now want to convert to DoubleSpace. How can I do this?

A: Microsoft provides conversion disks for a nominal fee for Stacker owners to convert from Stacker 2.x or 3.0 to MS-DOS 6.0 and 6.2. If you're using

> **If you encounter a problem you need help with, call Microsoft Product Support Services. The phone number should be in your MS-DOS manual.**

> **If you're still using version 6.0 of MS-DOS, you don't have ScanDisk, so you might want to consider using a disk-diagnostics utility such as Norton Disk Doctor to verify the health of your hard disk before compression. (Note: That's *before* compression; after you compress the disk, use Scan-Disk or another utility that's "DoubleSpace aware.")**

Stacker version 3.1, however, you need to either back down to 2.x or 3.0 and then convert or use the procedure described here. You can convert to Double-Space without the conversion disk by using the following steps. Note that you must have the *upgrade* disks, not the version 6.2 *Step-Up*, in order to do this.

1. Install the MS-DOS 6.0 or 6.2 Upgrade if you haven't already done so.

2. Back up your program and data files on all drives, using Microsoft Backup or a third-party utility. If you are using Stacker 3.1, however, note that your backup files or disks might become corrupted if you use Microsoft Backup. This happens because Microsoft Backup, in both Microsoft Windows and MS-DOS versions, handles data in 32-KB chunks. Stacker does not handle 32-KB units as comfortably. If possible, use a backup utility that is compatible with your Stacker version.

3. Create a bootable MS-DOS floppy disk. To do this, locate your original MS-DOS 6.0 or 6.2 upgrade disks; insert Setup Disk 1 in either drive A or drive B, change to that drive, and type a command like the one that follows:

   ```
   A:\>setup /f
   ```

   Important: After you type the above command and Setup prompts you to insert a disk to create the startup floppy disk, you *must* create that disk in drive A. Also, be sure that you choose to install on drive A.

4. Verify that the disk you just created is bootable by inserting the disk in drive A and pressing Ctrl+Alt+Del. If your system starts up, continue with the next step. If it does not, reboot from your hard disk and repeat step 3 until you have created a bootable floppy disk.

5. Format the compressed drive. To do this, type the following command at the A:\> prompt:

   ```
   A:\>format drive:
   ```

   where *drive* is the compressed drive.

   If you're formatting drive C, use the /s switch with the Format command to make the hard disk bootable.

6. If you formatted a drive other than C, skip to step 7. If you formatted drive C, you must now reinstall the MS-DOS 6.0 or 6.2 Upgrade. To do this, insert Setup Disk 1 in drive A or drive B, change to that drive, and type the following command:

   ```
   A:\>setup
   ```

   Follow the steps on the screen. If you used Microsoft Backup for MS-DOS to back up your compressed drive, be sure to reinstall Backup for MS-DOS when Setup prompts you to do so. (You need this program to restore the files from your backup disks.)

7. Install DoubleSpace. To do this, type dblspace at the MS-DOS command prompt, and then follow the steps on the screen.

8. Restore the files from your backup disks to your DoubleSpaced drive.

Q: I compressed my hard disk, but now my computer hangs when I try to start it.

A: You could have a problem with your compressed disk. Try the following steps. If you don't feel up to the task, call Microsoft Product Support Services.

1. Press F5 when the system displays *Starting MS-DOS*. This will skip processing of your CONFIG.SYS and AUTOEXEC.BAT files. If doing this corrects the problem, you probably have an incompatible or corrupted device driver or terminate-and-stay-resident (TSR) program. To find the problem, try rebooting and choose an interactive boot (with the F8 key). Skip one device driver or TSR and see whether the system starts properly. If it does, you've found the problem. If it doesn't, reboot and try eliminating another device driver or TSR until you find the problem file.

2. Press Ctrl+F5 when the system displays *Starting MS-DOS*. This will skip processing of CONFIG.SYS and AUTOEXEC.BAT and the DoubleSpace files as well. If this startup corrects the problem, you probably have a corrupted DBLSPACE volume. If you have the MS-DOS version 6.2 *Upgrade,* put Setup Disk 1 in drive A and run ScanDisk. (This won't work with the version 6.2 Step-Up disk unless you expand the SCANDISK files first.)

3. If the system still hangs with F5 or Ctrl+F5, your system files are probably corrupted. Start your computer with the MS-DOS 6.2 Upgrade Disk 1 in drive A, and press F3 twice to exit Setup. See if you can access your compressed drive. If you can, then the system files are probably corrupted. Sys the hard drive (or the host if C is compressed). For example, type sys a: c: (or type sys a: [*host:*] if C is compressed) at the MS-DOS command prompt.

Q: When I upgraded to version 6.0, I decided not to install the Windows versions of Microsoft Backup, Undelete, and Anti-Virus. Now that I've stepped up to version 6.2, I want those utilities, but I can't seem to get the Step-Up disk to install them. What's going on?

A: The version 6.2 Step-Up disk *doesn't* include complete copies of these utilities; it includes only the *changes* necessary to update existing version 6.0 copies (in your \DOS directory) to version 6.2. If you want to install either the Windows or MS-DOS version of one or more of these utilities, you have to install the version 6.0 utilities and then update them to version 6.2. The full procedure is in the file named README.NOW on your Step-Up disk.

Remember: To print a file, you can use the **Copy command** in the form *copy [file.ext] prn.*

Q: I used Step-Up to upgrade to 6.2 and now some of my MS-DOS files are corrupted. How do I reinstall?

A: Here's what you do:

1. Use the Setver command to set the version number for SETUP.EXE to an earlier version of MS-DOS—in this case, 4.00. For example, type:

```
C:\>setver setup.exe 4.00
```

2. Restart your computer.

3. Install the MS-DOS 6.0 Upgrade. (That's right, 6.0.)

4. Use Setver again, this time to remove the version number for SETUP.EXE that you set earlier. For example, type:

```
C:\>setver setup.exe /d
```

5. Restart your computer.

6. Install the MS-DOS 6.2 Step-Up.

It's a pain in the keester, but it's the only way.

Q: I just upgraded to version 6.2, and Setup told me I had less space available on my hard disk than I thought I'd have. What happened—did something get messed up?

A: Your system is fine. Setup uses its own means of checking out your system, and the method it uses to calculate available space on your hard disk may result in an inaccurate number if your hard disk is fragmented. To fix the problem, run Defrag.

Q: When I tried to uncompress a disk, DoubleSpace displayed an error message telling me that it couldn't uncompress the drive because I had the same filename in two places. It also told me to look at something called DBLSPACE.LOG on drive H. I don't know what DBLSPACE.LOG is, but when I tried the Directory command, I didn't see any duplicates. What's going on?

A: DoubleSpace can't uncompress a drive if it finds duplicate filenames on the compressed and uncompressed (host) portions of the drive. You didn't see any duplicates with Directory because the error involves either a SENTRY directory or a PCTRACKR.DEL file, both of which are created by Undelete to protect deleted files, and both of which are normally hidden from view. To see the cause of the problem, use the Type command. For example, if your compressed drive is C and your host drive is H, DBLSPACE.LOG is on the host, so use the command:

```
C:\>type h:dblspace.log
```

If the log file shows duplicate directories or files other than SENTRY or PCTRACKR.DEL, eliminate or rename each duplicate on the host drive and try uncompressing again. If the problem is either SENTRY or PCTRACKR.DEL, you'll have to delete one of the duplicates. Note, however, that afterwards you *won't* be able to undelete any of the files in the deleted SENTRY directory or PCTRACKR.DEL file. Be sure you don't need to recover any files before proceeding. When you're ready to remove the duplicate from the host drive:

1. Start your computer without loading Undelete. To do this, reboot and press F8 when *Starting MS-DOS* is displayed. Answer Y (yes) to each prompt *except* the prompt to process the Undelete command.

2. Use the Deltree command to delete the SENTRY directory or the PCTRACKR.DEL file from your host drive. For example, type:

```
C:\>deltree h:\sentry /y
```

or:

```
C:\>deltree h:\pctrackr.del /y
```

3. Run the DoubleSpace uncompress again.

Q: Under MS-DOS 6.0, I routinely used the Dblspace /l command to get a list of my drives. I recently upgraded to version 6.2, and now whenever I enter the same command, I get the message *Ambiguous switch - /l*. What's going on?

A: In version 6.2, DoubleSpace responds to two switches that begin with *l:*, /list and /lastdrive (which lets you set the highest drive letter you want DoubleSpace to recognize). You get the *Ambiguous switch* message when you type dblspace /l because DoubleSpace doesn't know whether you want /list or /lastdrive. To get the command you want, type an extra letter or two to make your intentions clear—for example, type dblspace /li to get a list but dblspace /la=[*driveletter*] to set the highest drive letter.

Q: I typed the Dblspace /host command to change the letter assigned to the host on my DoubleSpaced drive, but I got an error message saying *The drive letter* X *is not available for DoubleSpace's use.* Why isn't it?

A: One possible reason is that some other drive on your system is already using the letter that you asked for. To find out what drive letters are in use, enter the command:

```
C:\>dblspace /li
```

If the resulting report shows that the letter you asked for is already in use, try another letter. If that doesn't work, DoubleSpace probably thinks you asked for a drive letter that's outside the range of available (legal) drive letters it can use. To fix the problem, you need to change a line in the initialization file named DBLSPACE.INI, which tells DoubleSpace how to set itself up when it starts.

Follow these steps to change that line and correct the problem:

1. At the command prompt, type the following command, substituting the drive letter you want for the *j* shown here (you must manually edit DBLSPACE.INI under MS-DOS 6.0 to make this change):

```
C:\>dblspace /lastdrive=j
```

When you press Enter, you see the message:

```
DBLSPACE.INI has been modified.

For this change to take effect, you must restart your computer.
```

2. Press Ctrl+Alt+Del to reboot.

3. Now enter the command to change the host drive letter. For example, to change the host drive letter to *I*, enter:

```
C:\>dblspace c: /host=i
```

4. Press Ctrl+Alt+Del to restart your computer again. After DoubleSpace loads, the drive letter assigned to your host drive will be *I*.

Q: I just ran the Dir /c command on a file I know is compressed, but the command didn't report any compression ratio. Is something wrong with the file? Did it get uncompressed somehow?

A: The file is fine and is still compressed. What has probably happened is that some of the information MS-DOS uses to keep track of files somehow got corrupted. If you're not running Windows, run ScanDisk to find and fix the problem. If you *are* running Windows, you might not even have a problem: It could be that Windows simply hasn't gotten around to updating some of its records yet. If this is the case, start the Windows File Manager. Choose DoubleSpace Info from the Tools menu to check the file's compression ratio.

Q: I've installed version 6.2 on my computer. Last night I ran my favorite game, and it really acted funny. The graphics were all messed up, and the sound was horrible. Did my game get damaged? It took me weeks to find the magic sword, and I don't want to start all over again!

A: Your game is not damaged, and you haven't lost the magic sword. (To guarantee that you don't lose it, follow the game instructions that tell you how to make backup copies of your game files, and do so often.) As for your problem, many games use some special programming tricks to give you great graphics and sounds, but those tricks don't work well—if at all—on a compressed drive. The solution is to move or reinstall the game on an uncompressed drive and then to avoid loading DoubleSpace when you want to play the game.

To run the game, press Ctrl+Alt+Del to reboot your computer. When you see *Starting MS-DOS,* press Ctrl+F5 or Ctrl+F8 to tell MS-DOS not to load Double-Space. When startup's complete, run the game.

By the way, if you need to load device drivers or specify certain system settings to run the game, you can create game-specific CONFIG.SYS and AUTO-EXEC.BAT files on your host drive. When you boot or reboot, press Ctrl+F8 and then press Esc. This combination causes MS-DOS to start without Double-Space and assume an interactive boot. The Esc key then tells MS-DOS to carry out all commands in your game-specific CONFIG.SYS and AUTOEXEC.BAT files. To create the CONFIG.SYS and AUTOEXEC.BAT files you need, copy your existing files to the host drive. Then:

1. Start the MS-DOS Editor and edit each file on the host drive separately. (If you don't know how to use the Editor, refer to the chapter "Make a File with Edit," in Section 3.)

2. Remove as many lines as possible from each file, but proceed cautiously so you don't delete any lines that your system absolutely needs. The game's documentation may come in handy here. The safe way to go is to type rem followed by a space at the beginning of each line you suspect keeps your game from running right.

3. Save the edited files.

4. Reboot with the Ctrl+F8 and Esc keys mentioned earlier, and run the game as you normally would. If you experience problems, re-edit CONFIG.SYS, AUTOEXEC.BAT, or both. Unfortunately, from here on, you'll just have to keep working at it until your game runs smoothly. Good luck.

Q: I ran DoubleSpace on a computer with a hard disk and a RAM drive. Now my RAM drive, which used to be D, is drive I, and when I run Windows File Manager, I see all kinds of drives listed. What happened?

A: You're seeing DoubleSpace footprints here. What happened is that Double-Space, in compressing your hard disk, divided it into both a compressed drive (which remains your C drive) and a host drive (which you probably see as drive H, host for C). To leave plenty of room for you to connect to network drives or to compress additional hard disks, DoubleSpace "moved" your RAM drive higher up the alphabet and assigned it drive letter I. If you're not having any problems working with your compressed drive, don't worry about the extra drive letters you see. (You'll see even more of them assigned to disks if you compress a floppy or two.) If you want to check on your drive letters, use the Dblspace /list command to see which letter is assigned to what disk.

Q: Every once and a while I get DoubleSpace DoubleGuard error messages. What are they, what causes them, and what can I do about them?

A: These errors are probably caused by some conflict in the system; the exact cause depends on your particular system and what programs you have loaded. Often, the errors can be traced back to one of the various goodies that are loaded each time the system starts: screen savers or TSR programs—especially shareware—such as calendars and clocks. The command for loading the offending program is probably in your AUTOEXEC.BAT file. To find the program, press Ctrl+Alt+Del to reboot your computer, and then press F8 to perform an interactive boot. Load every suspect program except one. If the problem goes away, remove the program from your computer or at least remove the command to start it from your AUTOEXEC.BAT file. If the error message still appears, reboot your computer and press F8 again, disable a different program, and see if that does the trick. Repeat this process until you find the cause of the error message.

If all that doesn't work, your computer might have a bad device driver. Device drivers are normally loaded from your computer's CONFIG.SYS file. To isolate a suspect device driver, go through the same reboot/F8 process again, this time singling out individual lines in the CONFIG.SYS file. As before, keep going until you find the problem.

Finally, if the problem still persists, there's a chance that you might have a bad RAM chip in your computer. If that's the case, you'll have to take your computer to a qualified technician and have it checked out.

Q: I've had version 6.0 on my machine for a while, and I spent some time customizing my MEMMAKER.INF file to fine-tune my system. I've updated my system to version 6.2, but all those changes I made seem to have disappeared. What happened?

A: The version 6.2 update replaced your existing MEMMAKER.INF file in your \DOS directory with its own copy (which, incidentally, contains a couple of new entries—see the comment portion of the file). You can do one of two things. If you want, you can modify the new MEMMAKER.INF file directly. If you were perfectly happy with your system the way it was, you can overwrite the version 6.2 MEMMAKER.INF file with the one you used with version 6.0. Setup saved your old file in an OLD_DOS directory, probably OLD_DOS.1, when it ran the update. To restore your old file:

1. Check for OLD_DOS.1 with the command:

```
C:\>dir \old_dos.*
```

2. Assuming that your old version of MS-DOS is indeed in OLD_DOS.1 and that your current MS-DOS files are in a directory named \DOS, type the following command at the command prompt:

```
C:\>move c:\old_dos.1\memmaker.inf c:\dos
```

If your OLD_DOS directory is numbered 2, 3, 4, or whatever, or your MS-DOS files are in a directory other than \DOS, make the appropriate changes to the line above.

Q: Great Caesar's ghost! When I started my computer, it displayed some message about the hard disk being too fragmented and then the computer rebooted itself! Is my computer going to self-destruct?

A: Each time DoubleSpace starts, it automatically mounts all DoubleSpace compressed drives. If DoubleSpace thinks one of the drives is too fragmented to be mounted, it modifies some of its "housekeeping" files to compensate for the fragmented drive and then restarts the system to see whether it succeeded. If you unmount the fragmented drive, DoubleSpace resets all the information in its housekeeping file, and you'll get the same message later if you remount the drive.

Basically, all this means is that it's way past time for you to run Defrag on the drive to get it cleaned up. When you get any error message mentioning fragmentation, reboot your computer and run Defrag on the fragmented drive.

Q: My system has a CD-ROM drive, and ever since I upgraded to version 6.2, I get some error message saying the system can't cache the CD-ROM drive. The drive seems to work, though. What's going on?

A: Your CD-ROM drive relies on a device driver named MSCDEX.EXE to operate. In addition, your system probably uses the SmartDrive device driver to help boost system performance. In version 6.2, SmartDrive gains the ability to cache CD-ROM drives. For it to do so, however, Microsoft CD-ROM Extensions (MSCDEX.EXE) must be loaded *before* SMARTDRV.EXE. To correct the problem, use the MS-DOS Editor to edit your AUTOEXEC.BAT file—be sure the line that loads the MSCDEX.EXE driver precedes the line that loads SmartDrive.

Q: I keep getting a message saying *EMM Exception Error #06 or #12.* I have no idea what it means. Is this some kind of warning or does my computer have a problem?

A: It's possible that the cause of this message is a bad file on your disk drive or maybe even a problem with a program you're running. If the message keeps appearing, you might have a problem with the computer's hardware. Have the system checked by a qualified technician at your earliest convenience.

Q: I got an error message that said *Parity Error, System Halted.* This sounds serious, and I'm not sure I like the idea of anything halting my system without asking me first. What happened?

A: Parity is a built-in error-checking scheme that lets your computer check out data as it moves through the system to ensure that the data isn't being altered or corrupted along the way. The parity error-checking routine is built into—and controlled by—your hardware. MS-DOS and its programs cannot cause, control, or manipulate parity errors in any way. If the parity-checking hardware detects a problem, it seizes control of your computer immediately and forces it to shut down, displaying the message you saw. A parity error is almost always caused by a bad memory chip. Either a chip has failed somewhere in your system, or part of some recently installed memory could be bad. In any case, take your computer to a qualified technician as soon as you can.

Q: I tried to run Defrag to clean up my computer's hard disk, and I got an error message saying there wasn't enough memory available. Does this mean my hard disk is full?

A: No, it doesn't. Most of the time, your hard disk has nothing to do with your computer's memory, and the amount of free space on your hard disk is not directly related to how much memory your system has available. If you see an insufficient memory message from Defrag, try this:

1. Press Ctrl+Alt+Del to reboot your computer. When you see *Starting MS-DOS*, press F5 for a clean boot, which bypasses CONFIG.SYS and AUTOEXEC.BAT and so should allow the maximum amount of free memory to be made available.

2. Run Defrag.

If you still don't have enough memory, try this:

1. Press Ctrl+Alt+Del to reboot your computer. Press F8 for an interactive boot.

2. During the interactive boot, press Y (yes) to process *only* the lines containing HIMEM.SYS and DOS=HIGH. If your hard disk uses a special device driver, or if you use a third-party compression program, load those as well. Otherwise, answer N (no) to all other prompts.

3. Run Defrag.

If you didn't find your question answered, don't forget that HELP is only a phone call away.

STOP WORRYING!

HELP!

IS ON THE WAY!

ASCII and IBM Extended Characters

Standard ASCII Characters

Character	Control character	Dec value	Hex value	Character	Control character	Dec value	Hex value
ASCII control characters (displayed as graphics characters by IBM systems)				ETB	^W	23	17
				CAN	^X	24	18
NUL		0	00	EM	^Y	25	19
SOH	^A	1	01	SUB	^Z	26	1A
STX	^B	2	02	ESC	^[	27	1B
ETX	^C	3	03	FS	^\	28	1C
EOT	^D	4	04	GS	^]	29	1D
ENQ	^E	5	05	RS	^^	30	1E
ACK	^F	6	06	US	^_	31	1F
BEL	^G	7	07				
BS	^H	8	08	*Printable characters*			
HT	^I	9	09	(space)		32	20
LF	^J	10	0A	!		33	21
VT	^K	11	0B	"		34	22
FF	^L	12	0C	#		35	23
CR	^M	13	0D	$		36	24
SO	^N	14	0E	%		37	25
SI	^O	15	0F	&		38	26
DLE	^P	16	10	'		39	27
DC1	^Q	17	11	(		40	28
DC2	^R	18	12	)		41	29
DC3	^S	19	13	*		42	2A
DC4	^T	20	14	+		43	2B
NAK	^U	21	15	,		44	2C
SYN	^V	22	16	-		45	2D

Character	Control character	Dec value	Hex value	Character	Control character	Dec value	Hex value
.		46	2E	T		84	54
/		47	2F	U		85	55
Printable characters				V		86	56
0		48	30	W		87	57
1		49	31	X		88	58
2		50	32	Y		89	59
3		51	33	Z		90	5A
4		52	34	[		91	5B
5		53	35	\		92	5C
6		54	36	]		93	5D
7		55	37	^		94	5E
8		56	38	_		95	5F
9		57	39	´		96	60
:		58	3A	a		97	61
;		59	3B	b		98	62
<		60	3C	c		99	63
=		61	3D	d		100	64
>		62	3E	e		101	65
?		63	3F	f		102	66
@		64	40	g		103	67
A		65	41	h		104	68
B		66	42	i		105	69
C		67	43	j		106	6A
D		68	44	k		107	6B
E		69	45	l		108	6C
F		70	46	m		109	6D
G		71	47	n		110	6E
H		72	48	o		111	6F
I		73	49	p		112	70
J		74	4A	q		113	71
K		75	4B	r		114	72
L		76	4C	s		115	73
M		77	4D	t		116	74
N		78	4E	u		117	75
O		79	4F	v		118	76
P		80	50	w		119	77
Q		81	51	x		120	78
R		82	52	y		121	79
S		83	53	z		122	7A

Character	Control character	Dec value	Hex value	Character	Control character	Dec value	Hex value
{		123	7B	~		126	7E
¦		124	7C	Δ		127	7F
}		125	7D				

IBM Extended Characters

ASCII	Dec	Hex	ASCII	Dec	Hex	ASCII	Dec	Hex	ASCII	Dec	Hex
Ç	128	80	á	160	A0	└	192	C0	α	224	E0
ü	129	81	í	161	A1	┴	193	C1	β	225	E1
é	130	82	ó	162	A2	┬	194	C2	Γ	226	E2
â	131	83	ú	163	A3	├	195	C3	π	227	E3
ä	132	84	ñ	164	A4	─	196	C4	Σ	228	E4
à	133	85	Ñ	165	A5	┼	197	C5	σ	229	E5
å	134	86	ª	166	A6	╞	198	C6	µ	230	E6
ç	135	87	º	167	A7	╟	199	C7	τ	231	E7
ê	136	88	¿	168	A8	╚	200	C8	Φ	232	E8
ë	137	89	⌐	169	A9	╔	201	C9	Θ	233	E9
è	138	8A	¬	170	AA	╩	202	CA	Ω	234	EA
ï	139	8B	½	171	AB	╦	203	CB	δ	235	EB
î	140	8C	¼	172	AC	╠	204	CC	∞	236	EC
ì	141	8D	¡	173	AD	═	205	CD	φ	237	ED
Ä	142	8E	«	174	AE	╬	206	CE	ε	238	EE
Å	143	8F	»	175	AF	╧	207	CF	∩	239	EF
É	144	90	░	176	B0	╨	208	D0	≡	240	F0
æ	145	91	▒	177	B1	╤	209	D1	±	241	F1
Æ	146	92	▓	178	B2	╥	210	D2	≥	242	F2
ô	147	93	│	179	B3	╙	211	D3	≤	243	F3
ö	148	94	┤	180	B4	╘	212	D4	⌠	244	F4
ò	149	95	╡	181	B5	╒	213	D5	⌡	245	F5
û	150	96	╢	182	B6	╓	214	D6	÷	246	F6
ù	151	97	╖	183	B7	╫	215	D7	≈	247	F7
ÿ	152	98	╕	184	B8	╪	216	D8	°	248	F8
Ö	153	99	╣	185	B9	┘	217	D9	•	249	F9
Ü	154	9A	║	186	BA	┌	218	DA	·	250	FA
¢	155	9B	╗	187	BB	█	219	DB	√	251	FB
£	156	9C	╝	188	BC	▄	220	DC	η	252	FC
¥	157	9D	╜	189	BD	▌	221	DD	²	253	FD
Pt	158	9E	╛	190	BE	▐	222	DE	■	254	FE
ƒ	159	9F	┐	191	BF	▀	223	DF		255	FF

JoAnne Woodcock

JoAnne Woodcock, currently a master writer for Microsoft Press, is author of the *MS-DOS 6 Companion* as well as *Running Microsoft Works 3 for Windows,* the *Concise Guide to MS-DOS 5,* and the *Concise Guide to Microsoft Works for Windows*—all published by Microsoft Press. She is also coauthor of *Running UNIX* and *Microsoft Word Style Sheets* and a contributor to the *Microsoft Press Computer Dictionary.*

The manuscript for this book was prepared and submitted to Microsoft Press in electronic form. Text files were processed and formatted using Microsoft Word for Windows 2.0.

Principal editorial compositor: John Sugg
Principal proofreader/copy editor: Jennifer Harris
Systems technician: Carol Luke
Interior text designers: Hansen Design Company & Brett Polonsky
Principal illustrator: David Holter
Graphic design and layout: Polonsky Design
Interior color separations: Wilson Engraving
Cover designer: Rebecca Geisler
Cover illustrator: Kelly Hume
Cover color separator: Color Service
Indexer: Trisha Feuerstein of Integral Publishing

Text composition by Microsoft Press in Sabon and Univers Condensed, using Aldus PageMaker 4.2.